MANAGEMENT AND LEADERSHIP IN EDUCATION SERIES

Series Editors: PETER RIBBINS AND JOHN SAYER

TITLES IN THE MANAGEMENT
AND LEADERSHIP IN EDUCATION SERIES:

Headteachers and Leadership in Special Education

STEVE RAYNER AND PETER RIBBINS

CASSELL

London and New York

Cassell

Wellington House	370 Lexington Avenue
125 Strand	New York
London WC2R 0BB	NY 10017–6550

First published 1999

British Library Cataloguing-in-Publication Data
A catalogue record for this book is available from the British Library.

ISBN 0–304–33971–7 (hardback)
    0–304–33972–5 (paperback)

Typeset by York House Typographic Ltd, London
Printed and bound in Great Britain by Redwood Books, Trowbridge, Wiltshire

Contents

About the authors

Steve Rayner is Lecturer in Special Education and Educational Psychology in the School of Education at the University of Birmingham. He is at present responsible for fields of study in the Management of Special Education and Emotional and Behavioural Difficulties. He was formerly Headteacher of Penwithen School, Dorchester; he has taught in mainstream and special education and has worked in industry. His publications include articles on learning technology, the pastoral curriculum, residential special education, curriculum evaluation, and the management of special education. He has also published work on teaching and learning styles and been joint editor of the journal *Educational Psychology*. His current interests lie in three main areas: in teaching and learning styles; in emotional and behavioural difficulties; and in leadership and the management of special education.

Peter Ribbins is Professor of Educational Management and Dean of the Faculty of Education and Continuing Studies at the University of Birmingham. He has worked in a college of education, in an LEA, in secondary schools and in industry. He has published 22 books and over 70 articles. His books include *Managing Education, Developing Educational Leaders, Greenfield on Educational Administration, Improving Education, Delivering the National Curriculum, Headship Matters, Leaders and Leadership in the School, College and University,* and *Understanding Primary Headteachers*. He was editor of the journal *Pastoral Care in Education* and is editor of *Educational Management and Administration*. He has co-edited book series for Blackwell and for Cassell. His wife is an experienced secondary headteacher and his interest in the study of headship dates back to the mid 1970s.

Abbreviations

CEO	Chief Education Officer
CPD	continuing professional development
EBD	emotional and behavioural difficulties
ESL/E2L	English as a second language
ESN	educationally sub-normal
ESN(S)	educationally sub-normal (severe)
FAS	Funding Agency for Schools
GEP	group educational plan
GEST	Grants for Education, Support and Training
GMS	grant maintained status
GMSS	grant maintained special school
IEP	individual education plan
IIP	International Intervisitation Programme
INSET	in-service education and training
LEA	Local Education Authority
LMS	local management of schools
LMSS	local management of special schools
MLD	moderate learning difficulties
MSC	Manpower Services Commission
NC	national curriculum
NCC	National Curriculum Council
NCSE	National Council for Special Education
Ofsted	Office for Standards in Education
PMLD	profound and multiple learning difficulties
PRU	pupil referral unit
RE	religious education
SAT(s)	standard assessment task(s)
SCAA	School Curriculum and Assessment Authority
SEN	special educational needs
SENCO	special educational needs co-ordinator

SIMS	schools information management systems
SLD	severe learning difficulties
SMT	senior management team
TA	teachers' aides
TEC	Training and Enterprise Council
TVEI	Technical and Vocational Education Initiative

CHAPTER 1

Tales of heads: leaders and leadership in special education

Introduction

It is widely believed that headship matters a great deal in determining the quality of a school and the achievement of its pupils (Ribbins and Marland, 1994, 1–4). It is, therefore, not surprising that no other management position in the British education system has attracted so much attention from so many researchers over such a long time as has that of the head-teacher. However, whilst such a claim is most true of secondary education (*ibid.*, 3–5), it is much less true of primary education (Pascal and Ribbins, 1998, 1) and not at all true of special education. Thus, a sustained search of the literatures of special education and of educational management by the authors revealed very few references to headship in special education.

We believe that heads and headship in special education are worth studying. In this introductory chapter we describe, explain and justify how we undertook our research. It contains a preliminary analysis of key aspects of our conversations with the ten very different people whose careers are reported at length in the ten chapters which follow. Our approach to the study of leadership has led us, in talking to these headteachers, to take an intense interest in their personalities and characters, in how these have been shaped and developed, and in what all this means for the accounts they give of how they interpret and enact headship. In the section which follows we shall say something about how we conducted the study upon which this book is based.

Conducting the study

In preparing for this study we met several times to determine how it would be conducted, what issues it would explore and with which headteachers. Our key intention was from the beginning to 'enable heads to speak for them-selves' (Mortimer and Mortimer, 1991, vii) in a manner which, as far as we know, has not been attempted with heads of schools working with pupils with special needs. As such, our book reports on a series of face-to-face conversations with named headteachers. We took this approach because we wished to offer the reader a series of individual portraits based upon the accounts which individual headteachers give of their professional lives, each of which is reported in some depth. In addition, a face-to-face interview allows a much higher level of spontaneity and a more open process of agenda negotiation than is possible using other methods.

Given that we could not include a large number of conversations in the final text, it was never our intention to attempt to offer a representative sample, whatever this might look like, of all heads who work in schools containing significant numbers of pupils with special needs. As best we could we did, however, seek to include headteachers from special schools serving different types of special need along with some who work in mainstream schools. In addition, we tried to select people who we expected to be interesting, who had different life experiences, who were at a variety of points in their careers and who were drawn from across England and Wales. We are grateful to the members of the Special Education and Educational Psychology group in the School of Education of the University of Birmingham for their many helpful suggestions as to whom, in undertaking this study, we might approach.

Once all this had been agreed, we approached those selected to ask if they would be willing to be involved. This usually took the form of an initial telephone call which was followed by a letter which, inter alia, noted that those who agreed would be involved as follows:

1. They would have an initial conversation of about two hours with one of the researchers. The main themes of this discussion were listed in an interview schedule included with the letter. The schedule was intended as a framework, not a straightjacket. It would be possible for either party to identify further issues or sub-issues as the conversation progressed. If there were particular issues which the headteacher did not wish to discuss, this would be honoured.
2. The conversation would be taped and transcribed. One of the researchers would undertake a preliminary edit to ensure that it read fluently whilst remaining faithful to what the head had said and the way in which this was expressed. This transcript would then be sent to the head for any additions, revisions, excisions, etc. they might wish to make. As far as possible, these suggestions, subject only to their implications for word length, the laws of libel, the well-being of named individuals, etc., would be honoured in the production of the final published conversation.
3. It would be possible for any particular headteacher to withdraw at any time.
4. The headteachers involved would be named in the final text.

All those we approached responded positively, which had not been the case in our studies of heads in secondary and primary schools. As we discovered in earlier studies, of those who agreed to take part, some engaged in much preparation and came to the conversations with substantial notes whilst others relied upon a more spontaneous approach. None ruled out any particular topic from our schedule and almost all had important ideas for further themes which they introduced either before or during the discussion. Nobody asked to pull out at any stage.

We sent a detailed interview schedule to each headteacher before their meeting with one or other of us (see Appendix, pp. 51–3). The schedule was built around a number of key themes including:

1. the influence of family, friends, local community, early life, schooling, higher education, etc. on their views, values, lives and careers;
2. the influences which shaped their views/values as educators/ managers;
3. their reasons for becoming teachers; their reasons for becoming involved in special education; their views on special education;
4. their careers before headship; their reasons for becoming headteachers;
5. how they went about becoming heads; how well prepared they felt;
6. their vision for their institution, and how they seek to implement this;
7. the part they play in enabling effective teaching and learning, and with what effect;
8. to whom they are accountable, and who manages them;
9. their views on headship and the influences which have shaped them;
10. their key educational and managerial visions/values;
11. how they manage people and resources;
12. how they cope with stress, and where they find support;
13. whether they, as heads, are necessary; whether they are democratic.

These conversations took place during middle and late 1996 and the final version of the last of the scripts was agreed in April 1997.

Before turning to a preliminary analysis of aspects of these conversations we need to set this against a background of some of the most important ideas which have influenced our views on aspects of the relationship between personality and leadership.

Personality and leadership

For much of this century the characteristics of leadership have stimulated a great deal more interest than the character of leaders, despite the fact that studies and theories which attempt to describe, analyse and explain the personality of leaders have attracted the attention of many of the greatest of historians and dramatists over the last two thousand years. In these early portraits, the influence of a leader's early years in shaping his or her personality is often stressed. More recently, following Freud and others, this approach has been given an explicitly clinical spin. In thinking about the lives and personalities of the ten headteachers interviewed for this study we have been influenced by ideas drawn from this literature and, more specifically, by the work of Howard Gardner and Manfred Kets de Vries.

Kets de Vries (1995), like others before him, has had some hard things to say about the literature on leadership. He points to its exponential proliferation in recent times. Nobody has documented this in greater detail than Stogdill in *Stogdill's Handbook of Leadership*. His 1974 handbook listed 3,000 studies. By 1981 this had reached 5,000 and it has been accelerating ever since. But this is not the only problem with such studies. Kets de Vries regrets that 'the popularity of leadership research has not been equalled by its relevance. One of the problems is that too many theories about organisations seem to have had their gestation in the ivory towers of academia ... [they are] plodding and detached, often far removed from the reality of day-to-day life' (194). We share this view and have suggested that

> Much of what is written ... seems sensible and rational. It deals with the purposes of [aspects of education] and considers the advantages and disadvantages of various structures, roles, processes and the rest through which those purposes might be delivered. But much of it, however well meaning, seems curiously abstract. Little attention is given to the people through which the delivery must be made ... No wonder it is so often ineffective at the level of practice ... whilst sustaining an impressive facade of prescription ... To focus upon the management of 'people' entails being clear about how real people perceive and enact [what they do] in ... real institutions. (Ribbins, 1985, 12–13)

Happily, Kets de Vries believes things could be getting better, not least because an 'increasing number of scholars have become interested in going beyond the confinement of social science laboratory experiments to observe real leaders in action' (1995, 194). His clinical work with executives has led him to stress the importance of 'aspects of character' in making 'some leaders more suitable than others to taking on these roles ... the personality of a top executive influences the strategy, corporate culture and even structure of his or her organisation to a much greater extent than most people, particularly executives themselves, are likely to be willing to admit' (*ibid.*, 197). This is a claim which resonates closely with our findings both in this and in earlier studies of the impact of headteachers within all kinds of schools (Best *et al.*, 1983; Pascal and Ribbins, 1998; Ribbins and Marland, 1994). However, whilst we are interested in what kinds of people leaders are and what effect this has on how they perceive and enact leadership, Kets de Vries wants to go deeper and in doing so to explain the ways in which 'the behavioural patterns that make for effective leadership ... evolve' (1995, 197). In this, he shares an interest with Howard Gardner. Their views are instructive and will, perhaps, surprise some. Both place considerable stress upon the continuing importance of the deep-rooted influences which shape the personality of the leader as a child. It is to this aspect of their work and to its relevance to our study of headship in special education that we now turn.

Kets de Vries on the origins and implications of leadership personality

To study the origins of leadership personality, Kets de Vries (1995) employs a clinical approach and in doing so 'takes concepts from psychoanalysis, dynamic psychiatry, family systems theory and cognition'. He believes the 'shaping of an individual's personality begins early in life. Child psychologists have pointed out that the first three years of life are particularly critical to development. These are the years during which the core patterns of personality are shaped. . . . The foundations are laid for the kind of person we are going to be, and are likely to remain, for the rest of our lives' (205). The clinical term for this is 'narcissistic development' –

> a stage during which the growing child derives pleasure from his or her own body and its functions . . . The kind of treatment received during this critical period of development will very much colour his or her view of the world right through childhood. The role of parents or care-takers in the development of narcissism is obviously very important. Have they been supportive or inconsistent? Have family circumstances meant that the child has experienced a series of deprivations? The key question is has the child received a large enough narcissistic supply. Was a solid foundation laid for positive self-regard and initiative? Did the child have the opportunity to acquire a healthy dose of self-esteem? (205)

The nature of these experiences has an important influence in determining the kind of person which the young child becomes.

In some of his early writing (see Kets de Vries, 1989), Kets de Vries makes a

> distinction between people guided by [a] kind of reactive narcissism (individuals driven by a need to get even and to somehow come to grips with their past) and a type of constructive narcissism (individuals who are well-balanced, have a positive self-regard and a sense of self-esteem). Full blown reactive narcissists tend to have a grandiose, almost pathological, sense of self-importance. They habitually take advantage of others in order to achieve their own ends. They also live under the illusion they are unique . . . that they deserve especially favourable treatment and that the rules set for others do not apply to them . . . they are addicted to compliments . . . lack empathy . . . their envy of others and their rage when prevented from getting their own way can be formidable. (1995, 207)

His studies of leaders led Kets de Vries to conclude 'that a considerable percentage of them have become what they are for negative reasons . . . due to hardships encountered in childhood, they are driven to prove the world wrong. After having been belittled and maltreated when young, they are determined to show everyone that they amount to something as adults' (206). Happily, some reactive narcissists 'eventually overcome their feelings of bitterness and are motivated by reparation; that is, they try to prevent others from suffering what they have' (207).

Where this does not happen, Kets de Vries' studies of senior executives

> show that parallels can be drawn between individual pathology . . . and organisational pathology, the latter resulting in poorly functioning, or 'neurotic',

> organisations in which the 'irrational personality characteristics' of principal decision-makers can seriously affect the overall management process ... At the head of a 'neurotic' organisation ... one is likely to find a top executive whose rigid, neurotic style is strongly mirrored in the nature of inappropriate strategies, structures and organisational cultures of his or her firm. If this situation continues for too long, the organisation may self-destruct. (208)

In an earlier study he identifies five main types of 'neurotic' organization termed, respectively, the dramatic, the suspicious, the detached, the depressive and the compulsive (Kets de Vries and Miller, 1987). For a full and helpful diagram summarizing the key characteristics of each of these five types in terms of their organizational, executive, cultural, strategic and theatrical characteristics see Kets de Vries, 1995, page 209.

Gardner on the origins and implications of leadership personality

Howard Gardner, like Kets de Vries, in his study of leadership and in the account which he gives of leaders, draws essentially on a background of psychology and strives to derive and test his theories in the context of a close study of particular leaders. There are, of course, also important differences between them. Thus, for example, whilst Gardner (1995) takes a biographical and cognitive approach to the study of selected leaders who have spent much of their professional lives within the/a public domain and in doing so draws on evidence which has mainly been collected by others (13), Kets de Vries adopts a clinical approach to interpret mainly his own work with chief executives who have spent their careers in business. Even so the similarities in their theorizing are striking. We shall consider two aspects of this. First, Kets de Vries (1995), as we have shown, stresses the importance of their 'inner theatre' to leaders and to those they lead. Gardner (1995), similarly, emphasizes the significance of the 'stories' which leaders create, embody and exemplify and the ways in which they use these to supplant the 'stories' which had, hitherto, dominated the minds of their followers. Second, we shall consider the extent to which, in the writings of both theorists, 'inner theatre' and 'stories' alike are derived, essentially and typically, from the early life experiences of those who would lead.

Gardner identifies three kinds of leaders

> in terms of the innovativeness of their stories. The *ordinary* leader, by definition the most common, simply relates the traditional story of his or her group as effectively as possible. [They do] not seek to stretch the consciousness of [their] contemporary audience ... The *innovative* leader takes a story that has been latent in the population, or among members of his or her chosen domain, and brings new attention or a fresh twist to that story ... By far the rarest individual is the *visionary* leader. Not content to relate a current story or to reactivate a story drawn from a remote or recent past, this individual actually creates a new story ... and achieves at least a measure of success in conveying this story effectively to others. (10–11)

Such an approach is *cognitive* since it stresses that 'our understanding of the nature and processes of leadership is most likely to be enhanced as we come to understand better the arena in which leadership necessarily occurs – namely the *human mind* [or rather] *human minds,* since I am concerned equally with the mind of the leader and the minds of the followers' (15).

In this context Gardner (1995) explains that,

> Confronted with the phenomenon of leadership, a cognitively orientated scientist is likely to ask such questions as, What are the ideas (or stories) of the leader? How have they developed? How are they communicated, understood and misunderstood? How do they interact with other stories, especially competing counterstories, that have already drenched the consciousness of audience members? How do key ideas (or stories) affect the thoughts, feelings, and behaviors of other individuals? (16)

In developing these and related ideas, Gardner acknowledges that his approach is cognitive *and* cultural. Like most psychologically orientated students of leadership he is much concerned with 'the *personality* of the leader: his or her personal needs, principal psychodynamic traits, early life experiences, and relationship to other individuals' (17). However, he also views 'leadership as a process that occurs within the minds of individuals who live in a culture' which develops minds which have the capacity to 'gain nurturance from at least certain kinds of stories told by certain kinds of people' (22). What, then, are the characteristics of such minds and how are they created? Gardner identifies four principal factors including our primate heritage, the nature of our early socialization, the mind of the five-year-old and the attainment of expertise in domains.

Whilst this was not an issue we explored in detail, we were struck by what Gardner had to say on early socialization and the mind of the five-year-old child. Thus he claims that

> By and large, it has now been established that youngsters' initial notions about the physical, biological, and psychological worlds are remarkably robust ... in an uncomfortably large number of cases ... the five-year-old has already made up his or her mind. The theories and scripts of the young child are already consolidated and, in the absence of compelling circumstances that are repeated frequently, the growing individual shows little inclination to change. (27, 28)

This has significant implications both for the minds of leaders and for the ways in which they interact with those they would lead. When working with fellow experts within a specific domain, a leader does so indirectly 'by virtue of the work that he executes' but may also do so directly through the 'explicit communication of a message' (28). Things are different for those who

> presume to provide leadership across domains. Those who address a more broad-based institution like the church or a large and heterogeneous group like the inhabitants of a nation must at least begin by assuming that most of their audience members have a well-stocked five-year-old mind. So long as one traffics chiefly with theories and views already possessed by the five-year-old, one should be able to bring

about modest change ... when a leader seeks to promulgate a story that is more sophisticated ... she can succeed only if she educates the unschooled minds of the audience. (28–9)

However, educating the 'unschooled mind' is not easy. In this context, one problem is that relatively little is known about what makes leaders effective. On this, Gardner draws upon his theory of multiple intelligence to suggest what might be entailed. As he says, 'when ... linguistic intelligence is yoked to considerable personal intelligence, one has the makings of an effective communicator and, perhaps, a promising leader' (34). But how are promising, or for that matter unpromising, leaders 'made' and identified and what are the key characteristics of their life histories?

On the making of educational leaders Gardner points out that 'few systematic efforts have been undertaken to pinpoint the early markers of leadership ... Still, a few promising generalizations have been proposed' (1995, 32). These include (1) losing a father at an early age; (2) contrasting sets of relationships with their parents, especially where this is negative with one and positive with the other as in such cases as Gandhi, Lenin and Hitler. Gardner also lists the case of Stalin who detested his father and was doted on by his mother. Similarly, Kets de Vries notes the cases of Henry Ford and of Pierre Cardin, quoting in support of the latter Freud's dictum that a child who has been his 'mother's undisputed darling [will] retain throughout life the triumphant feeling, the confidence in success, which not seldom brings actual success with it' (1995, 207); (3) traits that make them stand out even at an early age either because of a striking appearance, an unusual personality or a remarkable life history; (4) inclinations from childhood to take risks and a willingness to go to great lengths to achieve their ends; and (5) an unusually intense desire for power and a feeling of being special.

In examining the life histories of leaders, Gardner stresses the importance of such key themes as their family background, education, personality and special feelings, early travel, willingness to challenge authority and take risks, the initial domain(s) in which they operated, early careers and relations to organizations, linguistic skills, the stories they advanced and the counter-stories they had to struggle with, personal characteristics, work habits and life, and ultimate successes and failures (327–41). In our studies of headteachers, and headship, in special education we have sought to consider their lives in terms of some of these themes. In addition, we have been influenced by research which has sought to construct typical life histories, or natural histories, of the careers of leaders. It is these to which we now turn.

A life and professional career history approach to the study of headship

Since the possibilities of such approaches to the study of leadership have been discussed fully in earlier books within this series (Ribbins and Sherratt,

1997; Pascal and Ribbins, 1998), we will restrict our observations to a brief summary of some of the key ideas involved. What such approaches have in common is the proposition that the professional lives of teachers and headteachers can be regarded as having a natural history and a developmental pattern. In the context of our research, the two frameworks which we have found most useful have both been derived from studies of headship. In the first, Gronn reports on a longitudinal, in-depth biography of a single headteacher. In the second, Day and Bakioglu discuss a survey-based investigation of a number of secondary headteachers.

From his study of Sir James Darling, Gronn proposes a life history framework of four broad phases through which leaders commonly pass (Gronn, 1993, 1994; Gronn and Ribbins, 1996). He entitles these phases Formation, Accession, Incumbency and Divestiture and we will say something about each of them in the sections which follow. Day and Bakioglu (1996) also identify four main phases: Initiation, Development, Autonomy and Disenchantment. Their framework deals specifically with the career patterns of heads in post and affords an elaboration of Gronn's phase of 'incumbency'. However, in using these frameworks as a means of describing the professional lives of the headteachers who are the subject of both this and an earlier study (Pascal and Ribbins, 1998), we felt a need to modify them. Thus, whilst both frameworks, Day and Bakioglu more than Gronn, appear to imply a pattern of creeping negativism leading to a final career exit (Disenchantment and Divestiture), our studies suggest that in some, perhaps even most, cases there is an alternative and more positive progression. It seems that despite the many changes and demands of primary and special education, the majority of the heads in our studies have managed to sustain their commitment and enthusiasm.

Given this, we suggest a modification of the original frameworks designed to allow for the expression of the kind of alternative progression we have in mind. It would accept the merits of a broad four-phase description of the pattern of development of the careers of headteachers in special education which remains close to Gronn's description but within our revised framework would be described as Formation, Accession, Incumbency, and Moving On (replacing Divestiture). Thus, although we accept that divestiture is about a progression to another state, our evidence suggests that whilst it does occur in some cases in the way in which Gronn describes, in others those who are anticipating or may be experiencing this phase regard it as a kind of re-invention or even a rebirth.

In addition, in our study of Incumbency, we make use of Day and Bakioglu's (1995) four-phase framework, including Initiation, Development and Autonomy but replace the fourth phase, Disenchantment, with Advancement. As we see it, this last phase may take at least two alternative and quite different patterns, one characterized by Enhancement and the other by Disenchantment. The suggestion is that it is possible to identify not one but at least two ideal typical professional life routes for headteachers. If this is so, then whilst all heads may enjoy broadly similar routes through much of their careers, their later experiences can be very different. This progression may be viewed as two routes as follows:

Route 1: **Career progression as potentially negative and destructive**
1. Formation
2. Accession
3. Incumbency: Initiation, Development, Autonomy, Advancement as Disenchantment
4. Moving On: Divestiture

Route 2: **Career progression as potentially progressive and creative**
1. Formation
2. Accession
3. Incumbency: Initiation, Development, Autonomy, Advancement as Enhancement
4. Moving On: Reinvention

In the examination of the careers of the ten headteachers which follows, this modified version of the framework will be used.

Making headteachers (Formation)

Gronn (1993), like Gardner (1995) and Kets de Vries (1995), suggests that prior to the assumption of leadership, there is a preparatory stage during which candidates shape themselves and are shaped for such a role. As part of this process of formation leaders are socialized into societal and institutional norms and values – into codes of taste, morality, values, beliefs and authority – by a variety of key agencies including, in particular, family, school and reference groups. Sometimes the individual experiences consistent influences and conditioning within and between these agencies, on other occasions inconsistency and even contradiction. Taken as a whole, these agencies, particularly those which exert their influence during the early years, shape a prospective leader's personality by generating a conception of self, along with the rudiments of a work-style, attitude and outlook. A comprehensive examination of the influence of the whole set of such agencies upon those who are the subjects of our book must await the production of much more detailed biographies than is possible from our research. In what follows we will focus instead upon selected aspects of family and schooling (and other levels of education) as key influences shaping the attitudes and values of the ten headteachers whose lives and careers are reported in the chapters which follow.

The making of ten people

The heads who are the subject of this book were drawn from a wide range of social, economic and cultural backgrounds. Some acknowledged their class roots. For example, Evans told us that 'mother and father were working-class, very much so' and Abrol that 'I belong to a working middle class. My father was an accountant'. Conversely, Haigh, the son of a policeman, describing the village in which he lived in his childhood, recalls 'a clear hierarchy among the families . . . There were the top families, the middle families and the other families, and it seemed if you were born into a marginal family that was your lot. A sort of caste system. It was fascinating.' Even so, he believed that 'the police were somewhere out in the wasteland in most people's view, so being a son of a policeman wasn't much of a help.' In describing a street made up of forty police houses he captures, vividly, what he regards as the essentially hierarchical nature of police life and the ways in which this can be represented materially:

> The street was on a hill, at the bottom were the PCs and they had a basic house. Up the hill were the Sergeants' houses. These had a wash house. Further up were the inspectors' houses, these had a small garage. At the top was the Chief Superintendent's house which had a double garage and a landscaped garden. It was a dreadful place to live. If you lived in the middle, as we did, you were above the people at the bottom and below the people at the top. The kids adopted this hierarchy physically and sociologically and psychologically.

Fathers and Mothers   The three headteachers quoted above all refer to their fathers. For several, the influence of their fathers, for good or ill, is recalled as a key influence in their lives and in determining their views and values concerning education and more broadly. Some of those who take a positive view, including Abrol and Sammons, describe this influence in, essentially, religious terms. Others, such as Evans, did not:

> Dad has always been a big influence on my life . . . He shaped our view on life and created a set of standards, moral standards and attitudes and values which we all shared . . . Dad was a 'Christian', not in the religious sense of the word, but in the sense that he was a good man. He'd do anything to help someone in a bit of trouble . . . He was basically a giving person who was prepared to help and support those who were less able or less fortunate. I mean 'Christian' in that sense. (Sammons)

> Dad could barely read, mum went to school until she was twelve and then went mornings at school and afternoons at the cotton mill. She was a fluent reader and would have, had times been different, gone on with her education. She was a clever lady. When he left the army . . . Father became a . . . driver and worked all hours to keep us. If he didn't work we didn't eat . . . But Dad really appreciated the value of education and worked and worked to let us have it – eighty or ninety hours of cleaning offices and coaches as well as driving to keep us at school. As children we were very conscious of this. So the biggest influences on us really were mum and dad. (Evans)

In contrast, Haigh, whilst his recollection of his mother is neither strong nor positive, still retains powerful, if highly negative, memories of his father:

> Inside [the family] there was a culture of ridicule, of always putting down. I remember thinking why don't my parents ever come to sports day, all the other

> parents did at primary school. I always assumed they would never be there when I needed them ... I never dared say anything to [my father] because there was always the threat of a significant thump. Once he picked me up and threw me into a radiator. I still can't lie down in the bath because I've got a bump on the bottom of my spine. It was heavy duty stuff ... but it gave me some sympathy for children with special needs ... [My mother] was devoted to my father. Whenever I criticized him I was told he was the most wonderful man in the world, if we could only be more like him we'd be all right.

Others have more positive memories of their parents. Hinchliffe, for example, recalls her father as 'a wonderful but old-fashioned dad', but also that he 'didn't want me to have a professional career of any kind. He thought that it would be nice for me to be at home with Mum'. Her mother, however, did want her eldest child to 'have a career'.

Members of the family   If fathers and/or mothers are regarded as key influences in shaping their views and lives by most of our heads, several identified other members of the family or extended family as having played a significant role. Examples of the former include brothers and sisters, grandparents and other family members. Ashdown was one who mentioned the importance of 'close aunts'. Another who did so as well was Ross who talked with great affection, as well she might, about her aunt. Her mother died when she was two and her father followed a few years later. This was during the war years and so she 'was one of many orphan children at the time ... It was not strange or unusual to be an orphan.' Even so, as she says, she and her brother were

> extremely fortunate to have had my mother's sister, who brought us up, and I must say even now as I look back, I think she must have been an absolute saint. My aunt had no children of her own yet within a couple of years she acquired a ready-made family of two stepsons, a nephew and a niece – all in all, a very disparate group. Although they were very poor, and accommodation was the two up, two down house so common in those days, there was never a hint of 'can't afford' or 'no room to take them' ... We had an abundance of 'love', which I must confess was never really appreciated until very much later.

Cases of more general support from the extended family were rarely mentioned. In this Evans is the exception. He recalls, for example, that 'I was virtually at university before I had a new set of clothes. It was usually handdowns from older cousins.' He also recalls that, when he was offered a place at grammar school, 'My parents couldn't afford a uniform. A conglomeration of aunties and uncles and Mum and Dad got me a blazer ... We were a close-knit, an aunties and uncles type, family'.

Local communities   If comments on the place of the extended family were rare, references to the influence of the local community were not. Evans, for example, like several others, stresses the support which he and his family received from, and gave to, the local community in a context in which

'Everyone was in each other's pockets. We helped each other out in hard times, they often were. Neighbours and relatives rallied round, we wouldn't have survived on occasions without that.'

Others recall the closeness and warmth of a local community and how much this had contributed to their lives as children. Rob Sammons's memories border on the elegiac:

> I really did have a lovely childhood. King's Norton was like a small village even though it was part of Birmingham. It was a 'village community', and where we lived backed on to green fields, the canal and a park. My sister and I were very happy throughout our childhood . . . Mum and Dad would let us wander – in a way you'd never be able to today. The council estate was built post-war, it was full of young kids . . . a good place, a good time in which to be children and to grow up . . . Dad . . . was very much the person who'd get involved in helping people. The street in which we lived, even the council estate . . . was a community. We would have, what seemed at that time, huge bonfire parties for the whole street, and other things like that, with everyone taking part.

If Sammons was fortunate in his family and his community, others were less so. Haigh, in escaping from a deeply unhappy relationship with his father, 'spent as much of my childhood outside the home as I could'. There, at least some of the time and in some of the many places in which he spent his childhood, he remembers 'wonderful . . . summers, I suppose children do, and lots of happy times'. As he makes clear, these happy times required a special kind of community since it always required being 'with other children, always in a gang'. Since he had always to assume that his parents 'would never be there when I needed them' this tended to 'make being within a supportive gang that had its own values and rules very attractive. There was a big wood we used to disappear into for twelve hours on Saturdays and Sundays. It was a *Lord of the Flies* culture. I found it comfortable, I knew my position. There was a distinct pecking order, that was curiously supportive.' He is well aware that there was a less acceptable side to all this, noting that for the first eighteen years of his life

> I really couldn't understand what it was all about. I knew there were some fundamental problems. I had no value system that made any sense. I couldn't understand what life was about. I often found it difficult to relate to other people. I divided the world into a small group of people who I rated and bonded with very strongly and then the rest who were of no consequence. It was a dreadful way of looking at things.

Haigh saw this as the first of three periods into which he could divide his life. The second was his three years in college, to which we will return in the next section. Not until well into the third period could he claim to 'have got over my childhood, it took twenty years of marriage to do it'.

Wives and husbands   Haigh identifies a number of factors which enabled him to recover from his childhood, the most important by far being his wife.

But even this relationship did not come easily since, as he put it, 'I met my wife at the end of my first term of teaching. I remember going through a year during which I recognized I needed her and she was all I'd ever wanted, an intelligent and able woman. I felt an incredible tension. I thought I do not want a relationship ... I can't cope with this ... I experienced an amazing see-saw relationship, but eventually we got married.'

Others also stressed the importance of their wives or, more rarely, their husbands in their lives and careers. Some are positive. These include Ashdown, who acknowledges the support which his wife gave him during his postgraduate studies. As he puts it, 'my wife Clare was very much a factor and a presence during this entire period. She was always in the background supporting and encouraging me, both at university as I pursued my PhD, and at Bristol during teacher training'. Later, it was she who persuaded him to apply for the first headship to which he was appointed when he had been 'in two minds about it'.

Some are less positive. Evans and Abrol are divorced, for reasons not wholly disconnected with their work. Abrol, on balance, did not find her husband supportive. The initial decision to come to England from India had been his. He had travelled first and in preparation for her arrival had got her 'degrees and qualifications accepted by the relevant authorities'. But whilst he seems to have been happy enough to accept her wish to pursue her career as a teacher, he was much less understanding when it came to appreciating her desire for promotion. Asked why she wanted to be a head, Abrol listed three possible reasons. In speaking of the second of these she said:

> it could be because in my marriage I was always being undermined, that made me a rebel inside. You know you've got the ability, why should you be undermined when you are not undermining others ... Many times I said to him [my husband] 'I want to prove that I am not what you think I am'. Many times he would ask me, 'What's so different between you and other ladies? They're satisfied with teaching. What makes you think you're so exceptional?' and I said 'I am exceptional' and to prove my exceptional nature and ability I wanted to go to the top position.

As we shall see, Abrol's confidence in her abilities had been generated in part by her relationship with her father and in part by her schooling. It is to this issue and the making of ten students to which we shall now turn.

The making of ten students

Attitudes to school   Each of the ten headteachers reported in this study acknowledge that their experience of schooling, primary and secondary, had a considerable influence upon their attitudes in general and with regard to education in particular. For several, if for a variety of different reasons, the experience was a broadly positive one. For others it was essentially mixed, some good and some bad, or negative. A few were sent to public primary and secondary schools, most attended state primary schools followed by grammar schools.

All of the three women heads to whom we talked remembered their schooldays with gratitude and affection. Ann Hinchliffe is particularly uninhibited. Her primary schooling took place at Nativity Convent in Leicester and she says of it that 'it was lovely. A very happy school. I can still remember vividly the smell of it. I can still see the little place where we could buy rubbers and pencils and tracing paper which was very exciting . . . I have terrifically happy memories of Nativity.' This experience clearly shaped her views on one of the great educational debates of recent times. Thus although Nativity 'was traditional and formal . . . Even so, within the framework of its formality, it encouraged us to be creative. The idea that formal must be dull and informal must be exciting is simply wrong. My education was very stimulating.' For secondary education 'I went to my mother's old school, Loreto College, in St Albans. I was very happy there but I hated being a boarder . . . I was almost twelve when I went. I loved the people and still have good friends from there. The school was lovely, being away from home was awful.' Finally, in spite of the fact that both her schools were 'lovely' private sector schools, Hinchliffe remarked in the interview that

> As I matured, I became increasingly disenchanted with the idea of private education. In my case it meant that I left school with a sense of superiority which was entirely unwarranted. While I was a speech therapist I became very committed to comprehensive education and to the feeling that all young people were of equal value. That appealed to my sense of what democracy should be about and that commitment is part of what I am.

Sudarshan Abrol also recalls her schooling in India with respect and affection. She is at pains to stress that her parents made the decision on where to send her to school on 'educational rather than on religious grounds'. She traces a lifelong concern for equal opportunities in part back to her time at Arya Samaj School, a school run by a reformist Hindu sect. As she says,

> I remember when I was seven we used to sing a song and I performed the role of a boy. The song had an equal opportunity message because it made a mockery of the traditional male role and expressed an appreciation of the role of the woman. . . . It showed that the school valued equal opportunity, that boys and girls should have the same role to play and they should be assertive in insisting on this. . . . When people ask me where I got my assertiveness from, I tell them I got it from my junior school.

Unlike Hinchliffe, she did not develop an antipathy towards private education and on being disappointed by the quality of education which she felt her daughter was receiving from a state special school, had few qualms about sending her to a private school.

The seven male heads, all of whom went to state grammar schools, were a good deal less unanimously satisfied with some or much of the schooling they received. Haigh does not recall his primary school with fondness. As he says, 'It was crowded. There were forty-nine children in my class. It was in an old-fashioned building with fully tiled walls, they didn't get dirty and you could wipe them down. The curriculum was dire: three years preparing for the eleven-plus.' He remembers in particular the casual brutality of the place:

> I was caned frequently, for being a nuisance basically. The head was forever grabbing my hair, pulling it in great yanks at the end of every sentence when he told me off . . . It was a brutal sort of approach. I got caned for turning round and talking to the kid behind me. This teacher had obviously got fed up with me and sent me to the head who caned me. He caned three of us one after another. It was like a conveyor belt, you popped up every now and then and got caned and came back. There wasn't much praise or reward. There was a lot of criticism and punishment.

Morgan and Craig also have negative memories of their schooling. Like Haigh, both experienced a good deal of corporal punishment and both, many years later, still deeply resented this. Craig is scathing and describes a bureaucratized institutionalized system of violence which seems somehow much worse than even the kind of casual brutality which Haigh recalls:

> There was an article in the *Times Educational Supplement* a couple of weeks ago written by a gentleman who had been educated by Jesuits in the same way I had . . . In particular, he referred to the ferula . . . It is a belt made of leather and whale-bone. We were beaten with this ferula as a form of education. We literally had knowledge beaten into us . . . The school I went to . . . had this system where the teachers were holders of 'cheque books' which were used to enforce discipline. If you misbehaved early in the day you were given a cheque which you had to cash in either at lunch-time or at the end of the day. It was like sadistic capitalism . . . a pretty inhumane way of dealing in discipline . . . In truth, I probably hated school when I first started . . . The supreme irony is that I am now working with kids who feel the same way and my job is to convince them of the efficacies of the educational system . . . with my problematic start to school, which on reflection didn't improve greatly during secondary education, I am well qualified for a career in work with pupils experiencing EBD.

If the disciplinary practices of individual schools were one source of disenchantment amongst some of our headteachers, another related to system-wide policies of selection. Most passed the eleven-plus and went to grammar schools where several found themselves separated from brothers and sisters and from friends and friendship groups which they had established in their primary schools. Asked what the eleven-plus transition was like, Evans, despite being happy at his grammar school, makes the point forcefully: 'Two things were difficult. One, I was one of very few going to the grammar school [from his primary school] . . . Two, my twin sister, who I was very close to and still am, didn't pass. We were separated for the first time.' His feelings were compounded by the recognition that, at his secondary modern, 'my brother who is bright but not academic was badly served'. For Evans this explains, in part, why 'I'm very pro-comprehensive. I am for a school for all abilities'. His knowledge of his brother's school came from going 'as a student [teacher] to the secondary modern [he] had attended. It was dreadful. The teachers were brilliant or dreadful. Too many would say, leaving the staff room, "What shall we do today? I'll get them doing some colouring, yes I'll do that".' Happily, on the whole, his memories of his own teachers are much more positive.

Attitudes to teachers   Asked to recall a teacher during their years at school whom they remembered, fewer could or would do so than in our studies of primary and secondary headteachers. Curiously, of those that did, almost all, even those whose experience of schooling had been negative, chose to describe a teacher whose influence was benign. In contrast, Hinchliffe, whose memories of her schools are amongst the most positive of all, had difficulty in doing so. As she acknowledges, 'I know this doesn't sound very good in a book about education, I haven't got a very strong memory of teachers, much more of . . . the excitement of being there and of learning rather than of any particular individuals'. Others who could not recall a teacher having particularly influenced them included Abrol, Ashdown, Craig and Morgan.

Those who did recall the influence of one or more teachers did so for a variety of reasons. Some stressed excellence and dedication. This was partic- ularly impressive when seen against the background of an otherwise poor educational experience. Haigh recalled just such a case:

> There was a teacher of English at the grammar school with low expectations who was inspired. She invented a story about a murder and we all had to work out possible next stages, and we wrote them all down, collected them and talked about them. We built up the story as a whole class, and then she took it away, twisted it a little bit and left it with a number of openings . . . We dressed up as different people in the Court. I was the Defence Lawyer and had an academic gown. Her lessons were like a shaft of light coming into the dark cavern that was our education at that time. It was a phenomenally exciting thing to be involved in, so she stands out.

Ross also praised, and for similar reasons, such a teacher. In doing so, she was the only one of our ten heads to recount an example drawn from her days in a junior school:

> Miss Lever [was] a talented teacher in my junior school. She used to write plays for children . . . the plays . . . were superb. They were the sort of plays that you would re- live again and again, as you become totally engrossed. All the children enjoyed them. They used to vie and fight and clamor to be part of them. It was very exciting and a tremendous boost to the imagination.

Yet others did so for the kindness and support they had received, even when the teacher was inadequate in other ways. Evans talked of Mrs Morris with great affection. She was his form teacher and had played an important part in helping him to settle into his new secondary school:

> She was a weak teacher in terms of discipline, even in the grammar school she had problems, but she was kind to me in so many ways. . . . My primary school gave me a [fountain] pen for passing the eleven-plus . . . I was very proud of it but it was stolen. Mrs Morris replaced it quietly for me. This was typical of her.

Evans and Ross also talked of one of their headteachers. Evans described his as 'a pompous man who was out of touch', one who 'didn't understand the situation in which boys who were very bright but very poor could find themselves'. Knowing this man 'for a long time . . . put [him] off all thoughts of being a head'. Ross spoke with respect and awe about her head. Miss Dobson had certainly not put her off wanting to be a head but Ross stresses that she could not have hoped to exercise headship as her head had done:

> For good or bad, I do remember vividly the headmistress of [my junior] school. She was a mountain of a woman . . . When she spoke, she put the fear of God into everybody, pupils and staff alike. There were three 'mortal sins' at Miss Dobson's school. They were telling lies, playing truant, and stealing. I don't think that anybody who attended Miss Dobson's school would ever lightly say an untruth, or pick up anything that didn't belong to them, without fearing the thunderbolt which they know would strike them down . . . Possibly . . . if there was more of that fear and awe in school today, you would not have the number of disruptive pupils who can't be managed . . . Miss Dobson would manage many of them!

Yet others recalled the influence of a teacher in helping them to make the decision to take up teaching as a career. In our related studies in primary and secondary schools, several heads make a similar acknowledgement but Sammons's example gives the case a new twist:

> I was not sure whether I wanted to go to art college or teacher training college. I remember taking the advice of a young teacher who'd just joined the school . . . He knew I was keen on sport, and suggested I go to his classes and help him in the final months of the sixth form. I ended up [doing so] and I liked it. I then decided to do student teacher work . . . then left . . . to go to teacher training college. . . .

The decision to become a teacher was, for those in our study, the first step in a career journey which was eventually to lead them to headship. It is to this we now turn.

Achieving headship (Accession)

Following Formation, those who in due course become candidates for headship, as with other leadership roles, must determine and enter their chosen career. They then characteristically seek advancement and in doing so finally engage in a period of preparation for promotion to headship during which they develop, rehearse and test their capacity and readiness by comparison with existing office holders and prospective rivals. Accession should, as such, be regarded as a developmental period geared to the accomplishment of two crucial tasks: the preparation and construction of oneself as a credible candidate for promotion and the acquisition of a persuasive performance routine to convince those controlling promotion opportunities. As leadership positions, at whatever level, become available, candidates learn to present themselves, to 'jockey' for position themselves and in doing so to compete with others for preferment. In doing so they come to rely on networks of peers, patrons and sponsors whilst awaiting the call to the next level of office. Furthermore, the lessons which had been learnt and the contacts which were made in successful, and unsuccessful, attempts to achieve promotion at any one level may be relevant to the search for further preferment. In applying these ideas to an analysis of this aspect of our research we shall focus specifically on the making of ten teachers and ten headteachers. In doing so we will draw upon those aspects of our conversations which consider aspects of the history of the careers of our headteachers as teachers and as managers and the extent to which all this was a preparation, planned or otherwise, for the achievement of their first headship.

The making of ten teachers

Why teaching? Rob Sammons's reason for becoming a teacher has been described above. As he recalls it, in his last year as a pupil he was given the opportunity to try teaching by one of his own young teachers and found he liked it. In this group of heads, few came early to the recognition that they wanted to be teachers, and some came very late to it. Haigh told us: 'I did not really decide I wanted to be a teacher until well into my second [teaching] post. Before then it was just something to do.' In arriving at this decision, several acknowledge a significant element of chance in determining their choice. Ashdown, although his father, mother and aunts were teachers, recalls that he 'didn't really have any thought of becoming a teacher' until he was undertaking his degree course at Cardiff University and found that he enjoyed the education option, becoming particularly interested in the 'child psychology course'. At school Clarke had not thought of teaching. He intended to be a pathologist but when this fell through, 'it was my mother, really, who organized my entry into teaching. She took me to the education office and sent me on my way.' Evans's choice was also influenced by his parents and teachers. In his case, however, he made the decision during his primary school years. Ross was another stimulated to opt for teaching, in part, by a suggestion from one of her teachers. As she makes clear, her initial reasons were not born of high enthusiasm or altruism:

> I went from school to teacher training college, not because I had any burning ambition to become a teacher, but on returning to the Sixth Form . . . we were faced with the expectation of making a decision about our career development. We were asked to make choices and I didn't have a clue. The headteacher advised me to come up with something, and she was talking to me about teaching as one example. She told me that if I was in an office . . . I could expect to earn between two pounds ten shillings and three pounds a week, but if I qualified as a teacher, I could expect to start on three hundred pounds a year. It was a very big incentive and there was no escaping the fact it seemed a well paid job. It all just fell into place, almost by accident, because the money was attractive although I didn't really have any desire to enter teaching.

Not all the others, or their parents, saw teaching as so lucrative and/or prestigious. As Sammons recalls, 'Dad would be very much motivated by success in business. He will still, even now, mildly disapprove of me not having a proper job. He would hope that . . . one day I would do something important and earn some money. Teaching has never been that kind of proper job ... He'd still put five pounds in my pocket because he thinks I need the money.' In contrast, whilst Evans's father did have a very high respect for teachers and teaching, he was much less impressed with his son's level of remuneration:

> I remember my first month's salary. It was paid in a wage packet, cash not a cheque. I handed it to my mum as my dad, brother and sister had done. It amounted to £53.00 net pay for my good honours degree and other qualifications. On the same day my brother handed over his week's salary, he'd been apprentice to a joiner and then got work as a skilled carpenter on the building sites, he drew £106.00. Exactly twice as much for the week's work as I earned for my first month's work ... When Dad eventually came home my mum very proudly showed him my first official wage packet ... He asked 'How much did our David bring home?' '£106.00.' I'll never forget, he looked at me and said 'Has it been worth it?' and I said 'Yes'. If you ask me that again today I would say the same ... He was pleased really.

Sudarshan Abrol is another who has 'regretted many things, including getting married, but never being a teacher. I have loved it, and I still love it even after all these years.' The explanation she gives for becoming a teacher is one of the fullest of all; it includes three very different reasons:

> First, it could be it was seen as a suitable profession for females. That is still a cultural thing because it is felt that if you teach you can also look after a family. Second, I remember somebody told me that a teacher is like a burning candle who enables others to burn and in doing so to increase the sum of knowledge. I was very impressed with this idea. Third, in practice, it turned out to be the most convenient thing to do.

Unhappy memories of schooling may have put some off the prospect of teaching but they encouraged others to show they could do better. Craig recalled a conversation 'with a couple of other teachers' in which they had agreed 'one of our main motivations for entering the teaching profession had been that we couldn't really do it as badly as some of the teachers we had when we were at school. We felt, quite strongly, that we would do it considerably better than most of the teachers we had known!' A similar motivation encouraged others to seek headship. Before turning to this issue, let us consider why, and how, they came to teach in special education.

Why special education?   In thinking about this question, we hypothesized that one possible reason for making a career in this field of schooling could be some kind of personal experience of a special need. In fact, this was true of only a small minority of the ten. Abrol's is the clearest example although even she, at the beginning of her teaching career in the UK, had 'worked in mainstream primary education for four years' and was 'quite happy there' before an event occurred which was to have a profound influence on her life and career: 'I had ... a girl ... She was born in 1964. When she was fifteen months old she had a smallpox vaccine reaction. I took her to India and then she had the reaction which is a very rare thing. It left her with left side cerebral palsy ... That made me go into special education. I wanted to explore it.' Of the others, Ashdown alone opted from the beginning of his career in teaching to work with children with special needs. Furthermore, uniquely, this decision was related directly to his advanced studies. Thus during his

> first year at college [I had an] involvement in a student group supporting young people who were mentally handicapped, as the term in use then described them. This involved regular time spent working with these young people where they lived within the hospital environment. I gradually became more involved in work with children who had severe learning difficulties ... This reflected a growing academic interest and a focus in my BA course on aspects of education relating to children with the same kind of disabilities and difficulty ... When it came towards the end of my PhD studies, I was in two minds whether to go into teaching or ... clinical psychology. In the long run, I guess I was really more interested in the teaching and working with youngsters experiencing severe learning difficulties.

Accordingly, he took up his first 'teaching post at Basildon at a special school for ESN(S) pupils'.

John Evans and Chris Morgan have not worked in special schools. Their interest in special education has developed, in part, as one result of their involvement in the management of mainstream schools catering also for children with special needs. They are, however, by no means alone amongst the ten in their experience of mainstream education. Indeed, the others all began their teaching careers in mainstream primary or secondary schools before moving on to special education. In many cases there was the same strong element of serendipity in the decision to opt for special education as there had been to plump for teaching.

The most common route from mainstream to special education amongst our set of headteachers came as a result of an early involvement, by no means always at their own initiative or stated wish, in some form of remedial education. As a case in point, Haigh recalled that 'at my first school, I was supposed to be doing English O Level and some remedial groups. This was not so much from choice, rather it was the only thing I could get to be honest, they just gave me the timetable and I accepted it.' In similar vein Ross recalls her 'introduction to teaching'. On arriving at her first school she discovered that

> there was a gentleman there who had just been appointed to take charge of the children who had difficulty with learning ... He took the older children who were all grouped together in a withdrawal class. I took the younger children who also had SEN ... I was given the 'naughty' difficult children, the 'slow learners' or disaffected in my first year of teaching ... in the middle of the first term, this teacher went sick, so I had the most difficult children together all in one class.

Others who began their career in teaching in this way were more positive. Hinchliffe, having held a senior post in a speech therapy department, was appointed to her first teaching post in a mainstream secondary school by a headteacher who 'gave me my freedom in creating a remedial department and all the support in doing this that I wanted'. Sammons also had cause to be grateful to a head who was willing to take a chance on him. His first post, teaching PE in a comprehensive school, he 'didn't enjoy . . . at all' so he 'went to play golf for about a year'. He then heard of a school that 'needed a man to teach some PE. I was asked if I was interested. I went along not realizing the school was for the physically handicapped. I said I'd do it, certainly up until the Easter, a period of six weeks. I stayed much longer. Thoroughly enjoyed it. Wonderful time.' Like all those who made the transition from mainstream schooling, he has worked in special education ever since. Once there, each worked in different ways, for different reasons and at different rates climbing the ladder to headship. Along the way, all but one experienced one or more periods as a deputy head.

Why deputy headship?   In a recent paper Ribbins (1997a) examines the literature and the research reported in this book and its companion texts to consider the views of thirty-four headteachers on their experience of deputy headship within a wide variety of special, primary and secondary schools (Pascal and Ribbins, 1998; this volume; Ribbins, 1997b; Ribbins and Marland, 1994). His findings suggest that if 'headteachers are interesting[,] deputy headteachers, it seems, are not . . . they have been, virtually, ignored' (295). Ribbins (1997a) considers three main issues: what heads felt of their experience as deputies; what they see as the role of the deputy; and how they compare headship with deputy headship. Drawing, in particular, upon the interviews contained in the chapters which follow, we will consider, briefly, each of these issues.

As might be expected, a variety of views were voiced. Craig expressed regret that he had not had the opportunity to be a deputy head, and others (for example, Ross) were positive about deputy headship. However, many recalled their experience of deputy headship without enthusiasm and the heads with whom they worked with less than unqualified affection. For several, it seems, deputy headship was seen as unsatisfying in itself and an unsatisfactory preparation for headship. Some were given little worthwhile to do, others found the demands they faced overwhelming, and yet others received little support from their headteachers:

> I found the step from head of department to deputy headship the biggest I have ever made . . . in my eighteen years of headship, five of the seven deputies I've helped appoint are now heads and good heads. I have always told them that the step to deputy headship is much bigger than that to headship. I think most of them would agree. (Evans)

> They [the heads she worked for] didn't overtly prepare me. I think they never thought I'd be a head anyway. Nobody expected me to be a head . . . Not even the head where I was a deputy. I can still see his reference, it was balanced, that's about it. Not necessarily saying I had the qualities needed for headship. He sat on the fence. Most of them did. It made me struggle. (Abrol)

If these comments offer some conception of the way in which some of our heads of special education regard deputy headship, none of them are as dismissive as those expressed by Mike Gasper, a head of a primary school (in Pascal and Ribbins, 1998). For him

> the job was absolutely thankless, the worst job on earth. Once I realized that, it was inevitable that I would go for headship ... I didn't like being in the position when I was the pig in the middle between the staff and the head and didn't have ultimate responsibility or control over where or when things were going on or how they were done.

In what follows we consider some of the other reasons these ten heads offered for seeking headship and describe how they prepared for and achieved their first headship.

The making of ten headteachers

In tackling this issue, we shall restrict our discussion to three themes: the reasons for seeking headship, how headship was prepared for, and how headship was achieved.

Why headship?   Earlier, we quoted Craig's claim that one reason he become a teacher was the belief that he could not possibly be less successful at it than some of his own teachers. A similar justification informed some amongst the ten heads in explaining their pursuit of headship. Morgan put it bluntly: 'I decided I had seen a number of people who I didn't respect professionally doing the job and I thought, I could do that job and I think I could do it as well if not better ... I think the underlying motivation for applying to headship was that I'm competitive and I wanted to prove that I was better than some of the people for whom I'd worked.' The other main reason he identified was pecuniary: he 'also had a family as well and wanted more money. Teachers don't get paid all that much money at the end of the day.'

A further common justification was the idea that only headship enabled those who wished to achieve this to influence change at a whole school level. As Ashdown put it,

> I feel that I would achieve a great deal with certain children if I was actually teaching in the classroom. But you know, I do feel overall that I've achieved a lot of things for a greater number of children than I would have done if I had remained a class teacher. I think the same thing applies to my involvement with families, and staff, and the school community. The school leader has a wider impact on things beyond the classroom, although quite obviously, his or her influence upon classroom teaching and learning is always of paramount importance.

Haigh takes a similar view although, in his case, he also believed that he could hardly do worse than the last of his heads during his time as a deputy and that he would welcome the opportunity to try to put into practice the ideas which he had developed during his studies of management which, along with his many-faceted experience, had prepared him for headship:

> I'd been on courses and developed a range of ideas on management, about how you could enable people to realize their potential by involving them in decision-making. I thought this would enable them to function at a higher level – it would make them happier and more productive, and therefore the children would get a better deal. I wanted the chance to put these ideas into action . . . It was almost coincidental that to do that I needed to be a head. It wasn't 'I want to be a head, I want to be in charge'. I needed a vehicle, a place and a venue in which I could use the authority of headship to shape a culture and to create opportunities for people to grow into new ideas.

Preparing for headship   Few of the ten admit to having worked to a planned timetable and programme of career development designed to lead ultimately to headship. Edna Ross 'wasn't looking to be a headteacher. It was not an ambition. I was not saying it was something I would be in so many years' time. I became a headteacher because I happened to be there as . . . deputy . . . when the headteacher retired.' Similarly, Sammons admits: 'quite honestly, I had no ambition at all. People pushed me in the right direction, and I've really relied on that to happen.'

Even so, Ross and Sammons, like all the other eight heads, made an attempt, in some cases slight, in others substantial, to prepare for headship. This preparation took a variety of forms, of which we shall consider two: attendance at courses and reflection on what they had learnt from those who had been their headteachers during their years as teachers.

The nature of the courses and what they entailed in terms of attendance and effort varied very considerably. Some were specifically aimed at preparation for headship; others had a more general management, or other, orientation. Some were award-bearing, others were not; some entailed substantial time and other commitments, others did not; some had made a considerable impression, others had not. In all these respects, Hinchliffe's experience may be located towards one end of the spectrum and Haigh's at the other.

Ann Hinchliffe confesses: 'I hardly ever go on courses . . . I don't go in for this in a big way . . . I did go on a "Preparing for Headship Course" which was run for deputies in the summer holidays of the year that I applied for headships in. It was run by the LEA.' The impact of the course could not have been very great since she goes on to admit that 'I don't remember much about it and I don't remember who took it'. In so far as these comments represent a less than ringing endorsement of the extent and quality of LEA provision with regard to headship preparation, they are echoed by others amongst our contributors. Ashdown felt that for him it would have 'been better to have had a distinct period of preparation for headship. It might have helped me get around some of the difficulties I actually faced in my first couple of years of headship. I do feel there should have been something in place, a course to prepare me for headship, as well as some formal induction procedure, such as ... is now offered by LEAs and outside agencies, and which are increasingly available for aspiring managers today.' For these and other reasons, he is cautiously supportive of initiatives like Headlamp and the National Professional Qualification for Headship, and he offers a thoughtful rationale for such courses – 'it will inevitably depend upon how well it is organized, but yes, I think the idea is good ... I also think that by going on courses, you have the opportunity as a professional to interact with and learn from peers who are thinking about the same sorts of things and doing the same job as yourself. I think that is a large part of the value of a course, as well as actually receiving ideas and information from the people who are delivering it.' In any case, one must hope that this provisions turns out to be a great deal more worthwhile than the four-day residential course which the LEA put on for its new headteachers out of which John Evans walked.

David Haigh, having been promoted in short order to a major head of department post, began to feel the need for 'an intellectual dimension to my thinking to enable me to do my job ... a framework that gave me greater insight and understanding so I did a [part-time] degree in Management ... It was trip to Damascus for me as regards changing my values and the way I looked at the world.' He followed this by studying for further degrees, MEd and then PhD, both also in aspects of educational management. Interestingly, he deliberately decided not to focus his further studies specifically on special education on the grounds that he 'wanted something rigorous and suspected Educational Administration would be far more intellectually rigorous and much less emotionally influenced. I enjoyed doing it'.

Most of the others also undertook further degrees and/or diplomas, usually, unlike Haigh, in some aspect of special education during the years before appointment to their first headship. Rob Ashdown is an exception: he had already undertaken his PhD, on a theme in special education, before taking up his first teaching post. Hinchliffe is another: study for a part-time first degree in history during her years as a speech therapist enabled her to take up a first teaching post even though she had no professional teaching qualification. Like Haigh and like many of the rest, she describes this experience as enjoyable and worthwhile, both in its own right and as a means of enabling career progression. Sadly, the same could not be said about the views they expressed on their initial professional teacher training course. Whilst all rated teaching practice as worthwhile or very worthwhile, most expressed negative or extremely negative views on the college-based aspect of their teacher training.

Most acknowledged that they had learnt something about headship from those who had been their headteachers. However, in common with the other studies of headship in this series (Pascal and Ribbins, 1998; Ribbins, 1997b; Ribbins and Marland, 1994) this tended to be more about what not to be and what not to do than the converse. David Haigh's interview can be used to illustrate this view. During his years as a teacher he worked for three heads. His account of one of them was amongst the most distressing we have reported throughout the series as a whole. Reflecting upon his experience in general he says 'I can't think of anything I learned from any of the heads I have known in terms of wanting to use what they did as a theme to put my variations on. None as far as I can remember did anything I regard as central to what I've tried to do. I can see a lot of what they did I've looked at and thought I must avoid doing. It's been what not to do, very much so. I can think of little I learned'. In developing his view, he presents one of the most negative portraits of a head we have heard. As he recalled it,

> I still remember my first day. At 10.15 the head called me into his office. I'd only been in the school an hour, he ranted and raved, said I'd got nothing to offer as far as he was concerned, it hadn't been his idea to appoint me and so on and on. I went out quite shaken, but one of the other deputies said don't worry, he does that to everybody. I was lucky he didn't do it in the middle of the corridor. He was unbelievable, he didn't improve during the ... years I was there.

Few other accounts approached this, but we did hear of heads who were, variously, manipulative, lazy, autocratic, ineffective, sly and unpleasant.

Happily, there are also a number of positive portraits. Ann Hinchliffe was particularly fortunate in her heads. Her first head 'taught me a lot. He gave me my freedom ... and all the support ... I wanted ... [He] taught me that if you are going to encourage staff you must give them opportunities to succeed. He also taught me that you can't change a school that does not want to be changed. It was a good lesson. You have to create the environment for change for change to be successful.' Her second head was also 'excellent' and she 'learned a terrific amount from [him] ... He had a passion for excellence before it became a fashionable word and in doing so ensured we achieved high standards in the classroom and in every other part of the school.'

Finally, Edna Ross stresses that it is possible to admire and respect a head without wanting to be or to act in every respect like them. Peter Lawrence

> was a wonderful person ... a tremendous character, who contributed an awful lot simply by his presence in the school. However, [as deputy] I seemed to do most of the organizing in school. When the school first opened we weren't even going to have a timetable, and each class teacher was going to be responsible for the daily programme of their own group ... the kind of approach I associate with an archetypal EBD headteacher, their philosophy would be reflected in an approach which would be about 'flying by the seats of their pants' or 'making decisions on the hoof', or facing the staff each morning and asking the question, 'What are we going to do today?' I couldn't accept this approach. I felt very strongly that we needed to have a structure for the curriculum, a firm foundation upon which to build an approach to teaching and learning. It was important that everybody knew where they were supposed to be and what they were supposed to be doing ... But as I say, Peter Lawrence was a super man, I felt involved and I felt that he appreciated my work. I must repeat that point. I really did feel appreciated. . . .

Against this backdrop, when it came to seeking promotion for headship, we were not surprised to learn that whilst Peter Lawrence had been very supportive, David Haigh's head had not. It is to this, and related issues, that we will now turn.

Achieving headship   In considering the views of our heads on achieving headship we shall focus upon two main themes: first, on the extent to which they found support from sponsors and patrons in the search for promotion; second, on the problems they encountered in the pursuit of advancement and their views on how headship promotion systems and process operate in theory and in practice.

In seeking and achieving promotion, ultimately to headship, many of the ten were assisted by three groups of mentors and sponsors: their head-teachers, officers and advisers from the local education authority, and academics. 'Mentors' we define as those who had played a significant role in enabling them to develop a conception of headship and a capacity to present that understanding in appropriate ways and circumstances. 'Sponsors' are those who exercised some power within the decision-making process which determines promotion to headship.

As we shall show, it is possible to be mentor and sponsor and mentors and sponsors can work closely together. In practice, heads frequently play both roles in advancing the careers of their staff and in doing so may co-operate closely with senior LEA staff. Clarke, quite early in his career, showed a fine understanding of the rules of the game by recognizing the potential value of working with a high-profile head. This led him to move

> sideways to an all-girls school . . . as head of science. I moved there specifically to work with the headteacher. She was a well known head who had a lot of charisma and style . . . It was a bit odd, looking back, to make such a sideways move. The motive was really to move forward professionally under this new head . . . She was very well regarded in the City and by other heads and the officers of the LEA. I guess I felt if I was involved with her and worked in her school, then I would be more likely to win recognition for good work. I felt that I might even gain extra recognition and move ahead of other people, who were as good as or even a little better than me, but who were not working in the same environment, with the same advantage.

Rob Sammons, as noted earlier, was one who did not regard himself as ambitious and so relied on being pushed forward by others. As such, like Clarke, although without the premeditation, he was fortunate to work for a highly regarded head. Asked to recall this head he responded:

> What I see is this little bloke who was held in such enormous esteem by everybody who came into contact with him . . . Wilson Stuart School in those days was a very highly respected special school in a period when Birmingham was a very highly respected LEA. Frequent guests to the school were people like Gulliford [University of Birmingham], Tansley [inspector for special education in Birmingham], Wedell [University of Birmingham] and others who were famous names, educationalists. They came to Mitch, worked with us, and so obviously held him in high esteem. It did not matter who you were in the system, everybody was a little in awe of Mitch . . . He pushed me onwards in the right direction. He encouraged me to go to Birmingham

> University – I took an advanced diploma with Gulliford. It was a great time . . . After I'd finished . . . Mitch told me about a deputy headship going at another special school where he was a governor . . . He said that I ought to be interested because I should go on to become a headteacher. Tansley had said the same thing to me – he was particularly good at encouraging people.

By his own admission, without the support and active encouragement of such people, Sammons would probably never have become a headteacher.

Edna Ross described how a head and an officer can work together. She had attended an INSET weekend for special education attended by an influential officer of her local authority. She recalls 'John Littson [the officer] chatting with me at the end . . . and telling me that he was very pleased and heartened by the way Peter Lawrence [her head] had spoken about me to him. I thought that was very good.' Even so, when Lawrence retired, she, as deputy, was not 'full of confidence' of being appointed in his place. In this case she feared she might be a victim of a gender prejudice since

> It had filtered through to me that they were looking for a man. They wouldn't be allowed to say that now, would they? They were looking for a man because it was principally a boys' school. They also preferred someone new coming into the school . . . I can only presume that the 'right young man' . . . didn't turn up . . . I remember saying to the Chief Education Officer a little while later that if I had gone to the interview and there had been a bearded gentleman in his mid thirties amongst the candidates, I wouldn't have bothered staying for my turn.

If there are clear hints in these last comments that things are not always as they should be, this is made explicit by others. Three cases must serve to make the point. The first is drawn from Abrol's account of her experience in seeking promotion first to deputy and later to head. On the one hand she identifies several people who acted as mentors and sponsors during her career including one of her headteachers, some of her university teachers and officers and members of the local authorities for whom she worked. On the other hand she found promotion difficult to achieve. As she recalls these years:

> I applied [for headship] several times without success. It even took a lot to become a deputy. I tried several times before I was finally appointed. You may take this wrongly but I'm telling you honestly how it felt. I said to myself 'This is a racialist country but in any case I'm going to prove I can do it' . . . So when I had been a deputy for about four years I started trying for headships . . . I tried in the Midlands, I tried in London, I tried in Bromley, I even tried in Clacton-on-Sea. I applied nine times and was shortlisted every time. But when I got to interview I was never appointed. It seemed my face didn't fit . . . I had good qualifications and good experience. I can only think that my name Abrol was confusing. If I had used Kaur maybe I wouldn't have been shortlisted.

In the second case, Haigh emphasizes that the checks and balances ostensibly designed to guarantee the fairness of decisions on headship promotion in general may, in certain particular circumstances, offer very little real

practical protection. His experience of this under the headteachers described above had not been a good one. These

> were unhappy years. He [the head] used to do things like say to people, 'I'll fix it so
> that you'll never get another job in this authority'. In my case I suspect it was true. I
> made seventy-six applications and got eight interviews. I'd a first class degree and a
> masters in educational management, experience of everything under the sun special
> needs wise, a history of rapid promotion, a lot of people saying nice things about me
> but it didn't help. It struck me again and again how fragile the system was. There are
> those charts that say if there's a problem you approach this person who approaches
> that person and all this suggests that the system as a whole maintains fairness and
> justice, but when push comes to shove there is a strong likelihood it doesn't work . . .
> I was not getting support from the authority. Some inspectors and officers even
> seemed to believe if a head says black is white, then it is and no argument. It was
> certainly put to me that 'You don't get on with your head'. For that person those who
> didn't get on with their head can't be a head.

In the third example, Morgan says some uncompromising things about
how local systems of promotion can be systematically subverted. In his
view,

> Merthyr . . . was regarded as a place where what political party or other 'fraternity'
> you might belong to, if it was the right one, would do you a lot of good in any
> promotion selection. Politics played a real part in career advancement . . . when
> Merthyr became part of the reorganized Mid-Glamorgan LEA, we were given a very
> enlightened District Education Officer . . . He was very fair and changed the system.
> People who were then working hard won recognition and promotion was a natural
> part of that process. There was an open discussion about an individual's professional
> development and career opportunity. The interview procedure was not a hidden
> agenda or prescribed selection. [That was what] I had experienced . . . I remember
> being interviewed by the 'old' Chief Education Officer and Chairman of the
> Education Committee. I actually had three minutes to answer two questions, and
> then I learnt I had been successful and was appointed the deputy headteacher of one
> of the biggest primary schools in Mid Glamorgan. It was farcical.

If both Haigh and Morgan had reservations to express about the nature of
the involvement of local authorities in the process of promotion to headship,
it should also be said that others spoke positively of their role in this. Thus
Ross felt 'appreciated' by her LEA and stressed the merits of being 'a part of
the LEA, a "family"' and Hinchliffe talked nostalgically about the days when
'local education authority officers got to know deputies who wished to be
heads and advised governors' accordingly. She also wondered 'how governors now choose' and doubted 'if some governing bodies have the skills and
experience they need in such important decisions'.

Of course, being appointed to a headship is one thing, enacting it is quite
another. It is to this latter issue that we now turn.

Enacting headship (Incumbency)

Career progression for school leaders in special education is influenced by similar factors to those which affect ascendancy to headship within mainstream primary and secondary schools (see Pascal and Ribbins, 1998; Ribbins and Marland, 1994). It is evident that stages of development, previously described in this chapter, are present in the stories of those headteachers we interviewed in our research study. Formation and Accession, the first of these developmental stages, naturally lead into the period of Incumbency. The individual takes up office, for the first time, or perhaps repeating a previous period of headship, and experiences a similar set of feelings, perceptions and understanding of the task facing them. There are, however, differences in the setting, and, given our interest in the leader's role in context, that is, the actual world of day-to-day school management, such contextual factors are important (see Gronn and Ribbins, 1996).

A second set of differences in the approach to the period of incumbency as a headteacher reflect the leadership persona developed by the individual through the stages of Formation and Accession. This profile, we suspect, will be largely intact by the time an individual faces their first headship. Experience and professional interest will have interacted to produce a particular vision and a set of beliefs, shaping both attitudes and behaviour, in turn reflecting individual personality and, more importantly, the professional persona.

What remains fascinating, and arguably of considerable significance, is the relationship between this professional persona and the nature of the school organization. The area of school management which is under-played in the theoretical literature, yet more or less accepted as a key to effective education (HMI, 1988; Ofsted, 1993), is the exercise of 'firm leadership' with its inferred notion of 'leadership personality'. It is as if, early on in the first period of Incumbency, the 'collective self-concept' of an institution, its identity, as reflected in an ethos and a culture, shifts to accommodate the management style of the new headteacher. Our research confirms this perception. Thus each of the heads talks of the importance of coming to terms with their new post in the first few weeks of appointment. The process continues throughout incumbency. The head's persona can gradually become synonymous with the reputation and identity of the school. This, it should be said, does not simply reflect the sole heroic charismatic leader. More probably, it does mirror the nature of school leadership, and the social psychology of the school system.

Management style is a useful construct through which to explore these individual differences, particularly as they are revealed during the turbulent challenge of the first year or so of Incumbency. While the rudimentary persona of a leader may well be intact on arrival, the experiences associated with managing change and establishing leadership in an organization inevitably lead to further shaping of that persona (Ribbins and Sherratt, 1997). A repertoire of management strategies continues to be built around the 'core persona', from which flows the style of management unique to that person.

In the various accounts of headship in special education, the four stages of Incumbency, while they may differ in the final stage, do in the first three stages remain easily identified. What does vary considerably is the period of time taken by a headteacher to move through each of these stages of Incumbency. An interesting outcome in our research was to discover that the rate of passage through these stages did perhaps correspond to the special educational context. Rayner (1995), for example, initially predicted that the emotional and behavioural difficulties context would encourage rapid progression, given the nature of work within this area. It is, by definition, volatile, turbulent, challenging and very stressful. The research reported in this study revealed this not to be the case. Clarke, for example, has spent a relatively long period of time in-post as an 'Incumbent Headteacher' in an EBD school. This is in contrast to his previous management career in mainstream schools, which is characterized by school change and progression. Indeed, Ross provides the best example of this 'longevity', having spent more than twenty years in the one EBD school, of which the last fourteen were as headteacher.

The special educational context does seem to affect general career progression and the development of leadership within school. Overall, it appears that turn-over of staff, and, more particularly, movement of senior staff within special schools, is slow, indeed, on occasion, dead slow. Several heads in our study have spent ten years or more in their present post, and for some, this is their first and only headship. The marginalization of special education, both for staff and pupils, is chronicled by O'Hanlon (1988) and should come as no surprise. However, to discover that this also applies to headteachers is significant, both as a further indication of a separateness which exists within the educational system and for the impact a slow or static career movement has upon the leadership cycle and institutional development.

An interesting implication of this developmental pace, in the professional lives of the heads in our study, has been the impact of 'staying put'. Their perceptions of doing the job reflect similarities between perspectives given by a head at the end of his first year (Craig) and heads who are close to retirement (Evans, Hinchliffe) or who have recently retired (Abrol, Ross). The stages of development offer quite distinct periods in a 'life cycle' which for some is repeated within the same school, while for others it involves moving on to a new school or even to a different job (Haigh). Underlying this regeneration is an awareness of being an agent of change and a sense of moving forward, as exemplified by Clarke's claim, 'It doesn't matter where you put me, I'll work for change and regeneration'. This dynamism features strongly, too, in the first stage of Incumbency, the Initiation or start-up of headship.

Initiation

The arrival of the post-holder marks the beginning of the first stage of Incumbency. The analogy which comes to mind is of moving house. The post-holder has accepted the offer of appointment and moving day involves taking possession of the keys of the building. Responsibility for the school is symbolically represented in the ownership of those keys and the management of the establishment. Edna Ross describes this sense of ownership clearly:

> I always felt that Slades Farm School was my school. You did feel, very much, that it was a place you enjoyed going to, felt at home in, because it was a comfortable place to belong. That sense of ownership, that personal feeling is very important. I know it's said that as a headteacher you shouldn't say 'my school' but should say 'our school'. I wouldn't deny the importance of staff belonging to the school. I think that all the staff felt in their own way that Slades Farm was 'their school' or, just like me, 'my school'.

From the outset, the early stages of Initiation are taken up with perceptions of management authority and credibility. The in-coming head is working, hands-on, with expectations, attitudes and a mind-set about the role and responsibilities of leadership and management. Indeed, in many respects these expectations lie at the heart of a constellation of forces, created by this mind-set, which crucially affects the running of the establishment as well as the shaping of the leadership function.

The first task, it seems, is to make a mark. The new leader must in some shape or form make a declaration of self, as a leader, which will embody professional expertise and express 'street credibility', as well as presenting a vision and philosophy for special education. Colouring this statement, and framing it, is the leadership personality. It combines an interface between the professional and the personal, characterized by attributes and traits which mark out a leader's persona and point to the nature of the management regime.

All of the heads interviewed described this experience. Sammons vividly recounted the first meeting he had with staff in his new school. He explained:

> I hoped they would call me Rob because I hoped we would be able to talk and work together as a staff. If I asked their opinion, I wanted them to give it, but there was another side to the coin, which was if they didn't express an opinion, I would assume they didn't have a view, and make up my own mind. I also said that if I didn't want their opinion I wouldn't ask for it, because I would have made up my mind and this would happen if there was an issue in which I very strongly believed.

Haigh described the same process, with a less easy feel to it, as the mark is drawn and the new leadership line is adopted.

> I sat down with them and said 'Over the next however long it takes I think these are the stages we will go through. A stage where you don't trust me . . . ' . . . I knew what

> I wanted and I had a framework and an understanding to work from and I shared
> this with the staff so that they also felt that they were working within a structure.

Other heads recall the same experience. Evans describes a direct approach
to making his mark, repeated in each school in which he took up headship.
He made it clear from the start who was the 'boss':

> I am willing to listen to anybody and to have regard to what is said . . . I will make the
> key decisions at my level. You'll often think you've not been listened to but you have.
> You have to know the difference between consultation and negotiation. On many
> things I'm not negotiable. I'll consult, I'll try and win you over. I know it would be
> useless to try and start something almost all the staff oppose but even on this there
> may be some things I hold so dear that I will try to make them happen.

Morgan tells a similar story. He began headship, he recalls, by bluntly
warning staff he was intent on changing things, and if they did not want this,
to begin thinking about leaving the school.

Ross, faced with a different role as incumbent, emphasizes a less turbulent
transition, yet nevertheless one which involved asserting and claiming the
role of leader. Hinchliffe's summary of this 'arriving process' vividly captures
the act of stamping a mark of individuality on the institutional mind-set. She
needed to find the head's chair, and perhaps more importantly, the head's
office, which involved evicting the school matron from her current accommodation!

The arrival of the head is followed by a period of Initiation, during which
the educational community, that is, pupils, parents, staff, governors, and
perhaps the LEA, look to the head for direction and purpose. A lead must be
given in order that the function of headship is fulfilled. A number of key
themes emerge from our research which characterize this period of development:

- *Preparedness* – Evans stresses the importance of readiness: gearing
  up for the job. This is exemplified by his three-point plan for his
  first headship and the view that if you don't prepare for an
  interview you don't deserve the job. Craig's awareness of his lack
  of 'preparedness', in the sense of not having been a deputy head,
  demonstrates the same point. He talks of the need for some prior
  experience of management and the insights or experience this
  would bring. He infers that this, in part, may have explained the
  fraught nature of his early months of headship and the 'steep
  learning curve' this involved. Conversely, Ross's experience of
  deputy headship, in the same school, is seen as a key factor in
  providing a smooth transition to headship.
- *Leadership style, self-belief and self-image* – each of our heads referred
  to the need for self-projection in the early days of headship. This
  was necessarily supported by an inner self-confidence and idea of
  what it is that ought to be achieved. Haigh, Evans, Morgan and

Hinchliffe all describe the certainty which they felt in the face of what they perceived to be a challenge. Others admit to apprehension and nerves when faced with the prospect of this challenge, which, Abrol tells us, repeats itself throughout headship. Ashdown talks about the experience of beginning a second headship contributing to self-awareness of management style and method. This sense of individuality is again, he reminds us, put under intense scrutiny in the first weeks of headship.

- *Professional expertise* – linked to the head's own concept of professional self, this reflects notions of particular experience and expertise. Perhaps equally important are perceptions of this experience and expertise held by other members of the school and the wider educational community. Craig talks very clearly about this, both in terms of his own staff as a head of an EBD residential school, and as head of a PRU (pupil referral unit) faced with managing a service to twelve schools. He describes the need to establish working partnerships, a point repeated by all of our heads, but goes on to neatly capture the essence of the greater need to project professional competency: 'I also need to have professional credibility. I think you have got to look the part – have street credibility. I don't say that lightly ... when I talk about professional credibility I mean you have to be able to back up what you say ... '.

  Ashdown describes a similar approach in taking up headship in his second school. Aware of the change in nature of the Severe Learning Difficulties (SLD) presented by the school population, he recalls deliberately enhancing his professional knowledge base. Several of the heads make this same point, but focus upon the need to remain a 'good' teacher, as part of a broader need for street credibility as a leader within the educational community.

- *Management expertise* is a part of this need for professional competence which is brought into sharp focus during Initiation, as interaction with people includes 'getting to know you'. The 'testing' a teacher expects in the early days of taking on a new class is repeated at a school level for the head. Much of this has to do with authority, expectations, role definition and ultimately purpose and direction. Yet more of this has to do with personal and professional inter-relationships: how pupils and staff, or parents and governors, can relate to the headteacher. A primary influence in shaping the individual head's person-management skills seems to have been their experience of being managed. As we have seen, some, like Hinchliffe, remember fondly an excellent head, who was responsible for inspiring their developing approach to management. Others, like Haigh, Abrol and Morgan, learnt what not to do, and shared with others a motivation that they could do a better job, perhaps, than those they had seen attempting school leadership.

- *Support structures and survival strategies* seem to feature less overtly than might be expected. Abrol describes her need for such structures, which in part reflects a personal perception of having struggled against the odds throughout her career as an educator. She refers to positive support from colleagues and LEA personnel. To some extent, her early period in school reflected a wider struggle in the community in which she lived. She explains, 'There is prejudice in our own community and the racialism is from the other side, it's three times the battle being a woman, an Asian woman in the male-dominated society and then in a racialist community.'

  Other heads make less reference to support, falling back on reserves of self-belief and conviction. While saying this, reference to home and family figure repeatedly, reflecting a much needed stability. Ashdown, Morgan and Ross provide alternative versions of this explanation, with Ashdown and Morgan laying great importance on home and family as a separate world, while Ross describes a life beyond education, involving 5 a.m. rises, and work on the farm. Many of the heads talk of staying at school to finish work rather than taking it home, and the value of a strategy which involves keeping the two worlds separate.

Overall, this initial phase of headship reflects the period during which the organizational climate of the school adjusts to reflect a new reality – the management style of the in-coming headteacher. Interestingly, the stories related by all of the heads at interview emphasized the need for change. This appears to be a necessary requisite for taking up appointment. Where it is not emphasized, and stability is identified as the order of the day (see Ross's comments), the school community is still expectant, waiting for change.

Most of the heads interviewed had appointments which pre-dated the Education Reform Act of 1988, yet all significantly profiled curriculum change, reform, and school development as a priority. Several describe their position as one in which they found it impossible to lose, with schools in a mess, there being no place to go, but forward and upwards, in terms of school improvement. The challenge facing them was simply to make it happen. The prospect was daunting for some, exciting for others, but nevertheless the same, with an inner conviction that their vision was right, driving them forward. An interesting afterthought, of course, is the idea that no 'movement' would have been failure. This did not figure in their thinking, or in any initial approach, which, to use a topical term, reflected an attitude of 'zero-tolerance' to failure.

Development

The management of change, not surprisingly, figures greatly in the minds of heads recounting their early days in post. This preoccupation with change is increasingly emphasized as the end of the first stage of headship is realized. The second stage of incumbency, a period of Development, is described by Day and Bakioglu (1996) as typically lasting from four to eight years, and marking out the period of sustained work aimed at school improvement.

A desire to come to grips with the job reflects in part the natural extension of an initial impression made by the head. Something has got to happen. Momentum is triggered during Initiation and must be harnessed and directed rather than lost or dissipated. This again is very much like the making of a new home. The first years of a new house are superseded by the desire to make a new home a better home. Priorities are sorted, plans are laid, and the development is organized. The headteacher, facing a range of possibilities, must alternate between 'strategic management', involving the decision-making process as a response to 'what to do', and 'operational management', involving the administrative process as a response to 'how to do it'.

The intrinsic desire to implement change and to improve the school is further fuelled by external forces – of national policy and new legal responsibility. The head, the school, the provision, must do the job. Indeed, since 1988, the need to respond to change has been a basic need for all schools. The issues generated by the educational legislation, which has unleashed a flood of reform, altering the educational landscape in what now appears to be an irreversible way, has affected the management of SEN in terms of both policy and practice (Walters, 1994; Riddell and Brown, 1994; Fish and Evans, 1995). Indeed, the issues of choice and change, as they face the head in a special school, are rehearsed by Chapman (1994) and Rayner (1995). An agenda for development has been, to a great extent, laid down by recent legislation. This has, for example, introduced the national curriculum to special education. It has created self-managing structures for the educational system. It has imposed a range of accountability, in the form of Ofsted, the Code of Practice, and LEA audits of SEN provision. It has reinforced parent power and rights supported by a formal system of appeal and tribunal.

This changing reality is evident in the thinking and approach to school improvement shown by our ten heads. Decision-making and the setting of priorities during the period of Development reflect the basic relationship between the personal and professional in the leader. A creative conflict is at play. A tension exists as the result of 'internal' drives, linked to philosophy, vision and a deeper-seated notion of what special education means or should be, and the external forces of government policy, funding realities, educational initiatives and resource.

Craig sums it up well when he states 'when we talk about special education, I think the biggest problem we face is that we've got a *finite* resource and budget and we've got *in-finite* needs. When we talk about the market economy, I think we fail to see the mismatch.' The implication, then, for heads in special education is that

> the challenge is there and the important thing is how we rise to meet the challenge, how we manage the provision. It's early days still here at Warrington, but the biggest problems for special education still remain lack of funds, and a lack of resource. What we must do here in Warrington is make the most of the opportunities that unitary status will offer us. To me, and crucially for the successful management of special education, by which I mean ensuring that we are about meeting the needs of pupils with SEN, this means all 'relevant' agencies working together – education, social services, health, youth services, educational welfare services, educational psychologists – to create a co-ordinated provision for children with SEN.

All the heads refer to this decision-making, which can pose dilemmas but also release energy for improvement. Ofsted, for example, is referred to by all of the heads, some less positively than others, but the overall effect is one of impact and change (Ashdown, Morgan, Haigh, Ross).

The period of Development is positively described by Day and Bakioglu (1996) as a time of vigorous activity. This is confirmed in our conversations with heads, in which they recount shaping the nature of their institution. A sense of movement is repeatedly mentioned, conveying the importance of momentum, and the idea of growth. Underpinning this perceived need are a number of developmental themes which characterize this stage of headship. For example:

- *Maintaining high expectations* vies with leadership as a key pre-occupation during this period of Development. Indeed, showing leadership, sharing a vision, and implementing policy in practice, sum up much of the activity taking place in the 'early middle years' of a headship. Facilitating this activity, making it happen, demands maintaining high expectations, and a collective sense of doing better.
- *Leadership and vision* represent the core function of the headteacher. The act of leading development fulfils this function in two main ways: it provides the school with a focal point for this development, which is collectively expressed in a statement of values, an ethos, a sense of mission or purpose, and a developmental direction (see Morgan); and it provides a catalyst for action, growth, adaptability and change, which are characteristics associated with an effective organization (see Clarke). The nature of leadership and vision described in this way is reminiscent of the interactive relationship in the curriculum between process and content. It is difficult to conceive of successful learning without both being developed, as it is inconceivable to imagine successful leadership without a clarity and quality of vision.
- *Team-building and improvement processes* represent the principal

medium through which educational leaders can hope to realize development. All ten heads make repeated reference to the value of staff collaboration and effective team-work. Well worn terms like 'ownership', 'enablement', 'collegiality' and 'empowerment' are used, but the tone and authenticity underlying these ideas belies suggestions of cliché. Involvement with all sections of the educational community features in this picture of institutional development. The working relationship of the head to the governing body is identified as central while the daily 'reality' of management and leading the school is perceived wholly as the purview of the headteacher (Morgan, Ross). A clearly established effect of LMSS and, in Sammons's case, GMSS, is drawn out, with a changing role for headship reinforcing wider institutional development. Sammons's development of the school management structure is one example of such activity, involving the establishment of a senior management team. Interestingly, no headteacher is emphatically negative about the change to self-management, and those like Morgan who recognize fundamental changes to their role as they develop LMS do not appear to be unhappy with the extra responsibility (Abrol, Clarke and Sammons). Rather, Morgan points to the problem of a diminishing unit of resource and the pressure this creates for maintaining a school budget and recent levels of educational provision.

- *Continuing professional development* is acknowledged as the fuel for the vehicle of school improvement and school effectiveness. While no explicit reference is made to the theory, notions of the learning organization (Schon, 1983) underpin much of what is stated by the heads in our study. Sammons stresses the link between institutional vitality and INSET: staff expertise is the life-blood of a special school. He refers to his own career and a continuing strand of personal and professional involvement in such activity. This began in the early days of teaching in Birmingham, and included periodic spells of secondment to work for the LEA, and partnership with higher education. Every head mentions this activity in various ways, with its significance carrying both personal and professional implications for their leadership style and for the ethos of management established within their own institution. Ashdown points to the importance of developing and maintaining a professional knowledge base for every practitioner. He describes much of his current work in terms of development, giving us a picture of reflective leadership which perfectly reflects the continuing activity of this phase of Development in a headship. This is exemplified by Morgan, who stresses the relationship between the school and its developing reputation for work in professional development at several levels, ranging from within school across the LEA to the national forum. All of this, he insists, is good for staff, pupils and school.

- *Personnel management* – in terms of managing staff-related issues as well as leading professional development – figures sharply during the period of Development. The head's approach to staff inter-relationships and a code of professional conduct is laid down at an early point, and is important as a foundation for development. Trust is a central issue in this process, and this is overtly emphasized in Haigh's account of development in his school, and his personal approach to a new role as an Educational Adviser. Issues of personal and professional need are shared with the head as part of a series of developing relationships which colour the ethos and climate of the school staff room, the school playground, and the classroom. Ross explains that a head must keep a finger on the pulse of the school and a weather eye on the well-being of staff as part of the working week. A stressed staff, it is inferred, will give less and less, in terms of performance and productivity. Underpinning this, of course, is the general management style and approach adopted by the head (see Craig, Ashdown, Hinchliffe and Evans).

- *Cycles of re-generation* form a final aspect of Development. They link the previously described developmental activity to the next stage of a head's incumbency, which is Autonomy. All ten heads referred to a notion of school development which reflected our description of career cycles for school leadership. Indeed, the two often appear to merge, as the rhythm of change in a school mirrors the developmental pattern of headship. There is a clearly stated need to see change as an endemic part of institutional well-being. In one sense, the idea that a school must remain adaptive, flexible, and alive, rather than fixed, static or stagnant, is captured in the notion of developmental movement described by Ainscow (1991) and Ainscow *et al.* (1994). This is expressed by the heads in various ways. Morgan describes the need to recharge professional batteries using INSET and ensuring CPD. He argues that this is as true for the head as for the rest of the staff. Evans is even more succinct and states: 'We need challenges. We must be on the move. If a place stands still, it is lost. I can't do with teachers who want to stand still ... I am willing to flog myself to death as a teacher and manager to get results in my teaching and in my management.'

It is, finally, an area of school life which is reinforced by the head's projected expectations and augmented by recruitment and appointment of new staff. Morgan, for example, refers positively to the impetus given to development by the introduction of new staff. Hinchliffe, too, argues that 'There are times when you need to introduce new people if you want to implement change. Unless the key people are interested and excited by the changes and really want to achieve them they will not happen.' The turn-over of staff contributes to the movement and change necessary to keep a good school moving. It may well be the case, however, that the head is then cast in the role of providing a necessary coherence and stability for continuity in development! The implications of this view are enormous for leadership in special education, given that there is little or no movement of staff in a special school.

Autonomy

The analogy of moving house for career progression is useful again in considering the next stage of leadership, Autonomy. This third period in headship incumbency is like that phase in home ownership which is summed up as maintenance and care. In other words, a leader is more concerned with administration and consolidation, fine-tuning, making sure things are in the right place rather than the right things are in place. At the risk of mixing metaphors, it is also like taking a journey in a new car. Early stages in the trip, in the slow lane, or driving up hill, involve lots of gear change, but this third phase of leadership marks a second phase of the journey, a change in pace, or speed, as the car travels in the fast lane. The driver, if there is one, can use cruise control!

Taking these two metaphors a little further, it is interesting that a feeling of satisfaction imbues the conversation when heads talk over this period of headship. While they all insist on emphasizing the nature of momentum and the need for continuing professional development, and this recurs as a key theme during this period, they also invoke a sense of confidence associated with control and competence. They are very much settled into a self-construction of professional role which they have successfully played. They are used to the role and feel more able to reflect on processes and approach. Clarke offers an interesting insight into this transition, as an experienced head of several schools, both in mainstream and then special education. He strenuously resists the notion that he has ever felt that he has 'arrived' and the work is more or less complete. Yet he comments, somewhat self-depreciatingly,

> I'm now old and ancient so things become blurred, a bit like failing eyesight. I probably do things differently now, maybe I've developed my own personal style of management which runs on automatic. I mean perhaps I have my own personal ethos, or aura, and therefore there's something that emanates from you, and if you go into a room, or a classroom, or a meeting, maybe there's something there which generates leadership. Perhaps I've become complacent in my old age and I no longer have to analyse how to do things in great detail – they automatically happen.

The less positive side of this period is a growth of complacency or familiarity which leads to less enthusiasm for the job. Day and Bakioglu (1996) report that seeds of disillusionment are sown during this period with the beginnings of a loss of commitment. Rather like the attention span, the inverted u-shape of a graph describing peak arousal illustrates this loss. A head works through this stage and may perhaps reach or pass the zenith, and experience a reduction in motivation, or interest, for the job. This part of the period of autonomy might be checked by further recycling of developmental activity, or simply trigger movement taking the form of career advancement, leading to either what we have described as professional enchantment or disenchantment. The length of this period of Autonomy is uniquely individual but in the special educational context appears to be the longest of our identified phases of headship.

A number of key themes emerge from our research which characterize this period of Autonomy:

- *Executive leadership* describes the transition from 'hands-on' head to a head who is more 'distant', who will work through people or a senior management team, and has learnt the utility as well as importance of delegation. Clarke and Evans, two very experienced heads, relate similar accounts of moving through this process. In Clarke's case, this is perhaps reinforced by a style of management acknowledged as innovatory rather than adaptive, in so far as he explains that he will come up with the ideas but needs other people to make them work. Management style continues to play an important part in shaping this enactment of executive leadership, with some heads retaining more control than others and a 'hands-on' approach. A balance between empowerment and control is clearly perceived as being required. The small nature of the primary and special school perhaps encourages a more direct control by the head (Haigh, Morgan, Ross, Sammons) but this is not necessarily the case (Ashdown, Clarke, Craig, Hinchliffe). It is also evident that an impact of local management has been the emergence of leadership functions more closely aligned to executive management (see Ross, Morgan, Sammons).
- *Continuing professional development* figures largely again in this phase of headship. Several heads describe new innovations as a product of having more time and therefore more opportunity to lead innovatively. Significantly, a great deal of this activity will involve the head in personal development. This involves creative use of secondment and higher education (as described by Sammons, Haigh and Ashdown), or, alternatively, increasing levels of extra-curricular activity which is professional in nature. Hinchliffe talks very positively about her involvement with a

professional association. Morgan refers to the balance between involvement in LEA initiatives and representation on various panels or committees. At an institutional level, organization and administration of school-based INSET reflects a regular topping up of the professional batteries identified by Morgan. Significantly, none of this CPD involves courses or training!

- *The institutional development plan* features more frequently during this period as a working document detailing and monitoring the effectiveness of school development. Several heads refer to this plan, albeit not always as a specific document, but rather as a process, and describe a re-visiting of previously identified targets as part of ongoing work. Much of this is delegated and requires a light touch as the main role of the head is to maintain an overview (Ashdown, Clarke, Evans). Hinchliffe's use of developmental 'themes' provides us with another example of the same feature, a system put into place, which is used to nurture continuing development.

- *Professional vision* also returns as an important feature in the head's approach to work in this period of Autonomy. The direction of school development is re-affirmed, perhaps in a wider frame of the school and its place within an educational system. Ashdown gives us an example of this resurgence of vision and leadership, in his second school, in a conversation about inclusivity and the place of the special school within the local school community. Responsibility for the 'survival' of his school is mixed with an idealism for special education, which has resulted in an expansion of the school as well as links with mainstream schools to help support integration of pupils with SLD. Other heads talk too about the importance of re-considering their vision, and Hinchliffe is adamant that you should 'keep your own vision'. In particular, she says, it is important that you should keep 'your own vision of what a child is, of what the developing adult is' and that you should not lose touch with your personal vision because you are immersed in a 'plethora' of detail.

- *New horizons* appear as a combination of the previous key features forming a wider field of reference for the headteacher. A widening of their professional remit in part reflects this growing interest in the policy-making of local and national bodies. The desire to renew their professional vision also contributes to a desire for fresh perspective and additional levels of professional or personal activity. Several heads describe the need to 'move on' as part of this process, and it may take place within the context of their present post, as described by Clarke and Morgan, or, as with Haigh, may involve a move into another career. Sammons describes his Ofsted inspecting in this light, as well as hinting that retirement might be a possibility, thereby releasing him to do 'other things'. Ashdown and Craig identify experiencing a similar need for change but respond to it as a need for a fresh challenge, a new position, or a new school. Ashdown and Ross also describe family life as essential worlds or horizons that help keep the world of work in proper perspective. Morgan gives us an interesting perspective, both on the importance of family life acting as a counter-weight to professional life, and the finding of new horizons. Success as a born again rock musician hitting the road at the tender age of – well let's say forty plus – is a perfect example of a new personal horizon helping to maintain the phase of Autonomy as a headteacher:

> It is a sort of get-out, which the sporting interests used to be, but it's only been going for six months or so, and yes, it is going well, maybe too well . . . we did one gig last week in a local pub, and it's led to five new bookings. People were there and saw it and liked it and now we're booked for performances in Bristol and in Swansea, so I suppose you could say we're on tour. That's got to be carefully managed, so that it doesn't run out of control. It has to remain an interest, a relaxation. Once it starts to create its own pressures, then it will have to stop.

It is perhaps true to say that some of the benefit of new horizons is as a safety valve or a kind of 'stress buster', whether it is professional, like Clarke's example of a temporary secondment to help close down a special school for the LEA, or a new interest, or even a long-standing pastime like Craig's tennis or Ross's farmwork.

It is towards the end of this period of headship that a fourth and final stage of incumbency is triggered. The nature of this Advancement will reflect the experience of Autonomy, and the degree to which personal involvement and investment is still being placed in the job. Other individual factors such as age, health, circumstances such as conditions and terms of employment, and family considerations, will also undoubtedly play a part. But, significantly, it is the level at which the individual is still engaged with the process of leadership which determines the nature of this transition between Autonomy and Advancement.

Advancement

Originally, Gronn (1993, 1994), Gronn and Ribbins (1996) and Day and Bakioglu (1996) all infer, as we have previously described in this discussion, a 'creeping negativism' in the 'twilight period' of headship, which accumulates and eventually results in a precipitation or 'fall-out' from the profession. Our studies do not necessarily support this – rather Advancement, as the final stage of Incumbency, and then 'Divestiture or Moving-on', which represents the departure of an individual from headship, can take the form of a positive or negative experience. An 'enchantment' with the professional role can result in a positive attitude and a desire for fresh challenge. It is possible, as with Craig, Ashdown, and Evans, to enter a 'loop-back' process at this point which results in change, a new headship, and a fresh challenge. It may be relevant to mention Craig's recent promotion to a new post as head of a larger Behaviour Support Service in Kirklees, thereby providing another example of advancement as enhancement.

Pascal and Ribbins (1998) cite Hubermann's four necessary conditions for professional 'enchantment', which reflect our own thinking about Advancement. They are:

- an enduring commitment to the profession;
- manageable job expectations;
- good relationships with colleagues;
- a balanced home and school life.

The actual factors that trigger advancement are individual and usually complex, in so far as there are often several motives and reasons for moving on to another place. Ashdown talks about family reasons for his move to a second headship, but, equally, places weight on having reached a 'modus vivendi' in his first school. He was ready for a new challenge. Craig, similarly, talks jokingly about a mid-life crisis, in professional terms, triggering his need to move, yet also acknowledges a frustration with his professional situation, fuelled by a desire for the challenge of management. Haigh, of course, provides us with a very good example of advancement as enhancement, with a move from headship to take up new issues and challenges that are perceived as part of the wider, more global management of provision for SEN.

Hinchliffe provides us with the best example of a head not yet ready for advancement nor the final stage of Divestiture. She describes herself as a 'very happy' head:

> I love my job. I'm a very happy headteacher. Not that I haven't been pushed to the very edge, the brink of feeling I just cannot take this any more. I love it. It's been a marvellous joy to me to have been appointed to this job at Ash Field. There has been, and still is, so much to do that there has never been any need to go on for another headship.

This is reminiscent of Ross's description of her final years as a head, but we will look at this more closely as we consider the ultimate part in the role of headship, leaving headship.

The alternative form of Advancement is one which is associated with disillusionment, tiredness, stress, and what might be wryly described as 'metal-fatigue'. Disenchantment with the job, its pressures, and its changing nature, is well chronicled in the educational press. The current high rate of early retirements for heads, particularly in the primary phase, draws an impression of mass flight from the profession. Our reference to Wragg's observation, listed in our interview schedule, that all of this suggests that you need to be as mad as a hatter to want to be a headteacher, reflects this perception of what might be described as a 'melt-down' in educational management. But our study, which by no means is presented as representative of the entire profession, reveals heads who, as a body, express a continuing satisfaction and a reward in the job. This is in contrast to other similar studies carried out by Ribbins in the mainstream phases of education. There are hints that the additional workload created by local management, or the mismatch created by the national curriculum and a diminishing unit of resource, will eventually lead to thinking about something else, but such comments are both exceptional and lightly expressed. Instead, all of the heads in our study describe a process of advancement as enchantment or perhaps advancement as enhancement, and even, in some cases, no advancement at all!

Leaving headship (Moving On)

Leaving headship is the final act in a head's period of office. We perceive this period as reflecting a progression from one state (Incumbency) to another (Divestiture). It should be added, however, that Pascal and Ribbins' (1998) distinction between divestiture and reinvention is wholly accepted. This distinction reflects a similar recognition of positive or negative ways for the head to leave office, which have been previously identified as features of the advancement of incumbency. In some respects, this movement to an exit can blur the boundaries between the final stage of incumbency and divestiture.

The first route to leaving is perceived as retiring or changing careers for negative reasons or natural causes such as ageing or ill health. Typically, heads taking this route see themselves as exhausted by the job: anticipating burn-out and planning for retirement. The second route, which Pascal and Ribbins (1998) call 're-invention', is regarded as a new beginning. Heads taking this route see themselves as continuing to exercise some form of leadership, perhaps still within the profession, and even as a headteacher. The latter option loops back to a positive advancement, paving the way for a career move or re-invention of the role of headteacher.

Clarke's vision for his school, and his perception of his role as an employee of the LEA, present an interesting example of this regenerative process, which enables him to continue enjoying the challenge of leadership and headship. More properly, of course, this represents 'advancement' rather than 'leaving headship' and 'divestiture', but it serves to illustrate the close relationship between the two. More accurately, accounts of leaving schools to take up new positions are given by Ashdown, Craig and Evans, in which they similarly adopt an approach which is positively connected to 're-invention' and further leadership with the world of SEN provision.

Ross's interview presents an opportunity to explore this phase of headship in her account of retirement from the profession. Ross does not describe an experience of Advancement in Incumbency, much like Hinchliffe, but she gives us a clear account of an approach to retirement which coincided with the first series of conversations taking place between her and the researcher. There is no simple division between a positive regard for her work and her school and a negative perspective on many of the changes she sees occurring in the final years of her headship. She talks about changes taking place in society, in education, and in the day-to-day task of leadership in an EBD special school:

> I also think that attitudes and values in society at large have changed which have made things harder in school. I think we reached the stage some time ago now where you take a professional risk of allegation and complaint if you give a pupil a dirty look. It seemed to me we also reached the point where there is no longer such a thing as an accident and somebody always must be blamed. I mean the kind of thing which involves an irate parent ringing me up to complain that their child has a bruise on their knee. Well, you know, so do I, as it happens, more than one, and it is all part of living.

She refers to a recent case where an ex-pupil has successfully sued a school for damages because he suffered post-traumatic syndrome as a result of bullying at school. She exclaims

> Common sense! Common sense! Common sense was my first school rule, and consideration was my second. This is a thing I repeatedly stated to the inspectors who came into my school, we exercise common sense. A lot of the strict prescribing of policy rules and guidelines would simply not be necessary if people exercised common sense. I'm sure that they are necessary to a far greater extent than I ever really thought, but in many respects, I do feel that common sense has gone out of the window.

and

> I find it extraordinary, generally speaking, to see the defences or excuses people will make now to explain away difficulties or alternatively how quick people are to seek to blame somebody else for a problem. Yes – I do think some of the additional pressures in school are very much reflected in the changes we see in society. I do think we have lurched away from 'Miss Dobson's day', when lying was a 'mortal sin' for which if you were found out you were publicly caned. We have moved to a way of life that involves making excuses, telling lies and getting away with it.

But this realistic appraisal of the changes to the job does not deflect from a basic enjoyment of the work, nor produce a negative, tired expression of disengagement from the post. Indeed, the reverse is true. Moving on for Ross actually involved an extending deferment to retirement that ran for several successive terms, as part of a transitional passing of the headship to a newcomer. True to her earlier start-up of headship in the same school, Ross was determined to see as smooth a transition for the school as was possible. Responsibility for her school was not easily relinquished.

Ross also alludes to the sense of status and power which accompanies headship. She candidly admits that she enjoyed both status and power. She explains:

> I very soon realized after I had retired that I was moving from a position which carried a certain amount of status to one of an unpaid labourer which was a long jump, from there to here. I suppose it probably encouraged me to carry on teaching for longer than I might have otherwise have done.

She does not present the divesting of office as a negative or positive experience but rather a mix of the two, and, in conversation since, has suggested that she misses some of the daily challenge of running the school. There is a sense too, in her conversations, of her still carrying a vision for individual children and their needs, which played a continuing part in motivating her approach to the management of an EBD special school. It is, finally, an account of retirement brought about by ageing, rather than a divestiture which is brought about by disengagement with the job. In this respect, she reflects an attitude to the task of leadership in special education held by the entire group of heads we interviewed.

A coda: does leadership really matter?

Are leaders as significant as we have assumed? Some think not. There are 'atheists', who believe that the importance of leaders in general and head-teachers in particular is much exaggerated (Davies, 1995). There are also 'agnostics', who, whilst acknowledging that heads might be as important as has been claimed, nevertheless contend that this, as yet, remains to be authoritatively demonstrated (Ainley, 1995; Hallinger and Heck, 1996; Scheerens, 1992).

The proposition that the importance of headship is overrated is a variant of the larger claim that the significance of leadership is much exaggerated (Pascal and Ribbins, 1998). There is a substantial literature on this latter theme. One influential strand has its origins in a classic study of leadership substitutes from Kerr and Jermier (1978) which has recently been the subject of a major symposium in the journal *Leadership Quarterly*. This symposium includes a review of subsequent research on leadership substitutes by Pod-sakoff and MacKenzie (1997) along with a final response by Kerr and Jermier (Jermier and Kerr, 1997).

Reporting on their empirical research, Kerr and Jermier (1978) claimed that the exercise of direct or indirect leadership by an individual had a decisive influence in rather less than half of the cases they had examined. In the rest, what transpired was, they suggested, better explained by a variety of substitute factors including the characteristics of the task, the subordinate and the organization. However, those who would use this seminal work and the research which it stimulated to celebrate the demise of superordinate leadership may be premature in doing so for at least three reasons: first, because, as Kerr and Jermier acknowledged at the time, in almost half the cases which they studied leadership did have a significant influence upon outcomes and performance in organizations; second, because the character-istics of substitute factors may have been influenced by certain kinds of prior leadership activity; and third, because, as Jermier and Kerr (1997) now accept, both their own initial research and almost all subsequent research in this area has drawn upon much the same psychometric methodology. Their call for further studies which adopt a longitudinal fieldwork approach has been answered by Gronn (1997) in the context of an exploration of a case of leadership exercised at a distance in the evolution of Timbertop, the mountain school campus of Geelong Grammar School. As he notes, 'The paper analyses the evolving delegated authority relationship between [J.R.] Darling [Head of Geelong] and the first head of Timbertop whom he appointed, E.H. Montgomery, and in doing so highlights the importance of a neglected substitute for the direct exercise of leadership viz, the leadership duo or couple.' Whilst this paper explores the development of an asymmetric authority relationship over time between two leaders working together within particular educational contexts, there are a growing number of studies reporting on more equal leadership partnerships. Examples of this include the innovatory models of leadership currently being developed at middle and senior management, especially co-principalship, levels in a small number of schools in New Zealand (see Court, 1994, 1997). It will be interesting to discover if such developments really do enable the kind of 'far more flexible, rotational, non-pyramidal style of school administration' that Davies (1990, 78) has called for and whether this will really make a significant difference to the nature of leadership within such contexts.

On this we remain unpersuaded and take our stand with Howard Gardner (1995). His view, he accepts, is 'conservative' in so far as 'it builds on the assumptions that there are individuals called leaders', a 'stance [that] will perturb those of a more radical stripe, who question whether leaders actually influence events, whether leaders *should* actually be allowed to influence events, or whether the conception of leadership itself deserves to survive'. Reflecting on his studies of such very different people as Robert Oppenheimer, Martin Luther King and Mahatma Gandhi, he argues that 'While acknowledging the rhetorical appeal of such accounts, I find them unconvincing in the light of human biology and human history. I invite those who question this enterprise to offer their own "leaderless" accounts of the success of the Manhattan Project, the early course of the civil rights movement, or the securing of independence for India' (18).

If some believe the importance of leadership to be exaggerated, others claim that, as exercised by individuals, it is undesirable. Those who take this view tend to be advocates of egalitarian and collective styles of decision-making and leadership. However, as Thody (1995) in a review of the Davies' book *Beyond Authoritarian School Management: The Challenge for Transparency* (1994) points out, 'the thinking emerges as polemics. The ... underlying and unquestioned assumption is that teams, democracy, non-competitiveness and total immersion of everyone in every management process is the only way to organise a school. One seeks in vain for this to be justified' (215). Are the virtues of collegial approaches to management so evident that they can simply be assumed? Numerous studies suggest not. Thus for Sinclair (1995),

> the great attraction of the 'bossless' self-managed team is the belief that it will be egalitarian. The mythology of a team of equals conveys the anticipation of dutiful turn-taking or, even more desirably, a dazzling synergy when creative individuals come together, each respecting the others' expertise. The evidence from research into groups is that hierarchies reproduce themselves in teams [and] exhaustive studies of participation indicate that participation in decision-making in teams in itself neither consistently leads to heightened satisfaction with work or better productivity . . . contrary to what some may hope, teams need leadership in order to develop independent functioning and some form of hierarchy is inevitable. To ignore or deny both in the hope that they will go away is likely to produce the opposite effect: a team obsessed with authority and with a covert, more oppressive hierarchy . . . Teams cannot be effective and leaderless . . . Effective team leadership might at times be exercised subtly and consultatively, at other times autocratically, but neither should be confused as evidence that teams are better off without leadership. (51, 59)

Noble and Pym (1970) also consider the impact of collegial structures of authority by examining relationships between participatory management and public accountability within an organization dominated by professionals. Reporting on a structure of decision-making based on a committee system composed, ostensibly, of status 'equals', they note its implications for the 'clients' of the organization who come to discover that 'wherever or at whatever level one applies to the organization, the "real" decisions always seem to be taken somewhere else' (436). They also found that 'formal equality of status was by no means commensurate with equality of access to these committees. In other words, powerful figures within the organisation could preserve their positions of power in the structure of committees, as witnessed by the domination of these committees by a select few' (Thorp, 1986, 420). The effects of 'collegiality', it seems, can be to enable senior staff to engineer consent amongst those within the organization whilst insulating themselves from demands for accountability from those outside it. It is surely not enough to dismiss this as 'pseudo-participation' (Nias, 1972) and, as such, a kind of pathology. Rather, we should face the possibility that attempts to introduce participatory structures and processes of decision-making and management can have the kinds of results described by Noble and Pym for the reasons discussed by Sinclair. As Brundrett (1998) concludes, 'collegiality, far from legitimating the decision making process, contains within its functioning the danger of creating yet another "repressive" mechanism in the management of schools'. For all these reasons, those who advocate the disestablishment of headship as we currently understand this in favour of collegial forms of management and decision-making within schools may face many more difficulties than they might imagine.

In our view it is more important to encourage a wider understanding of leaders and leadership than to try to do without them. As Gardner (1995) puts it, an enhanced cadre of future leaders can materialize only if we engender widespread appreciation of the principal issues that surround effective leadership . . . if we desire a leadership that is responsible as well as effective, we must do more than simply train a body of 'legitimated' leaders. The 'best' leadership training *for* potential leaders . . . should be the best training *about* leadership for all . . . in the sense of familiarizing the population with what is entailed in being a leader, and what can go wrong, as well as what can go right. (303, 304–5)

This knowledge he terms '*consciousness about the issues and paradoxes of leadership*. . . . No one can be expected to understand and master all of them, but familiarity with some can help individuals appreciate the *possible* and the *probable*, as well as the *problematic* and the *paradoxical* facets of leadership' (305). Such knowledge 'can be brought to bear when one considers the leadership that most of us deal with regularly [including amongst others] the leaders of one's . . . school' (305). Our research, and this book, attempts to identify such knowledge in the context of a series of individual portraits in some depth of the lives, as they see it, of ten headteachers who have been entrusted with the leadership of schools which cater for those with special needs. We believe that they are special and, as we shall argue in a brief coda to this book, that there is something finally and irreducibly 'special' about special education.

Appendix: Interview schedule
Heads and headship in the SEN school and sector

1. **Could we begin by your telling me about your personal background – home, school, higher education and people who have shaped the kind of person you are and have had a significant influence on your life?**

    How would you describe your life from your earliest years to the end of your full-time education? What influence did your parents and other members of your family, your friends and other members of your peer group, your teachers/lecturers and class and school/college/university contemporaries, and any other significant individuals or groups have in shaping your views on life, your values, your aspirations and ambitions and your actions? On reflection, how important and how compatible and consistent were these various influences?

2. **Describe your career to date. Why did you decide to teach?**

    How and why did you decide to become a teacher? Why did you choose to work with children who have SEN?

3. **How did your career develop to take you towards headship? What influences affected your decision to become a head and your early view of headship?**

    How would you describe your career in the years before headship? Why and when did you decide you wanted to be a head? What was your view of headship during these years and who or what shaped that view? How influential were the heads you worked for or have known in other ways been in shaping your view and practice of headship?

4. **How did you prepare for headship and for getting your first headship? How difficult was this?**

    How did you prepare yourself for headship? Did you have a career plan? How did you go about trying to achieve your first headship? How difficult was this? What are your feelings about the processes of selection and appointment you experienced?

5. **What was your early experience of headship like? And after this? To what extent do you think recent government-led initiatives will lead to better-prepared heads? What would you do to improve things?**

    What were your feelings when you were offered your first headship? What do you remember of your first day, week, year of headship? How well prepared did you feel? How confident do you feel now? What advice would you offer others considering headship?

6. **Describe your career as a head. How well have your development needs been met? What have been the high and low points?**

    How would you describe your career as a head? How do you approach the task of managing your school? What are your expectations for yourself and those who work with you? How do you measure your success?

7. **Describe the school(s) in which you have been head. What particular vision for the school(s) did you have and what part did this play in your headship?**

How would you describe the school or schools of which you have been the head? What was your vision for it/them and how have you gone about trying to implement this? How successful have you been? What are professional values and what is your vision for special education? How have these influenced your work as a headteacher? What is the effect of your vision and values for the school(s) of which you have been head? What has been their effect beyond the school?

8. **Describe the kind of head you are – as a leader – as a manager?**

What kind of a headteacher and leader are you? Has this changed over time and if so in what way and why? Has headship become less difficult as you have grown more experienced? How does a second headship differ from a first? Is it any easier and if so why and how? How do you enable others to lead?

9. **How do you enable effective teaching and learning to take place in your school? How do you know this is happening? Do you see any changes in the way in which you do this over time?**

What part do you play in enabling effective teaching and learning in your school? Are you satisfied with your contribution? How do you manage people and resources?

10. **To whom is a head accountable? Who do you answer to and how do you manage this accountability?**

To whom are you accountable? Who manages you? What do you see as the role of governors [especially the Chair of the governing body], parents, pupils, the local community, the LEA, the DfE in all this? How do you manage external relations?

11. **How do you manage to maintain your own professional well-being and development? Where do you look to for support?**

How do you keep up to date? How do you cope with stress and manage when things go wrong? Which aspects of the role do you most and least like? Where do you find support for you?

12. **Ted Wragg suggests 'You don't have to be a "nutter" to want to join the "barmy" army [of heads] but ... '. Do you think headship has become much more difficult in recent years and, if so, with what consequences? Do you enjoy it? More or less than you used to?**

Wragg's thesis is that 'demands on heads have escalated in the last few years' and the Government 'by drowning [heads] under brain corroding bureaucracy has side-tracked them'. Has headship changed radically and for the worse in recent times? Can you still be an educational leader? Do you still enjoy headship? Are you barmy to do so? Would you give up headship if you could? If so, why? What would or will you do? Would schools be better off without heads anyway?

13. **What changes do you think have taken place in SEN? How fundamental are these? Are they making things better or worse? What do these changes mean for your headship in the SEN school and sector?**

What changes have you seen in SEN in your time as a head? Do these changes represent an improvement on past practice?

14. **How do you wish to see your own school develop? How would you like SEN to develop? What will all this mean for heads and headship?**

What do you think and what do you hope the SEN school and sector will look like in ten years' time? What will this mean for headship? How will your school change?

CHAPTER 2

Pursuing equal opportunities: a passion for service, sharing and sacrifice

SUDARSHAN ABROL with Peter Ribbins

Sudarshan Abrol has for thirteen years been headteacher of Mayfield in Birmingham. Mayfield is a school for pupils with SLD which contains many children who are profoundly handicapped. It takes children from the ages of two to nineteen and is located on a split site, one catering for fourteen-to-nineteen-year-olds, the other for the rest. She was born in Pakistan and later moved to India, where for a time she worked as an Assistant Inspector with responsibility for sixty primary schools. In 1963 she came to England and was appointed to Brookfield I and J in Birmingham where she worked until 1967. During this time she decided to make her career in special education. She worked at Queensbury (a school for those designated as ESN), as Head of Remedial Education at Aston Primary, and as a Head of Department at Jane Lane School in Walsall, before becoming deputy head at Forest Oak School in Solihull (an all-age school for MLD pupils). Seven years later she was appointed to Mayfield.

PR   Can you tell me about your personal background; your home, your school, your higher education, the influences that have shaped you into the kind of person you are?

SA   I belong to a working middle class. My father was an accountant and my mother never worked. I was born in Pakistan. My mother's father was a headmaster but he died at an early age. They were all strongly in favour of education. That was why from the age of ten I wanted to be a teacher.

PR   Why?

SA   I spent most of my childhood with my maternal grandparent – with Nanny, a widow, and my uncles. Our family was very keen on education, and I was educated in an Arya Samaj school. I could have gone to a Sikh school but the standard of education which they offered was not as good as Arya Samaj schools. These schools were run by a reformist Hindu sect. My parents' decisions about my schooling were made on mainly educational rather than on religious grounds. As we talk memories of the school are coming back to me. I remember when I was seven we used to sing a song and I performed the role of a boy. The song had an equal opportunity message because it made a mockery of the traditional male role and expressed an appreciation of the role of the woman. In it, the woman is saying to the man 'What about you, why are you so lazy, you should get up and get things done'. It was a lovely song sung in Hindi. It showed that the school valued equal opportunity, that boys and girls should have the same role to play and they should be assertive in insisting on this. This idea is still important to me. When people ask where I got my assertiveness from, I tell them I got it from my junior school.

After Partition we moved to Jullundur, a city in northern Punjab (India). Again I was sent to a progressive school, because they were offering English at the age of ten as a second language. They offered Domestic Science but also the sciences and maths. It was a girls' school, unlike my first school which was a mixed school. This probably explains why I don't feel strange with any friends – Muslims, Sikhs or Hindus. During this time I did my matriculation in nine subjects including Maths, Domestic Science, General Science and Physiotherapy. I was encouraged to do this. As I said earlier, my family were working middle class and I was the eldest daughter, so my father treated me like a son. He wanted me to have a proper education and being the eldest he wanted me to be given all the opportunities I could cope with. At that time, his concern wasn't just with my eventually getting married.

PR   Was yours a large family?

SA   No, three in all. The others were born much later – there's a difference between me and my sister of ten years, and my brother of twelve years. Before Partition my mother did not spend much time with my father, he was always away on jobs and constantly moving from one place to another. The younger ones were much more loud and spoiled than I had been. I was the one given all the pomp and opportunities. I was the one who was pushed to get ahead. I was always encouraged to do things: I was never told not to.

PR   By whom?

SA   My father mainly. So after my matriculation I started teaching in the mornings in a Sikh school where my father was a member of the management committee. I used to teach junior classes during the day and studied in the evenings in Further Education. So I did my degree on a part-time basis whilst teaching in the morning. They used to pay me a full salary but out of this I had to pay my fees for my studies.

PR   What did you see as your key family values?

SA   From Sikhism I received the three 'S's: service, sharing and sacrifice. These were inculcated in me by my father. Although I saw much less of him, I had more real contact with and felt much closer to my father than to my mum. These three values have been the pillars on which I have built the success I have had. They are still important to me and they are still the core values on which I build my life. As a Sikh you share, you share your sorrows, you share your happiness. Sikhs also believe that if you don't sacrifice you won't achieve anything – that is where commitment comes from.

PR   By sacrifice do you mean not always putting your personal interest first?

SA   That's right. It is about always putting the interests of others above your own. Even now my daughter says 'Whenever anybody is in trouble they ring you, but when you have a problem nobody comes'. I say 'Yes, but only because they are confident that I can look after myself and I can look after them'. That has been my main concern, I don't know why, whether it is due to the influence of religion or because my father was like that. He would starve himself. If somebody was begging and he had his lunch with him he would give it away rather than eat himself.

PR   He expressed his values in his life as well as his words?

SA   He was a saintly man. My mother would sometimes say to him about some of the things he did which made life hard for her and for us 'Why do you have to do that?' but he would do it anyway. For example, when he lost his older brother and there was not enough money for the funeral, somehow he managed to pinch my mum's jewellery and took it and pawned it to get some money to pay for the funeral. When she found out they had a row. I was only thirteen at the time but I remember asking my mum 'Why are you angry, don't you think it's right what he did? He did not want his brother's body to rot away, why are you fighting? When I earn some money I'll give you more gold'. So the great influence on me is from my father – and it's still there. I wanted to protect him and when I started working the first thing I did was to buy a ring for my mum. Simple things like that taught me that your own interest should be secondary to others.

PR   Do you remember any particular teachers as having influenced you for good or for bad?

SA   I don't remember any of my school teachers having any great influence on me. But later on I did meet somebody who did influence me. After I had completed my degree and postgraduate training I worked as a school teacher for nine months on a temporary basis. The headmistress there had been my headteacher when I was in Middle Standards just before doing matriculation. She was a spinster at a time when there were very few spinsters, Asians particularly. She was a very gentle woman but could be very firm. Once she said to me 'If you have problems, don't get involved in trying to rectify them, come straight to me and be straight and firm'. I learned from her that it was possible to be discreet and firm. It was actually rather difficult to talk to her directly. She was the kind of old-fashioned head as dictator. You would not dare to do more than peep through her door and say good morning. You would somehow feel she always had a stick in her hand but her heart in the right place. I am a bit like her. Perhaps that's why I am sometimes thought to be very dominating. She was one influence. Another was the Director of Education for whom I worked for five years as an Assistant Inspector of Schools. Her name was Miss Sehgal, she's in her seventies now. She has been like a mother to me. I worked with her, I stayed with her, and she kept me under her wing. I was very young and so my father wouldn't let me stay on my own. She left her husband because he had been violent and made herself a successful career of her own. I learnt from her assertiveness, the need to protect yourself and to be self-confident. But I don't remember any of my class teachers having any great influence on me.

PR   Can you tell me about the early years of your career?

SA   I studied for a BA first, part-time, and then did the BT [Bachelor of Teaching]. This took four years. The BT had to be full-time. I had the money so I went on a year's study at the training college in Jullundar – it was very well run. From there I became a temporary Second Mistress for nine months and then worked as an Assistant Inspector looking after sixty primary schools in a variety of different districts in the area. This meant I had to travel to villages on a bike or horse's back. I also travelled in a variety of other ways including on a camel to get to one of the more distant schools. I was responsible for the work of over a hundred teachers. I can still remember writing up the log books. It was a very formal kind of activity. For the last five years before I came to the UK I was also involved in a great deal of administration, including looking after the salaries and budget for resourcing all these schools.

PR   What were the schools like?

SA   The schools were very much smaller than they are here. I remember small rooms and big classes with just a blackboard and chalk. There would be seventy in a class and the level of illiteracy was very high. The main teaching method was for the teacher to call out something from a book and for the class to repeat it. There was a heavy reliance on rote learning. But at that time in the villages the environment could be pleasant. The weather was good and much of the teaching could take place in the open or under the trees when shade was necessary. More often than not the teachers used to use a stick to write in the sand, it could all look very informal. But there was, and is, no compulsory education still in some States. As a result it was in effect available to only some people – those who could pay the fees. Compulsory education was only just beginning when I was there. In our State the schools were mixed and although there were men and women teachers the majority were women who had received only primary education. In most of the village schools there would be two teachers and one assistant.

PR   What happened next?

SA   I got married. The decision to come to the UK was made by my husband, or rather my ex-husband. I had helped him with his career, so he felt obligated to marry me. I thought I was in love. When you get older you become wiser. His parents didn't agree with our marriage, they thought I was from a different caste.

PR   So it wasn't an arranged marriage?

SA   It was in a way, and it wasn't in a way. It was our choice. His parents didn't agree, but my mother agreed, so he came to the UK. He thought it better to escape and then for me to follow him. Once I joined him his parents had to accept me. All this, probably, explains why we didn't get on very well. In any case I joined him in the UK after a year. I resigned my post which is something that I regret to this day.

Sometimes when you come to a new country, it's a struggle, a big struggle. There have been times when I have regretted that I came to the UK. Things seemed better in India once I came. In comparing, I may have been remembering the grass as much greener than it really was. I joined my husband here on the 22nd of June 1963. He had got my degrees and qualifications accepted by the relevant authorities. I obtained my DES number and was interviewed on the 9th July for Staffordshire. I then went to a second interview in Birmingham. Birmingham accepted me, they selected four out of the thirty-four Asians who applied. I started teaching in September 1963 at Brook-field Infant and Junior School.

PR   What made you want to be a teacher?

SA   First, it could be it was seen as a suitable profession for females. That is still a cultural thing because it is felt that if you teach you can also look after a family. Second, I remember somebody told me that a teacher is like a burning candle who enables others to burn and in doing so increases the sum of knowledge. I was very impressed with this idea. Third, in practice, it turned out to be the most convenient thing to do.

PR   Have you ever regretted it?

SA   I never regret it. I have regretted many things, including getting married, but never being a teacher. I have loved it, and I still love it even after all these years. I will be sixty shortly and will be retiring in a year's time. I will miss it.

PR   Your first teaching post was not in special education?

SA   No, not at all. I joined Brookfield Junior and Infant School. I taught
      the second infant age group there. I worked in mainstream primary
      education for four years. I was quite happy there. I had a child, a girl,
      she's now thirty-two. She was born in 1964. When she was fifteen
      months old she had a smallpox vaccine reaction. I took her to India
      and then she had the reaction which is a very rare thing. It left her
      with left side cerebral palsy. She is a capable young lady. She can
      drive, but still can't use her left hand, it's affected her badly, and she
      limps on that side. I used to bring her to the Nursery where the
      nurses were very good. It took another couple of years to make her
      walk or to do anything. That made me go into special education. I
      wanted to explore it. I applied for secondment in 1967, and got it.
      Sometimes you are just lucky. I worked with Mr Wright of West-
      bourne College. He was an inspiration. That time taught me the
      difference between English and Indian education. If you ask me the
      difference, I can tell you.

PR   What is the difference?

SA   I can't go into much detail, but in summary Indian education is
      based on a literacy model and English education is based on a
      development model. There's a subtle difference. My main ambition
      during that time was to learn to help my girl. Mr Wright was very
      helpful in this. He was the first Englishman whose house I went to.
      He invited us as a family. He said to me, 'Your English is very good. If
      you have the company of more English-speaking people in the upper
      class you will develop'. I said, 'How can I do that, they won't want to
      talk to me' because my husband was a postman at that time and we
      used to live opposite the Dudley Road Hospital. But Mr Wright made
      me aware of a possible scenario. I needed to meet some of the right
      kinds of friends, to keep the right company and develop the right
      knowledge. Doing this could have major implications for my career.
      Once I finished the course, I started to work in Queensbury School
      for MLD pupils. At the same time I got my girl into Wilson Stuart
      School. I wasn't very happy within two terms. As Mr Wright had
      suggested, my daughter needed physiotherapy but other than that
      she was an averagely intelligent girl. They were not stretching her,
      they were not giving her the educational opportunities she needed.
      When I asked them about this I was told that I was ambitious as Asians
      are. I thought that was not good enough.

PR   You wanted them to stretch her educationally as well as physically?

SA   That is right. They were doing a good deal of physical work with her
      but after that just letting her sit in a corner doing puzzles. I told them
      that she could read. OK, maybe I was ambitious. In any case I took
      her out and put her into a fee-paying school. She spent the next nine
      years in Four Oaks School where she was residential. This meant she
      had the best of both worlds. I would do most of the work for her at

home, while at residential school she would learn to do things for herself and this made her independent. Her inspiration made me interested in special schools.

PR   What happened then to your career?

SA   I decided to work in special schools, first at Queensbury School which was then a School for the ESN and is now for moderate learning disabilities youngsters. I did two years there and then came across Professor Kerr of Birmingham University. He was another inspiration. Maybe God makes it like this, I don't know how. I met him through Miss Sabon, who was then Head of Jane Lane School in Walsall. She was doing a Diploma in Child Psychology and we came into contact at an INSET conference we both attended. Her tutor was Professor William Kerr and she introduced us. He must have seen some potential in me and asked if I had thought of doing the Diploma in Child Psychology. I was attracted by that idea and thought I would if I could get another secondment. But that didn't happen there and then. So I worked from 1967 to 1969 at Queensbury. From there I was promoted to Head of a Remedial Department in Aston Primary School. I was Head of Remedial English. People used to ask the head 'Is it true you've got as Head of the English Department an Asian woman?', and he would say 'Yes'. I would say 'It's a Remedial department, not an English department.' I worked there for a couple of years. It was more or less working with SEN children in broader terms. It was a good experience. I had my own department and was able to develop some strategies. The *Break Through to Literacy* reading programme was introduced in schools at the time and this encouraged children to write as they talked. It did not matter if their spelling was wrong as long as they were able to talk to their script. Some of my youngsters asked me to write. I wrote as they spoke. A teacher came to me and said 'This is wrong, you shouldn't be doing it', and I said 'You're telling me because I'm Asian aren't you? That I can't spell, but this is a strategy from the "Break Through" method of teaching that I want to encourage the youngsters to use.' There were those kinds of differences of opinion around regarding English as being the monopoly of the English but I kept going and began to see some success. So this helped me to build up my confidence and self-assertiveness. I became abrupt at times because people challenged me for the wrong reasons. But I was firm in my thinking that they were wrong and I would show them. This teacher then said that she could not keep these books in the classroom because anybody looking at them could see that they had been wrongly written. I said 'I'm answerable, not you. If anybody says anything put them onto me and I'll explain why I've done it.' Things like that have shaped me throughout my career.

Later the Aston Primary School was closed. It was knocked down.

So they had to redeploy teachers to different places. I saw this as a chance to apply for secondment and to attend the Child Psychology diploma course. I said to myself 'If I get the secondment, then fine, if I don't get it then I'll go anyway. It will be much better for me to go on the course.' I know that if they just moved me to another school I would have never made this progress. Luckily I got another secondment, so I'm one of those privileged ones.

PR   To get two secondments, and one so soon after another, is very unusual.

SA   Yes, it is unusual. Mother Luck played a part. I did the diploma in Child Psychology for one year. After this, Miss Sabon appointed me Head of Department in her School, Jane Lane in Walsall. I worked there for four years. From there I went to a deputy headship in Solihull. I'm always getting chances, I don't know why. Miss Sabon was a chance because she knew me and knew Professor Kerr. He must have rated me because he told her 'There's a woman with potential.' So I got the job there as Head of Middle School. I then got the deputyship with Solihull. I attended for interview but at first I didn't get it, I was the runner-up. Then I had a call in the evening of the next day offering it to me. The person to whom they had initially offered the job had declined. So they had no choice but to appoint me. Otherwise they would never have appointed an Asian woman in Solihull. I was the lucky one wasn't I? I worked for seven years as a Deputy in Solihull at Forest Oak School. It was an all-age school for MLD pupils. I ended up looking after the middle and the secondary pupils.

PR   Had you decided by then you wanted to be a head?

SA   I have always wanted to be head. I found it very difficult. I applied several times without success. It even took a lot to become a deputy. I tried several times before I was finally appointed. You may take this wrongly but I'm telling you honestly how it felt. I said to myself 'This is a racialist country but in any case I'm going to prove I can do it'. I felt I had been pushed around at times. So when I had been a deputy for about four years I started trying for headships. My head encouraged me to keep on trying. I did, I tried in the Midlands, I tried in London, I tried in Bromley, I even tried in Clacton-on-Sea. I applied nine times and was shortlisted every time. But when I got to the interview I was never appointed. It seemed my face didn't fit. That's what I felt. I had good qualifications and good experience. I can only think that my name Abrol was confusing. If I had used Kaur maybe I wouldn't have been shortlisted. That was how I felt. When the Mayfield School post was advertised one of my colleagues said, 'Look this is a school in the inner city which has got a lot of youngsters from ethnic backgrounds, why don't you try?' 'OK', I said, 'I'm capable, I should be able to do the job in any school. But if that is the way to get in let me get in that way.' I was shortlisted but on the day thought that I wouldn't get the job. In the final interview three of us were called, my present deputy, another deputy and myself. I discovered afterwards that two of the governors were very keen to appoint my deputy, because they knew him. Of the two Conservatives, one was Asian luckily, that was sheer chance. I had one or two other supporters as well but it seems that as the discussion went on they were increasingly thinking of one of the others, who seemed to have more votes. Then my supporters said 'What's wrong with this young woman, why are you refusing her? Give us the reason why.' They couldn't find a good reason, so had to appoint me. I have been here thirteen years now. I did not want to stay so long, I think seven years is enough in one position. There should be a system for transferring. It gives you extra experience.

PR   How would you describe Mayfield?

SA   Mayfield is a school for severe learning difficulties. Since I came it has increasingly been geared to meeting the needs of the profoundly handicapped. About two-thirds of our children are profoundly handicapped and the other third have SLD. It's a big school for children between two and nineteen years. We are on a split site. One site caters for our fourteen-to-nineteen pupils. With the introduction of NVQs we can prepare them for vocational training. The other, and main, site has two departments, one for primary, including nursery, pupils and the other for secondary up to fourteen. The emphasis in the curriculum is on the development of self-help skills, self-development and cognitive development. Within that context we try to offer them a broad and balanced national curriculum modified as appropriate.

We try to integrate, as far as we can, with neighbouring schools like Heathfield, which is just next door, and our older youngsters go to Holte and Holyhead for their leisure pursuits. We are very much a local school. We have a good relationship with parents and they are welcome to come in. When I say we have an open policy I do mean an *open* policy. The parents really do come in. I know it can be sometimes inconvenient. If you have something else which is going on you can't always receive them. We have 106 children – mostly they are from ethnic minorities – they are a minority within a minority.

We are well off for services – provision is good. We've got a Mayfield Centre (paramedical services) on the premises which was opened in 1993 after seven years of effort with other agencies such as Social Services, Health and the Education Department. As a school we raised £100,000, as a whole it was a half a million job. It's a beautiful site and has a hydrotherapy pool and speech and physio provisions. From another project, with the MSC, I got a community room which is a base for our parents and serves as a toy and staff library. We are equipped adequately. Unfortunately, to achieve this we have mainly had to rely on charity. To be honest I think our children should be given the provision they need as a right. They would not have this without our charity efforts but every time you accept charity on their behalf you are undermining these youngsters. You are asking for pity. But that's the game I have to play, to get the appropriate provision for the youngsters in our care. We emphasize vocational training for all the youngsters – we use Handsworth College and Matthew Bolton. Our pupils won a youth award for enterprise recently. Mayfield is unique in its own way. It has challenges, but it has been a delight.

PR   At the time of your appointment to Mayfield, would you have minded going instead as head of a non-SEN school?

SA   No, but experience counts. Nobody takes any notice if your experience is not relevant for the position for which you're applying.

PR   Were you applying only for SEN schools?

SA   I was applying for special schools only. That was where my experience was. You can't go to another kind of school if you don't have the necessary experience. The idea that cross experience is a good thing is very new. At that time it wasn't like that, people were looking for people with experience of special schools.

PR   Why did you want to be a head?

SA   I'm not sure. First, maybe it's because I'm the eldest child, and you have this idea of dominating or leading. Second, it could be because in my marriage I was always being undermined, that made me a rebel inside. You know you've got the ability, why should you be undermined when you are not undermining others? That kept me going. Third, it could be a result of living in a racialist society, and within a prejudiced society of my own. Being an Asian and a woman did not make it easy. My rebellious nature kept me going. I wanted to prove to myself and to the community that I could do it. The only way I could do this is by taking on the top job and showing I could be successful. Wrong or right, that's what I tried to do. I knew I had the ability, I could do it. Even my husband did not help. Many times I said to him 'I want to prove that I am not what you think I am'. Many times he would ask me, 'What's so different between you and other ladies? They're satisfied with teaching. What makes you think you're so exceptional?' and I said 'I am exceptional' and to prove my exceptional nature and ability I wanted to go to the top position.

PR   You've worked for a number of heads. What did you learn about headship from them?

SA   There were things I learnt not to do. I rebelled because I didn't think that what was happening was right. One or two of my heads were very autocratic. Their word was everything, you could not challenge it. I felt this was not on, you should be able to challenge. If, as a head, you cannot take this then you are the wrong person for the job you hold. And the culture of staff rooms which just accept this is still around. I believe teachers should ask questions. They should speak out and interact, especially so in special schools. A good leader empowers the staff.

Interaction is an important factor in learning. That did not seem to be happening in some of the schools I knew. I wanted to show it could be done. When I came here I said to my staff 'I got this job, that doesn't mean I know everything, I am learning, I have to learn from you. Don't expect every answer from me when we have to make decisions.' They think that's my weakness in managing the school. But if there were negative things I learned from my headteachers, there were some positive things. Miss Sabon, for example, was very gentle, she would talk to people and she would do what can be even harder, she could listen. She has helped me out a lot. Others have helped me. Such people, especially if they are in the right place, can be very important in helping you forward. I remember how helpful the Inspector for Special Education in Solihull was. He liked me very much, not just as a friend but he liked the qualities I had. When I applied for the deputy headship there, he was very much in favour of giving me the job. Somehow some people do see potential, but he couldn't simply offer it to me. Solihull's way of interviewing is very daunting. There were twenty-one people sitting round a big table, and you are sitting there answering them, every one of them. As I said earlier, although I was at first runner-up I later got the job. Even then I might not have. The head wanted to appoint somebody else but the Inspector insisted that I was the runner-up and that I could do the job. His support at that point was important. He always supported me. He was the one who said later, 'Go for headship.' He was one person who helped me, another was Head of the Special Education Department in Birmingham, Dr Giles. At that time we had a separate special education department in Birmingham.

PR   How far did the heads you worked for prepare you for headship?

SA   They didn't overtly prepare me. I think they never thought I'd be a head anyway. Nobody expected me to be a head. Nobody, nobody expected it. Not even the head where I was a deputy. I can still see his reference, it was balanced, that's about it. Not necessarily saying I had the qualities needed for headship. He sat on the fence. Most of them did. It made me struggle.

PR   How did you prepare yourself for headship?

SA   I went on courses even before I came here. Solihull offered a management course of ten days. It was in my own time and I did it. I did an MEd as well during the years that I was deputy at Forest Oak.

PR   What did you specialize in?

SA   Again I was helped by the Solihull inspector. He saw I got the fees and half a day concession. I did the course over three years during which I changed job. I specialized mainly in special education. That helped me to get into Special Education. My dissertation was about maladjustment in children with learning difficulties. In this, amongst other things, I was interested in the possibilities of yoga in this context.

PR   Was all this useful in your subsequent work?

SA   My studies have helped me to reach a better understanding of children's cognitive development. Sometimes I say it is easy to teach the gifted child but to teach our children you need X-ray eyes. To prepare my X-ray eyes I have to go into detail and my studies have helped.

PR   What was your early experience of headship like?

SA   It was frightening. On my first day in I was shaking. I still do. I'm not going to stress the point but being Asian and a woman as well, you end up having to prove your worth all the time and that can be painful. You have to prove that you got the position because you deserve it and you can do it. That challenge is still with me every time. I keep on telling myself 'don't carry a chip on your shoulder', but the circumstances make it hard to avoid this. People are always challenging you saying 'I don't understand you' and I have to say 'English is my second language, if you don't understand ask three times, it doesn't matter.' They also ask 'Do you know what you're talking about?' and they don't pay attention to you. For all sorts of reasons they make me feel they think I'm not capable of doing the job, that's a challenge all the time.

PR   I remember something similar from the first Indian secondary head in Birmingham ...

SA   Mrs Rao, Vasanthi Rao. She has recently retired. She was a good friend. We worked together for UK Asian Women. Like her, I have had problems both from the white community and my own community. There is prejudice in our own community and the racialism is from the other side, it's three times the battle being a woman, an Asian woman in a male-dominated society and then in a racialist community.

PR   What was your school like when you first took up your headship?

SA   It was in a bad way, physically the fabric of the building had deteriorated. Expectations of the children were very low and provision minimal. Nevertheless it was a big school, with three Deputies and Heads of Department. I was told by my Inspector, 'You are going into a school with a snake with six heads, be careful mate'. There were more Chiefs than Indians, all sorts of problems. And when your first deputy had competed for the post, it would be unnatural if he didn't resent you. In this case it would have been even more understandable than would normally be the case because he had been acting head for nine months. Coming into that scenario was not easy. It was daunting, I was not as equipped as I am today to deal with things. During the early days it was difficult to act. I had some ideas but at that stage they were only theory, I knew little of the practicalities of dealing with and managing people. But I did have support from my inspectors and from one or two headteacher colleagues who were not in special education but in the consortium such as John Goss of Broadway. I had had another stroke of luck. I could go to him because somehow before all this happened I had got onto his governing body as a community member, so that helped me a lot. He helped me personally a great deal.

PR   He was a kind of mentor?

SA   That's right. At the time, there was no training available, so you just learnt mainly by your mistakes. I can give you one example of the kind of problems I faced. One of my senior staff had something rather like a nervous breakdown, he was having a family problem at the time. He put me into the image of the Asian parents that he had to deal with, the Asian mothers. He could not cope at all. The staff almost rebelled, my first deputy tells me now that he said 'No, don't do it. Give her a chance.' They could have walked out or done something else like it, but they didn't. But the person I was telling you about really got ill. In the end I gave him a reference which wasn't very good in terms of balance. I was asked by the office, 'Are you sure you mean what you are writing?' I answered 'Don't question me please, I know English is my second language but I am writing truthfully, I cannot support a person strongly who is not very good. I appreciate that I don't know him very well but I do know about his behaviour. I do want him to go so that he's out of my way and, as far as reasonably possible, I would like it if he gets what he wants. So if it's not balanced it's up to you, you can give another reference.' He has gone, thank God for that, but it was a difficult experience. That was one example, I have had other staff I have not been happy with and who I would never have appointed. I am told that there are competency and disciplinary procedures but that is a very risky road to go down. You can easily start them and then find that nobody is there to support you. As an Asian I would not expect anybody to come and rescue me if I got into trouble. Mrs Rao tried that. She stood her ground, and thought she could go through the appeals procedures and everything. She thought she would have support but she didn't get it. I thought I'm not going to get any support if I go down that road. So I did not begin with the staff. Instead I started by building up the strength of my links with my parents and the community. That proved to be a good place to start – so even our Ofsted has come out excellently, and it's thanks mainly to the parents and the community.

PR   That's where you get your support from?

SA   That's where I got my support from and some of my worst problems. Most of the Asians don't support you because they are jealous of your profession and your success. They think they're as good as you are. Why are you in that position when they're not? Nobody wants to listen to a woman's views, that's probably the reason that my marriage broke down. I'm not blaming only my husband, it may partly be me. I'm assertive and was challenging him. In an Asian family the woman is there to obey rather than to challenge all the time. It cost me something there, didn't it?

PR   Would the initiatives for training for new heads and for a national qualification for heads and aspiring heads currently being implemented have helped you?

SA   They would have been a great help. I would have a peer group, or at least one or two colleagues going through the same thing as I was. We could have worked together. I did join the black headteachers' association, we came up with that as well. So I did have some support from that source. I also got help from Mrs Rao, Carlton Duncan and others in Birmingham and then we all joined the national association as well.

PR   And there was Elaine Foster . . .

SA   She took Mrs Rao's position. First she was Deputy Head, then HMI and now she's gone back home. She was part of our effort, Birmingham's effort and with Carlton we developed the Black Headteachers and Deputy Headteachers Association. We have all been active members of the association and through that supported each other.

PR   So it was Carlton and yourself who really developed it?

SA   Along with Mrs Rao, she was its backbone. And Hazel Wright too from Grove Infants School, who died recently. We thought we needed a group we could rely on and cry on each other's shoulders. It has helped.

PR   Have any of your teachers gone on to be deputies or heads?

SA   None of my deputies have become heads, but several of my teachers have been promoted. One became deputy head six months after I came, I don't think I did much for her. She was doing an MEd when I arrived, subsequently she became a head. Kath O'Learey, who's Head of Fox Hollies at present, she went on from here to become a deputy and is now the head of the same school. When I came she was a teacher on Scale 2. She came as a PE trainer but I could see the potential, I always encourage others to go on courses and pursue their professional progression. That is one way of developing staff, and of getting their support as well. You have to have some carrots – you have to pull some strings, to win their favour.

PR   It was, in part, a way of winning allies?

SA   Kath worked well with me. What I told her, as I would tell anybody who came to me asking about headship, was that you need honesty and commitment. If you are not committed to the cause then don't go for headship. Headship is not easy, you've got to sacrifice most of the time. You've got to be able to bear the stress and the pressures that it puts on you. I saw in her that she had the potential to become a deputy and probably a head. I've told her that when I retire she may come back here at Mayfield, it's a bigger school. So that's what my message is. There's another young lady I can think of, a head of department, I encouraged her to think of headship in the near future. But I found over the years she was over-confident. She thinks she knows better than any of us. She has lost my support because she doesn't think she needs it. She applied for many courses but wouldn't give any feedback. You cannot work in isolation, you cannot say 'Me, I'm OK, I can do it.' You have to be part of a team, times have changed, we've got to be able to work with others and we've got to see how we can make joint decisions and take joint responsibility. She hasn't got that. I can think of another teacher, he's Head of Post 16, I have told him he could be a deputy any day. He doesn't want to although he has the ability and the dedication. Now we have a very destructive child, but he can work with him so there's the potential. He is running the department very well, independently most of the time. I have told him many times to go for headship or deputy headship. I told him he has the quality, because he's not thinking of himself. In special schools you've got to put your children first and that is what he does. He never thinks of himself, he is so gentle with the pupils. He can relate with people and he can get on with other colleagues, and he tells them as if it's their work rather than his own. He has even taught me. He said to me 'Mrs Abrol, sometimes you don't reward people.' I said 'Unfortunately it's my culture, in our culture we criticize more than we appreciate. He reminds me often that I should appreciate people more.' I want to be appreciated, I should appreciate people and get more out of them. He is excellent but doesn't want to be a deputy or try for headship.

PR   What kind of a head are you? How do you know?

SA   Ofsted has discussed this. They're saying that there can be different kinds of effective leadership. Nobody and no two situations are alike. So, if, as I am, you are an Asian female, this will effect the leadership challenge for you. I am effective, yes, in many respects. We have established a good school here, we have good support from the parents and from the community as a whole. If something happens in the area they don't automatically attack my school. I don't know why but it is true. I would say I am a 70 per cent to 80 per cent effective head. I still have problems, I'm not saying I don't, and I think I still have things to learn.

PR   What about in such conventional terms as autocratic or democratic?

SA It's a balancing game. Of course, it's nice to be democratic, to get everybody coming along with you. But being a head as the law is today can make this difficult. We still work in a hierarchical system and I am still responsible. So at times you have to be autocratic and to make decisions which are not popular. You have no choice. In addition, you are the only one amongst the staff who can see the overall picture when others can't. Many of them have tunnel vision. But as head you have the overview, so at times, yes, you have to work in an autocratic way and make hard decisions and take responsibilities. But that does not mean you can make any decision you like. You can decide this or that but if you don't take people with you nothing will happen. If people don't feel at least some ownership for a decision they won't implement it. I'm a good teacher, I am a model teacher. The quality of teaching within the school has come on wonderfully. This is not just my view. In our report, Ofsted found 90 per cent of the teaching they saw good. Leadership is very much a mixed bag.

PR What did your report say?

SA I would start by saying we got a good report from Ofsted. If we have difficulties here at present it's the curriculum area. We did not have time to develop schemes of work and the report said this aspect of what we do was a bit narrow. They are right and this needs looking into. We had to modify the national curriculum, and shape it to the children's needs.

PR You've been a head quite a long time now really. Has your view of headship changed? I was reading some research which suggested that very experienced heads tend to become more autocratic and more reluctant to change.

SA Thirteen years, I didn't want to be head for that long. I don't know if my thinking has changed but I do know that the way I do it has changed although I would not say I have become more autocratic or more reluctant to change. But if you are afraid or insecure then naturally you become autocratic and defensive. But if you are always challenging yourself and others, as I do, then you have no time to be afraid. You do, of course, feel fear, it's good sometimes to face some pressure and stress. I find this can be a positive experience for me. You must be able to take the pain. But if you can live in a stressful situation, as heads have always done, it's a good thing to work together. It's a matter of jointness, of working with others, in the Local Management of Schools, but it can also make you lonely. You can end up always working with figures and always looking for value for money, and forgetting everything else. That is not a good thing. You must be a leading professional not just a chief executive. When I look at LMS I judge what happens, I know its effect in the classroom.

If you look at it all the time as an accountant's job then you have trapped yourself in a tunnel. You must consider LMS in terms of its implications for the curriculum, for school development, and for school improvement.

PR   What's your vision for Mayfield and has this changed over time?

SA   No, it hasn't. I wanted a real community school and that is still my ambition. I won't fully succeed but we have been getting there. I wanted Mayfield to be a learning institution for life, where parents and children can learn at the same time. But I can't fully do this because I don't have the resources. Perhaps I might have been able to if we were a grant maintained school but this is an LEA school. I have wanted to change the attitude of the ethnic minority community towards the disabled but have not been as successful in this as I had hoped. I want to knock the doors down between the school next door so that we can work together, but I can't. As I say, I wanted to make this a community school but there is still some way to go in this. It will not happen fully in my time but I have made a start.

PR   Were you attracted by the possibility of grant maintained status?

SA   I was attracted towards it and we did consider it. We seriously considered it but the implications of going down this route could have been very serious. Under the 1993 Act LEAs are still responsible for SEN and if they stop referring youngsters to you where will you end up? If you don't get the youngsters then you don't get funding. But in any case the GM carrot is only for short term. If they agree with a project you propose they will give you a centre like the Mayfield Centre, or a Library or a Science Lab. But if in the long run the numbers go down there will be no one to protect you.

PR   I can see that although, as you know, there are some special GM schools.

SA   Yes, but there are none in Birmingham as yet. We were attracted by it, we wanted it, we wanted to have more independence. But I concluded that it wouldn't be possible because we also want a co-operative LEA. In any case, with SEN children you need direct contact with many other services like Health, Social Services. We have made those contacts. This is a strong point in my school.

PR   You seemed to have enjoyed the autonomy that LMS gives you. Some headteachers say it has forced them to become managers rather than professionals.

SA   But it's their choice isn't it? They do it because they want to. But it does make you think like a manager and I don't see why that is a bad thing. It makes you much more thoughtful and realistic on how you can best use the money available to you for the children, how can you manoeuvre things. It lets you respond much more quickly than in the past, things can happen quickly. It also makes you careful not to waste money. For example my second deputy, for health reasons, resigned in December 1995. This meant we had some money to spare. We had the money and could appoint core subject co-ordinators. So with LMS I could bring in core subject co-ordinators who could develop subject profiling. In the past I could not have done that.

PR   How do you enable more effective teaching and learning to take place in your school and how do you know it's really happening?

SA   I must start by admitting we have not yet fully formalized our system of monitoring. This may be a cultural thing. We have been considering a supportive approach to this. So we have an assessment policy and a reporting and recording policy, and people do undertake forecasts. Both of us, the Deputy and I, go through those forecasts every term and if we identify problems we bring the appropriate people in. We look at the lesson plans as well. We try to go in and observe, wherever possible, informally. We have had to make this more formal because of the new Ofsted guidance – 12/97 – on incompetent teachers. This means that we have had to be much more rigorous than we were in the past. In addition, we share forecasts, we will involve ourselves in annual reviews so that we know what's going on and can be sure that appropriate individual programmes are developed. The deputy and I keep in touch, we look at all this every term to see how it's developing. Then I am also involved in monitoring provision for learning resources. This takes place at a number of levels. For example, what is being ordered using requisitions and their payment. Of course, the Bursar does this or another teacher does it, but it goes past my eyes. You must know what is being bought and what is not. You must be directly involved. And then there are also the various new initiatives, things like Titan Partnership and City Challenge projects, which brings additional money and other resources. I am directly in touch because I like to deal with all outside contacts as a head. I also spend a lot of time on parental and community relationship and with outside agencies such as the colleges, social services etc. I don't know how I manage to do it, but I'm on the Corporation of Handsworth College so that I can get the maximum benefit for our youngsters. If I scratch their back and do something for them they will do it for me. That's how the network works, so that keeps you going. Although we have only recently begun to develop systematic and formal monitoring, you can do a great deal through informal monitoring that can be a natural part of taking classes and teaching. When you teach you find out a great deal about what the children are learning.

PR   Have you taken any part in Birmingham's Quality Development Initiative?

SA   We have. I sent my second Deputy on your Advanced Certificate Course at the university but, unfortunately, she has now left. Now I'm thinking in terms of Investors in People. I have talked about this to our adviser. I was considering including it in our post-Ofsted action plan. I said that if we wanted to sustain the momentum generated by Ofsted then one way of doing this would be through IIP. The adviser reminded me that it could well be a two-year project and that I would be leaving in a year's time. I answered that this didn't matter because my deputy would still be here and he could take it through. It would stimulate us to review our ethos, our aims and objectives. It might even encourage us to review other aspects of the work of the school such as teaching and learning. I know it will be a stressful experience, but as I said to you earlier stress is good sometimes. I am going to think about the whole thing more in the autumn term, and ask the people to come and talk to us.

PR   You talk about teaching and learning. Have you had a badly incompetent teacher in your school in your thirteen years at the school? What would you do if you came across a teacher who was thoroughly unsatisfactory?

SA   Luckily, we haven't anybody like that now. I wouldn't say I've never had one. I don't disagree with Chris Woodhead when he says there are some incompetent teachers around. Let's face it, there are. During my years here we have had our share. What do you do with them? There has never been a strong mechanism for doing very much about this. I've found this very frustrating. There's very little support.

PR   Would you get support from the LEA if you took a strong line? What of your governors?

SA   I would not get support from the LEA. From the governing body yes, but the LEA never have. In other words I have tried to take action in the past – after all there are competency and disciplinary procedures. But it's very difficult to use them in practice and you get little support if you do. I have come to believe it's a culture thing. These things do not give rise to the same difficulties in other countries. Maybe there is an English culture barrier.

PR   Do you mean there is a tendency to just put up with these kinds of things?

SA   It's a culture of it's my class, my kingdom, my territory and breaking through such barriers takes a lot of time and effort. Whenever you point this out and talk about the drawbacks it has, it always creates resentment. The defence mechanisms go up, you are a bad manager, you are criticizing. I find all this very difficult. I did end up taking disciplinary action some time ago. Even the union tried to throw it out. In the end I stuck to my guns and said, 'This is rubbish and you know it, you have got to see there are problems and these problems need to be addressed.' In the end the governors did give a warning but the problem was not resolved. I don't know why we put up with these sorts of difficulties, perhaps it's because we think those involved are good people. Well, they may be good people but they're not good professionals. I still find this very frustrating. I am not judge and jury and I don't want to be, but there should be joint action which enables objective decisions to be made and acted on as humanely as possible about the professionalism of a teacher. In the end, they should not be in our schools if they cannot do the job. If there is a system or method which enables all this I don't know if there is, it is unlikely.

PR   Can we return to your Ofsted inspection? What do you feel about Ofsted and about the inspection process you have just been through?

SA   The media gives a very negative view of it, which was frightening. But having met them I personally felt at ease. They were very good people and a team. They are people like us, and they try to do things properly. It's good to have an outside perspective. Having said this I also think there is a need for improvement, from both sides. I think it would have been even better if the team had been more experienced with our kind of children; they should have had more practical experience before they judge us. I don't think I am asking for too much. Some of them didn't have any experience of PMLD youngsters, and this did not stop them talking about them taking a broad and balanced curriculum – the national curriculum – and that worries me. I'm not saying those expectations shouldn't be there, but they must be there in relation to the youngster's needs rather than otherwise. But on the whole it has been a good thing.

PR   You think it's a useful experience?

SA   I think it's a useful experience, it puts you on the right track and keeps you going forward rather than sliding down. People do that, let's face it. They can get into a rut, and unless somebody tells them come on, wake up, they just keep going down. It's a good thing for professionals to have to face this.

PR   Some heads have told me that one of the uses of the findings of an Ofsted inspection is that it can give them the leverage to do things which they have wanted to do anyway.

SA   I had thought the same thing, that they would give me some ammunition to work with to do the things I have not been able to. But on the whole it doesn't, it doesn't work that way, it certainly did not work that way here. I accept that they identified some problems and made the people here more aware of them. But those who want to change would have done so anyway. Those who don't want to find ways of avoiding change and will continue to do so unless school managers put in place much more vigorous systems of monitoring, and unless the LEA comes up with much tougher disciplinary procedures and sets up much clearer and tighter targets to be met. If this happens, then you may be able to improve things. But my experience doesn't make me very hopeful. It tells me that those who want to change and they will do so with vigour and commitment, and those who don't, they will always find ways to avoid doing so. They will say there is a lack of resources, or a lack of time or that they are not well.

PR   You seem to be saying you need mechanisms to encourage such folk to go elsewhere?

SA   Yes, that's right. Such people should go. But there is little that somebody in my position can do about it.

PR   Who are you accountable to?

SA   I am accountable to my staff and, very rightly, to my parents. I have worked to empower them and when you do that successfully this can be helpful but it can also make your life more difficult. Even Ofsted pointed out that, your governors and your parents are not just puppets, they question you. I said, yes, that is true, I am proud of them. I am questioned every time. I'm accountable to my parents and I like this. I'm even accountable to my youngsters. They come and tell me 'Mrs Abrol, that's not on Mam'. Most of all, as a professional and as a headteacher, I am accountable to my governors.

PR   What do you see as their role?

SA   That's not very clear. I got some notes on this today from my school adviser. It says they should be a team with the head and that both should work together. They should be able to monitor everything they want to. Somehow the legislation has given them the real power. But we work as a team. I'm very proud that we are a team.

PR   What about your chairman of governors?

SA   He has been a governor for a long time. He was involved in the interview during my appointment. He was the secretary to the governing body. If you talked to him you would find that he is a good friend. We work closely together in all kinds of way. I have found him very helpful and supportive. He does not spend too much time in the school although he does come and when he does he often visits classes. In addition, I have got other governors, five or six are really active. I've got one who is very active, she works here as a dinner supervisor and is a parent governor. She's very active, she gets involved directly in the curriculum, so she will bring up issues. Another parent governor is an experienced bookkeeper. He's very helpful. He spends quite a lot of time here advising and checking how we deal with money. He's a good friend, if he doesn't like something he would say so and he would see that it is corrected. He helps me with the school funds. He checked all my books and audited them for Ofsted. He is very good. It is a good thing to have someone there to see you are not going astray. I've got some good people. Another has a good deal of experience of careers. I intro-duced him as a co-opted governor. He's retired now. He helps us prepare our youngsters for careers and that sort of thing. So there has been good support from these people from their personal experiences.

PR   What about the LEA?

SA   It depends on the person. I have had an adviser who really knocked me down, very much so. She wanted me to get out, she thought I was no good. But my present adviser disagreed. The LEA did an internal management audit which agreed more with my critical adviser than me. They offered me early retirement. But I said 'I'm not going now. I am not going to take retirement, not on those grounds.' They said 'So you want to be a martyr?' I said 'It's nothing to do with martyrdom. People like me are just not coming into the field. We need more of them, not less. If I go people will think that Asian people with a different background who come into high management positions cannot cope. That will be very demoralizing. I will fight this', and I did fight it. It was very stressful but it made me stronger. But they did their best to get rid of me. That's life. But I have always been ready to accept a challenge, I can take stress, people are astonished at how I cope.

PR   How do you cope? How do you keep up to date?

SA   That is difficult, but I still try to get up in the middle of the night and read and read because that has been my life. When I did my MEd my husband at first did encourage me to go for it, but when it came to actually sacrificing anything he couldn't cope. He would say 'You are studying for yourself rather than for me'. So I used to get up at two o'clock in the morning and work until five, and then go to bed and then go to work. So that has been the story of my study. Even in India I used to work at night, and then again in the mornings at teaching. That has been my hard working life, I'm used to it. Life makes you what you are doesn't it, and I'm used to it. Even now I will get up at five o'clock and go through my papers and read something. I did this morning. I was going through a special children's magazine and there was some material in it about assessment which I wanted to read. I made some notes on it and intend to do some more work on it. Then I read through the section on management issues. I also looked at one or two other professional magazines. That is the main way I keep in touch. I also talk to local colleagues and still go on courses. And then, of course, there is the Black Senior Teachers' Association.

PR   Do you belong to any other associations?

SA   I'm in the NAHT and I'm part of the Special School Heads and SLD Heads. They meet separately. It is a good way of exchanging ideas and information. I have also used one of my colleagues in my appraisal, so that has helped as well.

Stress is a new element, isn't it. I sometimes wonder if rather a lot is made of this. It could be that people like me, people from a different cultural background, are used to hard work and pressure. We think of it as a way of life rather than an extra stress. I am hardworking, I can work for twenty-four hours at a stretch and often have. There was a time when as well as my work in school, I also had to run a restaurant for my son in law. I am used to hard work, I find I don't melt away quickly.

PR   I remember one other head telling me that he coped with stress by working.

SA   That is what I do. It is a way of life. In addition to everything else, I do quite a lot of work for UK Asian women. I'm a workaholic. Working keeps me going. But I do enjoy my home, and my daughter is with me and my grandson. They are my life, they keep me going. It is something different to do and something different to look forward to. When I leave school I shut myself off, I don't take anything home. When I am at home I spend time with my grandson and my daughter.

PR   Ted Wragg suggests that you have to be pretty barmy to want to be a head these days.

SA   I don't see it like that, maybe because I'm from a different culture. There does seem to be a culture here of people who think of the job from nine o'clock to four o'clock. I don't think of it in that way. I still find headship exciting. I enjoy being part of a profession. I am sorry that the scenario seems to be changing, that there are no jobs and we are not able to prepare youngsters for jobs. But your profession is something you should enjoy, and I think it's exciting, not barmy. I love to take on challenges. I don't think it's barmy, it's interesting and exciting. You're dealing with money, you're dealing with people, and you're making such a difference. How can that be barmy? I still enjoy headship. If I can make some difference to a hundred children or a hundred people then I think I have done the job I came to do. I'm a candle, if I can burn ten more candles, ten will each burn another ten candles, and so on.

PR   Do you wish you'd done something else rather than be a head?

SA   If I hadn't become a head I would have wanted to be a teacher anyway. I regret I didn't learn better writing skills. I know I can speak very fluently but when it comes to writing I have some inhibition, so maybe that's what I would have tried to do.

PR   Can you tell me something about your conception of special educational needs? Has it changed much during your professional life? Is it going in the right direction?

SA   Changes can be for better or for the worse. It was a good idea that we should not be so ready to classify children with special needs, because in doing so you run the risk of marginalizing them. Brian Fraser, my tutor when I did the MEd, used to talk about a continuum of need. I still believe in a continuum of education. This is how it should be, I don't know why we still classify them so rigidly. We have changed the jargon but we haven't changed the concept. Much that has changed after the 1978 Warnock Report has not been for the good. That worries me. I don't think things are getting better. Now we talk about inclusion. There are youngsters who will never be part of an inclusive provision, that will not be possible, it's not practical. So we've got to talk about differentiation rather than about inclusion or integration or segregation. But I don't want to be too pessimistic. Some good things have happened. There was a time when if a child was assessed as mentally six months old it was thought we shouldn't be trying to do anything with that child. Now we will say that physically he is growing up and so his needs are different and we can do something about this. It's not good enough to be satisfied with treating him like a baby, giving him a dummy and that is that. That's an exciting change in perception. It's a matter of changing the attitudes of parents and teachers. As far as my school and its children are concerned, I find the attitudes of the parents and of the community much more friendly and supportive than it used to be. But there is still a lot to be done. People are still not as positive as they might be. But attitudes are changing for the better though.

I saw a programme on TV last night which did make me worry. They were saying that it is now possible to identify if, and to what extent, a child will be disabled when they scan the pregnant mother and that with this information parents should be given the choice to abort. They were saying that a child with spina bifida should have been aborted rather than going through all that pain. I thought to myself 'My God are we living in a society now where we are going to select ourselves and saying that this isn't a gifted child, a perfect child, so we'll get rid of it?' But against that it is important to raise awareness through information and to do so positively. To give more equal opportunity to the disabled to be able to say this or that is a good thing. So now I can fight on behalf of my daughter and try to make sure she gets the rights that she has never had before. So the legislation can help. It is a tool which we can utilize. It's the same as racialism and the legislation of 1976, but this has not been taken on board rigorously enough. But you can't do everything through legislation. But even so I welcome the 1996 Disability Discrimination Act. If it can play its part in helping change attitudes which define somebody as a man with blindness rather than a blind man then it will be worthwhile. This is beginning to happen with all kinds of disability. It is an exciting change.

PR   But you nevertheless seem to feel that extreme notions of main-streaming and inclusion can do more harm than good?

SA   They are not on. If inclusion is important, then within compre-
        hensive schools we may have to introduce selection again. If you are
        going to include children with learning difficulties then they are
        going to be selected within a selective system aren't they. They will
        become the minority of the minorities. Being realistic I think we
        should leave our options open. We are talking of compulsory educa-
        tion, the whole population, deviations are always there. Able
        children should be given a boost to develop as well, and the same
        thing goes for SEN. I don't agree that any one strategy will work for
        all. I don't see how you can manage differentiation if children with
        all kinds of need are brought into one kind of school. It will be even
        worse if they are all forced into one kind of class. It might be possible
        if we were to completely start again, to knock down every school and
        build new kinds of schools. I can't see that happening, can you?

PR   Do schools still need heads? Could schools get away without heads?

SA   You need heads. That's an attitude which comes from my culture. It's
        no good having a ship without a captain. You need somebody like
        that in any institution. A school is like an extended family. If you want
        an extended family to be able to work together then you've got to
        have somebody who can take responsibility and make decisions. I
        don't think you can exist without heads. But heads may need to
        change, they need to become like team managers rather than princi-
        pals and headmasters.

PR   When people come to you and ask about becoming a head, do you
        still say to them that's a good thing to go for?

SA   Oh yes. One of the heads of department here wants to go for
        promotion, I talked to her, and I said 'You've got the makings, but
        you must work very hard at it'. She finds it very hard to work with me
        or anybody else as part of a team. Without this she is going to find it
        very difficult.

PR   Do you still feel it's possible for you to be an educational leader?

SA   Oh yes, and it is vital that I am. But for this to be possible I must be
        clear about what my job should be about, i.e. teaching and learning.
        I do know something about managing our budget but it would be a
        very poor use of my time to spend a lot of my time doing this in detail.
        I have a bursar who does this with help from the LEA. My responsibil-
        ity is to manage our finances and resources as a whole. I do
        emphasize that these resources are there to improve schooling.

PR   What are you going to do in retirement?

SA   It would be nice to write or to undertake Ofsted training, to help the
        UK Asians to fulfil their ambitions. On the whole, my message would
        be: the pillars of my success story are hard work, perseverance and
        self-confidence.

CHAPTER 3

Facilitating teachers and enabling learning: the leadership task in a special school

ROB ASHDOWN with Steve Rayner

Rob Ashdown has been headteacher of St Luke's School for pupils with severe learning difficulties in Scunthorpe since 1989. He graduated from University College, Cardiff with a first class honours degree in Education in 1975. He stayed for a further three years to conduct research into new ideas on behaviour modification, investigating how they impacted upon teaching language skills to children with severe learning difficulties, and received his PhD in 1980. He has mainly taught pupils with SLD, except for a three-year period, when he taught pupils with language disorders in the Richmond School District of British Columbia, Canada. Rob has published a number of articles and has co-edited two books on special education.

SR Could we begin by your telling me a little bit about your personal background and perhaps anyone or anything which you think may have had a significant influence on your career?

RA I think for most of the time I have led a fairly contented, fairly sheltered life. I've always had a stable home environment. I worked through a normal school career; starting in primary school, on to grammar school, and then eventually to university. I completed my first degree at the University College, Cardiff. I then went on to do a PhD. After this, I went to Bristol, where I did my teacher training at Redlands Teacher Training College, as it was then, but is now part of The University of the West of England.

Home was in Egham, Surrey. Both my parents were teachers. My father is dead. My mother was very much the home-maker and my father was the 'wage earner', a teacher in the local grammar school, which I subsequently attended as a pupil. My father fell ill, and consequently my mother decided to train as a teacher to provide additional income for the family. They were both art teachers. I suppose that is quite a significant introduction to the world of education. It was reinforced at the time by my mother's teacher training. She was coming home each day, full of ideas, wanting to talk them through, and describing in detail her experiences on teaching practice. It was a very formative period, which coincided with my being in the sixth form and taking my A Levels.

There were also close aunts who were involved in education. In fact, my brother and one of my sisters also went on to become teachers, so it clearly runs in the family. I just hope it won't run in my own family! But that's another matter, and on current form, although I have not actively discouraged the notion, the children all seem to have other career interests and they don't much like school.

After grammar school, because I didn't do too well at A Levels, I spent a year at Weybridge Technical College re-taking my A Levels. I went from there to University College, Cardiff. Initially, my intention was to take a degree in French and follow a career in translation. In practice, my first year at university was a foundation year with courses in French, Italian and Education which was at that time a new degree course for Cardiff. I didn't particularly enjoy the French or Italian, but I did enjoy the Education. In particular, I was interested in the content of the child psychology course. I suppose, until that point, I didn't really have any thought of becoming a teacher, but I did decide to go on to take an Education degree in the final two years of my undergraduate course. The experience of the foundation course certainly played an important part in shaping my decision about my own education, and looking back, was a pivotal point in pointing me in the direction of teaching as a career.

There was another influence too, in the first year at college, which had to do with my involvement in a student group supporting young people who were mentally handicapped, as the term in use then described them. This involved regular time spent working with these young people where they lived within the hospital environment. I gradually became more involved in work with children who had severe learning difficulties, both in and out of hospital. This reflected a growing academic interest and a focus in my BA course on aspects of education relating to children with the same kind of disabilities and difficulty.

I was very much influenced at that time by the theories of behaviour modification which were in the ascendancy, and seemed to promise the earth, in terms of the possibilities of progress with these children. I obtained a first class honours degree and decided to stay at university to take an MA but soon converted to a PhD. I stayed at Cardiff, and Graham Upton, initially, was my tutor, and then subsequently Ron Davie. In actual fact, they both gave me a very free hand.

I was hardly involved at all in presenting seminars, or such other 'usual' activities which are frequently thrown at postgraduate students. Instead, I spent most of my time at the local 'mental handicap hospital' researching some of the new ideas in behaviour modification, investigating how they impacted upon teaching language skills to a small group of children. I came very much under the influence of the senior clinical psychologist at the hospital called John Clements, who has since moved on to do other things, and who is well known in the field of severe learning disabilities.

When it came towards the end of my PhD studies, I was in two minds whether to go into teaching or whether to go into clinical psychology. In the long run, I guess I was really more interested in the teaching and in working with youngsters experiencing severe learning difficulties. At that time, Bristol Redlands College offered a specialist postgraduate training course in teaching pupils who were then called the severely educational sub-normal (ESN(S)). I spent twelve months there and then moved to my first teaching post in Basildon at a special school for ESN(S) pupils.

I should add at this point that, of course, my wife Clare was very much a factor and a presence during this entire period. She was always in the background supporting me and encouraging me, both at university as I pursued my PhD, and at Bristol during teacher training, and both she and I wanted to see all the effort come to fruition. We were married throughout this period. Our first year of married life, in 1976, was actually spent as volunteer residents in a home for young adults with severe learning disabilities, which is not really the best way to set up home! She was a secretary for the student society that I had joined which gave opportunities to children and adults at the local mental handicap hospital. We both shared this common interest, although she was not particularly in training to teach. She actually works now in a local college teaching ESL students, so we don't really share a common focus in our work. In fact, I pretty much keep work to myself rather than talking about it at home.

SR   Was there anybody at Bristol who played a significant role in further shaping your ideas and attitudes about education or guiding your chosen career route into education?

RA   Yes – yes there was actually! Veronica Sherborne, who was our main tutor on the course and a leading exponent of 'Movement Activities'. Up to 50 per cent of our work was based around Veronica's ideas about movement and severe learning disability. Perhaps that's a slight exaggeration, but she was a powerful influence on me, not least because I discovered that I wasn't terribly good at movement activities and really had to work very hard at it. Looking back, although I found some of the ideas rather cranky, movement activities were really an excellent vehicle for work on communication with pupils experiencing severe learning difficulties. They were also very useful for fostering physical development and independence. She was really quite a big influence on my thinking.

SR   Would you say that the ideas are still relevant today for you in work with pupils who have severe learning difficulties?

RA   Definitely. However, whilst my first interest has always been in the language and cognitive functioning of such children, I still have an interest in the behaviour modification approach. I suppose Graham Upton should be blamed for that interest, as well as the clinical psychologist, John Clements, who I mentioned previously. I still feel that the tools offered by this approach, rather than the philosophy, can prove to be excellent techniques which can be used in teaching practice. What is critical for effective practice and good results is the selection of the right tools, and the ways in which these tools are used.

SR   You seem to me, at this moment, to represent a good example of a theoretician who has deliberately become a practitioner. Would you regard yourself in that way?

RA   I think I might. I still feel that the training in research is very important and I have very deliberately kept up to date with the research literature. I think I experienced a good training course at Bristol, and I certainly think that there isn't enough of this kind of training any more for teachers in this field. There's nothing like the postgraduate course I experienced now available. In that sense, yes, I would argue for a need to combine the theoretical and the practical to inform effective teaching and learning.

I am the first to admit, however, that there can be problems; for example, the work of pure theoreticians and researchers can seem very much removed from the practical context. A perspective which is clearly focused on the psychological research, in 'pure' or 'applied' terms, needs to lead towards validation in the school context. For this reason, in addition to several other reasons, I think that action research is very important. I accept that there are practical problems associated with such research (commitment, workload, finding the energy to run a project, etc.) but I do certainly think an awareness of research and the information it is yielding is very important. Indeed, it is encouraging to see more of a rapprochement today between those involved in the pure and applied research and people who are working in the classroom. I wish there was more of it. I think it would be fair to say that a concern for the two has been a feature in my own professional approach.

I've certainly had to work very hard at bridging the gap between theory and practice. I've recently completed a couple of units for the distance learning course at the University of Birmingham. One of them was about cognitive and intellectual impairments and I really had to delve deeply into the literature for that work. It was a very good exercise for me and it's amazing how much relevant information is totally inaccessible to the practising teacher, particularly teachers in the field of special education. I think it is important that people have the opportunity to do the same sort of thing, but unfortunately, in their professional context, too many teachers simply aren't given that opportunity.

SR   Could you describe your teaching career?

RA   My first year – in Basildon! I've been teaching mainly in schools for children with severe learning difficulties throughout my entire career. During the two years in Basildon, which obviously included my probationary year, I taught a group of pupils with profoundly multiple learning difficulties, and then within the same school, I went on to teach a more able group of teenagers with severe developmental difficulties.

The reasons I left the school were actually domestic rather than professional. We had had our first three children by 1981 and Clare's parents lived in Canada. We felt that it would be a good thing for Clare's parents to see something of their grandchildren for a while. We actually emigrated to Canada. For two years, I was teaching in a school district called Richmond which is on the outskirts of Vancouver. I was a peripatetic teacher or 'itinerant teacher', as the position was called in Canada, working with language impaired children in ordinary school. These children had language disorders, but fell within the range of average intelligence. It was useful for me in a great many ways, especially with respect to the fact that I was working alongside psychologists and speech therapists in speech and language programmes. I received an introduction to a whole new world of ideas which I found very valuable. Many of the ideas, unfortunately, I don't get the chance to apply in my work with pupils with SLD. However, if I was to begin to think about moving into a different field of education, I know the experience would prove extremely beneficial.

SR   It seems to have reflected your expressed interest in cognition and learning.

RA   Certainly. Yes! Yes, very much so. The work also involved teaching literacy skills, and that was interesting in itself. An introduction to Frank Smith, and the psycholinguistic theory of reading, which is a totally different world to the learning theory approach to language development and behaviour modification. That was an interesting time, but the main motivation for coming back was to teach children with severe learning difficulties. I wasn't working with these children in Canada and didn't see myself getting the opportunity to do so. There was an interesting system of special education in Canada, where the children were actually, literally 'mainstreamed'. They were placed in age-appropriate resource bases in a network of elementary, junior high and senior high schools. It was interesting to observe the system at close hand, although it was not without its problems.

I came back to a deputy headship at a small special school for pupils with SLD in Cambridge. The headteacher was a very nice bloke but unfortunately he was suffering from the after-effects of a serious illness. He eventually had to take early retirement on the grounds of ill health less than two years after my arrival at the school. Well, I applied for the headship, although I was in two minds about it. A number of people, including Clare, my wife, encouraged me to apply, persuading me it would be a good thing for the school, as it would provide it with continuity. I was appointed after the interviews, and was headteacher there for about four years before I came to this school in September 1989.

I suppose, on reflection, I became a headteacher after what was a relatively short period of time actually working as a teacher in this country. I had returned to a post in senior management and then quite quickly progressed to headship. In that sense, I suppose I was a 'young' or 'naive' headteacher, but not as 'green' as some because of my time spent in postgraduate study and then my teaching in Canada.

SR   To sum up, Rob, why do you think you decided to teach?

RA   I think it was because I was interested in how children learn and the way in which people can facilitate that learning. This might sound coldly academic, but I was also very interested in helping these children.

SR   If we move to focus a little more closely on the period in Cambridge and progress towards headship, in the final analysis, what was it that carried you forward to headship?

RA   Well – what really pushed me forward in the direction of senior management was the fact that as a class teacher, I had all sorts of ideas, which I had been wanting to try out but I felt I didn't have the clout to influence others and encourage them to try these ideas out. There are certain things which I believe children should be taught, certain values teachers should have and their methods should be appropriate. I guess, really, it's about wanting to influence things within school, and wanting to shape the direction of what's happening in school. However, you realize pretty damn quickly that it's not as simple as that in practice!

SR   Yes – I was just thinking the same thing, and I caught myself wondering about the true extent of the headteacher's influence on the daily 'exchange' of teaching and learning in school.

RA   Yes – I think there are times now, still, when I feel that I would achieve a great deal with certain children if I was actually teaching in the classroom. But you know, I do feel overall that I've achieved a lot of things for a greater number of children than I would have done if I had remained a class teacher. I think the same thing applies to my involvement with families, and staff, and the school community. The school leader has a wider impact on things beyond the classroom, although quite obviously, his or her influence upon classroom teaching and learning is always of paramount importance.

SR Are you aware of any particular preparation for management throughout the period of deputy headship at Cambridge?

RA Absolutely not – no! No! That was one of the things, with hindsight, which I have always felt was missing. I thought my headteacher in Cambridge was a good headteacher. He took time to talk to me about the issues. He was a good bloke with a well thought out philosophy of education and in many ways influenced my approach to leadership and school management. But I think he would have been a greater influence upon me as a manager if he had not been so unwell. There were several times during my first year, because of his illness, that I was thrust prematurely into the role of acting headteacher. It wasn't his fault, it was just the way it happened.

There was no accessible management course, whatsoever, no preparation for management like there is today. As deputy headteacher, and headteacher, I was very much given the impression that as long as things were going along 'quietly' and relatively 'happily', the LEA were quite ready to leave me to get on with whatever it was I felt fit to do as a special school headteacher. There was never a suggestion of offering me support of management training in the first year or so of headship. There may have been thoughts, but they were never put into any action.

One of the more useful influences in that respect were fellow heads, and in particular a colleague, who were special school headteachers. Keith Bovair, who was also a headteacher in Cambridge at a special school for children with moderate learning difficulties (MLD) became a useful foil and a good substitute for training. We built up a very good relationship, bouncing ideas off each other, and became friends outside of school. No, there was definitely not any preparation for management and in terms of domestic arrangements, I was at that time preoccupied with house and family. We had by that time five children and our hands full. I don't think I would have been too interested in twilight training.

SR Looking back, and using 20/20 vision, if you like, it seems fair to say that headship came on you quite abruptly, leaving you without a period of preparation or apprenticeship. Would you agree with this view and would it have been better to have had a longer period of preparation for headship?

RA I definitely think it would have been better to have had a distinct period of preparation for headship. It might have helped me get around some of the difficulties I actually faced in my first couple of years of headship. I do feel there should have been something in place, a course to prepare me for headship, as well as some formal induction procedure, such as the kind of training course which is now offered by LEAs and outside agencies, and which are increasingly available for aspiring managers today. There was one four-day course which I had the chance to attend, but this was in the third year of my headship. I did find it very useful. It introduced me to a range of literature about organizational skills, time management, and of course, personnel management. I do think the biggest thing about this job is managing people and sustaining good personal and professional relationships. I didn't really get any guidance at all in this aspect of management from the LEA.

SR   Do you think that this aspect of your experience relates to the new changes promised by recent government policy? I am thinking of initiatives like HEADLAMP and the new National Professional Qualification for Headteachers.

RA   Well – it will inevitably depend upon how well it is organized, but yes, I think the idea is good. I think preparation for headship is sensible. I also think that by going on courses, you have the opportunity as a professional to interact with and learn from peers who are thinking about the same sorts of things and doing the same job as yourself. I think that is a large part of the value of a course, as well as actually receiving ideas and information from the people who are delivering it.

SR   Were there any particular difficulties or challenges you faced in the early period of headship?

RA   Well – yes – partly because of my experiences and lack of preparation for leadership and partly because, I think, I'd been a deputy headteacher in the same school. I did take a final step across the 'divide' between 'staff' and 'management' that was reflected in people's attitude to me in school. There were a couple of teachers who seemed to expect things should continue exactly as before. I did feel that I had to take a stand on a couple of issues: for example, around about that time, the 1986 Education Act came into force, and introduced a requirement for schools to offer descriptions of the curriculum, information for parents, a school prospectus.

In school at that time, there was absolutely nothing written and available on the curriculum. I was trying to start movement in that area, while at the same time trying to exercise greater control over the curriculum. In contrast, staff were more concerned about the poor quality of their working environment and resources for learning. Of course, all of these changes and the issue of resourcing caused stresses for the staff and a few held me responsible and criticized my style of headship. In various ways, I suppose, I took it all personally, and that did not help. In the end we worked it all out, but I can't help feeling if I'd had more time as a deputy head and been given some training, I might have handled it differently.

There was also a very strong group of Teachers' Aides (TA) in the school, and two or three were as skilled and knowledgeable as the teachers and knew it. This extended to some believing that they knew better than the teachers what should be taught and how it should be taught, and this was not the case. There were clearly some staff who had no idea about the professional way of handling the issue and a difference of opinion. I found that this created very difficult situations, at times, and of course, while I don't think any of the staff had problems with me as a person, I was still learning people management skills and I definitely made a number of mistakes.

These experiences certainly reinforced for me that, as a manager, it is absolutely vital to pay due care and attention to procedures which settle grievances and underpin discipline. At that time the only written guidance I had was contained in the old burgundy book on teachers' conditions of service. I think, looking back, when I sought advice I was very well supported by the LEA and by some members of the governing body.

SR   It is interesting to hear you mention the TAs – I know from conversations I have had with colleagues when I was a headteacher, and this is going back now some three or four years ago, that TAs in SLD schools seemed to be a powerful and discrete group, which was in stark contrast to the same group of staff in a special school for children with emotional and behavioural difficulties (EBD).

RA   Yes, some of them, but for circumstances around the time of the 1970 Education Act, might have been and would have been very good teachers. One lady, in my present school, who is one of the best teachers I have known, actually came to teaching prior to 1971 but she qualified as a teacher some years afterwards. There were a number of TAs who could have gone down the same route, but for one reason or another didn't do so.

SR   It seems to me that the TAs represent a strong sub-group in the staff of SLD schools which probably doesn't feature in the same way in the rest of special educational provision.

RA   Well – to a certain extent, I think it depends upon the history of individual schools, the personalities and the actual make-up of the staff within a school. For example: the relationships between groups of staff in this school are very good. I admit that perhaps my management approach is better now, one hopes to improve with time and I certainly learnt some lessons the hard way. However, I think that relationships here are good mainly because the TAs, despite their occasional and legitimate moans, do not generate the kind of problems which quickly led to a cluster of people creating a 'them and us' scenario in the Cambridge school. Unfortunately, at the time, I was not experienced enough and 'directive' enough to deal with that situation promptly and effectively.

SR   How would you describe your first year of headship here, in what was your second school as a headteacher?

RA   I think it was an interesting time. There were one or two personnel issues which were not immediately obvious that soon floated to the surface. However, when I first arrived, the key issue was the introduction of the national curriculum (NC). Nobody knew anything about it, and I recall the very first couple of 'Baker Days' as I still call the INSET days we have, being devoted to the NC. I was very much taken up with getting these ideas across to staff, governors and parents and since then, work on the NC has been a central thread running through our professional development. Curriculum development has been a major aspect of our institutional development.

A great deal of the early period in a headship is spent getting to know people, getting to know class groups, spending time in the classrooms. There is a much more profoundly handicapped population of pupils here than at my last school, so while I had had experience of working with that population of pupils with profound and multiple learning difficulties in my first school in Basildon, the shift reflected a new dimension for me. It represented a new or perhaps renewed learning curve for me. I was lucky too when I arrived to find a very capable teacher working with that group of pupils.

I do remember one immediate problem which presented itself. I arrived to find that my deputy headteacher was due to leave two days later to begin her maternity leave. She's now back of course and in full swing, but the point was that her departure left me facing some rather pressing tasks which needed my attention with limited knowledge of the school and the LEA. In that respect, I was straight in at the deep end. On the other hand, with the exception of one new teacher who started at the same time as I did, there were no other new staff in the school, which was settled and well organized. The staffing at this school has remained very stable with little change occurring since 1989.

There were occasional troubles involving personality clashes between some staff which really had to do with discipline and temperament and I still found it testing and stressful having to manage these particular difficulties. Usually, we managed to resolve the situation and, on the whole, this is a happy school. Overall, in the scale of things, the first year here proved to be much more a 'honeymoon' than the one I had experienced in my first headship.

SR   What were the big differences, Rob?

RA   There was a very good governing body here which was immediately noticeable. There was a good governing body at the last school, but one or two key people left. I think it was also true to say that as a governing body, aside from the chairman, they didn't spend as much time with me as the head, as do the governors here. However, I suppose we should mention here that times have changed and encouraged the growing involvement of governors in management practice.

A second thing was the strength of the teaching staff; it is a great deal stronger here for various reasons – I am particularly lucky with my Senior Management Team (SMT). I have three colleagues who are well qualified, especially in terms of experience, who are my eyes and my ears. I have two team leaders and a deputy headteacher, a management structure based on what I inherited, which had initially been one team leader and the deputy headteacher. The second team-leader post was created as the school population increased in number. As a response to our lobbying, the LEA agreed to funding for the second senior teacher post. In my previous school, the number of teachers was smaller and the staffing structure was more straightforward. In that school, the SMT consisted of only myself and the new deputy headteacher, both of us relatively inexperienced in school management. I think another thing about my present school was that several teachers here had been relatively new to the school, prior to my arrival, and consequently were very enthusiastic about their work.

SR   Did you feel better prepared for the job the second time around?

RA   I think so, in terms of the experiences I had at the last school which taught me a lot. I think, with hindsight, at times, I was guilty in the past of letting a crisis emerge because I wasn't quick enough off the mark. Now I know to be quicker off the mark, can better spot things developing, and can act quickly to prevent a crisis from happening. I now know to make sure things are in place to remove the opportunity for mischief or misunderstanding. For example, one of the things I have introduced here is a school manual outlining professional responsibilities and procedures for all of the staff. We didn't at first have one in my previous school, and there were times when problems developed because staff could fairly claim they didn't know what expectations existed.

SR   What prompted you to move on to your second headship then, Rob?

RA   Family reasons primarily. By 1989 things were much more settled in my previous school. We had reached a satisfactory 'modus vivendi', and the difficult times had passed on with some staff having left the school. I think the school was actually beginning to 'tick'.

However, we had by that time a family of five young children. We were living in a three-bedroomed house, and on my salary there was no way I could afford a larger house in Cambridge. We started to look around in areas north of the Severn-Trent line for a cheaper part of the country, in terms of housing and the cost of living. Humberside is a very cheap area of the country and that played a big part in bringing us to Scunthorpe.

SR   Finally, perhaps, thinking about the transition from first to second headship, can you recall how you felt at interview and on taking up the new appointment?

RA   Yes, I can actually. I'd been to a couple of interviews beforehand. I actually liked the school and very much liked some of the staff I met while looking at the school. I felt very strongly that there was potential here. It is a shock, in a sense, when you actually make the move from a place you've got used to to a place that is new. I'll feel the same way when I move on from here sometime. You suddenly realize that you've got to start all over again. Of course, I was looking for a change; it wasn't only a move for domestic reasons, important as they were at the time. I was looking for new challenges, in various ways, although this school wasn't significantly bigger at the time nor did it represent a 'promotion'. However, it did represent change, and potential, and after a couple of years I did actually get promotion because of a dramatic increase in pupil numbers in school. It was importantly the opportunity to do new things.

SR   Did you clearly see an opportunity for the school to grow before saying yes to the appointment?

RA   No – I didn't initially have enough of a feel for the demographics of the area. I was struck by the space within the school, when compared to the one in Cambridge, although that has now evaporated under the pressure created by greater numbers as the school population has increased in size. We are now actually very cramped.

SR   Throughout your career, what, in particular, have been the high and low points of success which feature in your experience as a head?

RA   Right – yes – I think some of the low points are clear. Certainly, the disciplinary problems with some staff in Cambridge were amongst the lowest points of my career. However, there were also very many enjoyable moments during the first headship, you know; without doubt we achieved a great deal for the children. One thing which went very well and pleased me, and was only possible because of the support of the LEA and the school staff, was the integration of individual children between the age of five to ten or eleven years old into their local primary school. The LEA paid for taxis and additional staff time which allowed the integration to take place.

We were busy evolving our own curriculum. I saw it as important and I think the teachers did too, because we were evolving our own curriculum which was very interesting, involving and exciting. We were less regulated then by a strict curriculum framework and although there was a great deal of freedom, I don't think we were running a 'holiday camp' or 'respite care'. We were certainly teaching the things which interested us most of all, so that was good. Having said that, I think the introduction of the NC has been a good thing. However, it's been a very painful process introducing the NC into special education for children with SLD and I'm sure many people in this field wouldn't shed a tear if there was an abolition of the NC tomorrow.

Indeed, its introduction has truly dominated my headship in this school and I do regard the curriculum development here as a satisfying achievement. Talking through ideas with people, introducing new equipment, generating more opportunities for INSET and exploring new opportunities for the curriculum, have all resulted from the introduction of the NC and influenced a positive institutional development. I still think there are times when we are playing intellectual gymnastics as regards the relationship between the curriculum these children need and the curriculum as laid down in the statutory orders. I do get a bit fed up with end of key stage tests, with piles of boxed glossy materials arriving in school for these tests. I can't deny asking myself what the hell am I supposed to do with all of this and isn't it a waste of the country's money?

However, aside from that, I do think there should be an NC, although I do question whether there is such a thing as an NC for children with SLD because the appropriate learning targets for SLD just don't feature in the statutory orders. I do think that some of the National Curriculum Council (NCC) booklets and some of the more recent School Curriculum and Assessment Authority (SCAA) booklets are very good indeed. However, they don't prescribe in the same way as the statutory orders have attempted. I don't want them to 'prescribe' in great detail, but, and it is a significant 'but', they do not refer to or provide a model for an NC for children with SLD.

So – really we've been left to work out what suits us within the wider curriculum framework. It is only when it comes to Ofsted Inspectors or LEA Advisers dropping in to appraise us that it is all actually tested to see if it does meet national standards and expectations. I do think, you know, there should be a better way to assure quality. I think SCAA should be doing more to develop models. Teachers should be encouraged to produce more materials, and writing up their work, and the development should really move from the bottom up. There really isn't enough support for the sharing of ideas and collaboration in professional development.

SR   Did the Cambridge experience of mainstreaming reinforce your own convictions about integration and SEN provision?

RA   Yes – I think it did but I also think there were other things which were more important to me, which, if you like, contributed to the shaping up of a personal philosophy, such as the 'normalization' principle advanced by eminent workers in the field. There have been one or two good books: for instance, *The Politics of Mental Handicap* by Joanna Ryan and Frank Thomas, which has some excellent material in it. I think working with certain people in the mental handicap hospital in Cardiff had its impact. Perhaps it took a while for me to develop my own educational philosophy. The way I saw it, in the beginning, was that the 'patients' in the hospital were the way they were because that's the way they were. It took me a while to realize that it was the system and the environment that made them that way, that is, in terms of their behaviour and attitudes. I think since the mid seventies there's been a growing awareness that people with learning disabilities are a 'minority rights' group, and the principles of natural justice demand integration. That was the kind of philosophy which pervaded the student society in which I was involved and shared by most of the members in it.

SR   Do you think your professional practice reflects that philosophy? Have you held to it in your years of teaching and management?

RA   Well – I'd like to think so, but then, having said that, in this school, the finances are such that we can only afford the basic minimum of staff in the classroom, and what we consider a minimum standard of resourcing, and so we are not able to support a strong network of school links or an outreach programme. What we do do is to manage individual exceptional arrangements but not without depending on much good will and a resource 'stretch'. Of course I wouldn't stand in the way at all of parental wishes for children to be transferred to any school. I do think a majority of children could benefit from such a network of support provision. However, the financial mechanisms are just not there, the infrastructure is not there, even though the philosophy on my part is there.

In the first instance, I would really like to give all of our children experience of being integrated into schools, thereby furthering the process of 'normalization'. As I say we have no money for outreach work, but having said that, we have a number of visitors coming into this school, seeing what it is we do, picking our brains, and from time to time we do go out delivering INSET to people. But it is all rather ad hoc and carried out with no available funding to support it.

SR   What particular vision as a headteacher do you have for this school and how does it play a part in your headship?

RA   In this school, as a staff, we sat down and talked about the basic principles underpinning the school curriculum and what we saw as the basic entitlement for the pupils. From my own point of view, I would still like to think that we were ultimately working towards 'doing away' with special schools and children with SLD being educated in their local community school, with the appropriate resources being available to support their education.

Of course, the system we have at present will just not permit that to happen, because of the lack of resources, and the structure and funding of self-government of schools in the form of LMS. The organization of an SEN provision which would be truly inclusive demands extra money to make it happen, and would need to embrace the idea of locally organized educational systems which would support a 'mainstreaming of SEN'. There would also have to be changes made in mainstream school teaching approaches and curriculum. Organizing a system such as that would prove to be more expensive than retaining a system that simply segregates children with SEN in special school. Unfortunately, finances rather than philosophies appear to be the deciding factor.

SR   You don't think there's a contradiction there – a special school headteacher advocating the closure of special school provision?

RA   The reality, of course, is that unless there is much more funding and a commitment from the LEA, this vision for SEN provision will never be realized. I think the LEA envisages the need for this special school, or something like it, for the foreseeable future. I tend to think that's how the majority of people perceive things. It is a commonly held position that there will always be a need for a number of special arrangements. My own view is even if we don't achieve full integration into the child's local community school, given an appropriate level of funding, we ought at least be able to have resourced units forming an integral part of a network of primary and secondary school provision. Plus there needs to be a co-ordinating headteacher, and I think this would be a role in which I should be interested. I don't think it is going to happen, given the need for some considerable restructuring to make such a network function and the current arrangements for LMS imposed across the whole country. I think, in that respect, the tide of change is running in the wrong direction. There used to be 'double funding' which allowed a small number of these units to work, but this kind of 'dual funding' has all disappeared.

SR   What you seem to be describing is a vision of SEN provision which is 'global' and 'far-reaching', if you like, 'visionary', but how does this translate into the vision of the headteacher for St Luke's School?

RA   In reality, St Luke's School will continue to exist for my lifetime here. Therefore, I think we must be aiming to give the children experiences of various forms of integration. We aim to make a lot of use of community facilities, particularly with the older pupils, because it does become easier as pupils grow older and because the teaching and use of community facilities is equally increasingly important to them. It is not just a case of 'being seen out there', but it is also about enabling the children and their families to access things like the bowling alley or sports centre or shops and other aspects of the local community.

If I think of the youngsters in the nursery, similar opportunities are equally important to them. We have some children who may not remain with us, so visits and shared time with local nurseries is important. It is vital that we give them an opportunity to experience mainstream provision. Years ten and eleven also involve considering transitional arrangements for post-sixteen provision, as well as the individual pupil's future, which has led to extending our curriculum and to links with local colleges of further education.

SR   How does that vision impact upon your role as headteacher?

RA   Well – I think what we're beginning to talk about here is policy formation. One of the problems with policy formation has been the question of time. Inevitably, for some aspects of policy, I have to say this is how it is going to be, really as an interim measure, until we get around to discussing things more thoroughly. I know that's a rather bald characterization, but it is probably the most honest way of looking at it. In that sense, there's a certain amount of 'leading by the nose'; some people are far more willing to be led than others; and some people are galloping ahead of me.

For instance, as regards the school curriculum and pupil entitle-ment, we spent two INSET days on that, and a number of meetings subsequently, brainstorming what the school is about, its purposes, and what we ended up with was a written document about the school curriculum which we could communicate to parents. Time permit-ting, I would much rather have that kind of brainstorming approach occur throughout our policy development, and then synthesize the result into policy. I'd like to think that, certainly with respect to the teachers, it represents what they would call a collegiate approach.

SR   I want to ask you what is perhaps not an easy question and is related to this part of the discussion. How do you manage or measure your own success as a headteacher?

RA   No – it's not an easy question. I think this is where I find myself going back to around about 1989, and the work of David Hargreaves, and school development plans. I also think back to the course on Time Management which I attended while I was in Cambridge during my first headship. It is necessary to have an idea of where you want to be going and set realizable objectives tied to a specific time-scale, while being clear about your strategies. I feel we ought to be aiming for a similar professional approach to development for all teachers in this school. We ought to have a kind of personal development plan which would reflect the same ideas as the school development plan. This is where teacher appraisal makes a start, although it has by no means achieved what I would like to see happen.

So, if I have identified objectives, I can then see objectives being realized and that is very important. I can see policies being put into place, and I can see children having opportunities and specified experiences. The interesting thing is the difficulty posed by the measurement of pupil outcomes. For example, some of these children can barely move an arm or a leg and it is very much an adult-led encounter in the classroom. Just how do you measure the pupil outcomes, which by definition are going to be small and difficult to observe? We really do need to find measurable pupil outcomes to evaluate the impact of policy changes and teaching methods.

SR   I know you have inferred a collegiate style of management as an ideal but suggested that you can't afford to adopt this approach all of the time. Could you describe the kind of head you are – as a leader – as a manager?

RA   Well we just can't afford to have a full-blown democratic approach. There will be times when I have to respond to something very quickly and say, look this is what we are going to have to do. I'd try to explain why. I do actually try to give people some kind of written summary of my thinking, or if it is something from the LEA or national agencies, a written summary of that, so that there is always an explanation. Quite often, that will go into the school manual for ready reference.

SR   I know I have already said this, more or less, but I still have this impression of you as a 'thinking headteacher'. Would you describe yourself as a 'thinking headteacher'?

RA   I should hope ultimately that all headteachers and teachers think! I do believe that we ought to be able to articulate clearly what we are talking about and what it is we're aiming for in our work. I do tend to find it easier to do this on paper, rather than in the way we're doing it right now, out aloud and talking. Yes. I suppose in that sense, I would describe myself as a 'thinking' head. I do believe in consulting staff where I can, rather than saying this is how it will be, but I do find there are times when there is disagreement amongst staff which means I must intervene and say, no this is what I think and therefore we'll do it this way. I think enabling staff to do their job well is an important aspect of my job. I think this involves creating a good working environment, providing necessary equipment, arranging opportunity for appropriate INSET. In that sense, the headteacher must crucially be an 'enabler' as well as a leader.

SR   If I approached a member of staff, what do you think they would say, if I asked them to describe you as a headteacher?

RA   I think they would say they don't know me very well because I don't spend enough time working in the classroom or talking to them as people in the staff room. In fact, that's the big thing that worries me and I'm pretty sure nearly everyone would like to see more of me in the classroom. I don't think I'm spending enough time there.

I do think that part of the role as the headteacher is the 'school leader', is to know what is going on in the classrooms, and to provide feedback to the teaching staff and the governing body. I think that is definitely an area in which I'm falling down at the moment. I keep telling myself that I am at least now aware of it and I am moving towards changing that aspect of my work. I am now getting in to some classes more often, and I hope over the next few terms that this will continue to improve. I've become increasingly conscious of the fact that it's one thing to spend time formulating policy, but it is quite another thing actually to ensure that what goes on in the classroom matches what is stated in the policy statements.

SR   Is the main reason for your desire to access classrooms to secure accountability?

RA   No. I don't think the headteacher should be merely an inspector in residence. I do think it is about being aware, giving 'positive strokes' to people, a formative process. I really don't think I do that enough, perhaps partly because I'm not used to receiving them myself, because of the kind of job I have myself. I think that giving positive strokes to people, actually going in alongside them, and seeing what the problems are in terms of the delivery of policy, is not just about 'checking' that they are competent. If teachers can't deliver something for whatever practical reasons, you've got to make the resources available to them, or else change the policy. Now we can achieve that through the daily exchange of dialogue between the teachers and me, and we have at least one meeting per term on an individual basis, and all sorts of other opportunities to meet informally. We have our regular weekly teachers' meeting too. However, it is one thing to talk about an issue and it is another thing to actually see the issue in context. That's why I would actually like to be more involved in the classroom.

SR   I think this question, in large part, touches upon what you've been talking about but I'd like to ask all the same – how do you enable effective teaching and learning as the school leader?

RA   We spend a lot of time planning our work. We also aim to be in line with the requirements of the Education Act 1993, and the SEN Code of Practice. We use individual education plans which are an integral part of our assessment procedure. We also have the annual review system running, in which I am heavily involved as well as the class teacher. The assessment process also helps to shape the curriculum and there are issues which arise from this process which we follow up.

I would say that that is one approach to 'enabling' effective teaching. It is also about helping people to feel able to come to me with a particular problem. There are one or two more independent

	spirits, but generally most teachers do come and share with me, especially if they want to 'chew the fat' over a problem.
SR	In terms of the 'free spirits' who you describe as independent, how do you feel about the balance between collaboration and delegation and encouraging people to lead in the various areas of the curriculum?
RA	Well – I used the term 'independent spirits' euphemistically! However, in terms of enabling people to lead, that really takes place at several different levels. For instance: we have the Team Leaders of the two departments in school. They have delegated powers and responsibilities. They know they can take a lead within their own remit. I have given them substantial responsibilities, but also the benefits of being managers. They organize support staff, plan schedules for meetings and work on development planning, run departmental assemblies, etc., but they also have the opportunity to strongly influence things in their own department.
SR	How many teachers in the department?
RA	We're talking about four teachers in one department and five in the other department together with a large number of TAs. Obviously, we like to give Team Leaders non-contact time for planning and budgeting administration. We have managed to give a little to the department heads as well as the deputy headteacher, but not enough. We have a regular meeting of the senior management team, where we focus on issues of management. Wherever I can, I give them back-up in their own areas of management.

The deputy headteacher doesn't actually carry a leadership role within a department. She has the unusual position of being a class teacher and working to a team leader. That's because she did not originally have a class, but with an increase in pupil numbers and budgetary constraints, it was necessary for her to take up a class responsibility. She certainly isn't just a shadow of the headteacher; she has a very different set of responsibilities to me. She has specific responsibilities related to the Technical and Vocational Education Initiative (TVEI), the Records of Achievement INSET and Child Protection. There are a number of other things too, which form her remit. She's not very involved in the financial issues relating to LMSS but generally I would describe the management of the school as a partnership. I sometimes wonder, however, whether we have enough time to meet each other, because she only has two sessions of non-contact time a week, which is not much. She should really be getting a lot more. In fact, the deputy head and two team leaders are the only staff to have regular non-contact time.

This brings us on to the question of the subject co-ordinator, because the subject co-ordinator role is something we have been trying to develop here for the last two and a half years. We have moved to specify subject areas and match them to the strengths and interests of individual staff and allocate areas of curriculum responsibility. This has involved real management responsibility and opportunity, including budget control and resources administration and the leadership task for the particular area of the curriculum.

During the past several years, in our involvement in TVEI we have used over 60 per cent of the TVEI funding we received to release staff for participation in small working groups led by individual subject co-ordinators charged with developing policy and practice in various areas of the curriculum. I think that all of this activity has given people higher levels of 'managerial' responsibilities in the delivery of the curriculum. There are a lot of issues which have not yet been addressed, for example, 'time management', management of TAs and other staff, management of volunteers, and so forth. However, TVEI is coming to an end and it is becoming difficult to stretch the budget to provide regular non-contact time for the co-ordinator.

The teachers are also involved in running curriculum audits, in which they are required to answer the basic evaluation questions: Where are we now? Where do we want to be? How do we get there? How will we know when we get there? This forms the foundation for development planning, and I'm expecting them to clearly identify resources and INSET they think necessary to put policy into practice in their subject area. On the basis of that evaluation, I am then in a position to take a proposal forward to the SMT and then the governing body. We then decide what we can actually afford.

Now, there will always be more money allocated to some rather than other subject areas. For example, the amount of money allocated to the Art Co-ordinator is well over fifteen hundred pounds a year, because we spend a great deal on consumable resources. English and IT is another area which attracts a lot of money. On the other hand, Religious Education (RE) has a low spending requirement and has not attracted a great deal of money in the past few years.

SR   That seems rather ironic in so far as it lacks a 'divine justice', Rob?

RA   Well – yes – but if you are the RE Co-ordinator and identify an area of spending that underpins a development proposal, then the case is made and is put to the SMT, and to the governing body. In that event, RE will attract more money because it will be regarded as a priority for development. This is exactly the same for other areas of the curriculum. We are just coming up to the end of a four-year cycle of school development, and are beginning to work on the next four-year plan. The teachers are all involved in finding the best way forward.

This is why the forthcoming Ofsted inspection is really quite timely, and yes there is a certain amount of playing 'God' with the allocation of money, but I will always try to communicate to people how the money is allocated. I issue a bulletin from time to time giving an update on the expenditure. Each subject co-ordinator also receives a print-out detailing budget spending in their subject areas. Usually, I 'rubber stamp' their spending proposals, although I do insist on scrutinizing their plans, because there are occasions when I may know of another way of raising the money to buy an identified resource. We have spent a lot of money on the curriculum, admittedly with a lot of donations providing additional money. Last year overall, we spent twenty-five thousand pounds on the curriculum; this year we are now approaching fifteen thousand pounds. That is a significant amount of money, and puts previous years' budget management of a capitation allowance from the LEA into the shade.

SR   To whom is a head accountable? Who do you answer to and how do you manage this accountability?

RA   Well – that can vary from school to school and depends upon the governing body. I think, in truth, I'm accountable to all sorts of people in a variety of ways. I had some dealings with two unhappy parents yesterday who most definitely brought me to account. I think a headteacher has a good deal of power, sometimes I think it is a frightening amount of power with which to do things, but at the end of the day, there are systems in place which constrain that power. We have procedures for consultation with staff, we do have a governing body which has a number of structures in place, that is, various committees with designated functions. These are just a few of the 'accountability structures' which are laid down.

Then there is the 'Friends of St Luke's School Association' in which parents and others are involved. Its committee controls the spending of the 'school fund'. There is also a range of other LEA officers and institutions which have an involvement with school and exercise a varying level of accountability. There are all sorts of people, who in various ways can call me to account. At the end of the day, however, I think it is what we are actually offering the pupils in terms of quality of education that counts! I think the structures of accountability are there, and well established, and are there to be used by people who choose to use them.

I don't think that the governing body exercises its power to the full – they still virtually give me a 'carte blanche' with the budget. I know we consult on the budget, and costs are detailed and a plan laid before the governing body, but in truth they hardly question my advice.

SR   The relationship between the chairman of the governing body and the headteacher is crucial, I think, and in some cases is responsible for conflict and breakdown in school management. It is also perhaps perceived as responsible for an erosion of the headteacher's position. You clearly don't draw that kind of picture.

RA   The governing body has done a lot to become involved in the management of the school in the last three years, particularly since we have received delegated funding, and they have looked at the formation of sub-committees, and at the organization of working meetings. Whereas before there was a once a term meeting of the governing body, there is now another full meeting in the spring term, plus the Annual General Meeting with parents, and two or three sub-committee meetings each term. There is a considerable increase in working load and forms of accountability, but if I was unscrupulous I could still get away with manipulating the system. I do very deliberately try to reflect their views in our management practice. I do think there's been a marked change, in terms of accountability, and the role of headship, taking the form of a greater emphasis on shared responsibility. I think this is very true of headship in special education but I suspect it is equally true in all schools since the Education Reform Act.

Accountability is now coming at us in various ways. It includes for example, the Ofsted Inspection. We had one inspection two and a half years ago and we have another inspection due in a couple of months time. That's one form of accountability. Advisers these days are much more acute about what they're delivering because they've been through the Ofsted training process themselves. There's all of the accountability with regard to the internal auditing of accounts carried out by the LEA auditors, with checks, and records scrutinized for accuracy and good fit. We still have to justify our spending to the LEA.

There is the annual review system, the IEP planning, different forms of accountability which parents could indeed choose to exercise more fully. The Code of Practice for SEN didn't really change our annual review process, although it has changed the format slightly, but it does bestow a greater emphasis on parental involvement on assessment and their children's education. We no longer tend to just go through an annual review meeting merely reporting the teacher's perception, which was the way it could often be in the past. I do envisage a kind of unwritten contract with parents at the heart of the process, which is about what we are undertaking to do in the forthcoming year. It is about what everybody's discussed, agreeing on a set of priority objectives, and deciding together that this is what we are aiming for in the education of the pupil. I do feel that this is yet another important form of accountability of the school.

SR   What's your feeling generally about the parental role in this area of accountability?

RA   I'm not unhappy about it. What I am unhappy about is that it is always the same group of parents who tend to turn up for various social events or meetings. Most parents turn up for annual reviews, although a small percentage don't, and that level of good attendance pleases me. However, most of the parents don't really question us too closely. I do think more parent involvement would be a good thing; if I was in the parents' position, I would want to know more about the programme for my own child. I think parents could do a bit more to exert pressures on us, and it wouldn't break our backs. I think there are probably one or two staff in school who don't realize how dependent we are on parents, especially in this new educational market place in which we find ourselves. If you don't keep a child on roll, you're down a few thousand quid which is a sobering thought when it translates into people's jobs.

SR   Thinking about 'breaking backs' and the increased pressures of a burgeoning workload, how do you manage to maintain your own personal and professional well-being and development?

RA   I sometimes find myself taking a lot of work home. Actually, the IT can help with the workload, although it must be said that on other occasions, it does seem as if the new IT creates more work. I think what is important is learning to limit the amount of work that you do take home. I think it is very easy for your family to suffer in various ways. There are things like gardening, DIY about the house, trips away at the weekend. We don't tend to go on big holidays, but spend the time visiting relatives or friends around the country. We have had the occasional holiday in Canada, but a long break from work is the exception rather than the rule. I think, generally, that the break comes with my own hobbies and interests and family, and I am not averse to collapsing in front of the television and watching it for a couple of hours.

SR   Do you think it is becoming more important to manage stress?

RA   There's certainly more accountability on managers, isn't there? I also think there are higher levels of expectation but I don't know whether there is more stress. I wouldn't really like to say because I really found the initial years of headship stressful enough to seriously consider whether I wanted to get out of it and do something else, as friends of mine have done. I certainly don't feel the stress now, as much as I did then. However, I can think of times last week, when I wasn't too well, and should have stayed at home but I knew that if I was away, certain things wouldn't get done, and the results would be disastrous. I think that perhaps in many ways, that is a problem, the weight of knowing certain things will go short. I admit that in part this has to do with delegation, but there are some very real issues about workload to be addressed, and I don't think that delegation is about simply lightening the workload of the headteacher.

I think the tedious aspects of the job can be quite wearing. For example, form filling and paper-work. Some paper-work can bring with it an odd feeling of satisfaction, for instance, report writing and the annual review system. But the bureaucracy is increasing with a steady rise in the number of forms which need to be completed. I also have moments when I flinch at the idea of a forthcoming meeting with all those people talking out their viewpoint, when I would rather be doing something else. I mean I do it – but – I don't necessarily enjoy it, especially some of the 'people management' meetings which involve conflict.

On the other hand I do enjoy a great number of things about the job. I can honestly claim that no one day is the same. To have that variety is interesting and satisfying. I am also still very attracted to the idea of influencing events in a way that would have been impossible if I had stayed in the classroom. There is a satisfaction drawn from knowing that by and large this is a well run school, with a good team of people. It is very satisfying to know, in an enabling way, that I have played my part in that achievement.

I also enjoy the few opportunities I get for working with the children, usually a couple of sessions a week. At the moment, a lot of time has been spent gearing up for the Ofsted inspection, with my meeting individual staff and that's quite interesting, sharing perspectives, and acknowledging a gradual movement forward for both individual staff and the school. There are certain issues that depressingly recur, when you hit a 'brick wall'. We have real problems with accommodation in school at the moment, but the LEA is seriously looking at this question now. On most things, eventually, you do get a sense of moving forward and that is very important. If there wasn't that sense of forward movement, I would seriously be looking for something else, somewhere else.

SR   I felt earlier, rightly or wrongly, that you inferred being a head-teacher can be a lonely job. Where do you find professional support, and perhaps, personal support to help you carry on with the work in hand?

RA   In Humberside, there is a good network of special school head-teachers, particularly heads of SLD schools. In spite of the break-up of Humberside as a county we still meet from time to time, and we do keep in regular contact by phone. That has always proven very useful. I also meet regularly with Chris Darlington, who is headteacher of a local special school for pupils with Moderate Learning Difficulties (MLD). It is a very useful relationship. I also find one of the school governors very helpful and supportive, you always find one or two on the governing body! I've also found the SMT very supportive in a variety of different ways.

Then there are external interests I have, such as working on a book with Keith Bovair and Barry Carpenter which we have recently published on the curriculum in special education. This involved meeting various people from different sectors of education or reading their material, which helps in forming and re-forming my own professional perspective. Tomorrow, I'm going down to London, to the Teacher Training Agency where I am involved in a working party looking at national standards in teaching. The group is putting together some recommendations for teacher competencies. Although these things are professionally connected to my job, they do contribute to keeping a personal balance and a level of well-being. I think it is always good to meet people out of school hours, although I must admit when it comes to going to the pub or anything like that, as a school staff we do it at Christmas, but we tend not to otherwise do it. I'm far more likely to do that when I meet up with some of the other special school headteachers.

SR   Ted Wragg says 'You don't have to be a "nutter" to join the "barmy army" but … '. Do you think headship has become much more difficult and do you enjoy it?

RA   No! I don't think you need to be a 'nutter' at all. I think you have to go in with your eyes open. I think you have to be aware of all of the demands there are on a headteacher these days. I think the 'raison d'être' of the headteacher has broadened considerably, and I think people need to be aware of this change. It's not just about going in and running your own school.

SR   Do you still enjoy it?

RA   Yes! Very much! I do still enjoy it. I will admit there are times when I would enjoy doing what you're doing now, that is, academic research and lecturing. The only trouble is it wouldn't pay very well.

SR   I can vouchsafe for that fact.

RA   Yes. The reason I would want to do it has to do with my academic background, and it is a role which involves conveying knowledge to those interested in the field. However, there are still many things involved in being a head which interest me and from my point of view, I'm quite contented to remain a headteacher until I retire.

SR   What would be your words of advice to a colleague who was actively considering application for headship?

RA   I would say that first of all he or she should make sure they find some kind of mentor with whom they can talk through issues very much in the way that we've talked through the issues today. I think that the mentor should also be a 'critical friend' and provide advice on the way forward. I guess I feel that was missing in my preparation for headship. I think a lot of time should be spent with that person getting to know the 'job' and when it comes to your own professional development plan, you should be actively engaged in preparation for headship. There are certainly things you can only do once you're a head, but nonetheless there are major milestones en route which I passed by without making the most of them.

I don't think being a headteacher is an easy job. Every headteacher is going to have their strengths and weaknesses. I have certainly yet to encounter a headteacher who ranks as one of these charismatic leaders you read about. I am sure there are heads whose charisma carries them through everything, and takes everyone along with them. Whether that is a good definition of an effective leader, I don't know, but I know I'm certainly not a charismatic headteacher! I tend to think of myself as someone who has to slog away at learning various management skills, in a sort of cognitive learning process, and I think that must be the way it is for the majority of people.

SR   While you're saying you enjoy the job and are playing an important role, can we look at this from a slightly different angle? Does your school, any school, need a headteacher?

RA   Now then, I think we're drifting rather quickly towards a position where we will begin to argue for de-schooling society. In practice, why don't we have schools run by groups of teachers and have an elected leader who is in office for a fixed period of time? I suppose you would still need someone who would have a sufficient amount of time to guide and effect change, while preserving a continuity and progression in school activity. You couldn't have a rotating head-teacher where there was too much change built into the system. I couldn't see that working very well. I think a head-free school would need a revolution in structures and approach if it was going to work.

I think there will always be a need for a person, whoever that might be, and however they might be identified and appointed, who plays the role of the school leader. There will always be a need for someone to handle the inter-personal relations which form a major aspect of school management. I also think the school needs a titular representative to stand for the school and the headteacher is that representative. I think you also need the focal point that the head-teacher brings to a school, and that also involves a number of processes, such as facilitating, enabling, shaping direction, without which a school would probably drift, lacking direction, and perhaps even purpose.

I know you alluded earlier to the competing demands for financial allocation in our school budget, which gives us a practical example of what we're talking about. There is an observed need for someone to strike a balanced overview and to arbitrate or take a judgement. I am left wondering, and it would be one of these interesting social experiments you read about occasionally, what would happen if you created a system of elected headship rather than the current arrangement, which is an appointed headteacher.

SR   What fundamental changes do you think have taken place in special education? What does this mean for headship and special education?

RA   The NC is obvious – that's the major change. I think the change which has been far wider reaching, and if you like, far more insidious, has been the advent of LMSS. The 'pool of resource', like it or not, is gradually shrinking. I think schools are slowly being starved of funding because LEAs are in turn being starved of monies. LMSS is really in part about making funding more equitable between schools in an LEA, that is, all above board. I certainly see that as being a benefit of LMSS in Humberside. This school was one of the so-called 'winners' in contrast to 'losers' which in the past had been well resourced because they had had a headteacher who knew the 'ropes', in terms of the LEA system, which I am afraid used to reward those who knew who they should talk to and when to shout the most loudly. Funding is far more transparent now, and equitable.

But there still remains the fact that there is a shrinking pool of resource, and, in real terms, an ever increasingly smaller pot of money. It is this basic problem in terms of funding which reflects the insidious change in the educational resource. It is a drip by drip wasting of the core resource and of its effect upon the educational infrastructure. In this authority, the break-up of Humberside has involved some 'real' cost for us too in so far as the unit cost fixed for the funding of special schools had also dropped. North Lincolnshire, which is one of the four new unitary authorities created out of what was Humberside, is a cash-strapped authority. In the past North Lincolnshire was an area that relied heavily upon subsidies from Humberside. It no longer has that protection and this reality has impacted upon special education, for example, in the reducing cash value of SEN statements as part of the funding arrangements for schools.

I do think that, in real terms, resource allocation has shrunk. An education officer would probably disagree with me, but taking our own school as an example, our place element is made up of cash values tied to SEN statements. The cash value of these placement figures accounts for about 70 per cent of the school budget and is linked to the mainstream formula. The mainstream schools also attract a compensatory allowance for SEN. I do think they deserve the latter. I also think that SEN support services have been made more vulnerable, and they are certainly having to 'sell their wares' in what is a new educational market place. If they fail to adapt they will be left to 'wither on the vine'. I think that SEN support services which provide for pupils with low incidence SEN are less vulnerable, but they are not immune to the change, and I think they will increasingly feel the competition of independent or charitable institutions, who will offer educational support for children with disability.

I think there will also be another implication for special education in the shift to a small unitary authority which may well affect this

school. There are at the moment a number of out-of-county place-
ments, but I do not see the local authority wanting to continue to
fund all of these arrangements. This will probably result in an
increasing demand upon us, in terms of pupil numbers and range of
disability. We will probably see a trend in pupil referrals which
reflects a rise in a diversity of exceptional SEN. We will, for example,
probably see an increase of pupils referred with autism and other
disabilities associated with severe learning difficulties for which we
will need to cater.

So – two things, really, have had the greatest impact upon special
education: the NC and LMSS. I do think, however, that the next
piece of reform to hit us is fast approaching. I think this will involve
the whole question of teacher training and teacher appraisal, performance management, professional development, whatever you
want to call it, but it will be about various aspects of what is basically
a structure for assuring the quality of curriculum delivery, individual
professional competence and career development.

I think there will be a clearly drawn focus on the career progression
of teachers, a definition of expert teacher, of curriculum leadership,
and further down the road, school leadership. Performance evaluation
will lie at the heart of it! That will be one strand in the new development, but the other key strand which is equally important will be the
absence of specialist initial teacher training provision. I know there
were good reasons for their closure but personally I think it was a big
mistake. There are less than half of the teachers in this school who
actually had any specialist training whatsoever.

SR   Rob – that opinion seems to contradict your earlier statement about
'normalization' and an inclusive special education – doesn't it?

RA   I do feel there should be changes like teacher exchanges, integrating
educational experience through the teacher. You know the two years
I had in Canada, while I was working with SEN children, still gave me
an excellent experience and was a taste of teaching in a mainstream
school. I think there should be things like teacher exchanges built
into the system and teachers should be able to teach in different
types of settings. Equally, I think if children have complex learning
difficulties, then that requires teachers who do understand what are
the nature and implications of complex learning difficulties. I feel in
spite of the best will in the world, teachers who transfer to this work
from a background in secondary, junior or infant school are left
having to struggle hard in their first year as they try to come to terms
with understanding what SLD is all about. Now, I think people
should be coming to us having had an introduction to and an
awareness of SLD.

SR   So – does that mean there will always be a need for special arrangements and specialist staff, with a special expertise?

RA   Well – even if these types of schools didn't exist, yes, I do think there would be a need for special expertise. I wouldn't dream for one moment of putting myself forward as somebody who knows about the range of disability and teaching methods associated, say, with the hearing impaired. You know, I do have a lot of specialist knowledge on aspects of cognitive and language development in people with severe intellectual disability which I think is necessary and relevant for this kind of work. There is a need for specialist knowledge.

SR   How do you wish to see your own school develop? What will this mean for the head?

RA   There are some big issues in this school, which I expect the Ofsted inspection to highlight. These are issues for all of the staff, not just for me as the headteacher. One of them is the basic accommodation problem, and questions about the learning environment. Years of benign neglect are now coming home to roost, and it's going to cost money. There is also in this same context – and especially as we now find ourselves in a small unitary authority – some far-reaching questions which are going to be asked about the nature of SEN provision.

     The LEA will probably very soon consider the cost-effectiveness of a two-to-sixteen SLD special school and ask the question, can we afford it? This will be in addition to funding a three-to-sixteen MLD special school. With just two special schools, the thought might be: should there not be a primary-secondary split in a provision dealing with a generic classification of learning difficulty? Or even, and this is an idea I would not personally favour, some kind of monolithic area special school?

     The LEA has a number of issues to consider, and I think staff are beginning to become aware of the possibility of change. Doubtless, I will be involved in the process. At the same time the local authority is also looking at the possibilities of developing provision, to improve it, and this will involve a review of health services, social services and special education. I find that prospect exciting. It is one of the virtues of a new broom and a small authority that this might actually result in improvement. Although in the end, you know, it becomes increasingly difficult and a question of cash, rather than just a matter of good will, which is why you've got to get it right in the first few years.

     I think another issue is going to be the whole question of the ongoing development of the curriculum. We have by no means got it sorted in this school and it's axiomatic, isn't it, that a school which thinks it's got it sorted is dead on its feet! There needs to be a lot of development work in the curriculum and I want to get very much more into this question of monitoring for purposes of both evaluation and support. In terms of getting into the classroom, I think that's a really big issue for me over the next several years.

As I say, I think it will become more a question of performance management of teachers and teacher appraisal, which must be a supportive developmental process rather than a negative inspectorial process. I think this will come to the fore, and after all it's what makes for quality in education. It really should have been in place twenty years ago, but it does take time for these ideas to formulate and come through to schools. I think there needs to be a lot more done too in developing the role of governors and parents. I think, if they chose to do so and they were aware of doing so, parents and governors could exercise a good deal more power over schools than they actually do at present.

SR   Finally – in terms of special education, what do you see as the changes which will affect the future or are they the same as those which you have described affecting this school?

RA   I suppose I still think the world of special education is far too fragmented with people fighting their own corner, and I would like to see more cohesion being developed. I think you see a glimmer of it at times with small groups. For example, the Special Educational Needs Training Consortium (SENTC) group has managed to combine representatives of disparate organization to create an excellent report on teacher training, but then again you are left wondering how the representation on that group was decided. It would be nice to think that there was a chance of more co-ordination of interest groups within special education and special needs provision as a whole, including social services, health services and parent carer organizations.

SR   Do you see special education, realistically speaking, standing entirely separate from mainstream education?

RA   No – I honestly don't see it that way. What we should be creating is a continuum of provision to meet what is in effect a continuum of SEN. There are a considerable number of children with SEN, many of them experiencing SLD, in mainstream education. I think it's only right and proper that children and parents should have the opportunity of mainstream education open to them. I do sometimes feel that a tube of resource smarties is thrown up in the air, and parents are expected to grab as many as they can. Now that isn't fair for a number of reasons, not least, because not all parents are aware of the tube being 'up for grabs', and others, for whatever reason, do not feel able to have a go at claiming some of the resource.

There are children in mainstream schools with difficulties as severe as some children in this school. This is as a direct consequence of the parents having fought tooth and nail for the child's placement in a mainstream school. I know there are other parents with equal rights to make that claim, but they have not pressed their claim. I think developing inclusive education is where I would like to see the whole of special educational provision move, creating a professional and parental network which will be adaptable enough to meet the range of SEN which exists on a continuum. I would dearly like to see such a network lobbying for change in a positive and coherent manner. In the SENTC Report there was reference to teacher training for SEN, but I think the reality is that this government has its own agenda which doesn't include taking on board that kind of recommendation. I think special education, now, will be pushed to one side.

The challenge is really to mobilize that awesome amount of parent power and teacher power that does exist within special education, to effect change across the board. We do need a consensus because we have a lot of people firing on all cylinders but going in all sorts of directions. Not enough people are working together, pushing in the same direction at the same time. Special education does I'm afraid suffer badly from an acute form of parochialism. I think if we could reach above this and achieve a union of purpose and direction, it would be a very good thing for special education, and ultimately beneficial for the whole educational system. This takes us back to Deno's 'cascade theory', and the notion that special education interacting with mainstream education can produce considerable improvement in the latter so that the former ceases to be necessary, and, quite frankly, that is what we should be doing to find a way forward.

CHAPTER 4

Seriously seeking community education: making the special school special

MIKE CLARKE with Steve Rayner

Mike Clarke is currently Headteacher at The Lindsworth Centre, Birmingham. The centre is made up of a residential special school for pupils with EBD, with additional units including a unit for School Refusers, an Arts Therapy centre, and a Community Education Project. Mike has over twenty-seven years of experience in teaching, much of it in school management, in both secondary and special education. He has held several headships, all, with the exception of his present post, in comprehensive schools.

SR Could we begin by your telling us about your personal background – home, school, higher education and people who perhaps had a significant influence on your life?

MC Yes – I found the interview schedule fascinating and re-read it several times because I felt I couldn't easily answer any of the questions. My personal background – by which I presume you mean family background – was one in which my Dad was a policeman, then an insurance officer. His family were all police! My mum came originally from Derbyshire. I recall being evacuated for a short while right at the end of the war into Derbyshire, to my Mum's village. I guess that like most people, my family had a very large influence on me, at the beginning, during the middle and even now in the later stages of my life. I was brought up to think of others before myself as a general philosophy. I should think that's been with me for most of my life.

During my time at school, I was nothing out of the ordinary, perhaps slightly above average ability. I went to the grammar school. I left grammar school and went straight into teaching. I was initially going to be a pathologist. I attended an interview, and I understand from what was said later, that I had been successful, I got the job. But the arrangements fell through. I took time away from home, working through the summer holidays at Butlins in Skegness. When I came back from Skegness, it was my mother, really, who organized my entry into teaching. She took me to the education office and sent me on my way. I knocked at one door, was sent to another door, and eventually got a job as a temporary teacher. I started teaching in the September, and at the same time applied to teacher training college. The school was a junior school which no longer exists. It was situated near a railway line not far from Lea Hall in Birmingham.

SR   Your Mum played a big part in the early stages of your teaching career?

MC   Yes! Very much. In my family, my two brothers and I all shared Mum as the driving force, pushing us on to achieve heights she felt we ought to achieve. But for my Mum, we might have simply disappeared, sinking into the morass as it were. I applied for a place at teacher training college. My application came through that September and I was invited to attend an interview at Saltley College. I was asked to come into the office to speak to a Canon T. G. Platten. I can still see him sitting across the desk deftly crossing out the double 'n' I'd put in 'Canon'. As a matter of fact, I still wrestle with the same style of spelling.

I went to Saltley College where I was one of the last of the two-year trained teachers, as in the following year, the course switched to three years for teacher qualification, aimed at ensuring a better trained, more highly qualified teaching profession. I went from a two-year training qualification to an additional year, on secondment for science at Manchester. I subsequently began teaching science as a subject teacher in secondary school. My first post was in Birmingham, in fact, all of my teaching has been in Birmingham. I spent a number of years at a place called Cockshutt Hill teaching science. At that time the VEIA, and the UEIB plus O Levels were taught in secondary school.

SR   UEIB? I don't know what that means, Mike.

MC   I'm not exactly sure now – it was something like the University Entrance Institute Board. It's a long time ago. The papers were considered slightly lower in standard than the O Level. I'd give them to the fourth year (year ten), to tee them up in the run-up to O Level. This was around about the early sixties – I remember it was still policy then to award youngsters in assembly, and awards would be registered in their hymn book. Every pupil would carry a hymn book in their blazer pocket.

SR   Do you think there was any particular person who influenced your thinking during this period?

MC   No – only my parents. I think there were the usual influences which exist, both then and now, for example, you tend to read, there are one or two teachers who you get on with better than others, and therefore I guess they lined you up, particularly within the subject area. I remember the Zeta Project, a physics teacher was placed with us, who had worked on the project development. A Polish gentleman who didn't speak English that well, but it was interesting learning physics with him. I remember, too, that my early interest in biology owed something to the teacher of biology at the same time. No – overall – I don't think there were any particular influences on my thinking. I suppose going back earlier, I was in the Cubs, Scouts, all those things, the people, the characters involved in those activities had some effect on my thoughts and aspirations.

The Church was another significant part of my life both as a choirboy at the time, and later on, there was a vicar, Canon Crowson, actually, who was at Yardley, and had a big influence on lots of youngsters of my age. He was very active and a very charismatic person. The church was particularly active after the war, starting family camps and children my own age, fourteen or fifteen, were very involved. One of the things you'd aspire to was to be part of the advance party and go down with Canon Charles Crowson. If you were part of the advance party, you were involved in digging latrines, putting up the tents, and acting as general lackeys around the camp. But you were subsequently taken on a sailing trip on the Norfolk Broads. The church hired four sailing boats and the advance party was always rewarded with a week on the Broads.

SR   Did you often find yourself one of the advance party? Were you inclined to succeed – achieve?

MC   Well, there was no hierarchy, or specific selection for these things, but I suppose it would be true to say that, like 'dross', I would float to the top. When I was in the Cubs, I ended up being the 'senior sixer', and it was the same in the Scouts, I became a Troop Leader, and I'd captain other teams or groups, including school rugby and cricket teams. I enjoyed sport. I was reasonably good at it. I played both cricket and rugby to a fairly high standard, although not to inter-national level, and enjoyed it. I captained school sides on the way up through under fourteens, under fifteens, as you do. I carried on playing rugby and cricket after school, but just as a team member, playing in a league with county players, in what was a very good standard.

SR   Could you describe your teaching career? Why did you decide to teach?

MC   I've really said why I started on the road to teaching – in a word – my mother put me there! Having started on it – I didn't stray from it, at least not initially. It's interesting now to see children who have got through the educational process, and look back to realize that if you were trained to be a teacher, that when you completed the training, you were intent on becoming a teacher. Whereas, if you go on to take a degree, once you've got that degree, there is no specific route really down which to go, there is a great deal of variety and you are not channelled down one particular route towards a single career.

I started teaching, as I said, straight from college, at Cockshutt Hill. The school had a good reputation as a disciplined school, which it was, and it allowed me to develop a personal style of teaching because I didn't really have to worry about my own discipline. I suppose the discipline was there anyway, I mean the ability to manage discipline in the classroom, but I didn't have to work very hard at it. The school was a very good one, the pupils in the fifth year were coming out with six, seven, or eight O Levels. The standard of educational support for the children, who were non-grammar school, was very high. The school had a good set of staff, a good ethos. I didn't choose the school – it just happened – I was carried along by the current but found myself always rising upwards. Where I went was really irrelevant as long as it was upwards.

SR   Was staying in Birmingham a constraint or a requirement for you?

MC   Neither. That was the way it happened. My father was very ill. We had at that time a family grocery shop. We all supported Mum in the business. A year at Manchester was away from home but otherwise, I've had a fairly insular and protected life. I suppose while my family has played a big part in my life, I see myself as having been fairly well cosseted, yet not deliberately seeking that kind of protection. I had friends and colleagues at that time zooming off to the continent trekking world-wide, but that kind of activity never really appealed to me. Whether it was because I was involved in adventure-style outdoor activities, and the home environment slightly clinging, I'm not sure, but it reflected early life for me and my early teaching career.

After a period in my first school I left teaching and went into industry. My life, looking back, has been markedly influenced by money. Money was a motivation for moving from teaching. I had a friend who was in industry. He mentioned a vacancy and it offered a lot more money than I was earning at the time as a teacher. I went to work, initially, on the factory side, as a clerk, but very quickly got involved in the office side. It was nice to see the other side of the desk in the job. It all opened my eyes to a lot of things but at the time you didn't realize it. You just absorb it all as it happens. It gives you a number of different perspectives, which are valuable assets in seeing the wider perspective.

I remember people saying to me after I'd been in that job some time, that I looked really well, really much better than I had previously looked. It's not until – remarks like that make you realize that you do enjoy having lunch-breaks. Effectively, at that level in industry, when you finish for the day, you are finished. After a while I was promoted. I was probably the most academically qualified person in the planning office. The way I approached the job was slightly different to most of the other people in the office. I don't like mundane things. I was looking for opportunities to develop and change processes, and, I guess, be innovatory. I was moved from the planning office to a new foil mill to sell a process that we had developed. I am a fairly blunt person, honest and to the point, and I didn't fit into that role easily. I found that being a representative of the company meant being economical with the truth in order to maintain customer confidence and a market, even though things may not be working that well back at the ranch.

I left that job after a while and returned to teaching. All in all, I was out of teaching for about two years. I returned to a small secondary school. No other reason for choosing that school than that the job was there. It was a small two-form-entry school. The buildings are still there but it has been amalgamated with another school. I was the only person teaching science. The staff photograph taken in my first year there makes me look like Head Boy – the staff were all 'mature' and I was the only youngster in the staff room. I remember it being an Olympic year. It was an election year too, because I remember displaying cartoon faces of the political leaders which went up on the back of the classroom wall. I do enjoy putting up displays, and the Olympics and the election offered opportunity for some excellent work in form periods.

Another interesting thing which stands out in my mind was how we were always spending effort and time trying to raise money. I recall becoming very friendly with the woodwork teacher and using a plane from the woodwork room to clean up the science benches in the laboratory. We had antique benches which pre-dated the Ark. They were tatty and horrible, and I cleaned them up and re-stained them. We also made a very large periodic table for the laboratory. We made it with the children and it measured around ten feet length. We cut out all the letters and we had atomic weights to about five decimal points. I guess – silly – I'm not sure they were learning anything but it was a magnificent piece of work, having a periodic table that size displayed in the classroom. That was a fun time – most of the science which was taught then is considered unsafe now, for instance, ten separate oxygen preparations using potassium chlorate and manganese dioxide – and after that I moved and returned to Cockshutt Hill School.

I'd enjoyed it at Cockshutt School before and going back was a promotion. Well – I had had a stable time teaching there. It was a similar kind of institution. It was extremely well disciplined. There was a super atmosphere. I recall running the rugby and soccer teams, and cricket teams in the summer. It was, 'quote', what you would call a 'good school'. It provided the stability for my professional development, gave me time to be myself, and not worry about wrestling with children in the classroom. You maintained your own discipline as you watched some very competent older teachers, which I then perceived them as, going about their business, and earning tremendous respect from the children. It was fun!

I then moved from there to another secondary school as head of science. From there, I moved sideways to an all-girls school, again as head of science. I moved there specifically to work with the head-teacher. She was a well known head who had a lot of charisma and style, I felt that it would be good for me and she had suggested this to me. I knew some of her staff and therefore knew about her. She didn't actually say 'apply and the job is yours' – but I felt that she knew my worth and was very interested in having me on her staff.

I remember having applied for the post, I was told by the Inspector (Advisers as we call them today), that they were going to re-advertise the post because they wanted to make sure I had some competition. It was a bit odd, looking back, to make such a sideways move. The motive was really to move forward professionally under this new head. I was very impressed by the way she seemed to go about things. People knew her and events happened in her school. She was very well regarded in the City by other heads and the officers of the LEA. I guess I felt if I was involved with her and worked in her school, then I would be more likely to win recognition for good work. I felt that I might even gain extra recognition and move ahead of other people, who were as good as or even a little better than me, but who were not working in the same environment, with the same advantage.

SR   Did it happen?

MC   I don't know. Well – I can remember interesting things happening around that time. The school was affiliated to a boys' school, and the head of science in the boys' school retired, and I was made up head of science for both schools. It was an interesting challenge, and maybe, without the head, it would have been impossible. I got on very well with the head of the boys' school too, so maybe it would have happened anyway, I'm not sure. However, it was a case of running science in the two schools which was a very different job. The concept of one head of science for two separate schools was unusual and a useful experience.

It was not long after that, I remember, looking at the change in salary for heads of department, and seeing that promotion, and then later making the move to apply for deputy headship, would mean a drop in salary. I made a conscious decision to move for deputy headship. The procedure in those days, typically, was one went for small deputy headships before graduating to a larger one. I started to apply for deputy headships. I got a job in what was euphemis-tically called a comprehensive school, because in those days all

Birmingham had become comprehensive. It was a two-form-entry inner-city school. Teaching wasn't particularly difficult although the children were challenging. The staff were very young and enthusiastic and did better than merely cope with the job. The head was in his first headship – a year older than I was – and we made an odd pair. It was another good stable period and a useful introduction to management. The head had a quality, an ability to make people believe in themselves, I guess, both in terms of quality of work and our expectation of the children. He was also very good at dotting the 'i's and crossing the 't's and I would argue that we made a very good management team.

I was totally involved in the management of the school. The head shared the complete running of the school with me. The school was due to close and become part of a larger school. The head moved and I remained as an acting headteacher. I remember being quite astounded by the change one experienced from the staff. It was down to the change of title – nothing more! There was an entirely different perspective taken on by the staff. I didn't do anything different at the time. I didn't feel any change in my approach to work, except, as I say, the feelings and attitudes of other staff to me which amounted to a shift in the way other people perceive you.

The headteacher moved to another headship because of the imminent closure and I became acting headteacher. I moved from this school when it closed. I was offered a senior teacher post at another school but declined it. You have to remember that at that time in Birmingham, if you wanted to apply for headship, you had to complete a form that recorded your basic details, name the school, date it, and forward it to LEA. They would acknowledge it and that was that, your application was considered. As the school faced closure, I applied for headship, and for the first application I made, there were fourteen people shortlisted. I didn't get it. The man that did has only recently retired.

Instead I was placed in another school to act as a deputy headteacher, replacing the incumbent, who, in turn, had been seconded to pursue a degree course. I filled his space while I was applying for other deputy headships of large schools. Then, quite suddenly, during the summer holidays the head was taken ill, and I again found myself acting head. I remember finding myself looking at a pegboard school timetable hanging on the wall. I had a Renault 16 at the time. I took the timetable home because it hadn't really been used, and classes were accustomed to wandering around the school looking for an empty classroom. I remember, a number of pegs fell out, and I was left with no idea of the timetable, facing a school I didn't know, a staff I didn't know, and a school year about to begin. I went searching, anxiously, and eventually found a paper timetable, and managed to get it organized for the start of term. It was an interesting time, literally wrestling with the school curriculum, not knowing the staff, the children, the timetable, and working out how you were going to do it.

From there I moved to a deputy headship of a new school in Handsworth, a part of Birmingham. It was a very large school, initially a four-form entry, acting as a nucleus for an eight-form-entry school. It coincided with a time of great social unrest in the area. There was a lot of multicultural tension. We had race riots. For me, it was both an interesting and formative period. The school wasn't ready and we took an eight-form entry in a building originally designed for the four-form entry. I guess in the managing of the new school we made all the mistakes we needed to then, before moving to the new building. It was a peculiar set-up really, a four-storey building with only a single corridor linking it, meaning that you passed every classroom when you moved from one side of the building to the other. I was there for about four or five years. It was an eclectic period, picking up a lot of different experiences in management. The head was from outside the city. A lovely person, but he didn't have a lot of discipline or control, and in Handsworth, and at that time, with the particular mix of children we had, it was important you had some kind of stature and could maintain discipline.

It was a challenging time. I eventually ended up being acting head. The head resigned and this was accepted by the LEA. I was acting head for about nine months, but was applying for other jobs during this period. I got a headship of an eight-form-entry school in the south of Birmingham. The move was just before a contraction in the number of schools within Birmingham. There were twenty schools closed and twenty-six new schools opened as amalgamated versions of the previous schools. Hartfield School, where I was going, became one of those schools to be closed. It had historically been a split site, two schools. I remember my first impression, noting the number of pre-fabs floating around the grounds. In a sense this was my first real headship. I can remember walking around the corner of a building and seeing a group of children in whites playing cricket and think-ing, this is all right. Remember, I was coming to this school from a grammar school background, but had spent time more recently working in inner-city schools, here was an inner-city school which still had whites! It was throat-catching! It was very throat-catching. I don't mean an inspirational road to Damascus feeling – but it was a moment that sticks in my mind. I think it is fair to say that in all the places I've been in charge, I've never felt this is it, I've arrived. Hartfield closed. All twenty heads had to reapply. Hartfield was due to be amalgamated with another school. I was appointed head of the new school and it was called Nine Styles. It had 1500 pupils. All the staff were re-appointed from a wider pool of previously employed staff. I was responsible for appointing all of my staff. The procedure was time-consuming because of regulations governing the reorganization and re-appointment of teachers from the pool. We had to work from the top down, advertising top posts first, to allow those who had aspirations opportunity to apply. I remember it being like a cattle market. One of the schools which had been closed was used as a base for the interviews, which went on for days. I had to decide whether I went for continuity. I have to say, given time again in that situation, I would be a lot tougher, and would opt for fresh blood and quality, rather than continuity. The children didn't seem to be affected by the change, and certainly all of the staff that weren't part of the original school seemed to have more drive, more energy, compared to those that had been there for some time.

The headship went on for about two years. During that period the City appointed a man called Jim Munn, who was brought in with a brief to develop the amenities and recreational facilities of the City. His idea was to attach recreation to schools. I was at Nine Styles where I was describing a vision of schools sitting at the centre of the community. I had been pushing for that style of school and we got on reasonably well, so the consequence was that Nine Styles was the first development of that type in Birmingham. The school now has a sports centre, squash courts, bar, restaurant, astro-turf and grass pitches with changing rooms. It's still the only school which has all of this – it became a very big complex in what was a difficult area of Birmingham. It draws upon a large council estate which has a number of problem families. The school caters for a high percentage of difficult children coming from a less than desirable background. I'd gone there to raise the profile of the school. I spent a lot of time making sure we got a lot of positive press coverage. The school is very close to Solihull and we would make sure that positive information would cross the border into the next LEA. We were very keen to push the academic, pastoral and community aspects of the school. It was, I felt, very important to attract parents who wanted to drive their children forward. A lot of parents sent their children to Hartfield, then Nine Styles, because of the reception they received.

When I first went to Hartfield, the pupils weren't allowed off the premises at lunch-break. The procedure was all the children stayed for lunch. Staff would carry out supervision duty at the school gate. There had been a number of big fights, the typical scenario, with two or three hundred children jeering on the few actually involved in the fighting. I didn't want that kind of siege mentality. I'd rather attack the thing at its core. We no longer locked the gates. I remember using the cane around the same time – you could still be barbaric if you wanted to be. But I saw no point in keeping things closed that

	ought to be open. I'd rather try to deal with the trouble and opt for prevention, not reaction.
SR	The pattern seems to have been four or five years in a school, sometimes less, then a move?
MC	Yes – I suppose so – I enjoy change.
SR	And after Nine Styles?
MC	Well – I was there more or less minding my own business and I think developing a good school. I've said so before in conversation, I actually need people to cross the 't's and dot the 'i's for me. I'm not very good with detail. The seek and find mentality of management is around and I know colleagues who latch on to problems, pursuing them relentlessly. I understand that it needs to be done, but I need to have people around me who will do it. The same thing applies across the board. We developed some interesting policy initiatives at Nine Styles. I chaired a group of heads looking at the multi-function large-site city schools and the role of a community school. When I started the dual use of facilities, for example the swimming pool, we were always being visited by two or three councillors, officers or local dignitaries. The politics were important for the school, and for my headship, if I wanted to get things done. If I wanted to make things happen, I needed to ensure the powers that be were on-side. I've never really been able to do that as effectively as I would have wished. I've never really had the time, nor I suppose wanted to find the time to do the ingratiating bit. I've known colleagues to do that but I've never found myself drawn into the politics of the LEA.

Well – I was minding my own business when I was approached and asked to take on Lindsworth Special School. It was another school which had recently been reorganized. It was the result of an amalgamation of a special school for educationally sub-normal children and a residential special school for bright maladjusted children. The City hadn't followed its original plan of moving out all the educationally sub-normal children, replacing them with maladjusted children, and as a consequence, the result was a mish-mash of the two and to compound the problem they failed to appoint a headteacher. They had two or three goes at it and failed. So there were two special school traditions, one behavioural, the other therapeutic reflecting a psychodynamic method. The two were brought together and the person put in charge came from the residential school and imposed a psychodynamic regime on the new school. It was a mess. I was asked to see if I could pull it together, and this meant dealing with six major assaults on staff per day when I first arrived as well as talking children down from the roof-top.

SR	This is the first reference to special educational needs (SEN)?
MC	I suppose so – but all of the schools I have worked in have had pupils with SEN. Indeed, two schools had SEN Units attached to them, one

a unit for the hearing impaired, the second a unit for children with specific learning difficulties. However, there was no SEN factor involved in my decision to come to Lindsworth. Possibly it may have influenced those who asked me, but it didn't influence me at all because the process from my point of view was that I worked for the City, and not any one particular school, therefore if I'm asked to do something and I think it is within my capability, I will attempt it.

It was actually horrendous in the first few weeks. There were a lot of distraught staff, including teachers, support staff, care staff, classroom assistants, domestics, all going through a very difficult time. I was a bit concerned at first because as you rightly point out I didn't know very much about SEN. It suddenly dawned upon me that it was nothing at all to do with SEN, it was to do with organization and the management of the process. We're now ten years on, the school has tripled in size and has several aspects to it now, making it a bit more than a small EBD school. Ten years ago, I wanted to run Nine Styles and this school as a continuum of provision, and that was perceived as possible because reorganization was being considered by the LEA. I wrote a paper proposing that Lindsworth should be set up as a training centre and that was well received. One of the reasons I stayed was to do that but it never actually happened. To be fair, the City has changed beyond all recognition.

SR   Do you still see that as a possible development for Lindsworth?

MC   Yes in the sense that it needs to become a centre of lots of different provision in order to support these children because I think most people who work with children who have emotional and behavioural difficulties know that for most of the time, on a one-to-one basis, the children behave in a rational and appropriate fashion. It seems to me that the greater the diversity in provision on site, bearing in mind basic requirements like the national curriculum, the more chance there is of successfully meeting the academic and social needs of these children and that's good.

SR   Is the concept of the centre what lies at the heart of your vision for Lindsworth?

MC   Yes is the short answer. You are always fighting against the image of ten years ago here, and the fact that we deal with very volatile and difficult children skews people's views of this provision, even psychologists. So you tend to have the most difficult children referred, and unless you get children who are less acting out too, it can become extremely demanding and draining for staff working with the children. You need a way to break this circuit and develop a range of provision for a range of need.

SR   To sum up, are there particular aspects of your career which prepared you for headship?

MC   No – I don't think so but I can't honestly answer that question . . . as far as I am concerned you go into school and you do it. I'm going into a new school at the moment, a Junior Special School which is facing closure. I know the school. I'm going in for a fixed period and will oversee its closure as acting headteacher. I'll go in and talk to the staff on a normal basis – not interview – and I'll play football and ingratiate myself into the lives of the children, and just pick up the vibes and try to understand the people, the children, the staff, the ethos of the school, with the aim of becoming aware, and informed and moving forward. I guess I do that, and I suppose the fact that I'm facing that task next term throws me back into that process – it's one of making a start.

SR   You said you were going to close the school yet you describe the process in terms of moving forward. Isn't that a contradiction in terms?

MC   I said earlier that I work for Birmingham and at this particular point, it's a job involving closure. There's no head there and there's a group of staff who require support and that's what I'm going to do, and that means moving them on in the best possible fashion. The change is part of the city plan, involving a review and reorganization of the hospital schools. The building will remain but the status of the school will change. I shall actually maintain contact with Lindsworth and be running the two schools at the same time. The governors have agreed the arrangement.

SR   Your length of stay seems to have broken the pattern of movement which is reflected in your career development.

MC   I've been here too long! The skills I have, the schools I've worked in, all reach a point where the staff need to benefit from a new person with other ideas, a different approach. When I come up with new ideas now or a new direction, it's an old one because it's me producing it. It would be fair to say that if people look back over the ten years here, I've been continuing with innovation and change throughout that period. We continue to move forward in lots of different ways. You can continue managing change, but after a while people do not experience the same dynamism. It's like changing a girlfriend – it's new – there are new stories to listen to, to create an interest, and with the best will in the world, when you're old hat, it isn't as fresh. I don't think my drive has disappeared. We are still doing new things. But the change has become ordinary. It doesn't matter where you put me, I'll work for change and regeneration.

Someone the other day was discussing how to successfully reintegrate EBD children into the mainstream schools. It's very hard to do it successfully and it's becoming harder than ever. All my career I've worked in Birmingham but it's become harder because I know less heads than when I was in mainstream. As a head of a special school, you're given a different deference, a very much lower one, mainly because of the size of the school. When people knew me as head of Nine Styles, I was treated one way, but now I am the head of a special school, they treat me differently. When you're dealing with mainstream schools this can matter. I would say, in terms of managing reintegration that they should go back to the paper I produced ten years ago on the future development of Lindsworth. You need to give one person the oversight of several schools and create a continuum of provision which will benefit staff and children and cater for a whole range need. If you were to give me my previous school, the failing school and this one, we'd regenerate the failing school and create a very rich continuum of provision for a community of children.

SR   What particular vision for the school do you have?

MC   We would become the best kept village in the UK. We are a 23-acre site with 1930 buildings. We would go for developing a multi-faceted facility for children with EBD. We would also move towards building a provision for the community. It would become a fairly normal thing to do some shopping here. I don't mean attracting Sainsburys, but if you think about the craft shop we run, and develop it as a centre, a small or medium sized retail enterprise for small gifts to buy as souvenirs or Xmas gifts, that kind of thing. A community of a different sort, I wouldn't want us to become a community school of the type which focuses exclusively on the children, I'd want to attract the adults on to site, and to encourage the children to perceive themselves as part of the whole, together with adults forming a special community.

I occasionally have students placed here and they ask me a similar question about vision. I try very hard to think of an answer. My latest one, which fits into my current thinking, is to refer to my daughter who's been to Oxford. The thought of Oxbridge is one of a good place to go to and while we must remember we are providing for children with EBD here, I would like to feel that in terms of quality, we might manage to remove some of the stigma of an EBD school, and at the same time be the equivalent of Oxbridge for children with EBD. It's difficult though, because a number of pupils who come here haven't got EBD, not to put too fine a point on it, they're delinquent, they're perfectly secure within themselves, and difficult to reach. It can be very wearing, draining for staff working with them, and they can so often and so easily create the wrong kind of image for the school. We're sitting at the moment in a building earmarked to be developed into a therapeutic unit. What this will do is bring on-site a number of resources which will benefit the main nucleus of the school.

SR   Lindsworth seems to be made up of several units – do you see yourself as a centre rather than as a school?

MC   I want to provide a range of facilities for the children in what is a supportive environment. The starting point is and always was providing extra depth for children placed here but Birmingham will benefit from this kind of development. It is already beginning to happen, because we've attracted other people to the centre. We have a long-term truancy unit, which provides for Year eleven children across the city and is acting as a model for similar development. I'm old enough now to experience repeated bouts of 'déjà vu'. We've just set up a unit for practical, vocationally orientated craft-work, involving building and maintenance, decorating, metalwork, woodwork, which I think goes all the way back to Raising Of School Leaving Age days. It's perceived as innovatory, but I don't see it as that, I just see it as a spinning needle, in the sense that everything is coming around in a circle, again, again and again.

SR   How do you ensure your own success, Mike, as a head? Are there any particular highs and lows in your work or career?

MC   I can't see any really. We have a new Chief Education Officer (CEO) and he was asking me what I thought about the educational system in Birmingham. I replied I wasn't prepared to answer that question until he went away and asked people what they thought about me as a head. If he was prepared to do that and return with an answer, then I'd be prepared to let him know what I really thought about the system. Then – the answer might be placed in a context of 'supportive validity'. I guess he heard more about me than he divulged, that I was known as a person who had run three schools and developed three schools. I don't see any of those jobs being that different, albeit the schools were different, but they all needed bringing together and pointing in a direction and that direction involved the staff, the children.

SR   How do you manage your own success?

MC   I have no real answer for that question. I could waffle but if I'm honest, I just don't know. I guess I manage success by feedback and the perception of other people. Very often you get a skewed picture anyway, because people are talking to you, so I'm left with no direct or accurate assessment.

SR   Describe the kind of head you are – as a leader – as a manager.

MC   The trite answer is a benign dictator. I don't enjoy committees or committee work. I like to see other people doing things and moving forward. I like to facilitate successful people, and support less successful people and encourage others to play the same role. I guess I'm very much in control, which is a bad thing and a good thing. Again, I've listened to an officer talking about another school where a unit was not integrated into the mother school to the degree which was desired. I asked what the problem was, why weren't they involved. Her response was to tell me that the particular head liked to get behind the staff and gently nudge them forward, while she thought that my style was probably more like someone saying something like come on lads this is the way we go. I don't perceive that way at all but that was her view. So – I don't know what sort of head I am and to find out you need to go and ask other people.

SR   How do you enable effective teaching and learning which takes place in your school? Do you see any changes in this aspect of your work?

MC   We've had a sea change in special education for children with EBD in respect to the curriculum and teaching and learning. Coming out of mainstream, I was steeped in the curriculum and organizing the curriculum to help children gain success through the exam route. I've always been interested in pastoral care too but it always seemed that people's perceptions outside education on how well children were doing lay with bits of paper. Even for the less able, it was important, perhaps even more important that they felt they were successful. In all of the schools in which I've worked, it has been about trying to give their staff what they need to help them feel they have the knowledge, that they have the facilities in order to do the best they can for the children.

SR   Is there always an agreement on perceived needs and your own vision for the school?

MC   Well it's basically about what they want, not what I want. The thing tends to be a discussion, but discussion amongst them rather than discussion with me. I would not claim to be driving the curriculum. I would claim to be instrumental in pulling together the various threads to make sure the school is successful. If we take IT as an example, we've acquired more equipment but it's very difficult to get staff to feel more confident and flexible in their use of IT. There is little I can do apart from demonstrating the advantages of IT in their classroom. In an EBD school you've got staff who are willing to embrace that, but you've got staff who say no, because it disrupts the class, and they can no longer control the children. It's a case of allowing people to see benefits and providing the facility to have these benefits available if it's useful. I've seen too many occasions throughout my career when resources have been provided and they have been left in a cupboard. This still goes on because if you don't provide the opportunity the resources and other changes will never be used or take place.

SR   How do you keep your finger on the pulse, day to day?

MC   Once upon a time, I was involved in Heads of Department meetings. In this school, I don't because it is so small. A curriculum committee reports back to me. I guess I ought to be more involved than I am these days – I rarely teach, but I take assemblies frequently, and enjoy them. For successful teaching and learning with children who are experiencing emotional and behavioural difficulties, you need teachers with charisma and they are not easy to find. I would like more cross-curricular work but some people can't manage this approach with EBD pupils. I have a number of thoughts and ideas I peddle and I hope people will pick them up as we move along and run with them. I very much like the university style of teaching with key lessons setting up a programme of work, either in a subject or a programme of work or cross-curricular topics, and then the work can be supported by a range of adults who don't have to be teachers. This gives the teacher more time to work on an individual basis with each child. It allows us here to make more use of all of our staff, the care staff, classroom assistants, domestics. I think this approach really does suit EBD children, the less-able learner, and even disaffected pupils in the mainstream school.

When I first came here because the structure of the place changed, the ancillary staff and care staff were re-designated roles which barred them from working with children. Role definitions were rigidly drawn. Now it's taken ten years but we're finally breaking down these barriers. We're currently having a push on reading and a number of staff are listening to individual pupils read, working in the classroom, and this is bringing staff together as a whole team rather than keeping them apart in separate groups. There's a parallel in mainstream, I guess, I know I remember using ancillary staff, dinner ladies, technicians, and other people to get involved in the curriculum, to genuinely become part of an educational community.

SR To whom is a head accountable? Who do you answer to and how do you manage this accountability?

MC The children. I know it's a trite answer but it's true. I have no boss – except perhaps the CEO.

SR You've mentioned the LEA several times as your employer rather than any single school.

MC Yes but there's the governors too. But the very nature of headship in a large LEA such as Birmingham means there are a number of managers dealing with different aspects which come to focus in the school. You would go down different avenues depending upon what you wanted, so you contacted a person for day-to-day management, a person for specific curriculum issues, or other appropriate people for different problems or advice.

I guess you're rather more like an executive to the board, rather than part of a line management, as a headteacher. You have a number of threads which you need to bring together – in order that you can tie a knot in it! It's the same sort of process when you're managing a large complex. The teachers are your managers, and in an industrial analogy represent your management workforce, which is one of the reasons why a lot of industrial-style management theory or process doesn't easily or naturally fit the school organization. It isn't easy to generate the time to have meetings, you can't pull people off the production line.

SR   How do you manage to maintain your own professional well-being and development? How do you cope with stress and manage when things go wrong?

MC   I have no specific answer to that question. I have nobody I talk to or share with in educational terms. I go to colleagues, heads, and talk in general terms about issues and events, but there's nobody I share with in detail the worries, the anxieties, thoughts about potential trouble spots, or disasters you're heading off on a daily basis. I do carry the work around in my mind but I have a very supportive family, my wife and two daughters, which takes your mind away from work.

SR   Is that important?

MC   Very important!

SR   What would you advise a new headteacher on this question of well-being?

MC   It depends on the individual. To me it's important to have a family – I think it's part of the reason for my drive – to support them and keep them in the manner to which they have become accustomed. Family provides a purpose – it's an important part of the overall process for me.

SR   What do you like most about being a headteacher?

MC   I have no real answer – perhaps the exercise of power. But I'm not aware of liking the power – if that makes sense.

SR   But it occurred to you just then!

MC   Yes. But I'm now old and ancient so things become blurred, a bit like failing eyesight. I probably do things differently now, maybe I've developed my own personal style of management which runs on automatic. I mean perhaps I have my own personal ethos, or aura, and therefore there's something that emanates from you, and if you go into a room, or a classroom, or a meeting, maybe there's something there which generates leadership. Perhaps I've become complacent in my old age and I no longer have to analyse how to do things in great detail – they automatically happen.

SR   Can I ask a bit more about the power? You didn't seem comfortable with the admission about the power of headship.

MC   Well – it seems the wrong thing to say – doesn't it? To have the power over people – I presumably have a fair amount of influence over both my school and some of the things that go on in Birmingham therefore I have an influence over a fairly large tract or parts of the educational system. I have been involved with a number of schools at a fairly high level of management within these schools, and I have therefore affected a lot of children and adults in terms of their career. I don't really see the outcome, not often. I do what I do, and if it works, super, but I don't actually see the end product. I'm not ultimately sure I'm successful but because it's out there, I have a go, see if I can do better.

I don't really have any specific dislikes about headship. I enjoy doing what I do and I feel reasonably successful at it or I guess I wouldn't continue. But I don't see any nasty bits – I don't like attending to detail and I see that as a need and a professional failing but it's not a nasty bit, not really. If I have to do it, I can do it with the best but I don't like disciplining my mind to it. I'd much rather play with the broad brush which I find much more interesting. My success depends in great part on people who work with me, and finding the right people who will look after the detail. I've always felt that I succeed through people, I don't need the kudos, because if I get it right, I get the recognition anyway. It's very important to maintain support and offer the kudos to those people who are actually doing the work. It automatically reflects back on the school and therefore on the headteacher. I suppose if I am pushed, the bit I least like is disciplining staff. I don't shirk away from it but it is the bit I least like because I think it really shouldn't be necessary. I think people should be doing the job without having to be instructed or confronted.

SR   Ted Wragg says 'You don't have to be a "nutter" to join the "barmy army" but ... '. Do you think headship has become much more difficult and do you enjoy it?

MC   I think this is really to do with perception. If you have not known anything different it becomes part and parcel of the job. If you have new staff, people who have come through college and been trained to teach the national curriculum through the key stages and administer SATs, it really is part and parcel of the job. It's the older staff who have not been used to this particular aspect of education, and have gone through the dreadfully traumatic process to bring it somewhere to fruition, who are fighting it rather than people who have only known it. I think we can have a nice quote here. Pasternak says something like you can be uncomfortable at the beginning of a war but gradually you begin to get used to it. It is really about coping with change.

SR   With respect, Mike, you've already said that you're an older head – have you found it harder to take on board some of these recent changes? Has it become harder for you?

MC   No, not really because I've been able to slide around it. The schools I've been involved with more recently, in hindsight, have been difficult schools and I have heard the term 'trouble-shooter' used to describe me. It's all hindsight, 20/20 vision, rear-view perspective, but if you're dealing with utter chaos, people let you slide around a rigid framework. The framework is here. But I've not really had to get to grips with it, other people are having to dot the 'i's and cross the 't's.

SR   What about 'nutters working with nutters', Mike? Do you need to be a 'nutter' and crazy to be a head of an EBD school?

MC   Well, I enjoy chaos! I do like knitting 'fog'. I like to be stretched and this job can be said to stretch. When I first came to Lindsworth, I saw it as one of the most difficult places I'd ever been in, and you will appreciate I've been in one or two such places. I was being stretched by a store man who has whisky stashed away and other people being involved in drinking bouts. I had people who were doing laundry who didn't want to and were causing trouble. I had a seamstress, they were all strange new types of personnel who I'd never met before in my experience of management. I had a female teacher who took forty-eight hours to decide whether she had been assaulted by a pupil. Children were fighting left, right and centre. It was chaos. My mind was being stretched to assimilate all of these new people and events and crises and I thought how difficult the process was but now I've been doing it for a period of time, I still see the large school being more difficult than running this one. Although, I must admit, there may be a sense of growing into this job. I guess it quickly takes on an awesome prospect when you try to find someone to do this job. I'm able to do it because it has grown around me.

SR   I'm curious about the similarities and differences between the two management roles in the special school and the large comprehensive. Do you still think the large comprehensive was more difficult in spite of the intensity of work in a special school for children with EBD?

MC   Yes – I think you're right in so far as you're closer to staff in a smaller school. I've had experience of both. Somewhere in the interview schedule, you ask the question about the most difficult bit of preparing for headship. Well – the most difficult bit for me was persuading people to understand or accept that I could actually cope with a large complex, because my experience was mostly in smaller schools. It was difficult to convince an interview panel that if your experience was mostly small, that you could work with large. One of the big differences is that in small if you don't watch it mountains can grow out of molehills extremely quickly, whereas in a large school, you just don't get anywhere near the same thing happening. That's true for any small school, and you recognize it in a larger school, but you realize that all of these things aren't coming to you, basically because they're being filtered out before they get anywhere near you. I suppose I do use this now as a deliberate strategy. I stay away from staff. Just the other day a member of staff said people think I'm not involved enough, again . . . .

SR   I suspect that is largely deliberate?

MC   A lot of it is deliberate but . . . a lot of it's to do with having lots of things on your mind and because a very important issue, from the staff perspective, that is, yourself and your overt acknowledgement, tends to drop as a priority and it ought not. I'm going to have to, over the next fortnight, get off my backside and in and around some of the classrooms! But again, it's not just that straightforward, I was talking to another member of staff from another school and they were saying that the head there never visits the lower school. From the head's point of view if you're based in the main school, when you go down to the lower school you get in the way. I've even gone to the extent of organizing my own room in lower school when I was in a similar situation, so that I could go somewhere, or otherwise, with the best will in the world, you become a disruptive influence in the school. You can go and take assemblies, work with the children, but that's organized rather than popping in, which usually ends up with you being a spare bit. People want you but they don't want you. They want your recognition, a feeling that you know what they're doing and approve, and you need to be able to achieve that, but if you don't watch it, then as things go on you draw away, not because you want to but because you're avoiding disruption. It is an interesting balance that you need to achieve.

In this particular school – I had to teach a difficult group for when a member of staff had a nervous breakdown. I was timetabled for half a year. The staff had the chance to see that I could teach. It was very important for the staff at that time, not for me, I didn't have any worries about coping, but for the staff, and really you can't do both indefinitely. I suppose that there might be criticism of that position and I could possibly reduce the number of other ventures and developments we're involved with and focus on the main school.

SR   What fundamental changes do you think have taken place in special education? What does this mean for headship and special education?

MC   Certainly the national curriculum has had a big impact upon special education for EBD children. Or it seems that way to me, because coming out of mainstream into this, and finding the lack of curriculum provision was something that I instinctively changed. The idea of academic in the morning and play in the afternoon is probably a good concept but I think the children miss out. You have to draw a line, in terms of what school is about, and when I came here the academic emphasis was very weak and expectation low. We've raised expectation and consequently achievement, but it needs to go higher and perhaps we're into the need for new blood again. It's this business of being drawn into the process again, going native, I suppose, and having your sights lowered rather than raised.

SR   Is the curriculum important for children with EBD?

MC   Well – I think it's more important for the staff so that they will strive for a standard they'd otherwise not work toward if they'd just got behavioural targets in place. It's a difficult issue. It is hard to decide for each child how much you can excuse academic underachievement because of misbehaviour – there's no doubt you can because it does have a number of obvious effects – but it can be a case of the chicken or the egg coming first. And it's important that you continue to strive to encourage academic achievement.

I think you do need to create an academic ethos to demonstrate to the children this kind of achievement. However, when you're dealing with EBD children, children who often have a reading age four or five years below their chronological age, their access to worksheets, books, text is limited. This can take us back to the discussion on IT. The children are often very good at picking up things visually and verbally, rather than with reading. It's a kind of learning that's not so easily recorded in terms of achievement as measured outside school. And unfortunately that's the important bit – kudos for the children – and if you don't have the curriculum and you don't work to levels by which other people will judge them, then you are ultimately failing them. In that sense, it can be therapeutic. What is difficult to maintain is to provide them with all that they have missed in ordinary child development and still manage to get the curriculum into the day. It is important that a lot of these children play, just play with one another, play with water, play with sand, play with games and just interact with one another rather than wind each other up and fight. Now – that doesn't fit easily into the workload one's expected to get through in terms of the national curriculum. I guess one ducks and weaves, and talks about visiting rather than staying in various areas of the curriculum. I'd turn that around the other way too, and say that if you've got a teacher who can maintain the children's respect and dignity and have control, then it seems to me that the level of work you can get out of the children is extremely high.

SR   Are there any other aspects of recent change which have impacted upon your job?

MC   I'm not sure this impacts directly on headship, but the nature of the children now being catered for in special education has changed. The SEN have become more exceptional, and more extreme. It has changed quite dramatically. A lot of pupils you now find in special schools some time ago would not have been in school at all. They might have been in a remand home or a psychiatric unit but they certainly would not have been receiving a full-time education. The levels of difficulty in EBD provision has increased considerably, especially in terms of violence. On top of this, you have the effect of levels of violence increasing generally in society, which I think has perhaps reinforced this trend.

It's obvious that if you get children from this school into mainstream they are going to be better off than they would staying here.

But because of the increasing difficulty of social expectation and pupil behaviour has increased, and I think it has, you're now facing a really vicious catch-22 because if you reintegrate children into mainstream, more often than not these days they fail, and then the only place for them is back here and they don't want to come back and again experience the difficulty level of other pupils who are placed here and you just lose them. We have this happening here at the moment. A pupil has just failed – he's had two reintegration attempts, both initially very successful, but his behaviour gradually deteriorated as he became himself and he could no longer be tolerated in the mainstream school because of his behaviour. He was doing all the things a teenager might, not dramatically serious, but not appropriate or acceptable in a school. His return has been marked by abscondence. He's voted with his feet, we can't keep him and he is worse off as a result of our trying to reintegrate him.

SR   Do you see any other effects on headship from recent reform legislation, for instance, self-management?

MC   I think it has made quite a difference in the way you can now look at the fabric of the building and the provision of materials for the staff. It is possible to vire monies now and it makes the management of the school more closely linked to costs. I am now able to authorize immediate repairs rather than wait, which is very important in an EBD school, because you need to prevent rapid deterioration with a quick response or you'll end up with a demolished school. It's far easier to do this now rather than wait for the LEA.

However, I'd argue that it's other people who do most of the work associated with the reform and changes associated with it. I have a general oversight of the finance and care of the site, but I don't dot the 'i's and cross the 't's, other people do it. If you've got good people, good at doing that then it doesn't require me to do it – I just need the overview of the budget. There has been an increase in workload but not necessarily my own workload or my own time.

SR   How do you wish to see your own school develop? What will this mean for the head?

MC   Well – I don't see grant maintained status (GMS) for the school. If I'd been in mainstream, with the financial benefits being offered, I'd probably have opted for GMS. But now those inducements are diminished and the LEA monies are devolved, it makes it much less worthwhile going GMS. I don't see any moral or practical contradictions for special schools and GMS, it's not very different from the independent special school, is it? I think the important thing is weighing up the advantages and the longer-term benefit.

I'd like to see the school become the focus for EBD provision in Birmingham, but that would be quite a leap forward. It's already happening to some extent. Lindsworth was a small EBD school for up to thirty children and is now a centre for up to ninety-five children, plus a unit for long-term truants, and a sixth form which has grown out of this, catering for about sixty pupils, together with over one hundred and twenty children involved in what I describe as the 'Newsome Process' in the centre for Arts Therapy which takes clients from the age of two to ninety-two years old. It's involved with social service offering a provision which is clearly meeting a need. If it goes on in this fashion than it will be providing a flagship for the LEA in the way that it can assess and resource an EBD provision. At the moment, I think that maybe we ought to look at this question of the EBD-delinquency categorization and do something about it. The only way you can do that, I think, given the financial constraints, is to actually have more children so that you can run a lower, middle and upper school. You would effectively have three schools for which this site is ideally suited. Each of the schools would have a therapeutic and delinquency emphasis within it. To move on from one school to the next would involve a major review, so there would be an expectation that a pupil would only remain in one school, and then return to mainstream provision. I guess, ideally, if I want to be a mega-lomaniac, I'd like a mainstream school to run at the same time in order to create this continuum.

To make this kind of provision work, you need the control in the hands of practising people, practising what they preach. People who end up administering from an administrative centre have less credence than a person who is actually working and can demonstrate their ability to do a job. The latter are more likely to be listened to and worked with than someone from outside. There is also the issue of Local Management of Special Schools (LMSS) offering a power base that you didn't have before. There is a pot of money that needs to be used to enable, in terms of priming things, setting things up, developing new ways and moving forward, developing a plan in discussion with the governors in order to really achieve something. That seems to me to be a more powerful place to be, there's that word power again, to make things happen. These sorts of things are happening already, it would therefore be a continuing process, taking a set of ideas, a vision, which seems to work and just *perpetuating* them. It worked in mainstream and it could work here. In mainstream in the tiny two-form-entry comprehensive, we were one of the first schools to have people from industry teaching in school. We made the link with Lucas Industries. We had their Training Officers coming in to teach our children. We made that direct link then and we're talking about sixteen years ago.

It is difficult to break down traditional barriers and set things off. This is why I'm driven to the idea of one person in control. I've always said it doesn't have to be me, it could be someone else, but you need one person for whom the workforce is working, and you create less barriers. Each time I've run a school, I've experienced this same problem. At Nine Styles, I had a manager who was not responsible to me, and consequently I spent a great deal of wasted time kicking down walls which were being built by his staff. Their reticence at being involved in the school was a problem. Eventually, we persuaded them that they could walk down a school corridor, as staff, and that this brought them kudos, and an authority which they could take with them back into the Leisure Centre. This meant when the schoolchildren came into the centre, they were less likely to misbehave, because the staff had a rapport with them. They were also less likely to get involved in bad behaviour because the centre staff were perceived as part of the school.

There are a whole range of things that could happen here, but you do need a person controlling the purse strings who has enough faith to put the money into the development. We may manage to do it under LMSS but I guess it'll be a long process, unless someone else sees the vision too.

SR   Do we still need headteachers?

MC   I didn't really understand this question. You do need someone who understands what's going on. I don't know whether someone who hasn't taught can actually really understand the process. I think people who aren't 'born teachers' can be taught to teach, but I think there's really something in the genes, I think teachers are born to teach. I think you might be born a leader too. If I'm involved outside of school, I usually end up leading the group but I don't particularly want to do it. It just tends to happen without my striving for it. What we need is someone who knows the job leading the way. The common trend seems to be towards the idea that if you have a knowledge of management theory, the processes and the strategies which make up this theory, this will enable effective management and good leadership. But I still think there's the question of individual ability and personality. You've mentioned the analogy, previously, with soccer, well if we take that example, if I'm a team manager with professional experience and expertise, and I also have innate leadership qualities, there is a much better chance of my being successful. I will have a better idea of what's going on in the game. The same thing applies to teaching and leadership in special education.

CHAPTER 5

Finite resource meeting infinite need: starting up an EBD support service

PHIL CRAIG with Steve Rayner

Phil Craig is Headteacher of the Warrington Tutorial Centre, the only pupil referral unit (PRU) in Cheshire. He has taught in mainstream and special education in both England and Canada, but has spent most of his career working with disaffected pupils experiencing severe emotional and behaviour difficulties. Phil has previously held posts of responsibility within a secure special unit and as a headteacher within a residential special school. He has also studied and lectured at a postgraduate level in both countries.

SR   Could we begin by your telling us about your personal background – home, school, higher education and people who perhaps had a significant influence on your life?

PC   This sounds a bit like I'm in the psychiatrist's chair being interviewed by Jonathan Miller. Well, in terms of deciding upon a career in education and becoming a teacher, I think I was not unlike many people in the 1960s or the early 1970s. It was almost pure serendipity. I didn't really know what I wanted to do. I went to college in Leeds in 1970, and studied Physical Education and English. I completed a certificate of education in three years and then had the chance to go to Canada and complete a Bachelor of Education degree in Physical Education. I was the first student from the Leeds college to go on the exchange. I was a kind of pilot study to test the idea to see if it had merit. There had been some discussion about setting up a reciprocal arrangement, and I was the first student on the scheme.

   I went to study for the BEd at the University of Alberta in Calgary in September 1973. I arrived to find myself in a very different educational environment to the one I'd left behind. It was very much like what it is now in university education here. I had to complete a set number of modules for the course in an open-ended period of time. I also had to find the money to pay for the course. I completed the required number of modules for the degree in about a year, which was pretty good going. I also did reasonably well – I was offered a scholarship to study for an MA. They in fact paid me to teach undergraduate classes there as well and I did a bit of research for professors, which all helped to pay my way. I think that happens in Britain now, but not then, it would have been unheard of back in Leeds. I completed the MA in 1975 and then a few months later returned to Britain, I think, around the beginning of 1976.

SR   Can I ask you to go back a little before this period at teaching training college – to your own schooldays? Were there any particular influences that looking back you might feel had some influence on your decision to make a career in education?

PC   It's funny you should ask that – I had a similar conversation to this recently with a couple of other teachers and we concurred. We all felt that one of our main motivations for entering the teaching profession had been that we couldn't really do it as badly as some of the teachers we had when we were at school. We felt, quite strongly, that we would do it considerably better than most of those teachers we had known! I think when I look back at my own schooling – do you really want me to go back to school?

SR   Please do – from the smile on your face I think it might be interesting.

PC   Well – yes. I suppose it is when I look back at it. There was an article in the *Times Educational Supplement* a couple of weeks ago written by a gentleman who had been educated by Jesuits in the same way I had and it brought a smile to my face. Many of the experiences he described were familiar. In particular, he referred to the ferula. The ferula is from the Latin. It is a belt made of leather and whale-bone. We were beaten with this ferula as a form of education. We literally had knowledge beaten into us. It wasn't an experience for the weak of heart.

The school that I went to in Glasgow also had this system where the teachers were holders of 'cheque books' which were used to enforce discipline. If you misbehaved early in the day you were given a cheque which you had to cash in either at lunch-time or at the end of the day. It was like sadistic capitalism. You had the sword of Damocles hanging over you all day and you were paid, literally, in physical punishment. It seems to me – when you are talking about eleven- or twelve-year-old kids – that it is a pretty inhumane way of dealing in discipline. Well – the writer talked about the ferula, and the experience of a Jesuit education, and how really it was in spite of the teaching that we learned anything. The conclusion was that for all our different backgrounds, we knew we could do better.

SR   Could you tell us a little about home and early life – do you recall any events or experiences which perhaps had shaped or encouraged the idea of what you might want to do in life?

PC   In truth, I probably hated school when I first started. I remember, vaguely, running away from infant school on more than one occasion and had to be returned by my parents. Perhaps I was a good judge of what schooling has to offer right from an early age! The supreme irony is that I am now working with kids who feel the same way and my job is to convince them of the efficacies of the educational system. I guess that perhaps, with my problematic start to school, which on reflection didn't improve greatly during secondary education, I am well qualified for a career in work with pupils experiencing EBD.

I suppose looking back the seed of an idea that I might consider teaching as a career took a long time to germinate. If I am really honest I drifted into Teacher Training College without really knowing if I wanted to pursue a career in education.

SR   Was there really a point at which you chose teaching as a definite decision?

PC   I think it gathered momentum while I was at college because as you worked through the course, and experienced teaching in the classroom, you began to feel, increasingly, that you could do this, and what's more, you enjoyed it! It is when you feel that you are 'connecting' with the kids, especially when you are working with a pupil who has a specific problem, is failing, one way or another, who can't understand something and you help the kid through the difficulty. It gives you a buzz! You get a physiological reaction. It's that real.

I get a buzz from watching kids' self-esteem grow or from watching kids work through an achievement. If you are part of that process, and see a kid achieve GCSE English when everyone had written him off, and the kid himself didn't think he could possibly do it . . . there's a magic moment when they realize they just might do it. They begin to work, part way through the course, in marked contrast to before they started, when they simply couldn't even begin to think seriously about taking GCSE. They had been branded a failure and they had lived being a failure all the way through school, when they managed to turn up for school. The turn-about is when you have made that connection. I'd say it was sometime in my second year at college when I began to feel this connection and enjoy actual teaching. I felt then, that yes, this is what I wanted to do for a career.

SR   Previously – you weren't sure at all?

PC   No – I don't think so. That's right. It was about falling into it – for me.

SR   Was there anybody at college – a lecturer or a friend – who helped influence that decision when it finally occurred?

PC   Certainly when I went to Canada there was a lecturer who did – and yes – there was a lecturer at Leeds called Jean Williams. She went to Canada to do an MA and was largely responsible for initiating this scheme I mentioned a few moments ago. She was still there when I did the BEd. She persuaded me that to go to Canada was a good idea. I didn't really need that much persuasion. I regarded it as an opportunity not to be missed. There was also Margaret Talbot. She is highly involved in national curriculum PE at the moment. She was a lecturer on my teacher training course, very motivated, very committed, dynamic and interesting. She helped to keep me on track during that period. There was also a Canadian lecturer – I think his name was McGregor – he inspired me. But – it was all such a long time ago!

SR   I'm curious – thinking of what you have said – I have the impression that teaching practice played the greatest part in influencing your decision to carry on with the idea of a teaching career. It was instrumental in helping you to realize that this was something you enjoyed?

PC   Yes. Yes. I think that's right. I think so – you can sit in lectures and you can talk about child development and about Piaget, and it's all very abstract. It's when you actually go into schools and you're in front of a class of kids and you either survive or don't survive, that you know. You have your good days and bad days and you think about both afterwards, think about what you might have done better because you're locked into the process. I suppose in a sense, you are hooked. That's when it hits you that teaching is a good idea, or maybe, no, this is all a bad idea.

    Overall, I think a lot of it comes down to core personality. I'm not saying that's the only thing that's important, but if you can connect with the kids and if you can project your personality – it's a head start. And it is always part of the equation, even if it is not the whole answer. I do think that the subject you teach at school is not the key factor in successful teaching and learning, but plays second part to the relationships you build with the pupils. A lot of kids like the subject because of the teacher. In my opinion, and experience, it is this relationship which features, consistently, in the accounts of school disaffection with which I work. I currently interview pupils on the threshold of exclusion and one of the questions I ask the pupils is which subjects they like and why. The response is almost always the same – 'The teacher is good' and 'I like the teacher because I get on with them'.

SR   Can we move on and return to your own teaching career in this country? Perhaps you could give us some idea of your own teaching experience?

PC   Serendipity played its part again. I returned from Canada in 1976. I arrived well qualified but with no experience in the British system – so I was *special* right from the start. I was married with no children but faced the future with no money, no job, no home. I looked in the

Times Educational Supplement and saw a job advertised for the Kingswood Special Schools in Bristol for an experienced PE teacher to work in the secure unit. The work was with young people with severe emotional and behavioural difficulties – well that's how we would describe them today. The label in use then was 'disturbed'. They were kids who had murdered, raped, or committed other violent crimes. It seemed to combine the psychology and PE background which reflected the main part of the two degrees I had completed in Canada. I didn't have the experience but I had the motivation. It also seemed interesting.

I also have to say the job offered a house – a three-bedroomed semi in the school grounds – as part of the package. That was a good thing and a bad thing because it was convenient but it trapped you. It trapped a lot of people because the rent was low but you were living on campus, living right on top of the job. I actually only lived there for about eighteen months, then bought a house of my own. I was very happy at Kingswood Schools for a very long time. I stayed too long.

I was there for most of the time through the period from 1976 to 1994/5. It must have been about twenty years, off and on. The work changed dramatically during that time, involving me in a number of different roles, and the actual job itself changed just as dramatically. A number of different and quite significant things happened – like the Children Act in 1989. I also had an opportunity in the late 1980s to further my professional development – I realized by this time that I wanted to stay in special education.

SR   Why was that, Phil?

PC   Well, I had realized I worked quite well with children with problems and if I'm totally honest, when you get to a certain level in special education it becomes almost impossible to transfer into mainstream education at the same level or higher, because you don't have the necessary experience. There are lots of good people out there with that experience. If people were to take you on in the mainstream context, they'd be taking a chance, a gamble, and the educational profession is not a gambling profession.

SR   What about the challenge of working with children who present serious problems? Were there any particular aspects of the work you enjoyed?

PC   I think it was the variety. I really think it was the variety. It was also the size of the teaching groups – they were very small – often individual. You get to know the kids very well and they get to know you very well indeed. They really do get to know what you will and will not accept. In that sense, I think an important part of work is about teacher-student relationships. I mean, I do think, looking back, that in excess of 90 per cent of the actual work kids produced, they produced because of the relationship between the teacher and themselves. They really did do it for you, and then of course for themselves.

SR   I think you were going to say that an opportunity occurred for you during this period.

PC   Yes. I was very fortunate. I realized that if I was going to *escape* from the secure unit I would have to do something about it. I had qualifications but I felt I needed something more if I was going to move on in special education. I looked into professional development opportunities at Bristol Polytechnic. I didn't want to plunge straight into an MEd, given the nature of the job at Kingswood. I was working extraneous duties, which were fifteen hours per week. This meant that I was working the equivalent of two extra days every week, and juggling that with family commitments, and sporting pursuits, and sanity, I thought it would all be a little too heavy.

I opted to take a BEd in Special Needs at Bristol Polytechnic, which during that same period became the University of the West of England. I thoroughly enjoyed the degree course. I learnt a lot and was persuaded to continue to do an MEd which I also enjoyed. I finished the latter in 1994. I think the MEd was probably a catalyst for change in my career, particularly as a vehicle for progression to senior management. I think having worked through it, and looking back, although it was intrinsically worthwhile, finally completing it, remaining in the same job would have been both silly and frustrating. But I must emphasize that I was ready for a change anyway.

SR   The change came?

PC   Yes – it did – but I should mention 'escaping' once before from the secure unit which I've overlooked. I served a short period of headship at an independent residential special school in Somerset in 1987. It was cut short when I was involved in a car crash. I started the job at the beginning of 1987 and was badly injured in the car crash on the first of May 1987. I was lucky to escape with my life. I would say, in career terms, that the episode set me back by two or three years.

What I did learn, however, is that things can't change overnight. I inherited a very difficult situation in the school when I took up the appointment. The pupils were presenting serious behavioural problems and were literally out of control. More seriously, staff morale was virtually non-existent, they felt powerless and stranded without effective management or support. I learnt the hard way and quickly that effective management of change is slow but deliberate, and that you need to work to a medium-term action-plan, say three to five years, and importantly, you need to create a sense of movement which is felt throughout the period. The staff as a group need to feel that they and the school are moving in the right direction. I think you also need to empower staff – give them a say, a stake in the planning and decision-making. An effective manager cannot do everything – I think I learnt quickly that I needed to lead a team and, in that situation, build a team. Leadership then meant sorting out the priorities, realizing that we couldn't do everything but that we had to work towards achieving everything which was fundamental and did need to work. I had to sort out quickly what was short-term goals and what had to wait – in essence, to prioritize. I also had to lead from the front, by example, and I do recall that aspect of re-building confidence and re-taking control of direction and purpose as a very real issue in the early part of my time there. I wouldn't have been able to direct affairs from an office even if I had wanted to be that kind of headteacher.

I was very fortunate, looking back, in that I was able to return to work at Kingswood Schools after the car accident. I started work again fairly soon during the period of convalescence and recovery. I began with part-time work and gradually returned to full-time work. I had a number of different operations and treatments for the injuries caused by the crash.

I've lost my thread ... yes, I was only there at the school for about six months, about a term. But as a result, I was facing what I saw as a problem with my Curriculum Vitae, I mean my career path. The crash set everything back, and I felt I had to recover some professional credibility. When it came to writing a letter of application, and it came to writing down, 'involved in a serious car accident and now fully recovered', well, there's a doubt, isn't there? The words are there on a piece of paper and can be easily negatively interpreted by a selection committee.

SR   In terms of career progression, then, the crash was a tragedy?

PC   It was a serious set-back. I had an opportunity to do something in Somerset which through no fault of my own was stopped. Then, through the operations and everything, that set me back two or three years.

SR   And towards the end of this period? How did you make your next career move?

PC   Well – again – it came down to looking in the *TES* for possible job opportunities. It was interesting – thinking about a different direction. As you know the first Pupil Referral Unit (PRU) was actually set up as recently as 1994. I took up this post in April 1995 and this is the first PRU in Cheshire. We are a pilot scheme set up in the first instance to run for three years. In many ways, the job is literally evolving as we speak and if we look to other areas in Cheshire – there are six distinct administrative areas – Warrington is the only one with this kind of provision. There seems to be an inevitability about further development of this provision in the near future.

SR   Did you consciously set out to look for headship as a way of escaping the secure unit?

PC   Certainly I wanted management at some level and something differ-
     ent – a new challenge. The concept of the PRU interested me – the
     rationale behind the approach which in my view argues that even
     within the focused 'part' of the SEN continuum which is EBD, there
     exists a great diversity in pupil need.

     The available provision prior to 1993, which was uncoordinated,
     some would say chaotic, was made up of a patchwork quilt of units
     and special schools, often serving the same or very similar functions
     but described formally, and organized in very different language. For
     example, there were adjustment units, assessment centres, inter-
     mediate treatment centres, psychiatric units with education, young
     offender units, secure units, stage 5 centres. Different names and a
     mish-mash of provision.

     The movement to PRUs at least reflects an awareness and an
     attempt by the government to make better sense of this area of
     special education by bringing off-site units under the one umbrella.
     This has coincided with a very obvious trend which has gathered
     momentum during the past four years, to maintain as many young
     people with SEN as is possible in mainstream education.

     I think, if I'm honest, it was both advantageous and a disadvantage
     working at the Kingswood schools, when I consider what I do now.
     Kingswood was a very specialized provision, with kids presenting
     severely challenging behaviour, kids who Hoghugi, the ex-principal
     of Aycliffe School, and a well respected 'expert' in the area of secure
     special education, described as having arrived at 'the end of the line
     with nowhere else to go'.

     Well, no matter how much you try to prevent it, you do to some
     degree become distanced from mainstream education when you
     work in special education. Particularly the specialized provision
     which serves young people with needs which lie at the end of a
     continuum, whether or not they're described as extreme or excep-
     tional or troubled or troublesome! If you have a young person who
     ends up in secure provision, there is an extremely remote chance
     that the individual is going to reintegrate into mainstream school.

     One of the ways we did maintain contact was to go out as part of
     INSET arrangements and observe 'good practice' in mainstream
     schools. I spent a term's placement teaching in an inner-city compre-
     hensive in Bristol. We were continuously involved in GCSE
     administration, so we went to moderation meetings, attended cour-
     ses, and met and talked to colleagues about marking, administration
     and teaching content. But – notwithstanding all of this – it's still kind
     of artificial. It doesn't represent the kind of experience shared by
     colleagues who have taught in secondary education throughout their
     careers.

SR   Perhaps I can move us on to consider whether during your career there were any experiences or events which prompted you to decide you wanted to become a headteacher?

PC   No – at least not for a long time. I actually had no ambition to enter senior management. I was quite happy doing the job I was doing at Kingswood. One major factor here is that working in special education and what's more, in the heavy end of the EBD market, means that you are well paid. I am talking, literally, from day one earning the equivalent of a deputy headteacher in a small secondary school. Now – given that I loved the job, I felt that I was suited to the job, and that it didn't feel like I was working for a living, there was a very powerful disincentive to move.

I can remember for years thinking that this is ridiculous! I'm getting paid, and paid well, for this! Another factor was the state of mainstream education. You looked at the deteriorating morale of colleagues in mainstream schools, and this went on during the late seventies and eighties, becoming increasingly more pronounced. I would go to moderation meetings or INSET days and talk to very unhappy, disgruntled people and yet I wouldn't feel the same way at all. The pressures were very different and the educational changes buffeting mainstream education were not having the same effect upon us. I was well paid for doing a job I loved. So – that suppressed any need for change or any motivation to further my career.

A third factor was that I had a very good headteacher. He gave me a lot of autonomy. Looking back that was a very big factor. I've discussed this with my wife, and we both agree that if I had not had such an accommodating, perhaps enlightened headteacher, I would have probably progressed much more quickly, in terms of my career. I would have been less happy and moved on, whereas in fact, I did not move for a very long time. In one sense this was a mistake. However, having said that, when you do love the job you are doing, and you do taste success, and you feel you're making a difference, and this is acknowledged, and you are committed to working with young people who have extremely serious problems, difficulties which appear intractable, and you are helping them to progress and to grow as individuals in a number of different ways, well that's a tremendous amount of job satisfaction!

SR   When did you reach a point when you felt – look – it's time I moved up the ladder into management?

PC   I think it was all tied up with a mid-life crisis. I would have been around about the age of thirty-five or thirty-six years old. I remember thinking what am I going to do for the rest of my life? Around about the same time, I was contacted by a colleague who I had worked with at Kingswood Schools who had just taken up a post as headteacher at a residential special school in Surrey. He asked me to apply for a deputy head's post which had come up at his new school. I went and had a look. There were particular problems in this establishment, as there always are when you move into a management position, especially in EBD provision.

He was a forward-looking individual, and I was ready to go there. Surrey wasn't particularly a place I wanted to move to because it's expensive and near London. But in fact it didn't work out. I applied, was interviewed, but I didn't have the necessary experience. Another candidate had the experience, he was a deputy head in another residential special school for children with EBD, and he got the job. Looking back, I can see that the experience of applying and interview sowed the seeds of change. The ground was perhaps fertile, freshly turned maybe, but attending the two-day interview opened up the idea of promotion, and management, in terms of a professional career.

SR   Do you think things could have happened in a better way to prepare you for headship? Or was your experience the best grounding for management in special education?

PC   No! No – I definitely think I could have managed my professional development in a better way. There are gaps in my experience that it would have been better to fill. I would have preferred to have had a more linear development. I mean, I really passed by the period and experiences of deputy headship. I don't think this was ideal, by any stretch of the imagination. In both periods of headship, in Somerset and now, it was very difficult during the early part of the job.

To some extent I guess I jumped in at the deep end. But I managed. I managed successfully although looking back I'd say it was in spite of the circumstances. Some of my previous experiences as I have already said did help. I had undertaken management responsibilities, additional duties which are usually associated with 'departmental' duties and senior teacher status in a secondary school. I had managed budgets, for example, not total budgets for the unit, but specified allowances which were quite substantial in comparison to budgets in a mainstream school.

When you are working in a small specialized unit, you find yourself undertaking a variety of management responsibilities – duties which in lots of ways were in fact preparation for a management role, although this may not be immediately obvious when it comes down to writing a CV. For example – I managed the GEST funding, I was the examinations officer, responsible for timetabling, which not only included the school day, but co-ordinating with care staff to build a 24-hour schedule, I ran the English Department, was responsible for Personal and Social Education.

It was when you had a visit from Her Majesty's Inspectorate that you truly realized how much managing of the curriculum actually took place. All of this kind of activity, additional duty, started fairly early in my time at Kingswood, so I suppose I quickly became accustomed to various levels of management accountability. The level of responsibility gradually increased throughout my time there and I thrived on it.

However, overall I do think a period as a deputy headteacher is a valuable thing. I would advocate it. It is a necessary preparation and most people would need it. Perhaps one of the things about being a deputy headteacher is, if you do it for a number of years, it gives you a better insight into the job of headship. You get the chance to see if you really do want to take the next step. You would be in a better position to make up your mind about the challenge of headship. Or, at the very least, the time would help shape your attitudes, values and approach to the task of management.

SR   Did you feel that the fact that you had not worked as a deputy head had any lasting impact upon your attempts to become a head-teacher?

PC   No, I guess not, not really. I think what you write down in your letter of application and Curriculum Vitae either enable you to get an interview or not and I then think it's a different stage of the application. I think in my situation, the hard part was to get an interview, the easy part was the interview. At that stage, you either sell yourself or you don't. It might come down to selling yourself well, but in the final decision certain gaps in your experience are a given and it's up to the selection panel to weigh this up.

Really, as an individual I can't arbitrate for that, I can't control that, and I don't think it should really figure in my thinking. And I don't think it did. I'm not aware of it counting as such, although clearly certain kinds of experience are going to be sought by the interview panel. In that sense, ideally, and probably often, it will ultimately come down to the best fit. As we mentioned in conversation this morning, I think there's probably a place for a national qualification as part of continuing professional development aimed at aspiring headteachers. We should formalize preparation for educational leadership.

SR   How would you describe your first year in your present post?

PC   Fraught! Certainly not easy at all.

SR   Were you prepared for it – ready for management?

PC   I think the trouble with working in special education and particularly in the area of EBD is that the powers that be – some politicians – pay lip-service to valuing these young people but when it comes to the crunch, when push comes to shove, these kids sit at the extreme end of the educational continuum and they are unwanted. I mean, the politicians talk about valuing these young people but in most cases they are finally perceived as a problem and a nuisance as 'naughty' kids who need a firm hand and a little old-fashioned discipline. I think, you know, that there's more than a spadeful of irony in the recent spat about the return of 'caning' advocated by Gillian Shephard and other members of the Conservative Government!

Nationally, I think the facilities that are offered are second rate – just look at the Ofsted report on PRUs – the overriding factor was the inappropriateness of the buildings and the lack of resources given to those working with these children. I think the problem is that very often, no appropriate facilities exist and there is no money with which to spend on building new provision.

I guess I wasn't totally prepared for management – but who is – in reality. When you talk about PRUs, you are talking about a concept in its infancy. We know there is a need for some kind of provision for these disaffected pupils but there are over three hundred PRUs in the United Kingdom and very little liaison or commonality between them. This liaison is slowly beginning to happen but it has got a long way to go. Each PRU is attempting to respond to local need and this does account for some differences in provision but nevertheless, they are serving the same client group, the same purpose, and lack guidance, definition and I have to say, very often, credibility.

To take a slightly different slant and to return to the question – yes – I was ready to again enter management in so far as it felt right to move into the role and take up this appointment. I really didn't quite know what it was I was going to manage and the 'what' has evolved and the centre will in every likelihood be a very different institution, say in a year's time. The process of growth and change is continuing at a remarkable pace. I do see that continuing, and perhaps even accelerating, as Warrington takes up unitary status in the planned reorganization of local government.

SR   Do you think the issue of resource provision in the management of PRUs is true generally?

PC   Well – it's one issue but it is enmeshed in several issues which all have to do with the way we manage pupils with emotional and behaviour difficulties. We've seen an increase in exclusions across the country which is quite extraordinary, starting from just three thousand per year in 1990 to fifteen thousand a year in 1996 – a fivefold increase in the first half of the nineties. We can take all day to talk causes but the fact is that while some schools are doing good work with these young people and spend a disproportionate amount of time and effort and resources on them, there is an ever increasing number of kids who are having to be excluded.

Some schools are managing the process better than others, but at the end of the day when the education of the other pupils is threatened, exclusion is used as a strategy. In very few cases are we talking about a pupil being a physical threat to teachers or peers, very few cases. It's true to some extent in Warrington that there is a magic roundabout running which sees kids excluded and passed from school to school. This is compounded by popular schools filling quickly and then not having to take excluded kids from other schools. Nationally the disaffected, the truants, and the excluded are groups of pupils with SEN who are not really being provided with an effective national system of education. It's a mess, in my opinion. It really is a minefield.

SR   What was the actual first week like then Phil, as headteacher of a new PRU?

PC   You know, it's interesting you should ask me about the first week. I had no base then, nowhere to go, no desk, no telephone, nothing. On day one, I was actually asked to report to county hall, twenty-seven miles down the road from Warrington in Chester. I was there talking about where I should be based. The building which had been leased was not ready. I obviously had to be based in Warrington because that was the area designated for the PRU. I had no infrastructure. Nothing.

It was a case of starting from zero and working up creating a service for the twelve schools in the Warrington area. I set my own agenda and decided my first task was to visit the schools and introduce myself to the heads and discuss what it was they thought a PRU should be and what it should offer. I wanted to share with them my vision for the PRU and involve them in the development of the service. I remember enjoying this and getting a great buzz from it. I also started writing policy documents at the same time, based on the six-pack of circulars dealing with the education of 'problem children' produced by the DfE. I knew roughly what I wanted to do, and I made further use of an LEA paper which addressed the issue of the development of a PRU provision in the authority. I think that this served as a useful model even though it was policy-bound, written by an officer on the third floor of county hall, rather than a description of effective working practice.

I think, as a matter of fact, that this is a scenario you would find repeated across the country. It might not perhaps be exactly the same, but there would be more similarities than differences. I think the basic problem with a PRU is that government legislation is responsible for the re-designation of a variety of special educational provision, but the reality is these units initially remained adjustment units or assessment centres. The same building, the same kids, the same staff, and the same practice. I have the advantage there in so far as I have none of those problems here in Warrington. On the other hand, at least some provision existed in these areas rather than none at all. These establishments also have some LEA support and guid-ance in the transition to becoming a PRU. But the practice leaves a great deal to be desired. I visited one such PRU where I recall talking to a twelve-year-old pupil who had been at the PRU since he was five. A special unit doesn't suddenly become a PRU no matter how well managed. In a sense, starting with nothing had some advantages, although the lack of planning has perhaps meant the disadvantages outweigh the advantages in the final analysis.

SR   If I was an LEA officer looking at the process of setting up a PRU and I approached you for advice, what would you say to me?

PC   I think if you take troubled and troublesome kids from different schools and put them together what inevitably happens is initially the group behaviour doesn't improve. It actually deteriorates and is generally determined by the less well behaved individuals in the group. It almost becomes a competition in misbehaviour. I think the way forward must rest with developing effective support services which maintain young people with problems in mainstream school. I also think that when you're talking about a PRU working with small groups of children in a very different way to mainstream, aiming to give them skills to survive in the mainstream, I think it is a nonsense to assume these kids will transfer those skills from this setting into another setting. I think if we are to stand any chance of success, we have to work on a part-time basis, supporting the pupil in the mainstream, and enskilling both the pupil and the school staff.

Managing the support successfully involves working in partnership with staff, and, in my own position particularly, working with the heads of each school. I certainly need to be a politician. I also need to have professional credibility. I think you have got to look the part – have street credibility. I don't say that lightly ... when I talk about professional credibility I mean you have to be able to back up what you say and deliver effective strategies in behaviour management, or stages of behaviour modification. It has to be delivered in ways which are accessible for staff and will work. In Warrington, the PRU faces twelve different heads in twelve different schools, and each of them wants to know what you're going to offer their school. Each school in the area has individual needs, let's call them special needs, and each school will have a different set of demands to make of the PRU.

The rights and wrongs of this approach are open to argument. One opinion I've heard expressed is that we're all in it together and we should pull together. But when you reflect upon how this government has encouraged open competition amongst schools, for pupils and for funding, and reinforced this with accountability that labels a school a winner or a loser, it is not surprising that heads first look hard for what their own school is going to get from an initiative or activity. If you sell behaviour management, you've got to talk to the heads and show how this will work in their school. You have got to actually deliver the goods. It is no use at all simply talking a good fight. You have got to work with their kids and effect some sort of change.

SR   Is your own experience in secure provision an advantage in working with the children and managing staff dealing with these same children?

PC   Yes. For example, it has influenced the assessment and referral system we have developed. We have devised a referral form and we require detailed assessment of a pupil's behaviour together with a record of intervention stages 1 and 2 described in the SEN code of practice. We regard ourselves as a stage 3 intervention and we think it is very useful and important that detailed information is kept as part of an assessment, including information from individual subject teachers, which we analyse, using a computerized program we have developed. We have found that this methodical approach to referral and planning is absolutely necessary for successful support and intervention.

Recently we began working with an individual pupil from one school who was experiencing severe emotional and behaviour difficulties resulting in an intolerable level of disruption. The young man's party piece was to leap on to a desk in nearly every lesson, and make monkey noises for the amusement of the class. I took the class for a social skills lesson, during which I tackled the behaviour head on, giving the pupil the opportunity to perform. He thought I was 'insane' and refused. But this allowed us as a group to move on to talking about why he was disrupting lessons and misbehaving.

I was able to encourage the class to focus upon the attention-seeking behaviour, and we were able to see that desire for self-esteem and attention from peers was being sought by this young man, at any price. Even negative attention from staff was better than nothing at all. We were able to work through this together and as a consequence, not only did this pupil not repeat the behaviour during his time attending the PRU, but to my knowledge he has not done the same since returning to his mainstream school.

SR   In terms of your own experience of headship during this first year, are there any particular times you can identify as high or low points in your work?

PC   It's a story of little victories, I think. Recently, I visited a local school where I was involved in an INSET day on behaviour management. At the end of the day, a young female teacher introduced herself. She was a form tutor for a young man who we had been working with and said what a wonderful job we had done, and how he had returned a different lad. That was heartening, although we don't profess to offer a magical cure.

I guess that working with people is an important part of my work, which I enjoy. A lot of the work is with individual kids and with staff, and the process of building a relationship figures very much in what

I think is good management practice. I think it would be fair to say that managing the PRU involves very close proximity to staff and kids, and that you become immersed in a series of individual relationships.

I teach! I'll be teaching this afternoon. It is very much like this in special education. You were a headteacher in a special school – you know what I'm talking about – you probably washed the cups in the staff room. I remember the time you painted the staff room with some colleagues because there wasn't the money from the LEA to do it. You worked with children and you taught. You did it all! There is no real distance.

SR   How do you measure success in your work as a headteacher?

PC   There have been small successes, or little 'victories', I think I called them a moment ago, throughout this year. A small number of schools wanted to send their school rejects here and have them stay. Full-time! I call it 'respite'. A number of schools were looking for respite. I have certainly locked horns with a number of people over this issue. We're not full-time any more after an initial period at the start of the year. The building here won't allow it. Anyway, I don't believe full-time is the way to go forward. In fact, we operate a point 5 placement at the moment, with linked support in mainstream. We're working closely with the local college of further education, the Warrington Collegiate Institute, which is great. It helps us considerably in terms of resources and facilities. We also offer an additional half day of support which entails going into each mainstream school and working any way the school wants us to with individual pupils. It might be support in the classroom, it might be withdrawal, it might be teaching social skills, it might be counselling (with a small 'c'). It can be any one or more of these things which we negotiate with the school. That's the package we have developed and are working to improve.

SR   Is this in fact a description of your vision for the PRU?

PC   Yes.

SR   How was this vision developed during your headship?

PC   It has evolved. If I had been given a disused junior school, for example, as is sometimes the situation when a special unit is set up, a building with an outside play area, and scope for organizing a school day, I'd have probably been far more flexible about medium-term off-site placement, both in terms of taking kids and retaining them. But I would still insist upon putting a time limit on length of placement. You asked about the first week in the job. Well, in terms of placement, the LEA had this model of the young person being placed in the PRU for eight weeks, I asked why eight weeks? I think the number had come from the top of somebody's head. They thought eight weeks sounded like a sensible period, but it could have been ten, thirteen, twenty weeks.

I asked them then, well what do you expect to happen by the end of this period? One outspoken head declared that if there was a stage 17 in the code of practice, a pupil he wanted to refer to the PRU would have breached it! He wanted the kid out of his school and helped. He should not be in his school. I asked what it was exactly people were expecting at the end of a short period in the PRU. This particular pupil was very difficult. He'd been diagnosed Attention Deficit and Hyperactive Disorder and was in a mainstream class year seven with a reading age less than six. The lessons didn't make any sense to him. He was causing mayhem. We initially had to work hard at developing a realistic expectation and appropriate use of the PRU.

SR   What do you expect of your own staff and how do you measure their success?

PC   I have been here right from the start and I have appointed all of the staff. I've been very very fortunate – the staff are excellent. We've got a really strong cohesive team with what could really be described as 'Tenko' spirit, a backs-against-the-wall camaraderie, an esprit de corps which reminds you of Colditz, the Blitz, perhaps I exaggerate slightly but I've always been prone to hyperbole. But it is true to say we have all experienced some difficult times in this first year, and now we're beginning to see a chink of light, we're still here and we're united in a good team.

My management style is aimed at maintaining a team approach – it's about open-door management and delegation. I don't want to take everything on, I want to delegate. I also want to be surrounded by competent staff. I know people who have taken a position of power and then appoint people who they feel they can manipulate or dominate. I don't want that at all – I'm not in the least interested in megalomania.

SR   Do you get a buzz out of exercising power?

PC   I enjoy decision-making but not necessarily exercising power. If people call me 'boss' I still get embarrassed.

SR   Do you think you would tackle a third headship differently? How has this post influenced your approach to management?

PC   I've learned an incredible amount in a year in this post. The experience has involved a steep learning curve. I can't say I've enjoyed all of it. It's almost like learning to cope with what you can or can't change. What you have no control over, you must learn to recognize, and not to worry about it. There was a time when we first opened when I could have gone under, as problems were flying at us thick and fast. There was a lot of pressure. I acknowledge that. I had to sort of 'helicopter above and look down on the scene' to take perspective. It wasn't easy and there are still a lot of problems but I now feel I'm better able to manage the process.

SR   How do you manage to ensure good teaching and learning takes place in the PRU?

PC   One very important aspect of working in a PRU is the small size of the teaching group and the total number of pupils in the building. We can talk curriculum differentiation until we're blue in the face but the reality here is we have differentiation thrust upon us. I wanted the schools not to just throw a disruptive pupil into the PRU for however long, but to accept the responsibility for continuity in the curriculum and producing work which we could continue with the pupil, albeit in a different setting.

We work one to one, small group, whatever's appropriate. I recently worked on an English project with a pupil and we were able to work one to one, then he transferred to using IT with another teacher on the same project. The outcome was a very professionally presented piece of work – an achievement this pupil had never ever realized before in school. The pupil was able to take this project back to his mainstream school and he subsequently received an 'A' for the work from his subject teacher. I think that this aspect of special education, that is, small numbers, individual attention and curriculum flexibility, especially as it appears in a PRU, enables me to have a clear idea of the standard of teaching and learning taking place in the service we offer. I think this is probably because of the closeness involved in working in a PRU.

I think another thing we haven't touched upon is that special education teachers are very definitely a discrete type of teacher. They are very individual and I do believe, although it's a generalization, but I do feel a special education teacher is not afraid to go into the staff room at coffee break and say he or she has had a terrible lesson. You don't get that in mainstream so much – it's far more defensive – the inference is that you do not go in and talk about your failures because this would make you less of a teacher in the eyes of your colleagues. In this context, you're sometimes dealing with very defensive teachers. I mean, if I talk to less experienced staff, I'll say something like, if you're having a problem with Jimmy Smith, everyone will be having some sort of problem with Jimmy Smith, whether or not they admit it. We work very closely in the PRU and I can't imagine even beginning the same conversation by saying, as I have heard several times in a mainstream staff room, 'He's never any trouble when he's with me!'

SR   How do you manage your own professional well-being and professional development?

PC   I think my professional development began very early in this particular headship. I was invited to join the heads' association (WASH). I am now a fully recognized member of that group. I began by learning on the job and coming from special education to this situation was certainly straight in at the deep end. I am now fully involved in the decision-making forum, although I think it would be fair to say that I do listen and learn more than I speak. I am in a position where I do know what's going on in the Warrington area on a day-to-day basis.

As I have stated earlier, we also have local government reorganization taking place and Warrington will become a unitary authority on the first of April 1998 and that's very exciting. There's a lot happening within this process of change and nobody is quite sure about how it will all end. To gain some idea of this you have to remember that Cheshire is a massive shire county with a population of just less than a million. Warrington and Halton are going unitary, and that means Cheshire will lose a third of its population. Warrington has a population of around one hundred and eighty thousand people, and will be a fair-sized unitary authority, much bigger than some of the Welsh authorities, some of which are around a hundred thousand people.

In terms of professional development, I'm visiting all twelve schools in the Warrington area and looking at good practice. It's quite a privileged opportunity. I'm also currently considering the use of GEST money I can spend. I was successful in a bid for monies in January 1996, and I plan to spend it over the next three years funding the secondment of teachers from mainstream schools to teach in the PRU. Now – it's going to work on a two-way basis, because we're going to offer them training and support in developing an expertise in behaviour management and behaviour intervention and they are going to contribute to broadening our academic curriculum. There are some exciting times ahead. I really am in a unique and rich environment, in terms of professional development opportunity. It's exciting. There are some frustrating twists to the work but it is nevertheless very exciting.

SR   What about specific INSET for management? Headteachers are notoriously bad at looking after their own specific training. Do you spend INSET money on yourself?

PC   In terms of management training, no, I don't. In terms of more general professional development – I've just put in for a couple of English courses which I thought looked interesting. Possibly management-orientated training may appear later on my agenda. I think if I had my time again I would probably have thought about completing an MEd in Educational Management instead of Special Educational Needs.

SR   Ted Wragg says 'You don't have to be a "nutter" to join the "barmy army" but ...'. I know this is more or less the end of your first year here, but do you think headship has become much more difficult and do you still enjoy it?

PC   I think he's right – but I think he's really talking about secondary heads, and perhaps not so much heads in special education. I'm guessing but it's more likely – no – in retrospect I think he's talking about all heads and headship.

SR   So – do you think you might be less barmy than some colleagues because you've had the sense to stay in special education?

PC   Well – no. No! I wouldn't say that exactly! I've always said this job is not easy. When you're working . . . particularly with EBD kids, and – well, do you know the working definition for EBD? It stands for *Ever So Bloody Difficult.* I suppose we could just as easily apply what I'm going to say to secondary heads, but headship is the type of job which can ruin your health. It can literally kill you. We all know 'horror stories' of headships ruining people's lives and leaving them physically as well as mentally shattered.

Yes – I think it has got more difficult. I think a lot of the changes the government has introduced recently don't make any sense. I think the changes were brought in by people who know very little about education. I think this is even more true of special education than it is of mainstream, but you can apply it to both. I mean, when you stop and consider cost-effectiveness and economies of scale, pupils with SEN are simply not cost-effective. They are a financial liability. They are very expensive. EBD kids are not as expensive as some other kids with SEN, but you're talking of a placement in the secure unit I worked, and admittedly you're talking about young people who are a danger to society, you're talking about a cost of a hundred and twenty thousand pounds per child per year. I would imagine for hearing or visually impaired kids, or kids with severe learning difficulty, or autism, an out-of-county placement will probably cost you around sixty to seventy thousand pounds. You simply cannot look at a market economy in terms of that kind of reality.

I do think there are rewarding and exciting aspects to headship, and leadership still represents a challenge to which people want to respond, and they are still willing to take on the job. One exciting and stimulating aspect of the leadership role I have discovered in the last two years here is my involvement in the creation of a 'new' 'LEA' for the new unitary authority of Warrington. This has run in parallel and often coincided with the development of the PRU. The two really cannot be separated. I am, as I think I have already explained, a member of the WASH and I have also become a member of Warrington Borough Council's Working Group looking at the provision for SEN in the new 'LEA'.

To sum up, I regularly have the realization that I am learning so much in such a short period of time that it is breathtaking. It is also very very exciting. It is also gratifying to feel that I am making a contribution, albeit a small contribution, in policy-making and the management of what is going to be far-reaching change in the area's educational provision. There is a sense of reward and a motivation in this which helps to keep you on track, in spite of the many pressures which Ted Wragg does rightly point out are also a very real part of the day-to-day task facing us in the educational world.

SR   So – would you say you're still enjoying headship in spite of these pressures?

PC   Yes – I think this appointment has given me a new challenge. I needed a different challenge at this point in my career. I am confident that it is right for me and I'll move forward, build on my time here at Warrington.

SR   Finally – if we think about the many changes we've experienced in the last few years in special education, can I ask, how do you see the future for special education and its management?

PC   I think that people have got to come to terms with the reality of special education. I feel that there are a lot of people who are not practitioners who talk about reintegration of pupils whom practitioners know couldn't be successfully reintegrated. There isn't a way back for a very small percentage of children. I do feel that a lot of theorists were talking about children being included in mainstream when, unless mainstream education changes significantly in the way that they operate, and I personally don't see a great deal of hope of schools radically changing how they operate, reintegration for some children will not work. The mainstream schools may tinker and to some extent accommodate children, and make no mistake some schools do very good work with children experiencing less severe needs, but there will always be a need for special provision.

SR   OK – where does that finally leave you, looking forward to the next four or five years, as a head of a PRU?

PC   For me, a PRU cannot operate in isolation. The PRU has got to be part of a wider behaviour support system. It's got to be really flexible, it's got to respond to the needs of schools and individual children. For example, if a head has an urgent problem, they've got to be able to get to the phone and we have to be able to respond. Now – whether it's a matter of our going in and providing support, or whether we take the young person out of school to disarm a powder keg, a situation which can often occur, we do need to be flexible and quick in our response.

The PRU overall must remain part of the wider behaviour support system which exists in an area. We should really be looking at a schoolgirl mother and baby unit being part of this system, we should be looking at school phobic kids, there are not really many true phobics, but they are out there, we ought to be looking at a key stage 3 element and a key stage 4 element. This is important, because one of the big things is that it is a completely different ball game for each of the key stages. I would operate each completely differently.

Educationally, philosophically, you're working towards very different objectives in each of these key stages.

SR   Where does that leave the headteacher of a PRU in relation to the job task and shaping up a service in a rapidly changing educational world?

PC   I think the headteacher of a PRU has got to be very strong, offer firm leadership, and must, on a personal level as well as a professional level, accept what they can and cannot do. They cannot be all things to all people. When you look at staffing, you look at the limited number of available staff, the number of hours in a day, the number of kids out there that need help, you've got to prioritize, and you've got to be strong.

One of the things I did, early in my time here, and looking back it was very helpful, perhaps a watershed, or a turning point, was when we felt pressured into looking after a cohort of pupils on a full-time basis here, and I said 'enough'. Now – very early on in the process I realized this isn't the way it should be, I made a commitment to myself that this did not make sense, it was not good for the staff, it was not fair to the kids. I would not again accept any full-time attendance programme in this building. I returned to my vision for the unit as a service which offered part-time support in mainstream with an emphasis on working together with schools in order that we maintain 'mainstream' education for these pupils, not compound its destruction. I see that approach as being the way forward.

SR   Any final thoughts, Phil, about leadership in special education?

PC   I think when we talk about special education, I think the biggest problem we face is that we've got a *finite* resource and budget and we've got *in-finite* needs. When we talk about the market economy, I think we fail to see the mismatch. I see people making decisions about provision for pupils with SEN and they're heading towards a nervous breakdown because of the pressure it is putting upon them. I'm not talking about myself here, I'm talking about dedicated, able professionals in special services, in LEAs, going to appeals and tribunals and having to say to people, to parents, no we're not able to do this, we can't afford it.

The government has led parents to believe that there are no limits, that the pot is bottomless. They have a parents' charter stating parental rights and not surprisingly, parents think they can have what they want. They can think they can nominate a residential special school charging eighty thousand pounds in another county or sometimes even another country and the LEA must fund it.

SR   So – a considerable challenge facing anyone involved in leadership or the management of special education?

PC   I think so – the challenge is there and the important thing is how we rise to meet the challenge, how we manage the provision. It's early days still here at Warrington, but the biggest problems for special education still remain lack of funds, and a lack of resource. What we must do here in Warrington is make the most of the opportunities that unitary status will offer us. To me, and crucially for the successful management of special education, by which I mean ensuring we are about meeting the needs of pupils with SEN, this means all 'relevant' agencies working together – education, social services, health, youth services, educational welfare services, educational psychologists – to create a co-ordinated provision for children with SEN.

CHAPTER 6

In praise of inclusivity: managing special education in a large secondary school

JOHN EVANS with Peter Ribbins

John Evans has for fourteen years been headteacher of Bodmin Community College, a large mainstream secondary school for students aged eleven to eighteen. In line with Cornwall's 'policy' on inclusion, there are over 120 children with some kind of designated special need within the school including 27 who are located in a special SLD unit. After studying chemistry at university, Evans worked in a technical school and then a comprehensive school before moving to teacher training at St John's College in York and Newman College in Birmingham. He then taught in Cumberland and Derbyshire, as deputy head. After two years of deputy headship he was appointed to his first headship in Kirklees. Four years later he moved to Bodmin.

PR   Can you tell me about your early life and its influence on you?

JE   I was born in Oldham, one of three, a twin sister and younger brother. Mother and Father were working-class, very much so. Father spent most of his life in the army. He ran away from home at twelve to join the Royal Horse Artillery as a stable lad, stayed until just before war broke, was recalled and served until 1946. He was a Welshman who came to Oldham because his older sister, the person who held the family together, was moved there. Mother and Father were each the second youngest of eight children. We were a Victorian family, they were old parents. My dad met my mum in Oldham and they got married just before the war. The three of us were born during the war. We were a close-knit, an aunties and uncles type, family, certainly on my mother's side.

PR   What of their education?

JE   Dad could barely read, Mum went to school until she was twelve and then went mornings at school and afternoons at the cotton mill. She was a fluent reader and would have, had times been different, gone on with her education. She was a clever lady. When my dad left the army, we lived in a two up and two down terraced house with an outside toilet and a cobbled back yard. Mum and Dad were in their forties when we were born. They had no skills. Father became a lorry and coach driver and worked all hours to keep us. If he didn't work we didn't eat. I was virtually at university before I had a new set of clothes. It was usually hand-downs from older cousins. But Dad really appreciated the value of education and worked and worked to let us have it – eighty or ninety hours of cleaning offices and coaches as well as driving to keep us at school.

As children we were very conscious of this. So the biggest influences on us really were Mum and Dad. Mum with her reading, she encouraged us to read, I was a member of two free public libraries. I used to go to the library every day and read and read. My sister did the same but was not quite so academic.

PR   What do you remember of your primary school?

JE   It was a little back street Lancashire primary school with separate infants and juniors as well as a senior school, the secondary modern, which was above the top floor of the juniors. Everyone knew each other. Our next door neighbours' kids and the kids across the road all went to the same little school. Everyone was in each other's pockets. We helped each other out in hard times, they often were. Neighbours and relatives rallied round, we wouldn't have survived on occasions without that.

PR   There was that strong sense of community?

JE   Oh yes; and school was good. I enjoyed it. They didn't have many eleven-pluses. I think I was the first for several years. I then went to the grammar school. I was very nervous. I had a stutter all through my schooldays, especially when excited. I had therapy and it did help. Even so I still talk rather quickly, trying to get the words out. Summarizing, I have got a lot of love for my mum and dad. They were the main influences on me. I also found some of my primary school teachers very helpful. It was at that time that I decided to be a teacher. Well an accountant, a barber or a teacher. I might have ended up as an accountant but for the respect in which my dad and mum held teachers.

PR   What were the key values of your family?

JE   Work. Work and friendship and helping each other.

PR   What was the eleven-plus transition like?

JE   Two things were difficult. One, I was one of very few going to the grammar school. I did know somebody there, a neighbour. Two, my twin sister, who I was very close to and still am, didn't pass. We were separated for the first time. Other things made it difficult. My parents couldn't afford a uniform. A conglomerate of aunties and uncles and

Mum and Dad got me a blazer. All the rest were hand-me-downs.

Two things happened which helped to settle me in very quickly. First, Mrs Morris, an English teacher, our form teacher, helped me. She was a weak teacher in terms of discipline, even in the grammar school she had problems, but she was kind to me in so many ways. Second, I made two good friends in the school straight away, two boys. One is my life-long friend. He has been married to my twin sister for over thirty years. He was in callipers, a poor little boy.

PR   So he had even greater problems?

JE   Yes, he used to have to be carried around, because the school wasn't equipped for disabled children. He is one of my heroes. If people said he couldn't do something he'd show them he could. When he was told he wouldn't walk unaided he said within two years he would walk! He did and became a champion runner and rugby player. By the time he was fourteen he was free of his callipers. At fifth form level he was told he wouldn't get many O Levels but got sufficient to get him into the sixth form where he followed the course I did. He was then told he shouldn't apply to university but for college. He was interested in becoming a teacher. But he went to Liverpool University and gained a science and maths degree and then we came together again to do our PGCEs at Manchester. I had real fun but the PGCE was a bit of a waste of time. My brother-in-law was then and always has been since a major influence on me.

PR   Can you describe the grammar school?

JE   It was mixed, with a three-form entry. My primary school gave me a pen for passing the eleven-plus. A fountain pen, unheard of in those days. All through my school days it was ink, biros were just coming in. I was very proud of it but it was stolen. Mrs Morris replaced it quietly for me. This was typical of her. I didn't dare tell them at home it had been stolen. I'd have been accused of not having looked after it properly. I think my mum knew. I enjoyed my time at the school and did quite well. When I got to the sixth form I came into my own academically. The primary school had warned my parents that although I had done well to get my eleven-plus, when I got to grammar school I would have to accept I would not be top dog anymore. I didn't expect to be but turned out to be quite bright. For me, work came first, and so I did very well at O Level.

PR   Were you top dog at primary school? Did you see yourself as this?

JE   No. It has always come as a bit of a shock to find I am better than I think I would be. I know people reckon I can sort problems out. I put this down to being prepared to work very hard rather than being clever. That's how I've got on, hard work.

My grammar school experience was marred slightly at the end. From thirteen I worked with my dad and brother washing coaches and offices and cleaning cars, weekdays and weekends, to put money in the family coffers. Mum didn't work, she was semi-invalid from the cotton mill with lung disease. I worked to help keep the family and continued to do so during the sixth form. I had done it and had still, to my surprise, been made head boy. I think they recognized I was a good organizer. So these years were one of the best periods of my life. But it was all rather spoiled because the head, a traditional grammar school head, didn't understand the situation in which boys who were very bright but very poor could find themselves. I had done my exams and there were five weeks to the end of term. My father had organized for me to work at a coach station for four weeks, return for the last week of term, and then work through the summer to put together a nest egg for clothes for university. At the time all I had was on my back or in the wash. He was proud I had won a place and wanted me to be able to go like anybody else. But when, on the morning of my last A Level, I told the head, he was very upset. I made it clear I intended to return for the last week to undertake all the formalities which went with being head boy. I wouldn't miss that for the world, I had enjoyed being at school. But I stressed how necessary earning this money was. Anyway, in the morning post my dad got a letter from the head threatening to withdraw his references if I didn't continue to go to school. He thought it appalling and was determined I would go to work. So, for the first and only time ever, he visited the grammar school. He may have been illiterate but certainly wasn't inarticulate, a Welshman with the gift of the gab. Mum was frightened because he was a very, very tough, physical man. She was frightened he'd hit the head or swear at him because he had a full vocabulary from his thirty years in the army. But he was well behaved. He said if I had to come back to school, I would do so because he didn't want to spoil my record which had always been excellent. But he made it clear that he was very angry and said to the head 'If my son comes in, he has to work, he's not going in just to sit about, make sure he has definite work'. That didn't please the teachers because they had to make special arrangements to teach me. When it was learnt I had won a state scholarship, the school had only had four in twenty-five years, the head was full of the honour of it. He had always thought this and that of me. I remember feeling the sense of hypocrisy of it all.

PR   What did you learn from this?

JE   For a long time it put me off all thoughts of being a head. I had been at the forefront of what was happening in the school for two years, I'd been prefect and head boy. You'd think he would know something about my family and its situation. Most of the teachers did, some helped me out. They would say 'Save your bus fare I'll drop you off, I'm going to my brother's anyway'. It was a very close community in some ways.

PR   They understood but he didn't?

JE   He was a pompous man who was out of touch. But this was not true of many of the other teachers. I respected them and was not put off teaching. Early on, I went as a student to the secondary modern school my brother had attended. It was dreadful. The teachers were brilliant or dreadful. Too many would say, leaving the staff room, 'What shall we do today? I'll get them doing some colouring, yes I'll do that'. To this day I believe that my brother who is bright but not academic was badly served. He now holds a responsible position in a nationally reputed civil engineering company and is highly regarded, but this owes little to his schooling. Even so the teachers there taught me a great deal, good and bad. That is why I'm very pro-comprehensive. I am for a school for all abilities in which the head and teachers know as much as they can about the background of the children.

PR   You did your degree then trained as a teacher. That was not a memorable experience?

JE   In terms of the time I spent at the university it wasn't. In terms of the time I spent in schools on teaching practice it was. I was allowed some choice and picked a big secondary modern in Oldham for my main practice and a technical high school for my shorter practice. I was known in both. My sister went as a thirteen-plus transfer to the high school and I had attended functions there with her. She was quite high-profile in the school. I enjoyed my teaching practice there and met some very good teachers. The experience reaffirmed my preju-dice in favour of the comprehensive school.

PR   What happened then?

JE   I was offered jobs at both schools and chose the latter. I lived at home and could help out financially. I remember my first month's salary. It was paid in a wage packet, cash not a cheque. I handed it to my mum as my dad, brother and sister had done. It amounted to £53.00 net pay for my good honours degree and other qualifications. On the same day my brother handed over his week's salary, he'd been apprentice to a joiner and then got work as a skilled carpenter on the building sites, he drew £106.00. Exactly twice as much for the week's work as I earned for my first month's work, outside all the moon-lighting I'd been doing. When Dad eventually came home my mum very proudly showed him my first official wage packet as a teacher, £53.00 net. He asked 'How much did our David bring home?' '£106.00.' I'll never forget, he looked at me and said 'Has it been worth it?' and I said 'Yes'. If you ask me that again today I would say the same.

PR   Did he look surprised?

JE   He was pleased really. But I had to continue moonlighting at the travel agency and bus station trying to put money together to get married eventually. After I'd been teaching for four years, two years in technical high school, two years in comprehensive school at which I got my first promotion, I was offered the post of general manager to a big travel agency and bus company at three times the salary I was earning as a teacher.

PR   Were you tempted?

JE   A little, I was looking for a change. But I said no but carried on helping the company during the holidays and at every weekend. I would finish school at four on a Friday afternoon, go straight home and have my tea and then be on the five o'clock bus to Manchester where the bus station was located. I would start work there at six and finish at two on Saturday morning. My dad and brother also worked in the garage: they cleaned the coaches whilst I was sorting them out. Then dad would drive us back home to Oldham in a coach and I'd be up again at five in the morning, back at the coach station at six and work until six in the evening, then go back home and back on Sunday morning for four hours. I did that for my first eleven years. It was the only way I could put money together. But I enjoyed the work. It goes back to the work ethic I talked of. I was working alongside my dad and brother and we were all doing it for the family, not for ourselves.

I was then tempted to go into teacher training, partly because I wanted to be more academic. I was still quite a powerful academic chemist. So I got a job in St John's College in York, but didn't like it. Although those immediately around me in the science and maths department were real and strong people, I didn't really like the College. I liked York, I did a bit at the university education department but left after a year. Then tried to get a job back in schools but the salary position had changed. I had gone quite high up the salary scale by moving into college education. To match that I had to apply for jobs in school at a higher rate than my experience allowed. In the end I took a Senior Lectureship at Newman College of Education, Birmingham, to start up chemistry in the science department. I have never regretted this. I was there for four and a half years.

I got heavily involved in the Nuffield Secondary Science Project. I did a lot of in-service work up and down the country on behalf of the project. I felt I was on a winner. You had good stuff to work on, good equipment, you couldn't lose. There was real talent behind it with good writers. I enjoyed this aspect of my work but it was hard to attract science students. I liked college life. I was Chairman of the Common Room Association and elected by the student body for four consecutive years to be Secretary of the Social Club. I can't say I liked teaching practice and didn't enjoy the teaching much. I did a lot of voluntary teaching in schools on Nuffield. You would take an in-service course and the teachers would say although they liked the ideas 'They wouldn't work in my school'. I would reply 'I'll come and show you'. I rarely had any problems. Even so, eventually, I got fed up even with this and thought I must get back into a school. At the time, I had no ideas about being head but just wanted to go back to a comprehensive school with real children. I went to a school in Northwest Cumberland. Why there I don't know except that it came up. Really it was a secondary modern school, there were still grammar schools in the neighbouring towns. I was appalled to discover that some staff moved house to get their children into the grammar school area. I enjoyed my time in Cumberland. It was a small place like Bodmin. It was very run down. There was 35 per cent unemployment. It was a big community school doing a good job on the outskirts of a small town. Not a lot was happening, so we formed a club. It was called a boys' club, this got better grants, but it was a mixed club really.

PR   What post did you hold there?

JE   Head of Science. I did lots of community work in the town. I was very busy. There was no time allocation for my post. We were desperately short-staffed in the science department. I took double classes, sixty children in a class for practical science which wasn't easy. I'd teach in the dinner times or the evenings. I'd said to the head I'd stay for four years. During that time my own boys attended a delightful, all-age, village-type school. But by the end they were beginning to outgrow that. But that was only one problem. Mum had Alzheimer's disease and dad was struggling to cope. My brother was still in the area but my sister had moved to Essex where my brother-in-law had become a deputy head. So we needed to get a bit closer to home. I looked for advisers' jobs particularly on the teaching of science to less able children. I talked to my head and asked him what he would suggest. He suggested a deputy headship. I said 'No, its not for me. I'm not the man for checking up on the toilets and lining boys up in the yard. I'll do more than that, I'm going to be an adviser.' I thought I had the contacts, working for Nuffield up and down the country. He replied 'You don't want to be an adviser. You need to be able to see a job right through. As an adviser you have the ideas but have to leave them to other people to bring to fruition. That's not you.' So I said 'I'll apply for a couple of advisers' posts at the same time as a couple of deputy headships'. The first thing that came up was in Glossop in Derbyshire. So I went there as deputy head.

When I got to Derbyshire I found a new head had been brought in to tighten up the school. He was a Yugoslavian who spoke heavily accented English. He was a tough man but his problem was the staff weren't with him. I found the step from head of department to deputy headship the biggest I have ever made. I'm proud of the fact that in my eighteen years of headship, five of seven deputies I've helped appoint are now heads and good heads. I have always told them that the step to deputy headship is much bigger than that to headship. I think most of them would agree.

PR   It was more than lining boys up and checking the toilets?

JE   I was surprised at the expectations of you that other people held. In part this might have been due to the set-up in that school. I and the new head were appointed at the same time but after a few months he had a serious road accident followed by a stroke. He never returned. The previous deputy was made acting head and I was left to get on with my responsibilities. The expectations staff had of us were high. He was probably the best educationally, socially minded person I've worked with. He really knew kids, working-class, white, coloured, whatever and their families. He was a good classroom teacher and enjoyed the regard of the staff, but wasn't, in my view, the most effective manager or leader. A lot was thrown to me at that time and that's perhaps why I say the step from head of even a big department to a deputy is so great.

If that was one shock the other was to find I was good at it. I enjoyed it. I enjoyed working long hours. My colleague spent a long time as acting head but when they made the position substantive I talked it through with him. It was only two years but I said I was going to move on. I started to apply for deputy headships at bigger schools and one or two headships, in the area my mum and dad lived. Mum was worse by this time and Father was having a difficult time looking after her. They were in their seventies and he was still working part-time.

PR   When did you really realize you wanted to be a head?

JE   I slipped into it. I was looking for a change of job really. I was fortunate to get the first headship I was interviewed for. I applied for four deputy headships and three headships in the Lancashire/Yorkshire area. I remember my first interview. You had to convince the officers on the first day to get to the second day with the Education Committee. There were twelve of us on the first day with four to be selected for the day after. This was in Kirklees, salt of the earth Yorkshire folk. It was Tory then but with some serious left-wing Labour people. I was first to be interviewed. It was an aggressive interview, I was asked straight off 'Teachers waste money don't they?'. I was ready for that. I can be quite aggressive and I'm best when I'm being put on the spot. I said 'You'll have to prove that to me. I can certainly show you waste in local government. If you want to get down to cases, let's discuss cases.' I got the job.

PR   Were you surprised?

JE   I was amazed. There had been a long wait before the interviews got under way and the four of us were chatting. Two disagreed with the other two. The issue was should you give the answers you think the appointments panel want or those you really believe? My view was headship was going to be such a tough job, particularly in the school we were being interviewed for, that you had to be true to yourself. You would regret promising things you couldn't deliver. I wouldn't want to be in a job that was against my core beliefs and principles. One agreed with me, the others didn't. I reckon to this day it was between me and him. My dad believed in honesty and truthfulness. I've a reputation for being blunt here. Partly because of my accent, in Cornwall I am thought of as John Evans 'The Blunt Yorkshire Man' and not 'The Warm Lancashire Lad'. I think I'm fairly warm as a person, as you would expect from a Lancashire lad!

After this, the deputy chair of governors ran me down to the train. I remember thinking after I have told my wife and family, we would get into the car and drive straight over to my mum and dad to tell them with a bottle of whisky. I was quite shocked to get it.

PR   How did you prepare for headship?

JE   This is the advice I give. First, I write the best letter of application I possibly can. I write a letter for the school I'm applying for, not the job I'm doing now. I identify eight or nine key areas in which questions might be raised, like discipline and curriculum. The higher up the scale you go the more general the areas need to be. In those days you had two very different audiences to persuade. There was the professionals, the officers, the advisers and I could usually get past them. I could talk their language. Then there is a completely different audience, the councillors, the governors. That day in Kirklees I got there an hour early and walked the streets around the town hall practising my replies to the areas I had prepared. With an accent like mine you don't come over as glib. I can't do glib anyway. If anyone tells me, as did one of those interviewed with me for my present post, 'I don't prepare for interviews' I would think 'You don't bloody deserve to get the job'. I have found of the areas I prepare I usually got a chance to talk of five or six. What I say is carefully thought through in anticipation. This does not lead me to lengthy answers but enables me to make the points I want to make. Preparation is important. I've undertaken quite a bit in preparation for our interview today. But I'm no good from notes. I stumble and stammer. I'm better thinking things through and then tracking this into my mind. It is the same with assemblies. I am often asked 'You don't refer to a note in an assembly taking fifteen minutes?' I say 'That's because I've spent an hour preparing it'.

PR   What was your first headship like?

JE   It was in a split site, formed from the amalgamation of two single-sex grammar schools and two single-sex secondary modern schools. The buildings were old and battered, the furniture and equipment were dreadful. Prior to interview we spent day one in the school and had a chance to have a good look round. I knew it was going to be tough but didn't doubt I could do the job. My experience in Derbyshire had proved to me I could relate to what teachers want the boss to be. I knew there would be a lack of cohesion given that four schools had been put together and that not all the staff would want to be there. They had come from small, single-sex, selective and non-selective, single-site schools into a large, co-educational, comprehensive school on a split site. In the four and a half years I was there the school went from one hundred to eight hundred Asian, Muslim children. I enjoy working with Muslims, sometimes the culture clash could be difficult but during my theological studies at King's I had learnt quite a bit about Islam, and some of the kids were delightful. But the staff weren't prepared for them. For some this was the last straw.

I had three main things to try to do, none easy. First, to get some organization into the place. Second, to cope with a rapid expansion in the numbers of Asian children, some from fundamentalist families many unable to speak English. We had a massive growth in the staff through Section 11. Third, to do something with the curriculum which was based on what had happened in the grammar schools. It was called a comprehensive but wasn't. There was a big tail of indigenous Yorkshire children with special needs, there was a massive tail of E2L children with learning and language difficulties.

I got stuck into this. I tried to get the management organized. I did lots of work with heads of department and others, to show them they had a managerial role. I don't see myself as a theorist but I am big on practical suggestions about management and, in particular, the management issues related to those with special and ethnic needs. Let me illustrate this with a case. The best student I ever taught was there. She was a young Asian girl who came to this country with her family. She joined the school at thirteen and went into an E2L class. In two years she had progressed sufficiently in her English to join a mainstream class. Later she joined my CSE chemistry class. There were twenty-six Asian children and half a dozen white children. She was one of eight girls and got a grade one. It was clear she was a very intelligent and articulate young woman. But at sixteen she was going to leave school, her marriage was arranged. It is hard to see why girls in this situation should want to try at school. This girl did, she tried and she tried. It became obvious she was very academic and very bright. I persuaded her father to let her stay on into the sixth form college. I had to do some work from a distance because I'd left before she went to the sixth form college. The marriage was put back. Eventually I persuaded the dad by correspondence and with the support of colleagues from the college that she should go to university. Her dad took her to university in Bradford every day. Now she's graduated and she has children. I still correspond with her.

During those years, I became very involved in the National Association of Multi-Racial Education, I was the local chairman. I organized a massive One World week across all of Kirklees which I'm very proud of. I was trying to get people to appreciate the Asians. I had nearly thirty years in youth work, so ran a club in the place where we lived and helped to run another at school. This was an all-Asian youth club. I was brought on to the Community Relations Council and then it began to break my heart. We had a fifteen-year-old Asian girl raped on school grounds by three of our students at half past three in the afternoon. She was tied to a tree and raped. That upset me more than I can say because I thought I was beginning to break through with the English teachers, to persuade them our Asians had a lot to offer to us. I was also at the Community Relations Council trying to persuade the Asian people they were respected. Then this happened and it coincided with two other things. First, an upsurge in anti-race activity, pigs' heads in the mosques, kids coming to school armed. We had to search children and found knives and iron bars on fourteen- and fifteen-year-old boys. We had to have a police presence at certain times in the lunch hours. I'm a toughie, not as tough as my dad, but I found that hard. The last straw was when one of our second year boys was sexually attacked. He was on his way home from school, on his second week of school, and was abused and murdered and his body was left in a dump. I went to the home, the police were in the school for three months because they thought it could have been part of a pederast ring, we didn't know those terms then. The attack took place in September, but the boy's body wasn't released until the new year. I went to see the parents regularly. I went to the funeral. The mother collapsed, the boy's photograph was turned to the wall. I can still hardly talk of the experience. I decided to apply elsewhere. I was running away.

PR It sounds a dreadful experience.

JE My family was supportive. I looked for a new job somewhere very different. Cornwall seemed an obvious place. I wanted to be head of a bigger, eleven-to-eighteen school with a sixth form not under threat. I wanted to avoid the worst effects of the growing competition I foresaw. I anticipated falling rolls and guessed this would mean much more competition. I can fight as dirty as the rest but didn't want to be in that position if I could avoid it. I wanted to be in a one-school town so that I could develop some ideas about community education. Put those factors together, it has to be a place like Cornwall.

By then my mum had gone into a geriatric hospital. She couldn't feed herself, couldn't speak, couldn't recognize anybody. Her lungs were giving problems. Dad said 'You had done what you can. You can't help your mum any more. Go where you need.' It had been different when I was in Yorkshire, every other Saturday I spent the day in hospital with her. She didn't know. I was supporting dad. He was going three times a day to sit with her for an hour. No recognition. I was a bit freer, I could look elsewhere. I had five interviews: in North Yorkshire, in South Yorkshire, in Cumberland, one in East Yorkshire and in Bodmin. I didn't get the others but since coming I have never regretted this.

PR   Do you remember the selection process?

JE   There was a local deputy and five experienced heads shortlisted. Few of us struck me as typical of the image I had of Cornwall. Not many locals applied. They thought Bodmin tough. By Cornwall standards it was. It was the only school in Cornwall with a sin bin, an EBD unit. That attracted me.

PR   You have worked for several heads. What have you learned from them?

JE   I learned from the first, that I must know the children. I will always be grateful to the head who advised me not to be an adviser but a deputy. It was a very big school run by the heads of house and the deputies. He was a remote head but I used to enjoy talking with him. He used to walk the job very occasionally. I enjoyed the meetings with him, the formalized structure of meetings. That is when I first began to realize the purpose of meetings. They were rare in the olden days. But I didn't learn a lot from him really except the very good career advice which was a one-off.

PR   It seems he knew you better than you might have thought?

JE   I think he knew my family background. He knew my regard for my mum and how much I respected my dad. He knew a little about me personally. He respected all I did in the town. The Yugoslavian head I did not know well or long. But my office was next door to his with thin walls. I've heard teachers in tears. I thought that's not the way. I get quite short-tempered myself and have to watch this. But, again, what I learnt was mainly negative. He had high expectations without giving direction. My current first deputy is superb but doesn't want to be a head, he's my age, been here, done every job, worked his way up through the school, he's a superb deputy. He once did the timetable and struggled somewhat, that wasn't his fault. I blame myself because I didn't give him sufficient steps to move to. I used to blame the Yugoslavian head for doing the same thing. He tended, in effect, to say 'I want this doing yesterday but I'm not going to give you any help or advice or support. Get on with it.' He would chat with the staff but wasn't popular or well understood. I don't have many social chats. I don't go and sit in the staff room at break time and have social chats but do welcome people coming in to see me.

I haven't learned how to do headship from anybody else. I've had to learn for myself. I read and you've seen my library. I must average three education or education management books a month. I devour the *TES*. My working week is longer than eighty hours if you count my reading time. I still relax quite a bit. I also learn from courses and conferences, both those I go to myself and those which others on the staff go to. I like listening to good people, to learn from the knowledgeable. My idea of a good course is five end-on lectures a day. I am not keen on hearing 'Let's go and have a workshop in which we'll think about our problems'. I've got plenty of real problems, I don't want to waste my time on artificial ones.

I found, early on, I was good at making decisions and solving problems. In Kirklees I learnt how to work with staff and parents as a senior manager in a quite short time. They put all the new heads in Yorkshire into a new headteachers' training course. It started in my second term there. The first of four residential days was held in Wakefield. I'd just moved to my new school and had a great deal to do. I had staff to bring together, I had to get some organization into the new school, I had to resolve split-site issues, and I had to do something about the curriculum. I had a lot on. I probably went to the residential with the wrong attitude. We had a number of keynote speakers on the first day. The speaker in the session between tea and dinner said at the start of his talk he was going to create a crisis at some point and that he'd be interested in people's reaction to this. He started talking, it was quite reasonable, I was making a few notes, then in mid-sentence he sat on the table and just stopped. I had just come to the conclusion he hadn't really prepared a full talk when suddenly he stood up and walked into the corner of the room. He stood with his face to the corner of the room, ignoring the audience, thirty-odd of us. I and others thought this is odd. There was a growing level of whispering. After a bit, I thought to myself, I have had enough. If this is the crisis and he wants a response to it, mine would be to conclude he did not want to talk to us any more. That was fine, I didn't want to listen to him any more. I said 'I'm going'. I got my briefcase. The lady next to me said, in real Yorkshire, 'Ee lad and I'm coming with you'. Then the course organizers began to chase after us. We had become part of the crisis. The other course members thought it was a put-up job, that we two had been inveigled into the act. I drove all the way back from Wakefield. Later the Chief Adviser phoned me up at home and asked me to return the next morning. I did and I stayed for the rest of the course but didn't find it very useful. I have often wondered what others made of that course.

PR   What did you expect to find at Bodmin? What did you hope to achieve?

JE   The understanding that the governors and the County Council had of the school was misplaced. They thought it tough but by the standards I had known, it wasn't. Some of the kids here are as bad as

I have met anywhere but there's only three or four of them in a year group, not thirty or forty. I think they wanted somebody tough. Tough in the sense of being able to get the discipline side of things organized as quickly as possible.

The curriculum, when I came, was badly out of date. It was dominated by a traditional grammar school ethos, there was a split curriculum. So my elder son, when he came here as a second year, did two foreign languages and Latin compulsorily but virtually no craft or a creative subject. Yet he was expected to pick one of those subjects at the end of the third year in the option system. The curriculum badly needed working on. They wanted somebody with fresh curriculum ideas. I had been a curriculum deputy so did a lot of work on the curriculum and the timetable myself. I did a great deal of consultation.

We were one of the first two named community schools in Cornwall. That was largely due to my work. I didn't take all the staff with me but enough, with the governors, to make it work. That was my vision. To create a meaningful curriculum, to sort out the problem they perceived to be having with discipline (I didn't see this as that bad), and to do something about community education. We have been successful in most of these aims. A lot of this has been the result of raising expectations. The best teachers and managers I have known have been people who have high expectations.

All the five deputies I appointed who went on to become heads were outstanding classroom teachers. They all had high expectation of the kids. I recall the first deputy we appointed in Yorkshire. He took the top set for English in their fourth year, and was determined they would do well in their O Levels. He was accused by parents and kids of being above their heads, of working them too hard. He got many letters of congratulation when they eventually did very well in their O Levels. Remember this was in a school which was not really a comprehensive in its intake. He was an outstanding teacher, as is the deputy most recently promoted to headship. She is an outstanding classroom teacher with high expectations of behaviour and work. The other deputy here, another aspiring head, is also a brilliant classroom practitioner. Such people are good at enabling people to do better than they think they can. They don't do it in a wagging finger way but through their quiet and determined expectations. One thing guaranteed to drive me up the wall is to hear 'It's Bodmin. What can you expect?' We have fought against this. The expectations our teachers have of all their children has risen. We have some really good teachers now and are getting better and better results. If I could wave a magic wand I would ask that all teachers have high expectations of whoever they teach.

PR   You have described your vision for what needed to be done. How did you go about achieving this? What kind of a manager and leader are you?

JE   I border on the autocratic. On my first day here, I said 'I've done five years as a head. I am willing to listen to anybody and to have a regard for what is said.' And I do, it was my dad's way, to listen to anybody and have regard for what they say, but, in the end, he would make his own mind. So I said this and stressed that ultimately, 'I will make the key decisions at my level. You'll often think you've not been listened to but you have. You have to know the difference between consultation and negotiation. On many things I'm not negotiable. I'll consult, I'll try and win you over.' I know it would be useless to try and start something almost all the staff oppose but even on this there may be some things I hold so dear that I will try to make them happen.

PR   To what extent do your managerial values match your educational values?

JE   I want challenge and success at every level. I want teachers to be challenged and to feel success. I want kids to be challenged and to feel success. I'm very much a didactic teacher. The head of chemistry has been here for thirty years. He works on learning science as a process; I work on learning science as a product. I try to get the body of knowledge over to children in whatever way works best. I work very hard at it. I do so partly because I enjoy it so much. I love teaching. I have been offered jobs at county hall at various points in my career but I've never been seriously tempted. It would mean giving up teaching children.

I enjoy learning of innovation, development and good practice. I say to the staff, 'You are busy classroom teachers, one of my jobs as head is to do a lot of the educational reading that many of you don't or won't do and to transmit what I have learnt to you.' I laugh with them when I tell them something and hear 'He has been reading again'.

When I gave up being chairman of the Cornwall Association of Secondary Heads, many heads wrote and thanked me. You feel flattered when people consult you and ask you what would you do in this or that circumstance. Often as I helped solve others' problems I would find I had solved my own. I am glad to have problems. People say of me 'If he can't find someone to argue with, he'll argue with himself'. We need challenges. We must be on the move. If a place stands still, it is lost. I can't do with teachers who want to stand still. There's always something worth challenging yourself with. When faced with a problem, I try to spell out several possible ways and reduce these to just one best way. I think I'm aware of my faults. I am not necessarily the most egalitarian of teachers or managers. But I am willing to flog myself to death as a teacher and manager to get results in my teaching and in my management.

PR   Can we turn to special education? When you came to Bodmin you presumably had some idea of Cornwall's 'policy' on special education. What was your view at the time?

JE   The authority is proud of the fact that most special needs children are in mainstream schools. But to be honest before Warnock and the Act they did not have many special schools and so, by default, children with special needs, who in other authorities would be in special schools, were mainly in mainstream schools. Their policy of not having a policy has put them in the very forefront of fashionable thinking today. You could say that pre Warnock they did not have what was then thought of as proper provision because they were unwilling or unable to fund this. They value education and special education but didn't want to spend more money than they had to or, perhaps, than they could on these things. They had a very low-cost school base.

Even so, Cornwall's 'policy' was a plus factor for me. It meant children with special needs were for the most part in mainstream schools. I thought it absolutely right they should be. When they decided to expand the severe learning difficulty provision in Cornwall they had two main options: to extend available residential provision or to link people into a mainstream school. I did all I could to encourage the latter option and so they placed an SLD unit here. My criteria for this development was that it should be done openly, the unit wasn't to be a shed situated at the bottom of the school yard. So the unit is situated right within the main building. I was determined that as far as possible the children were going to be full members of the college community. They dine with the rest of us, they attend mainstream lessons as appropriate. I didn't want a system that gave them constant support in lessons in order that they could always be in mainstream classes. I always had reservations about this. We studied it very carefully for the first two years and discussed it fully. We were blessed with a very experienced special needs teacher who was formerly a deputy head of the College. She retired and returned as our SENCO. She is Cornish herself, and has grown up over the years with developments in special needs policy and practice in Cornwall, and knows the ropes. I thought her knowledge, experience and talents were wasted before I came. With her help, and with help from outside we got things started. We got in the then Adviser for Special Needs and the LEA officer responsible and made a study of the provision of in-class support.

The way traditionally this had been done is by a system I call 'teacher mop up'. Such and such a body in the English, Humanities or Maths Department who had some free periods would be detailed off to support a number of classes. There was little planning and no coherence to this. Some good work did go on but it was a matter of luck when this happened. In most cases there was little commitment. There was nobody with a particular sense of ownership for such special needs children. They moved from subject teacher to subject teacher with different or no support teacher. If they were lucky it was a special needs trained teacher but that often did not happen. If I was one of these children in a first year class I might see one support teacher in one maths lesson but a different one in another maths lesson and yet another in an English lesson. Furthermore, there were no individual learning programmes against which to assess progress. We had a major study done by the maths adviser. He spent one hundred hours studying our maths work and organization here of which a quarter was on special needs maths teaching. He wrote a separate report on our special needs maths teaching. As a result and because of my own views and interests in learning, I took the step of having a small withdrawal group in each of the first three years with a single designated special needs trained teacher, who was to develop coherent programmes for the children in these groups based on individual learning plans. What this means is that when the bell goes, the rest of the school might change from maths to English, but since these children are on individual learning programmes they might not change. To make this possible a lot of money has been put into computerizing the support of special needs learning and it is beginning to work. That particular special needs teacher is attached to that group of fifteen/sixteen children and teaches them exclusively, with ancillary help, for between half and two-thirds of the week. So they will mix for half to a third of their class time with children in mainstream classes. They will also mix on a whole variety of other occasions which I will say something about later. But overall they will have the support of a single designated special needs teacher. It seems to be working. We've done it for four years.

I had found teaching the wide ability fourth and fifth year science difficult. Not that I did not enjoy teaching low ability groups, after all I had made my name at it through my involvement in the Nuffield Secondary Science project. But I found it difficult because children with learning difficulties in mainstream classes, without adequate and coherent extra support, tended to slip further and further behind. We did psychometric and other tests on them which demonstrated this clearly. Even though I had some help in the classroom and tried to prepare special work for them I and they were struggling. I could manage it but only because I had a small teaching load. I knew other teachers weren't coping. That also was something that convinced me that such a system would not do.

PR   Can you say something about the history of your own developing knowledge and thinking and views about special needs?

JE   I think it starts from my father's problems with literacy. He was a real salt of the earth man who I dearly and greatly respected. Why should he be regarded as different because he couldn't read and write properly? He was no less a person for that, in fact he was someone to be admired. If this was one influence there have been others. First, the lack of understanding of the background of his pupils that I found in my grammar school head. Second, my growing commitment to the concept of the community comprehensive school. I believe comprehensive schools should cater for everybody, hence the severe learning difficulty unit here. I've done quite a bit of reading on this. My knowledge tends to be second hand because I've never taught exclusively special needs children. I've taught many special needs children mixed in with others of low ability. So reading about and talking to people I respect has shaped my views. Third, I have also been influenced by a number of special needs teachers over time. I could mention several but have already singled out one, our former deputy now our SENCO. Her example has been inspirational. Like most special needs teachers I have talked to and worked with, she has tended to formulate her views through training or practice rather than from extensive reading. I don't know whether our special needs teachers do a lot of reading. They keep themselves up to date by course attendance or by meeting other special needs teachers.

Cornwall's policy on special needs and the way in which it organizes funding causes real problems for us. Some schools in Cornwall with much smaller numbers of children with identified special needs have as much additional support as we have with our much bigger numbers. It's the way the system works. It is possible for these schools to give their pupils the kind of coherent, individual, in-class support we cannot.

PR   Can you describe how the funding works?

JE   Since LMSS, and this is our third year of having a devolved budget on this, we have the same funding as if each special needs child in the SLD unit were part of a Cornwall special school. We have twenty-seven children in the unit and they count as the equivalent of two classes in a special school. If there were a Cornwall special school with six classes, we would get the equivalent of one-third of the total which they would get in such a school. That comes as a single lump sum. Our budget for the unit is about £100,000. How we deploy this is up to us. Those with statements in the main school are counted and funded like any other child but the unit is considered as if it were a two-class special school. So there is nothing which says you must have X number of teachers, or ancillaries, etc. It is all up to us. In fact, we probably spend more on ancillaries than the county ratio would entail. Pre LMSS, when we had one class in the unit, the allocation was ten children equals one teacher plus one ancillary. If it was agreed that a child from the unit should come out into the main school for X hours a week there could be an allocation against that child which would allow X hours extra of ancillary provision. Relatively this was a more generous provision than we have now.

PR   How else does the LEA support this aspect of the school's work and how well?

JE   A concern I have is that when we agreed to take the unit, a condition was that we should get full assistance from the support services. This has not really happened whether it be psychology, social, educational, health services or whatever. We get lots of input from the advisory teachers for special needs but not much from others. We were promised more than we got. This is reflected in the quality of the office provision we have made available. It has never been fully used. If we have a real problem they do come but beyond this they tend to rely on the review, or double review, process. By this I mean the regular statementing review *and* the review of placement. This can mean movement out of the unit into our mainstream if somebody comes who has a greater need. But we do want to have a level of integration and it is possible to use our small withdrawal groups as an interim between the unit and mainstream classes. In general terms, then, LEA support rarely comes if we don't press for it. Our SENCO sometimes comes to me on this if she needs a 'heavy'. She has excellent networks herself and is very respected but even so a heavy is fairly often needed.

PR   Can you say something about your views on integration and inclusion?

JE   I think a great deal of theory and practice on this has been dominated by a commitment to the belief that it is wrong to single out or to segregate. But that's often been done on social grounds without the necessary educational back-up. In my view, educational considerations should be given priority. You can achieve a high level of social integration quite easily by simply insisting on mixed-ability settings for all but a tiny number of the most extreme cases. You could then argue that you are meeting the social needs of all children. But if this is your only consideration then don't be surprised if it does not meet everybody's needs educationally. What schools who have gone down this route in the past have done, what this school has been doing, is to concentrate on the social and to neglect the educational. I'm trying to reverse this. Let us put education first. But this can mean that some of the children for some of the time are going to be segregated from other children. We need to minimize this as far as we can. We need to look as imaginatively as we can at ways of integrating socially as far as we can where this would not be educationally damaging. Part of that long study I told you about earlier showed us that to stress social integration meant that the educational needs of those with special needs tended to be neglected in the classroom. Let us take a case of a fully mixed-ability year nine Geography class with twenty-five to thirty kids of which four are special needs children. Now they may have part support, part not, whatever, it wouldn't be coherent support. For this to have any chance of working, of meeting the needs of the four, it would be necessary to create the necessary educational environment. We would have to work very hard at differentiation. We need to be reasonably sure we can do this before we just put them all together for reasons of social integration. It sometimes seems that some people think that if you get social integration that educational integration will somehow necessarily also happen. I think we need to switch that argument around. If you get educational integration right then worthwhile social integration will happen. On our experience, I think I can now prove that the provision of coherent provision for children with special needs who work with trained, qualified teaching for a significant portion of the week on individual learning plans is better educationally for them than just dispersing them into mainstream classes. Even so we need to enable them, in so far as they can benefit educationally from this, to spend as much time as they can in mainstream classes. We must also work as hard as we can to enable them to integrate socially in all kinds of other contexts around the school.

PR   I understand there are over 120 children with some kind of designated special need of which 27 are located in the unit (Greenfield) and 96 in mainstream classes. Can you describe your provision and how you make decisions about who goes where?

JE   The children come into year seven and we sort out what we think are the fourteen or fifteen with the greatest learning difficulties. There will be more than that who have statements but we sort out the people who we think would most benefit from working with a trained special needs teacher covering the whole curriculum.

PR   That's in each of the years?

JE   In each of the years that teacher will cover maths, English, history, geography and possibly the modern language aspect of the national curriculum.

PR   What's the justification of that approach?

JE   In making these decisions we rely in some cases on testing and in others on what is set out in the statement. In addition, our Head of Special Needs visits schools extensively over the summer term and collects information from them. After long discussion, looking at test results, statements, information from primary schools we identify the fourteen or fifteen. That's not a fixed population. For those for whom this is appropriate, usually about two or three, they are relocated to mainstream classes.

PR   They all spend some time in mainstream classes, don't they? What's the balance?

JE   In a thirty-period week, they spend on average about twelve to fourteen periods as a group with the special needs qualified teacher covering the five curriculum areas I identified earlier. In doing so they would not necessarily be working in a standardized way. They should each have their individual learning plans. In other subjects, say science, they go out with that special needs teacher in one of two groups to fully integrated, fully mixed-ability classes in the lower school. So they are taught in a wider group but the teacher with them is their home tutor. There might also be further support from an ancillary. So they would be a full class, along with the other children, along with their special needs teacher, the science specialist and possibly an ancillary. Then for the rest of the curriculum, for the art, technology, music, drama, PE and so on, they'd be fully integrated into smaller groups in mixed-ability classes. We tend to have smaller groups for the creative, technical, practical aspects of the curriculum. They would work with the subject specialist and with some ancillary support in some of those lessons.

PR   You monitor how they develop as time passes and take the action this entails?

JE   You might find that a particular child develops well in, say, maths and so we say when it's maths on everybody else's timetable you will go out and do maths in one of the mainstream classes. That means they will only spend nine periods instead of twelve in the special group and as part of their learning development plan. They go initially on a trial basis. If we think her maths is good enough to be placed in a lower mainstream set then we let her try. Our plan would be to try the maths that they would be doing when they move into that set in their own group first. This helps to give them a start.

PR   Some people would criticize what you are describing as essentially separatist, others might argue that it is not very inclusive. What would your response be?

JE   I might compare what we do with say Penryn School Community School. It is a much smaller school with an intake of 120 compared with our 250. They have twenty-odd with statemented special needs. We have a much bigger number but they have a much bigger proportion. They are struggling to give support to these children. Whatever system they try to use they have difficulty in supporting the 20 per cent of their entry who have statements of special learning needs. It would be much easier for us given our bigger numbers and smaller proportion of special needs children to undertake such work. They are pretty well bound to have to try full integration or else to have full segregation. They simply do not have the numbers to practise our kind of withdrawal policy.

This year two of the county's secondary MLD units closed. One, at Redruth, was bigger than our SLD unit here. I don't know if they did this because they think integration is the thing or because they thought the unit system wasn't working. Mainstreaming may not be that straightforward. Our SLD unit is, I think, significantly different to an MLD unit.

PR   Could you say a bit more about that? When I was last here talking to you and the head of the Greenfield Unit I got the impression the unit has been taking in increasing numbers of children designated as SLD and that is causing significant changes in its nature?

JE   You're dead right to say it is becoming more SLD in proportion and bigger. Partly that's because of its success. We have a waiting list for it with three and four times as many wanting to come as we have places for. And the number is drifting up. If we are forced to take more than thirty in the unit then we really do need more provision. I think the waiting list has gone up because parents see this as a way of placing their children in a mainstream school, one which takes integration seriously. All this is very attractive to parents. They are reluctant to send their children to the special school when they think they can go to the big comprehensive school.

PR   The same as everybody else?

JE   That is part of the attraction. My worry is that we are not, and the Ofsted Inspection picked it up, as well orientated educationally as we might be. That's not a criticism of the staff. With the older pupils we have work to do educationally. We are successful in the unit on the social integration side. We can now teach these pupils up to nineteen. When the unit was opened it was supposed to be only for pupils from eleven to sixteen. We argued with county officers at the time because we knew parents wanted their children to stay here beyond sixteen. We agreed some definitely needed to move on because they would benefit more from a further education environment. Others we knew were not ready for this. We have had people come in from elsewhere and some who have asked if they could stay on longer. There is special provision in both the major FE colleges but some have wanted to stay on here post-sixteen. We do not cling to them. It's what they need that matters. Even so it brings out the softie in me. Each morning as I drive in I see our former first student in the unit. He is twenty and stayed with us until he was nineteen and will need support and protection all his life. He waves pathetically to me as he waits with his mother for the taxi to take him to the FE college. He is a sad figure. He was much happier here. I also see another. He can go in on the college bus but stands isolated twenty feet away from twenty other students also waiting. Nobody speaks to him. I am not saying all are like these two. Others are ready and should be encouraged to go. After much argument, we successfully kept some here until nineteen.

I don't think, as yet, we have fully met the challenge of providing an appropriate education, particularly in terms of integration, of all these sixteen-to-nineteen-year-olds. We haven't got many yet but the number is increasing as the children grow up through the unit. We face a strong and growing demand for post-sixteen from parents who don't want to see their children travelling the distances which, in Cornwall, are sometimes needed to get to a college unit.

If I had to identify the biggest challenge in our unit it would be post-fifteen, the latter key stage 4, educational provision. What's been helpful is the number of people, teacher and student, including sixth form students, who like to help out in the unit. The number is growing. It's not done just for altruistic reasons but because there is a feeling that there is something worthwhile taking place there. In addition, we are asked by all sorts of outside bodies to take a trainee for this or that reason to work in the unit. I am particularly interested to see what happens when children from the unit go outside it. What happens when they go to a PE lesson or an English class or a drama lesson? Teachers in these classes feel increasingly prepared to see them. Some of this takes place on an official basis but a growing amount is agreed unofficially between the teachers involved.

PR   To what extent would it be appropriate to describe the Greenfield Unit as a special school located within a mainstream school?

JE   We have to be careful of that. The children do spend a good deal of time in the unit but mix with other children in a whole variety of formal and informal ways. They mix in the corridors, in assembly and in the dining room. They mix at various points in the day and in various parts of the school, the tuck shop for example. But there is a real danger that they don't mix as much as they could. But it can be difficult, particularly with the older ones, to make the interactions meaningful educationally. We do try to encourage this when we can. An English teacher might, for example, tailor an aspect of her course to produce a coherent unit of work over, say, six or seven lessons, in such a way as to make it possible for selected children from Greenfield to attend supported by an ancillary. And the Unit staff would prepare these children to make the most of this. That is happening, but not as much as I might hope. I could try and force it more but I think this would probably be counter-productive. There is growing support for children with special needs in the college from all kinds of mainstream children and teachers. There could be even more but you risk what has been gained by trying to go too fast. In any case, we are facing a change in the kind of children who come to the Unit. In the past they have mainly been children with learning difficulties but increasingly we are also getting children with major physical difficulties coming. As an example of the former, at the beginning of this academic year we have a multiply-handicapped young lady, a thirteen-year-old, coming in. Now that worries some staff. They have learnt to work with children with learning difficulties, even with behavioural difficulties, but now have to learn to work with children who might be seriously physically handicapped.

PR   You mention the Ofsted inspection. The report, although largely very positive, expressed some reservations about aspects of the Greenfield Unit?

JE   It took place in 1994. They were not happy generally about some of the work within the unit. Not so much about the quality but the range of the teaching and the levels of achievement. They were a bit more neutral on the extent of integration. They felt that the diversity of the curriculum under offer there was too low as were expectations of achievement. The main issue for action was on the quantity and quality of provision for statement children. One problem was that group budgeting, as I have described this earlier, meant that we have had an increase in numbers of pupils but not in budget. In addition subsidiary special needs issues which we are working on include the need to keep action plans based upon individual learning plans and of the lowish expectations for the children in the unit from teachers and ancillaries. Initially, this was questioned by our specialists here who suggested what do they expect? But they have come around.

In accounting for the money we get for the unit, one item is the extent to which this is used to support its children working in mainstream. There is a belief that there is an element of funding in the total package to enable this. In conjunction with the other three schools with units in the county, one SLD, two MLD, we have agreed to try over the next three years, year on year, to outline our outcome expenditure patterns on that part of the budget. So ancillaries are now being asked to log the time which they spend in mainstream classes. This is the main cost.

PR   Is it your policy that the children in the unit stay in GCSE classes until the final January?

JE   It was my policy. It is part of my attempt not to label and to raise expectations. I have no problem with setting children. But I do have problems to do with parity of esteem. Other than the two in the unit, I do not have exclusively special needs teachers. Teachers who teach these children also teach their subject a proportion of their time in mainstream classes. They do not get labelled special needs teachers. This means also that they keep pace with what is happening in mainstream. If I am teaching one of these withdrawal classes for twenty periods a week the rest of the time I will be, for example, teaching two mainstream English classes. If the teachers are not labelled as special needs then the children may not be either. Doing this also enables these teachers to keep a firm grasp in making assessments about what can be achieved in such classes and by such children.

PR   Does this create a problem for the two teachers who do spend all their time in the unit?

JE   I feel guilty that we have not really managed to make some personal reflection time available for them. We did appoint somebody to help with this but because of a financial difficulty when a member of staff left, we had to use this teacher to take classwork and not relieve those in the unit. I hope we will be able to do something in the future. I hope they will then have time for reflection and also to talk more to mainstream teachers and by doing so to facilitate more integration. Now and then we have made time for them to go and visit the other units but they rarely seem to find anything which could be worth applying here. We do make some extra staffing available and it is up to the SENCO to say how she wants to use it. She tends to support the older children and to help them to leave with something. We had, for example, three lads last year who got a grade B in GCSE Technology. They sat no other subject. She was bought in extra time to support them.

PR   What's it like managing a mainstream school with a large number of statement children?

JE   If you measure a headteacher's joy in the success of his kids then there's more joy when you've got the fullest possible range.

PR   It's part of your definition of what it is to be comprehensive?

JE   When I came I set up a system of rewards, they're real rewards, I won't reward like confetti. It's part of a policy of trying to catch people being good. We were keen to get the mums and dads involved in this, to get them to come in and to show them. This didn't necessarily go down well when I first brought it in. We have three major presentations a year and smaller ones in between these. I remember the second time we did this. As came to be usual we had all kinds of children receiving awards. They included children from the unit, other children with special needs as well as children from mainstream classes. All were there to receive their awards. One parent said to me as we were taking refreshments after the event that he believed achievement should be real achievement and by that he meant scholastic achievement. Instead, we had been giving awards for effort to all kinds of children who had achieved very little as he saw it. Another father was standing next to us. I'd never spoken to him particularly before but he said 'My lad is one of the brightest lads in the school and I am glad to see him being rewarded for being a high achiever but it meant more to me to see my lad being recognized as a high achiever in a school that also recognized the achievements of children at the other end of the ability scale.' It was simply and quietly said, but meant a great deal to me.

PR   How do you feel about managing staff?

JE   Managing the children is a joy. Managing the staff can be difficult especially in trying to overcome the 'It's Bodmin' view. My reading has shown that the teachers have a cut-off point for designating children as slow learners which is some way short of even the most stringent of official definitions. This can mean defining well over half the children they encounter as of less than average ability. This can happen even in selective schools. I believe a true comprehensive must be able to cater for everybody. It shouldn't write children off. So one of our targets for next year is to look at the achievement of lower achieving children. That got rather lost in the debates on the national curriculum. There was a lot of good work going on with low achieving but much of that seems to have got lost. We need to look again at developments in terms of modular courses, different forms of certification, short-term learning gains. I've a filing cabinet full on this. You will remember that Keith Joseph, towards the end of his tenure at the DES, began to take a major interest in slow learning children, but not much has happened since then. The real task as I see it is to get teachers to recognize that they are quite capable of teaching slow learners. Too many say too easily that we have too many special needs children here. But what do you mean by too many? I accept that there can be difficulties if you don't have the resources to cater for them but too many? You can't have too many children who require teaching, that's what school is about.

PR   You have focused, understandably, on staff who don't regard themselves as expert in coping with the special needs of such children. What about those who do?

JE   They are simply expert, they're superb, they're the best.

PR   What happens when there's disagreement on aspects of special needs provision between you and such staff? There seem some hints of this in your Ofsted Report.

JE   Yes, that's right.

PR   The Greenfield staff seem less persuaded than the Ofsted Inspectors or even yourself that their expectations are lower than they might be in terms of the levels of integration which would benefit children in the Unit. How do you manage that kind of problem?

JE   I'm trying there to use other staff with special needs expertise not involved directly at Greenfield. I have tried to encourage a higher level of involvement for them in the unit.

PR   One of your policies is for no teacher, other than the two in the Greenfield Unit, to work exclusively with children who have remedial or special needs? They all also teach mainstream classes and, in doing so, work with very able children?

JE   It is a deliberate policy. The Greenfield system is a little out of my control in the sense that although we have an input into who comes, at the end of the day it is a provision for all of North Cornwall and is therefore funded separately from the main college budget.

PR   But under the more recent LMSS arrangements, this is a fund you control?

JE   That is right. This is the third financial year this has been so. That helps in some regard and I've actually put more staff provision in than would otherwise have gone in. So I have used some of the general budget to increase the staffing provision of the unit. But decisions on which children should be accepted is largely decided by a panel who decide on entry on the basis of county criteria. I don't necessarily want to be the selector but without this the possibilities of conflict increase. Particularly, if there is a change of policy. This is not always made explicit. I think there has been a change, particularly with regard to the kind of older children who come to us.

PR   You have had wide and long experience of headship within mainstream secondary schools. You have been responsible for large numbers of children with a diversity of special needs. Much more, probably, than the vast majority of your mainstream headteacher colleagues elsewhere. What advice would you give those likely to have to cope with increasing numbers and types of children with special needs in their schools?

JE   My maxim is knowledge is power. So first, prepare yourself as I do through reading and course attendance. In preparing for things like this you need to try and find out what is involved, you need to know your own school and yourself, you need to know what other schools are doing. I would advise them to read widely, go on courses and visit schools which have some experience of the kinds of development which you face. Don't wait until the last minute, don't jump into things. So know as much as you can. Second, try to anticipate as much as you can. Don't work on the basis of what a good idea it will be to meet problems as they arise. You need to look at your existing systems and structures and consider what your options are. So do the analysis before you start. Things may be less difficult than you think. There are a lot of myths about special needs I think. Third, meet and mix with the children themselves to know and understand them.

PR   Have your views of special needs been changed significantly by your experience of it?

JE   I have come to realize these children can do far more than is often expected of them. It really is not enough to label them as thick and give them a Mickey Mouse curriculum designed to occupy and mind rather than educate. You have got to plan carefully for them. It is, for example, the hardest possible work to draw up suitable individual learning plans and assess children against them. To achieve the level of differentiation which is necessary you've got a lot more planning than would be the case in a mainstream class. The planning capacity of competent special needs teachers and their ancillaries has to be immense. It cannot be a case of drifting and teaching these children as the mood takes. A teacher who isn't interested in such out-of-classroom planning will not be effective. In addition, what I've learnt is that it is not enough to be child-centred, to have a sympathy for slow-learning children or children with learning difficulties. You've got to be an expert planner. That is one of the most important things I have learnt here.

What I feel I have been less good at is, perhaps, in checking up on the academic progress of children with special needs. Social progress is one thing, participation in educational provision can be quite another. I know I tend to look at this in terms of participation rather than progress. I do look at individual action plans. I was keen on this long before it became fashionable. I believe fervently that it is very important to record carefully achievement. I have grumbled at the special needs people here asking where are the detailed learning records? what is the target, to what extent have they achieved it, what is your evidence, have you reassessed it, what will you want next? can you show me the practical working record which every child should have? If this is true of the unit it is also true of the withdrawal groups and, probably, special needs pupils of all mainstream classes. As far as the children in the unit and withdrawal groups are concerned I want their activities to be coherent, recorded, analysed and I want this to shape what they are offered in the future.

PR   Have you enjoyed headship?

JE   My grammar school head couldn't survive now. Even so, it's a superb job. Unlike Ted Wragg, I don't think you have to be barmy to want to do it. It can be tough. Some of my best headteacher friends have retired because of illness or stress. I am talking of people I rate highly who are not just looking for a way out. To survive you've got to be much tougher than in the past. I'm a diabetic with serious stomach problems and think this is stress related. It's part of the job. But it's still the most rewarding job there is. How can people prepare? The mentoring scheme is good and HEADLAMP can be useful if a bit late. The key task remains selecting the best people to do the job.

I cannot think of anything I would rather do than be the head of a big comprehensive school. But it must be a true comprehensive which caters for everybody. You shouldn't write people off. One of our targets at Bodmin is to look at the achievement of lower-achieving children. That got lost in the national curriculum. One of the joys of headship is it is still possible to take a lead on important things like this. I still look forward to it.

CHAPTER 7

Exorcizing the ghosts: life, leadership and special education

DAVID HAIGH with Peter Ribbins

David Haigh has recently taken early retirement. His post before this was as an Inspector for SEN in an LEA within the Midlands. Before that he was for six years headteacher of an EBD secondary special school. Since qualifying as a teacher, he has taught in five education authorities in the Midlands. Through his experience of three comprehensive schools and three special schools he has worked with children aged two to nineteen across the whole range of special educational needs. He was seconded for two years to the University of Birmingham to undertake an evaluation of the effectiveness of his authority's INSET programme, a project which was incorporated into a PhD.

PR   Can you tell me something about your early life and times and the extent to which key influences from those years have shaped the sort of person you are?

DH   I was brought up in Yorkshire. My father was a policeman. We often moved which made life difficult. I went to several schools – a fractured pattern of forming friendships and moving on. This became increasingly difficult with each new move, particularly in my adolescence. I went to three secondary schools and avoided a fourth only by going into digs for the sixth which did a lot for my education and little for my exam results. There were problems with home as well. Looking from the inside out, it seems to me policemen have a distinctive view of life which is very convergent, authoritarian, structured and rule bound. As I grew up I found this more and more difficult to understand. My relationship with my parents got more and more distant, they became less and less of an influence on me. When we parted company I think it was a relief on both sides. There seem to be two approaches to dealing with a very discipline-focused father. My older brother spent his time trying to stay on his right side and I took the opposite approach. Neither of us are now in contact with him, so it seems both failed.

PR   How about your mother?

DH   She was devoted to my father. Whenever I criticized him I was told he was the most wonderful man in the world, if we could only be more like him we'd be all right. Looking back I seem to have spent as much of my childhood outside of the home as I could. I remember wonderful sunny summers, I suppose children do, and lots of happy times, but this was always with other children, always in a gang. We lived in a mining village in South Yorkshire. It was tribal, an amazing culture. I often think of it.

PR   What do you mean by that?

DH   There was a clear hierarchy among the families in the village. There were the top families, the middle families and the other families, and it seemed if you were born into a marginal family that was your lot. A sort of caste system. It was fascinating. Streets of the village tended to band together and to have a distinct identity. If you lived in one street that was your group. I suppose it's a bit like Northern Ireland. People took up very strong positions. Of course the police were somewhere out in the wasteland in most people's view, so being a son of a policeman wasn't much of a help. As I say the happy times were always outside the family. Inside there was a culture of ridicule, of always putting down. I remember thinking why don't my parents ever come to sports day, all the other parents did at primary school. I always assumed they would never be there when I needed them which tended to make being within a supportive gang that had its own values and rules very attractive. There was a big wood we used to disappear into for twelve hours on Saturdays and Sundays. It was a *Lord of the Flies* culture. I found it comfortable, I knew my position. There was a distinct pecking order, that was curiously supportive.

PR   Did moving a lot mean that you sought membership of a new gang every time?

DH   When we moved away from that pit village I felt disorientated for most of the three years we spent at the next place. It was forty miles away and very different. It was a very urban setting, and I did not like that at all. I felt adrift – I didn't have a particular group of friends, I always felt on the outside of everything and very unhappy. I started going to church but it didn't work. I got confirmed but it didn't provide what I was looking for. We then moved to a mill town and I greatly enjoyed that. My parents moved again at the end of my lower sixth year but I stayed in digs. I had a group of good friends and am still in contact with one or two of them. It was where I moved from childhood to adulthood and I thoroughly enjoyed that period.

PR   Did your parents allow you to stay?

DH   It was a relief all round. My father had been promoted again, he was in charge of the South Yorkshire Crime Squad – a plum job. I said I wasn't going and they said fine. We had reached the end of the road.

I don't think we had communicated in any meaningful sense for a couple of years. He had stopped thumping me by this time, but I never dared say anything to him because there was always the threat of a significant thump. Once he picked me up and threw me into a radiator. I still can't lie down in the bath because I've got a bump on the bottom of my spine. It was heavy duty stuff. That didn't help, but it gave me some sympathy for children with special needs.

PR   You seem to have found compensations for an unhappy home life in the community, and especially with other children.

DH   Particularly when I started having girlfriends, there were two or three girls I went out with for periods of six months and that started about my third year of secondary school. I found that very supportive, somebody actually found me attractive. Somebody who wanted to hear what I'd got to say. I remember being overwhelmed by my first girlfriend who seemed to be quite interested in me.

PR   Did your father's occupation isolate you as a family from the local community?

DH   In the mining village we lived in a council house. There was real poverty. I used to visit the houses of friends. Even then, when what you see is what you accept as the norm, I recognized it was pretty dire. I saw broken lino on the floor and the smell was quite distinctive in the houses. But when we moved we lived in a street of forty police houses near the police headquarters in Wakefield. The street was on a hill, at the bottom were the PCs and they had a basic house. Up the hill were the Sergeants' houses. These had a wash house. Further up were the Inspectors' houses, these had a small garage. At the top was the Chief Superintendent's house which had a double garage and a landscaped garden. It was a dreadful place to live. If you lived in the middle, as we did, you were above the people at the bottom and below the people at the top. The kids adopted this hierarchy physically and sociologically and psychologically. I remember discovering if you stuck your back brake on your bicycle it swung round and made a lovely skidding sound and lots of smoke and dust shot up. When I did this in the street my father rushed out, dragged me into the house and started ranting and raving about showing him up in front of all the street. It was just a normal adolescent thing. It was like living in a permanent examination room.

PR   Have you recovered from your childhood?

DH   I thought about this when I was preparing for this interview. I think there are three periods in my life. My wife of twenty-six years is my foundation and everything else is arranged around her. The first eighteen years, I really couldn't understand what it was all about. I knew there were some fundamental problems. I had no value system that made any sense. I couldn't understand what life was about. I often found it difficult to relate to other people. I divided the world into a small group of people who I rated and bonded with very strongly and then the rest who were of no consequence. It was a dreadful way of looking at things. Then there was the three years I was a student where things fell apart. I was drinking heavily, but managed to stagger out with a bare pass and finished up as a teacher. I drew a circle around where my parents were living and applied for jobs more than 100 miles away. I got a job on the penultimate day of the summer term. Once I left college it seemed as though I had broken the link and life settled down again.

PR   Things became more normal?

DH   I met my wife at the end of my first term of teaching. I remember going through a year during which I recognized I needed her and she was all I'd ever wanted, an intelligent and able woman. I felt an incredible tension. I thought I do not want a relationship, I can't be tied down, I've got to be a free-wheeling agent. I can't cope with this. So I experienced an amazing see-saw relationship, but eventually we got married. I think I have got over my childhood, it took twenty years of marriage to do it.

PR   You've exorcized the ghosts? If home life was a source of unhappiness, what of school?

DH   I think I have exorcized the ghosts, but only since I got the PhD. I remember my primary school. It was crowded. There were forty-nine children in my class. It was in an old-fashioned building with fully tiled walls, they didn't get dirty and you could wipe them down. The curriculum was dire: three years preparing for the eleven-plus. We did IQ, English and Maths tests over and over and over again. We had the same teacher for three years, a fanatic for wild flowers. That was nice. We knew the names of all the wild flowers. He had a system with the *I Spy* books of giving certificates. You brought in a wild flower to prove you had collected it so the rare ones in the district disappeared!

PR   At least he communicated . . .

DH   Yes, he did. He took us on long nature walks which was very nice because once you turned your back on the mine the area around it was superb. There were lots of ancient sites. There was a Cistercian abbey just by the school which we used to go and look at and draw and measure.

PR   What kind of a school was it? What did you see as its values?

DH   I was caned frequently, for being a nuisance basically. The head was forever grabbing my hair, pulling it in great yanks at the end of every sentence when he told me off . . .

PR   Did you deserve it?

DH   I don't know. I took it as part of life's pattern that adults did that to you. Everybody else did it so why not the head. It was a brutal sort of approach. I got caned for turning round and talking to the kid behind me. This teacher had obviously got fed up with me and sent me to the head who caned me. He caned three of us one after another. It was like a conveyor belt, you popped up every now and then and got caned and came back. There wasn't much praise or reward. There was a lot of criticism and punishment. This made the wild flowers seem all the better, but that was only within a sector of the day declared as wild flower time. The rest was grey and mono-chrome.

PR   Presumably you passed the eleven-plus? What happened then?

DH   Yes, I passed. The first grammar schools I went to I really enjoyed. I enjoyed it because it was a new start. It was different and I stopped being a nuisance.

PR   You had been successful? You had passed your eleven-plus when others didn't?

DH   Thirteen passed out of the forty-nine, but then there were two other classes. It was a big primary school. The secondary school was a new start. As soon as I arrived I could almost tangibly feel the change of values. It was my first experience of middle-class values and assumptions. I remember talking to the elder brother of a lad who'd gone up with me from a very poor family and he was going to university the next year. It suddenly struck me, 'if he's going why can't I?' Also we were doing all these new and different subjects. We were learning Latin, proper history as opposed to, I don't know, say the history of the dandelion. It was structured, it was meaningful. I remember French, it was magic. I did really well those two terms. I had just settled in and started to make friends with children from the surrounding villages who came to the school and had met people who hadn't branded me as a troublemaker, when I had to move. Looking back before this, I think I had been a bit of a bully, which is hardly surprising – kids who are thumped tend to thump others. It was a new start, and it gave me the chance to change into the kind of person I wanted to be. But of course then we moved to the hierarchical hill street in an urban setting which I described earlier. I found this difficult to accept. I had become used to playing around, making camps and pretending to be living in a stone age village for the whole of the summer holidays. We used to rip all the bushes up and pile them up into a sort of Namibian desert type shack and live our own values. And then suddenly I found myself in an urban setting set in concrete, I found that extremely distressing.

PR   What kind of a school was it?

DH   It was dreadful. The kind of grammar school where if you got four O Levels it was regarded as a real achievement. They had very low expectations. It was utterly unlike my previous school which had much higher expectations. The staff saw it as essentially a grammar school for workers' children. The bullying got worse, my bullying of other kids. I was very much a loner there. I felt bereft. I thought 'My God, how long is this going to go on for?' I was very pleased when we had to move again. I found myself at my third grammar school, a boys-only school. Strangely enough in the second school I'd had a number of girlfriends although I was only in the third year. I suppose I was precocious in that sense. As for the rest of the package, I was relieved to get away. But my third grammar school gave me an opportunity to start afresh and I changed again. I remember saying, 'Right, this is what I want to be, this is what I'm going to be'. I gave up hitting kids again, settled in reasonably well and was as happy as anybody of that age can be. I got on fairly well with most of the staff. I was in the first fifteen at Rugby which helped. I did get suspended for a week in the fifth year for something I still feel outraged about. A kid whose father was the Principal of the local FE College did something far worse a couple of days before and got a ticking off. When I popped up I found myself suspended for a week. Maybe I deserved to be suspended for it, but the inequality got to me. Apart from that I did reasonably well I think.

PR   And when your father moved again you asked to stay there?

DH   I didn't make a fuss, I simply said I didn't want to go, and he said 'Thank God'. I remember the first time I took my wife home. Afterwards he ran us to the station. He said goodbye to my wife and then turned to me and back to her and said 'God you're welcome', and walked off. That about summed up our relationship.

PR   What happened then? You took your O Levels presumably?

DH   I took O Levels and managed to get four and went into the sixth form where I rapidly collected some more. Then my motivation began to flag. I was living in digs. The others went to the pub every night, there was a lot of distraction. Early in Upper Sixth I was offered an unconditional place at the college to train to be a teacher. Well that's that, I thought and stopped working. I got one E at A Level. I could have worked extremely hard I suppose and scraped a university place, but simply gave up on that as an idea. I was always in the middle range and maintained one subject in which I came top – usually Geography. As long as I did I was happy, I felt I had let them know I could do it if I wanted to. For the rest of the subjects I was happy to be in the middle of the middle of three forms. Some of the more caring teachers recognized that that was the case. There were some quite pleasant people there, and one or two of them tried to take me on one side and tell me that if could pull my act together I could do well. But I didn't.

PR   Can you say a bit more about your life at college and also how you got your first job?

DH   There were times at college where for my self-respect and to prove a point, I tried to do really well. One was in my dissertation for the history course on the Battle of the Somme. This was in advance of the times. I interviewed old chaps in pubs and collected a lot of original material. The tutor was impressed. I didn't want them thinking I was dim.

I got married in 1970, at twenty-three, and by 1977 we had two children and suddenly life took on a shape and meaning that had eluded me and I got ambitious. By then I'd achieved rapid promotion at work. In those days there were five scales from basic teacher to biggest head of department and I was promoted to the fifth scale in five years. That did a lot for how I felt about myself. I am still grateful to the third of my heads, a very warm, very human sort of chap who told lots of stories in which he was the butt of the joke, I admired him tremendously. It was then that I began to find I needed an intellectual dimension to my thinking to enable me to do my job. I needed a framework that gave me greater insight and understanding so I did a degree in Management at the University of Wales at Wrexham College and got a First. The course was over nine weekends a year which suited family life. It was trip to Damascus for me as regards changing my values and the way I looked at the world. I came to realize a whole set of beneficial influences had been at work on me – my wife was head and shoulders above any other, but through the sixties I listened to a great deal of Bob Dylan, the ideas he advocated were diametrically opposed to the values of my family. That made them even more attractive than they might have otherwise seemed. I still remember the first time I heard Dylan sing, it was like an electric shock had gone through me and after that everything he did, every record he made, I listened to over and over. His theme that justice should be above all other values, I took on board. I thought the times were changing. I sometimes wonder if I married my wife because she'd got all the Dylan records I hadn't got. If we put them together we had a complete set, which seemed a very good reason for getting married!

PR   What happened next?

DH   Studying for the degree in Management alerted me to concepts like organization and development. I felt energized, changed and enabled. It was a wonderful period. Then I did the year with you on the Administration MEd in Birmingham which took my thinking forward and gave me confidence and understanding – that was wonderful.

PR   Why did you do a doctorate?

DH   Why does a mountaineer want to climb Everest? Because it is there. You want to try yourself against the ultimate. In my mind doing a PhD was the ultimate. It was to try to find out if what I had suspected all along was true, that I had it in me. I didn't do it in my field, Special Ed. I wanted something rigorous and suspected Educational

Administration would be far more intellectually rigorous and much less emotionally influenced. I enjoyed doing it but I'd had a really rough time in the eighties from the job point of view. When I'd finished the MEd I went to work at a school in which I wasn't happy at all for a number of reasons and I found it very difficult to get out. I didn't get on at all well with the headteacher. Subsequently, I heard and read a number of programmes and journal articles on the bully at work and realized that that was what I was experiencing. This chap had been appointed head of a small Special School with a clearly defined group of children who were physically disabled but intellectually able. His school then suddenly become all things to all people. It increased by about 500 per cent in terms of the number of children, and went from a staff of half a dozen to one of over a hundred and he was totally incapable of managing it. He used to use classic phrases like 'I don't need a management course, I manage by the seat of my pants'. It was patently obvious he was inadequate and hated people with qualifications. We had a lot of eminent medical consultants coming into the school to do clinics and his pet activity was to find some tiny reason for sounding off in public (always in public) and he'd shout and bawl at them. This made life difficult. As for the PhD I did it, partly, because I needed to prove to myself I was still able to do something useful. Everything I tried to do within the school, he allowed to go forward until it began to develop and then deliberately pull the plug, he'd sabotage it. He did this to everybody. The number of nervous breakdowns within the staff was significant. What he did to me wasn't personal, he did it to everybody. The state I was in as a result of six years of this treatment was probably the worst possible in which to do a PhD; by the time I'd finished it I was fairly near a breakdown.

PR   Who amongst your own teachers do you remember and why?

DH   There was a teacher of English at the grammar school with low expectations who was inspired. She invented a story about a murder and we all had to work out possible next stages, and we wrote them all down, collected them and talked about them. We built up the story as a whole class, and then she took it away, twisted it a little bit and left it with a number of openings. It was a bit like the stories that became fashionable in the eighties where you could choose different ways through or different endings. We dressed up as different people in the Court. I was the Defence Lawyer and had an academic gown. Her lessons were like a shaft of light coming into the dark cavern that was our education at that time. It was a phenomenally exciting thing to be involved in, so she stands out.

PR   At what point did you decide you were going to be a teacher, and why?

DH   I went to college because I wanted to be a student and I wanted to enjoy three years. I hadn't decided to teach at all, in fact I had great difficulties getting through the teaching practice. I had to repeat at least one of them, I think I had to repeat two of them, but then taking into account the state I was in at the time that was not totally surprising. But I did stagger through, and ...

PR   Should they have failed you?

DH   Without any doubt. I once came across a Ministry of Education Circular, when I was doing the MEd, which had been sent to college principals, which said the natural wastage on teacher training courses is X per cent of the intake. This is far more than we can cope with so under no circumstances fail anybody. I thought, 'that's how I passed!' I did not really decide I wanted to be a teacher until well into my second post. Before then it was just something to do. I had been remarkably unimaginative. It was more a case of total inertia than anything else that kept me in it. My first school, a large co-educational comprehensive in a depressed area of the West Midlands, was a strange place. The staff were very idiosyncratic, hand picked characters, a bizarre bunch of people. I drifted through it.

Then I went to a well managed, extremely large comprehensive school at the centre of a large, recently completed housing estate in the West Midlands and began to realize that there was something magical about teaching. I started getting the hang of it and by the time I left three years later I think I had begun to be quite good at it. I also had a chance to see what it was to be very good at it because I got to work with the head's wife, the other half of the Remedial Department, she was a truly gifted teacher.

PR   It sounds like you rather drifted into remedial teaching?

DH   Well, at my first school, I was supposed to be doing English O Level and some remedial groups. This was not so much from choice, rather it was the only thing I could get to be honest, they just gave me the timetable and I accepted it. That's how I operated at the time. I never questioned authority. It was only later I started to question.

PR   In your second post, you knew you were applying to work in a remedial department?

DH   I did. There was myself and another chap I became good friends with. In those days there was a desperate shortage of teachers. At the end of the interview the head said 'I am not going to give you that job, but if you agree to do the remedial work I'll give you an extra scale'. I had applied for a job with two extra scales which was the sort of cheeky thing people could do in those days. In that sense, I chose to do remedial work. I got the extra scale which did my confidence much good, over the next three years I perfected being a teacher. But it was only after about a year of being at that school that I actually finally decided that teaching is what I wanted to do.

PR   And you worked with a superb teacher. What made her so good?

DH   She was warm, caring and had a highly structured approach setting herself and others very clear targets. She had a clear view on what remedial teaching was about, there was no ambiguity about what she wanted to achieve. Not a sergeant major. She just did the basics but very, very well indeed.

PR   What do you remember about the head?

DH   He had his strengths but could be manipulative. He knew what he wanted and didn't have too many scruples about getting it. At the end of the day the children got a five-star education and that's what it should be all about.

PR   Do you mean to some extent the end justified the means in his case?

DH   To an extent. He played a dirty trick on me which took a while to forgive. I applied for a job which he knew I'd get so he offered me an extra scale to stay. Only when I'd withdrawn did he tell me 'Of course, it's up to the governors'; I never did get the higher scale. He was capable of doing things like that, but at the same time the children got an excellent service. I think he tended to put the interests of the children first. I don't think anything gave him more pleasure than seeing one of them succeed at something they might not have been expected to achieve. They did succeed at a very wide range of things. We had children appearing in television programmes. When there was a drama presentation costumes were hired from the West End. This cost a great deal and everybody had to contribute to raise the money for it. It was a big school with over 1,600 kids, and big ambitions. Everything was done with style and quality.

PR   What of your third school?

DH   This was a community school in the north of the West Midlands conurbation and was a wonderful place with the full range of facilities found in community comprehensives. It was brand new. It had an open-plan layout, and took a mixed-ability, inter-disciplinary approach, with groups of 120 children taught by a team of teachers. It was wonderful. I co-ordinated a team of fourteen who did nothing other than provide learning support across the curriculum. As an LEA inspector now I go round trying to fan flames of development less ambitious than we achieved then. People think they are discovering something new and exciting, obviously I don't tell them, but we were doing such radical stuff then and had the setting and the resources to make this possible. We had triple levels of capitation and, on top of that, in the first three years I managed, through the Inspector concerned, to get £5,000, at 1973 prices, as extra grant. We ran out of things to buy. We had special machines such as synchro-faxes and language masters which enabled illiterate children to read work sheets, to do the questions, even though they couldn't read and write.

PR   How successful was all this in enabling pupil learning?

DH   Very successful. Each year we took in 240 kids, 60 of whom had very significant reading difficulties, and about a dozen who were total non-starters, and by the end of the year all were reading. Many put three or four years on their reading age in that one year. To have lived in an intellectual desert for ten to eleven years and then suddenly to bloom meant that potentially some of them were high fliers and all could do much better than had previously been expected. That told me a lot, it formed my views on education and remedial education.

PR   How far did the head contribute to all this?

DH   As far as contributing to the development of the theory that underpinned the whole operation, it was virtually nil. He'd come from a boys' grammar school where he'd been deputy head for fifteen years. But he did recognize that the fourteen of us knew what we were doing and had a lot of sound ideas and so gave us anything we asked for and, in that sense, enabled it to happen.

PR   Where did the ideas come from?

DH   Some I'd developed at my previous school in a limited way. But I could never persuade the head there to a total commitment to such an approach. At the open-plan comprehensive we were given possibilities by the design of the new school. Obviously somebody believed in an open-plan approach and gave the architects their brief. It wasn't the only school there to have that design. It was good and helped what we tried to do to succeed. But all things are relative. It didn't work as well as it could, in part for historical reasons. It was a new school but had its origins in the last of the secondary moderns set up in that Authority. As such it had the most difficult catchment area in terms of children who were socially and culturally deprived. It had staff, some in key head of department positions, who had worked at this secondary modern for up to fifteen years. They brought with them attitudes learnt in their previous school. So there was always a tension between those who were totally committed and those who were totally uncommitted to the kind of things I have described above. Ultimately the uncommitted won in the sense that after four years the builders turned up and put walls up and turned the open-plan layout into conventional classrooms. At that point I left.

It had been a time of a massive expansion of thinking and practice in terms of the nature and quality of meeting the needs of children with learning needs in mainstream – if we started again today it would take a long time to get to where we were then.

PR   Where did you want to go to next?

DH   Career wise the next step would be either to be a deputy head of a comprehensive or to be something else. I really didn't fancy being deputy head of a comprehensive. So financially I moved sideways to the deputy headship of a relatively big MLD, 165 children, school in the same authority. I stayed for two years, technically three, because I did a year on secondment. In 1981 I moved to another large special school in a neighbouring LEA in the West Midlands with the intention of eventually becoming an Inspector. By then I'd become more interested in this than anything else.

PR   More interesting than being a head?

DH   Yes. So I moved to a second deputy headship to gain experience of those elements of special needs I hadn't covered. I'd done mainstream and MLD special, the new school gave opportunities to work with physically, mentally and sensorily disabled children.

I still remember my first day. At 10.15 the head called me into his office. I'd only been in the school an hour, he ranted and raved, said I'd got nothing to offer as far as he was concerned, it hadn't been his idea to appoint me and so on and on. I went out quite shaken, but one of the other deputies said don't worry, he does that to everybody. I was lucky he didn't do it in the middle of the corridor. He was unbelievable, he didn't improve during the six years I was there. I was on the payroll for nine years in all but was on secondment the last three. I think the authority recognized there were significant problems. They were unhappy years. He used to do things like say to people, 'I'll fix it so that you'll never get another job in this authority'. In my case I suspect it was true. I made seventy-six applications and got eight interviews. I'd a first class degree and a masters in educational management, experience of everything under the sun special needs wise, a history of rapid promotion, a lot of people saying nice things about me but it didn't help. It struck me again and again how fragile the system was. There are all those charts that say if there's a problem you approach this person who approaches that person and all this suggests that the system as a whole maintains fairness and justice, but when push comes to shove there is a strong likelihood it doesn't work.

PR   Nobody ever took a grievance procedure out?

DH   I thought of doing so and was advised to, but remembered something I'd been told by an inspector about a deputy who took a grievance procedure against his head. Everybody recognized that the deputy was in the right but he never got further promotion. It may be good for everybody else but it may not be for you. I concluded that what I had to do was to grit my teeth and get out, but that proved to be difficult. Eventually I got secondment and did the research that led to the PhD. I then returned for a short time under a new head, by this time the other one had gone, but was offered a headship.

PR   How did that happen?

DH   I'd come back and the new head, I think he'd admit, didn't want me there in the sense that we were coming up to LMSS and he couldn't see the purpose of having three deputies and so was happy for me to go. We discussed it, and one day, literally, the Inspector walked in and said 'How would you like to be a Head?' This after seventy-six applications in which I had tried for everything going.

PR   Including some headships?

DH   Some headships within my own authority. But I wasn't getting interviews and that really was corrosive because it meant, presumably, I was not getting support from the authority. Some inspectors and officers even seemed to believe if a head says black is white, then it is and no argument. It was certainly put to me that 'You don't get on with your head'. For that person those who didn't got on with their head can't be a head. It was as simple as that. Happily, not everybody in the authority shared his view. As I said earlier an inspector turned up and said, 'There is a school, would you like to be the head?' I said 'Yes, yes'. He then told me 'It's a very difficult situation, the head has asked to leave, the kids have wrecked the place, there's no curriculum, there's no materials, are you sure?' I said 'Yes, yes, yes. No problem whatsoever.'

PR   Did you know the school?

DH   I'd visited it once. It was pretty awful, but that was three years earlier. I didn't care what it was as long as it wasn't where I was. When I got there I found a demoralized staff and several dirty old settees along the main corridor on which the kids seemed to lounge all day taking no notice of any bells that sounded, and so it went on.

PR   Can I ask you first when and why you realized you wanted to be a head?

DH   I'd been on courses and developed a range of ideas on management, about how you could enable people to realize their potential by involving them in decision-making. I thought this would enable them to function at a higher level – it would make them happier and more productive, and therefore the children would get a better deal. I wanted the chance to put these ideas into action. I wanted to try them out in special education by creating a community in which the children were also involved in decision-making, where their inappropriate behaviour, lack of confidence, feeling of no worth, was transformed into a feeling of empowerment. A situation in which they could make a linkage between what they decided to do, what they did and how this improved their lot. I wanted them to see this happening in very concrete terms. It was almost coincidental that to do that I needed to be a head. It wasn't 'I want to be a head, I want to be in charge'. I needed a vehicle, a place and a venue in which I could use the authority of headship to shape a culture and to create opportunities for people to grow into new ideas.

PR   You encountered many heads as a pupil and teacher, what have you learned from them?

DH   I thought a lot about this when I read your questions. I can't think of anything I learned from any of the heads I have known in terms of wanting to use what they did as a theme to put my variations on. None as far as I can remember did anything I regard as central to what I've tried to do. I can see a lot of what they did I've looked at and thought I must avoid doing. It's been what not to do, very much so. I can think of little I learned, apart from the head who was a very human character, warm, and told jokes against himself.

PR   At least one was effective if somewhat manipulative and sometimes ruthless?

DH   The ruthless bit I could live with. On occasions I have been ruthless as a head, but I preceded this by saying 'These are our values. We've agreed them over time.' We posted a set of basic values on the staff room wall in very large print. Whenever we got into a discussion in staff meetings and were splitting up into opposing groups advocating very different views we could say 'let's look at the wall, let's go back to basics, what's this school about? This school is about these things.' Whatever we did had to relate to these values. That meant if somebody said 'I just don't want to do this or that, I don't like it', this was ruthlessly put down and I would say 'I'm sorry that isn't acceptable, that isn't a reason for not doing it'. Maybe I'm living in cloud cuckoo land but I genuinely believe that the staff group we were working with thought like this. This did not mean we always came to quick and easy decisions. Some discussions went on for nine months.

PR   To what extent did you lead the decisions they arrived at?

DH   In the early days far more than later. I identified three types of decision when I first got there. First, executive decisions where I say what we are doing, if you don't like it, that's tough, that's what's happening. Second, collaborative decisions where I say by the end of this session, in an hour and a quarter, we are going to make a decision, let's explore the possibilities. We would identify options and at the end I would make the decision, but would have consulted. Third, participative decisions where we operated a Quaker-style meeting and carried on until we arrived at a consensus we could all go along with. Over the six years I was there, the number of executive decisions dropped to nil, the number of consultative ones reduced and the number of participative ones soon increased dramatically because people became used to that way of operating. At first it took a long time to arrive at consensus because people were not used to this under the previous regime.

PR   An alternative explanation might be that over time they'd come to accept your values or the dominating group's values and those who disagreed moved on.

DH   Well yes, there was that first alternative. The second is less plausible because the staff group was very stable. Although they'd had a rough time many had been there for between ten and twenty years and weren't moving. They'd lived through several heads and all sorts of stressful situations over the years. Being in an EBD school was by definition stressful, but they'd stuck it. Over the six years there was one retirement through medical breakdown; all the others were normal retirements.

PR   Did you feel ready for headship when it finally came?

DH   Very much so. I never doubted that I could do it. When new situations came up, I had a framework of research to fall back on. When people did things that other people might have thought, my God, it's personal, they don't like me, I just thought this is the stage we are at. I actually sat down at one point with the staff and said, look, this is where I think we are at. And we went through an exercise in which they described where they thought we were at and how they felt about being there, and what they wanted to be done.

PR   Can you say something more about the school?

DH   It was for Emotionally Behaviourally Difficult Children. It's a day school for secondary children, there are two others in that LEA but they are residential. It's on a 1960s small housing estate, located cheek by jowl with the community. When one of our kids sneezed a dozen people living around knew. That made life difficult at times because it is a deprived community, so some of the children's behaviour in school was mirrored by adults across the road. You didn't know which group you were dealing with at times.

There were problems with pretty well every facet of the school and our relationships with the community were poor. We had fights in the middle of the street when I first went there with the children and the local people. The police were there regularly. I invited the staff to analyse this when I arrived. There were three assistants, seven teachers, a deputy and the head. I sat down with them and said 'Over the next however long it takes I think these are the stages we will go through. A stage where you don't trust me and will think I am doing things for all sorts of reasons which aren't acceptable. A stage in which you will start to understand what we are trying to do and a stage in which you will start to trust me.' After a couple of years, I said 'We are now at stage three, we have accomplished this and this, you now trust me. You didn't believe me when I said the school is going to remain open. It's done that. You didn't believe me when I said I was going to get resources we needed. We now have these resources.' So you constantly look back to remind them of progress spelling out where you were going to. The MEd and BEd were an excellent preparation, they enabled me to do all this because I knew what I wanted and I had a framework and an understanding to work from and I shared this with the staff so that they also felt that they were working within a structure.

PR   In one sense you had little to lose. If the school did not survive and prosper, you could hardly be held responsible.

DH   It did cross my mind that they might be trying to kill two birds with one stone. But no, as you say I was on a winner. In fact the officer who encouraged me said 'You can go there and you're not going to lose'. I found the staff desperate to have something that would give them self-respect, identity and credibility. Inevitably they said 'You've never worked in an EBD school'. The fact that I had been in a tough mainstream school and an MLD school with some EBD kids was not enough. I had the same problem when I went into PhD work and when I moved from mainstream to MLD. Every time I was told I didn't have the particular skills required. There is a lot of this in special education.

PR   There are so many kinds of special education, and a tendency to believe that if you don't have a specialism in the particular area you intend to work in you can't be relied on as a professional.

DH   This is one of the problems of special education. Some staff seem to feel the 'special' tag refers to them and not to the pupils. They feel their skills are very, very special. In fact if you analyse what exactly these are you are left wondering in many cases. In my present job I talk to SENCOs in mainstream schools all over the Midlands and am often impressed by the quality of their understanding of curriculum and how it can be analysed, differentiated and organized. Sometimes I go into MLD schools and think there should be more emphasis on the curriculum and more emphasis on understanding how a curriculum actually works, and I find that an area that needs development.

PR   You were at the EBD school six years. What was your vision for the school?

DH   To create a community, a place where children with significant behaviour problems arising out of their experiences could have the space to say 'I want to change, and I want to change into this. I want to change into somebody who takes hold of my life.' I wanted to create a school which would support them in making this a reality. A school capable of organizing their own learning and of teaching them to be able to negotiate with a teacher and say 'I accept that over the next fortnight I've got to do this amount of work in these subjects. I'd like to do this subject today, that subject tomorrow, and then come back to this.' As such, for pupils their curriculums are planned out as negotiated exercises and the social and organizational skills, the understanding of how you set about learning something are intrinsic elements of such a package. In such an approach the teacher is an enabler, an organizer, a provider, a support, a critical friend, rather than a didactic authoritarian figure. In fact the education process is seen as something that happens every single minute of every single day within the community.

This was true of other aspects of life in the school. On the school budget, for instance, we reached a point in which the children had the right, and knew they had the right, to take part in decisions on allocation. We had a School Council made up of every child and member of staff and it was explained to the children that there were three elements in the budget. There was that which you had to spend, that which you didn't have to spend but if you didn't you'd find life difficult, and the rest, and they discussed each budget item and the category to which it belonged. We introduced things like form funding. Each term each form got £250 and £25 for each child which generally worked out at around about £500, they collectively could decide how that was to be spent. They could organize trips, buy furniture, organize events, have their room decorated, whatever. The money was held in the 'bank' for a term, every time anybody swore in the class 25p was knocked off, if anybody bullied somebody £2, if anybody got excluded £10, any damage (accidental or otherwise) the money came off to pay for it. The first couple of terms we tried this they finished up minus £300. But after a year or so they cottoned on and only lost maybe £100 over the term. One class decided they would employ the caretaker at £10 an hour, she bought the paint, and they wanted their room decorated according to their colour scheme. They then saved the money for a couple of terms and over the summer holidays ordered furniture which was grey and scarlet. When they came back after the summer holidays there it was, it didn't get scratched, marked or anything for a couple of years. Other classes bought tropical fish tanks or music centres for use at break or whatever, not one piece of equipment was damaged. Now you would think it unlikely that EBD secondary-age boys faced with delicate machinery like music centres would cause no damage for three years but this is what happened. The best term we had on the vandalism front we spent only £154 from September to Christmas on all sorts of damage. To get this in perspective: every time the caretaker had to rub some graffiti off the wall she charged a minimum of £10. Graffiti was eradicated and vandalism virtually vanished.

We identified a number of criteria by which we would measure our success. Swearing was still something of a problem when I left, but when I got there the children couldn't put more than five words together without a couple of 'f's and a 'c'. The tolerance children showed each other greatly improved. In the case of bullying, I kept thinking it has to be a lot worse than it seems. I searched for examples and so did the staff. We came to the conclusion that the kind of bullying which consistently and deliberately sets out to make somebody miserable day after day simply wasn't happening. I find it difficult to say this because nobody's going to believe me. Even I find it hard to believe that in an EBD school for secondary-aged boys this sort of bullying isn't going on. But the amount of supervision of the children was very high. The staff didn't take breaks so seven teachers and six assistants in my last year were around all the time. This made possible a whole range of activities – there was a kids' café which was a mini-enterprise and we had a school farm. We had pigs, chickens, hens, geese, rabbits, a horse and all run by the children up to a point. The caretaker supervised, but the eggs were produced for the kids' café and so the profit paid for the farm, it was all very nice.

PR   A system based upon valuing children and also staff. You achieved IIP didn't you?

DH   The IIP people first came in July and had a chat with us and did a health check in September. The only thing we had to work on from the twenty-four criteria was to improve our induction process for new staff. We had started doing that when we learned the OFSTED inspection we had been expecting wasn't going to happen because they couldn't get a team together. This took the steam out of IIP because we had seen it as a bulwark against OFSTED. But in the following February I said we might as well finish so we did another four weeks' work on it. And then a guy came, assessed us and passed us, so we'd got IIP. That nicely confirmed that the framework I'd taken to the school worked.

PR   What were your views on the curriculum at the school when you first came?

DH   There was no real curriculum. The timetable was basically about keeping the kids in your room with you – a primary school model – you and ten kids in a room, shut the door and keep them there. What a lot of the teachers seemed to do was based on their own hobbies. If you'd got somebody who liked making model aeroplanes their kids spent most of the time making model aeroplanes. There was a guy who spent vast amounts of time making models. The kids loved it but I'm not sure they learned anything. To change this meant re-educating the staff to the notion that they were teachers, that teachers taught children, and that the curriculum is basically what a state school, even an EBD school, is about. I wanted to persuade them that the national curriculum was a superb instrument, compared to the alternative of not having anything, for doing it. That was the first stage. The second stage was enabled by the extensive contacts I had made during my secondment with many of the staff development tutors the authority had appointed. I got them in. We spent a lot of staff meetings considering, 'How do you teach children effectively?' We gradually moved away from the notion you just tell them things, and if they don't listen you shout, to a notion of sharing in the process. We then moved in that very simple way into issues of pedagogy. All the time I was recruiting staff because when I arrived three of the eight teachers were on supply. Some on long-term supply, people at the very end of their careers – nobody else wanted them so they went to the EBD school. So my first task was just to get some staff who had elected to be there and who had something to offer. Ironically it was only as I was leaving that the final pieces of the jigsaw were put in place and I finished up with a team, all ex-mainstream, all ex-comprehensive in challenging areas, all subject specialists with significant experiences and, most importantly, all of very significant ability. I'd made it over the six years. We had a maths specialist, an English specialist, an RE trained person who did the Humanities, a music teacher with a very high standard of musical ability who was also fluent in French, an art specialist and two technologists. We had a better teaching team than some small comprehensives.

PR   How did you know what was going on in classrooms and corridors at the school?

DH   It was a small school so I went into every classroom every day. I was seeing what was happening. I also talked to many children in classrooms and elsewhere. At staff meetings we shared perceptions of what we were doing and how and how effectively. There was an openness. One of our beliefs was there was no blame – nobody blamed anybody for anything. Instead we sat down and analysed how things could be done better. I never heard anybody saying 'That was your fault. If you hadn't done that . . . '. We talked and talked about what we were doing, and how we could do it better. Within each form room every child had a piece of board about four feet square, that was their territory and they pinned up on it their best examples of work. We asked the children to write what they thought about different aspects of what we were doing. 'I like school because . . . ', that sort of thing. They could put up pictures of their dogs, cats. It was their board. We had a sophisticated reward system linked to school trips. If children didn't achieve in various ways consistently over the term they didn't go on the trip, that was ruthlessly applied. It presented very challenging situations until the children realized we really meant it. They would kick the side of the minibus and have a tantrum and pull the windscreen wipers off but eventually they just quietly accepted the fact that they hadn't earned whatever it was, they hadn't performed to the required standard, and the standard was set by the children themselves within the school council. They negotiated all sorts of anomalies like if somebody had been away ill and hadn't got the required number of points, what would we do about that? All this gave us many opportunities to monitor their ability to cope with a wide variety of situations. I would go to a school council and say 'I think I have decided that I am going to exclude him for doing this. What do you think?' And the children would spend twenty minutes very rationally and objectively and calmly discuss the rights and wrongs of excluding him.

PR   And did they sometimes say you shouldn't? Would you accept that?

DH   Fifty per cent of the time I accepted it. At other times I'd say no, I don't accept what you say and I am making the decision and the kid would be sitting there, and they took it, and that was an indicator that what we were doing was working. Everything we did was spelt out as group management theory tells you it ought to be done – transparent but not manipulative. You might be perceived as ruthless, but they know you are going to be.

PR   So it is open and transparent in a certain sense, but it's also highly structured, and almost behavioural in other ways. It sounds like a form of behaviour management.

DH   I suppose so. It was certainly consistent. Now you've mentioned it I suppose it was behavioural. That's inevitable because I lived through the seventies and eighties in special education when behaviourism was rife, elements within behaviourism do make sense in certain situations. It's when you start employing it across the board that you get problems. But whatever else, I was trying to put in place a system, and that's what the staff and children needed. Before that they had no shape, structure, consistency in their lives. Everything was an ad hoc happening at school and at home. Some of our pupils had been abused in all sorts of ways. We had a girl, although we didn't have girls after the first two years, who witnessed the murder of her mother's lover on the hearth rug while she was sitting on the settee. We had all sorts of children. They needed structure, they needed to know when they'd finished kicking the waste bin down the corridor and ripping stuff off the wall and hitting their head on the door you were still going to be saying 'no'; eventually they stopped doing those sorts of things because they knew what was going to happen. You could say to them, look, we are here, we are going to there, if you do this in between it won't make a bit of difference. They knew you were right.

PR   I have often been told about the importance of the annual review process for children with special needs. Is this less the case in the kind of process you set up?

DH   We had a daily review. But we have a formal annual review but in an EBD school I don't think anybody looked at any statement because it didn't tell you anything. So as far as the review goes it was a very minimalist approach. We were seeing the parents on a regular basis. All the teachers had a 20 per cent non-contact timetable to enable them to maintain very close links with all the agencies and the family. I expected all parents who had a phone to be contacted twice a week to just have a chat. Quite often the chat was about Grandma's bunions or the pet rabbit's problems, but it established a level of continuing contact. All too often the parents' experience of being in school as kids and being a parent of a kid in school was very, very bad indeed.

PR   Was there anything dear to your heart you didn't achieve? Why did you decide to leave?

DH   I can't think of anything I wanted to do and didn't do. I can think of a number of areas where I didn't do enough. I achieved all the key things I wanted. I created the School Council, the form funding initiative, the school farm and developed the kids' café, and many other similar things. I'd got all the staff involved in decision-making. We'd got the children involved in decision-making. I could have taken some things a lot further. For instance the school grounds. We had a £160,000 development project. We'd had professional land-scape architects do us a beautiful plan. We were starting to involve the community in development of the school and its grounds as a community. We had the whole of the estate involved so the school would become an integrated element of the whole estate which was the next stage. Had this happened, I would have become a sort of community leader because the estate was small enough for that. I could have stayed and continued that process and it would have been very exciting and new. Pay-wise I was on Point 28 so I actually took a pay drop to move to become an inspector. I think that after six years no matter how successful, in an EBD school you are exhausted. You are absolutely simply finished. It's like being an ageing boxer, you know what to do but your hands and feet won't do it any longer, you are . . .

PR   You're punch-drunk.

DH   Not punch-drunk. That suggests you've lost the direction of where you are going. That's not it at all, I still had a very clear vision, but dealing with children who are by their nature extremely challenging is exhausting. It's exhausting because you can have something happen at quarter to nine and if you do the job properly and you do the counselling and enable the child to analyse their own actions and then do the necessary reparations and go and apologize to the necessary people, it can take you up to lunch-time. By which time the report that you've got to do for the Education Department has still got to be done, so you do it at nine o'clock at night and over the years it simply knackers you.

PR   I am sure that is true, but you've hankered after being an inspector haven't you? What's the attraction of an inspector's job? How would you compare it with headship?

DH   It's certainly less stressful on a day-to-day basis. Nobody is going to be swearing at you or throwing chairs at you. There are far more opportunities to operate intellectually. There's far more variety. You are dealing with a whole range of people. You are working on a much bigger scale. And that's one of the things about the EBD school towards the end. I felt more and more constrained. It was small. What I was doing was valid, no doubt about it. Probably the most meaningful job I've ever done, but it was small, and intellectually I wanted something bigger, and I've got that now. I'm operating across a whole borough, in fact across a region because since I went to my present authority we have started talks with surrounding LEAs, to discuss regional provision and the distribution of kids with special needs, and the distribution of units where they can be catered for. There is the prospect of rubbing out the boundaries and seeing what patterns emerge. Now that is exciting. That is intellectually challenging.

PR   It's some months since you've taken up your new post. Looking back, what kind of a head were you? What sort of a leader? What would your staff or others say on this?

DH   It depends who you ask I suppose. I think as a leader I was totally committed. I am sure my wife would say that. She feels, I'm sure, that I always put the job before her, and I suppose if I'm honest, I did. I always forced myself (and sometimes it was difficult) to be reasonable and calm with staff and pupils even when they made some silly mistake or had done something that was so stupid. I never, ever lost my rag with staff. I've witnessed how destructive that could be personally. I was always reasonable. On rare occasions I would say to staff 'Let's leave this until after school, I need a couple of hours to think about it'. During which time I would sit on my own and think, well, what can possibly be the picture from where they're at? I would force myself to go through that process. Sometimes I would be totally nonplussed as to why they had done what they had done. Whichever, when they came I would explain that I have gone through this process and I've made this list of four things that describe what it looks like from where you're at. Is that right? And just the process of showing them that I had actually tried to understand often defused some quite challenging situations.

PR   Was there a fit, do you think, between the values that underpinned your educational vision and your vision for the school and the way in which you operated as a manager?

DH   I believe there has to be harmony between the management style, the administrative system, the curriculum, pedagogy and all of the other elements of the school systems.

PR   To whom are you accountable and what was the nature of that accountability?

DH   I found this very difficult actually, because legally you are responsible to the LEA, or the LEA is responsible for ensuring things happen in a certain way. But in practice, in the EBD school authority, the LEA's role was so marginal at that time. For example, I decided I wasn't having girls any more in the school, and I told them, and that's how it happened. So if the head of a school can decide whether he has girls or not without consulting the LEA then the lines of accountability there cannot be onerous. Basically, I don't think the LEA cared less as long as nobody finished up on the front page of the newspaper. It was that sort of a set-up at that time. As for the inspector, we must have had at least six or seven different ones in the six years that I was there, and most of them had very little specialist advice to offer. So again, as far as support or a feeling that you were responsible to the LEA, it was very tenuous. I felt a strong responsibility to the children really. That sounds ever so gooey, but . . .

PR   No, that comes out clearly. What of the governing body? You haven't mentioned them.

DH   When I first went there wasn't a governing body. There hadn't been a governing body meeting for over a year. Eventually we got a number of people together, but really the governing body was just a legal device. They meet regularly now as they ought to, and there's five, I think, now on it. They turn up for meetings but don't come into school for any other reason. I had good relations with them. For virtually all the time after we had reconstituted it, they were extremely supportive. They gave me seven pay points. That's fairly indicative of their level of support. And they let me go a couple of weeks into the term where I should really have stayed to the end of the term. I would give a very fulsome written report to the governing body, in a sense that was to my advantage because it rather decided the agenda. The only governor to come into school was the chair. The rest of the governors were very much once a term, well, actually, three times a term sometimes. They seemed to like meeting, but it didn't indicate a high level of involvement. Their involvement was marginal if supportive.

PR   How do you keep up to date? How do you cope with stress when things go wrong? How do you stay sane in what sounds a little bit like an insane job?

DH   You are surrounded constantly by children who are, up to a point, very much on the edge or even close to being over the edge. Now and again you come across kids who are psychiatrically disturbed. It is very stressful in that sense. How do I cope? Well, my wife is *the* point of sense and strength. It must drive her round the bend, but I go home and talk things through with her. She is a very wise and sensitive person and full of understanding kind of person, and she always has the ability to say 'Yes, but if you take these other things into account it does start to make some sense, doesn't it?' And she puts it into a context that makes it possible for me to cope with. Her support is tremendous and ongoing. She keeps me sane. In addition, I go for walks, dig the garden, I've got an acre of garden so by the time you've dug it once it's the end of year.

As for keeping up to date, I find reading hard work. I've always found reading hard work. I don't read for pleasure. I used to as a child, but somewhere along the line I lost out. I only read to gain information. I rely more and more on journal articles from which I just pick out the key points. It's all very superficial, but I've reached the point in life where I have an in-depth framework and can quote bits of research, however out of date, in support when I need. I can relate incoming information to this overarching conceptual network. That's one of the benefits of being fifty not twenty-five.

PR   Are you a member of the NAHT or the community of special school headteachers?

DH   Off and on. I have been a member of the Association of Special Education but don't always find it a source of intellectual inspiration, this is one of the problems of the whole area of special needs. When I did the MEd I studied aspects of the three elements of curriculum, special education and administration. I found curriculum and administration intellectually challenging, very connected to eternal truths if you like, and gave you a lot to think about. Special needs, I found, was always desperately looking for solutions.

PR   Its focus was on content rather than process?

DH   That's right I suppose. It was always claiming if you do this, it will be all right. I was always left thinking but if you don't do it in that individual context it won't be all right. The strategies, such as Conductive Education for example, were context-specific and worked, maybe worked, because of staff commitment as much as anything else. I never found any satisfaction in what they were saying. I never found it of much use.

PR   If headship was so hard why did you do it all that time?

DH   It enabled me to do what I wanted to do. I wanted to have a place where there were a group of professionals and a group of children who had needs, and I wanted to create a distinct operation according to a coherent set of values which were linked, I suppose, to a number of inspirational influences. These included Summerhill. I know lots of people claim this but the set of ideas it expressed really were a source of inspiration in determining what I tried to do within the very real constraints of a local authority school.

PR   Given the demands of headship today, is it possible to be an educational leader?

DH   If you've got the guts to do it. If you've got the vision. You've got to know what you're talking about because if an inspector comes into your school asking questions and you don't have well thought out, theoretically related, philosophically sound answers, then they're going to feel free to start suggesting you do things some other way. But if an inspector comes and you demonstrate the strength of what you are doing and why you are doing it, and you've got evidence to show that things are working better than a year ago, and much better than when you arrived, then things are different.

PR   What do you see as the key developments in special education? What of the future?

DH   There have been two key developments, both from the Conservative administration. First, the national curriculum has transformed special education. It has taken it out of the hands of the well intentioned amateurs and given it a proper focus – the curriculum. When I first went to special education people said 'What do you want to worry about the curriculum. We are here to love the kids to bits.' So the national curriculum has given us a framework and ensured that special education remains a part of a continuum of schooling.

Second, and it's wonderful, is the Code of Practice. It confirms, if twenty years later, what we were doing in the mid seventies. It's opening up the possibility that schools will start to do a range of things. One of the things I'm working on at the moment as an inspector is encouraging secondary schools to see the role of the SENCO as a real co-ordinator; a teaching and learning consultant for the school. In addition, that within each department there is somebody with the dual function of looking after the children with special needs whilst still a full member of the subject team. This would enable thinking on the curriculum in three areas. First, on that which is essential to the subject in making it what it is – the range of skills, experiences and content that is central. Second, on the sub-concepts branching off those key concepts that are very important. Third, the rest which is the detail that gives colour, meaning and shape. By undertaking such curriculum analysis, you are improving the process of curriculum transaction, pedagogy and structure of what you are doing. You are enabling teachers to be more effective across the whole range of ability of children, whilst also enabling the writing of subject-focused IEPs. If a child is to learn 25 per cent of what the average-ability kid does, let's make sure it's the 25 per cent that enables the development of a framework on which for the rest of his life he can hang further information. That's a notion from the Code of Practice, it seems to me.

PR   What of the implications of Warnock ideas?

DH   I've always felt out of step, an oddball. I've never felt comfortable in meetings made up entirely of practitioners from special schools. My interests in, for example, the curriculum and its analysis aren't the traditional things people in special education focus on. When I was at the school for physical disabilities people seemed to take such pleasure in collecting all sorts of understanding of obscure physical conditions and lots of long words that end in 'isis' or 'osis'. I always felt they were substituting what they should be good at by trying to be good at something else. They wanted to be special and different and were in danger of abandoning education. Education, albeit, for a child in a wheelchair, in which, it seemed to me, the wheelchair was regarded as central. That was probably a source of friction between myself and the head. He, unlike me, was comfortable focusing on non-educational things.

PR   Have recent developments pushed special education more into your line of thinking than it used to be: educational issues are more centre stage and special issues further back?

DH   Absolutely. I feel I have been ahead of the game for the last twenty years. What I'm trying to do in my work at the moment is to develop a flexible and responsive continuum from mainstream through special schools through a series of units. My authority is blessed in having an unusually large number of children with special needs located in units attached to mainstream schools. They've got them for EBD, MLD, visually impaired, hearing impaired, etc., so part of the infrastructure is already there. I am trying to identify ways of making it far more possible for children to go into special education for specific reasons and specific lengths of time whilst remaining on the roll of the mainstream school. This would take place on a kind of contract basis. I find it hard to understand how support from a support team going into a mainstream school, working for a couple of hours with a mainstream teacher, can be made as effective and economic as other uses of the same resource which can be made. Clearly the role of the MLD school needs to be developed so that the boundaries between it and the units and mainstream are very permeable and children dual funded. So children might be in the MLD school, and in the extreme cases might be there for several years, but would still remain on the roll of a mainstream school and, wherever possible, should spend time in the mainstream school. There's a whole lot of ideas being explored along those lines. I think that's what will happen over the next five years. Every single authority in the country as far as I understand it is massively overspent on the special needs budget. Two Directors of Education have been sacked essentially for not doing something about it. We had a consultant who works with many authorities all over the country come and speak to our inspectors and he explained all this very graphically. We have to move resources upstream, so that we are not spending it on people on stage 4 and 5 of the Code of Practice. Rather we're spending it on stages 1 and 2 and 3. In that way you then make statementing an activity which becomes almost redundant. Even so, if we go down this route, it will be necessary to be clear about the mechanism we use to replace statementing as the means by which we access kids into special schools. So I don't want to do away with special schools but on the other hand I do want to think about the mechanism by which you get kids into them and, more importantly, the mechanism by which you get them out again. Because the last thing you want is keeping them there from age five to sixteen.

CHAPTER 8

Empowerment through communication: an integrated approach to special needs

ANN HINCHLIFFE with Peter Ribbins

Ann Hinchliffe has since 1984 been headteacher of Ash Field School in Leicestershire. Ash Field is a school for young people aged between four and nineteen with physical and sensory disabilities. Between 1959 and 1974 she was a speech therapist. During this time she worked in Salford and Berkshire before being appointed as Head of the Speech Therapy Services for Leicestershire. Between 1974 and 1984 she held a number of teaching posts in three mainstream secondary schools in Leicester and Leicestershire. At Stonehill High Schools and Brookvale High School her responsibilities were mainly for remedial education and at South Wigston High School she was for three years a deputy head.

PR What are the key influences which have made you what you are – family, friends, local community, peer group, school, higher education, whatever?

AH I am the eldest of six. My father was a general practitioner. I come from a family many of whom have been medics since the end of the eighteenth century. Many others have been involved in other services like law or the fire brigade or the police. So I come from a family with a strong service ethos. I share that ethos. That is how it all began for me and that is where I come from.

PR Did you have a happy childhood?

AH I did. I was born in Ireland but came to England when I was very young. My education was entirely private. For my secondary education I went to my mother's old school, Loreto College, in St Albans. I was very happy there but I hated being a boarder. I suppose the happiest part of my school life was at Nativity Convent in Leicester, and so I count Leicester very much as my home city. My father didn't want me to have a professional career of any kind. He thought it would be nice for me to be at home with Mum, but my mother did want me to have a career. As a boarder, I wanted just to be at home with my family again.

PR　What was your mother's background?

AH　She never had a job, which was why she wanted me to have one. She came from a professional family, her father, two of her brothers and her sister were doctors. Another brother was a lawyer and became the Attorney General of Ireland. She was the youngest girl who had ambitions later on.

PR　How would you describe your father's views?

AH　He was a wonderful but old-fashioned dad. He died when I was in my early twenties.

PR　Do you come from a family that values education?

AH　Yes, very, very much.

PR　Do you remember your primary school?

AH　Nativity Convent, it was lovely. A very happy school. I can still remember vividly the smell of it and the feeling of it. I can still see the little place where we could buy rubbers and pencils and tracing paper which was very exciting. The rubbers were gold. I have terrifically happy memories of Nativity.

PR　Was it run by nuns?

AH　Yes it was. Strangely, and I know this doesn't sound very good in a book about education, I haven't got a very strong memory of teachers, much more of a feeling of the excitement of being there and of learning rather than of any particular individuals.

PR　What were its values as a school?

AH　It was traditional and formal. I have never had any experience of education which you might describe as progressive and informal. Even so, within the framework of its formality, it encouraged us to be creative. The idea that formal must be dull and informal must be exciting is simply wrong. My education was very stimulating.

PR　There's a big debate taking place on the supposed benefits of interactive whole class teaching in the primary school. Was what you experienced something like this?

AH　It was certainly whole class teaching. When we eventually did some science we broke up into little groups. But I am not sure how far I can generalize usefully from this because I can't really be sure of what the range of ability was in the classes in which I was taught. So since I was on the brighter end of the spectrum it might be that a great deal of the teaching was pitched at people like me. I don't know how the less able fared. We tend to be able to speak from our own perspective in these matters.

PR　You don't remember any of the teachers from Nativity? Not even the head?

AH　I remember a nun called Sister Anne, not because she taught me but because she had to have an arm amputated. She was an artist and had done a kind of relief sculpture for the little chapel in the convent and I thought it was so really horrifying that she had to lose her arm when that was the kind of thing she loved doing. I also remember Sister Agnes. She sold the pencils and rubbers. But even if I do not remember many of the teachers I still think it was a very loving and caring school.

PR   Why were you sent to a boarding school?

AH   I think it was partly because my brothers were going away to school. I had read books about it and it seemed exciting. But, for me, the idea turned out much better than the reality. Of course, mum had been to the school I was sent to. She'd been one of the first pupils there. I suppose I felt I was going back to where she'd been. I was almost twelve when I went. I loved the people and still have good friends from there. The school was lovely, being away from home was awful. Even at eighteen I was very reluctant to leave home.

PR   Were you a successful secondary pupil?

AH   I was one of those children who want to be good. I wanted never to have order marks, or since you got them if you were bad perhaps they should have been called disorder marks. I was frightened of being bad. I could have had much more fun if I'd realized that it didn't really matter if I was a little bit bad sometimes. Even so, I think now that the idea of wanting everything to be good and nothing to be bad is what I want for Ash Field. So maybe the feeling of wanting to be good has had good results. In any case this wish is deeply rooted in my personality.

PR   Were you successful in the public exams?

AH   Not particularly. But I got my O Levels. I was in the Latin group – if you were at the lower end of the ability range you did Art and if you were brighter you did Latin – so you kind of knew you were OK if you were doing Latin. Eventually, I was almost seventeen when I was interviewed for a place on a speech therapy course. I felt quite proud of getting into the School of Speech Therapy in Leicester. They preferred you to have a year in work, so when I was seventeen, much to my relief, I left my secondary school and came home.

PR   You didn't do A Levels?

AH   I didn't do A Levels. For a person doing the sort of job I'm now doing I am almost without qualifications. Nor have I been on many courses – I'm not a great lover of these things when they are connected with work. Fancy saying this to a man like you whose bread and butter depends on people doing courses – never mind!!

PR   Ah well. Why did speech therapy attract you?

AH   I became fascinated by communication and the way it can empower. That is with me still. Everything I now do stems from this belief. I believe the principles underpinning empowerment through communication are fundamental to education generally, and indeed to democracy as a whole.

PR   Was it a good course?

AH   Parts of it were good; parts of it were desperately tedious. But compared with what some people on the old teacher training and PGCE courses were doing it was fine. I was very grateful that it was well structured with high expectations of us. It had a high failure rate in final exams which I always thought was a good sign. It ensured high standards. A high failure rate is considered a bad sign nowadays.

PR   But why speech therapy?

AH   It was about teaching children who couldn't speak to speak and it was local. I could achieve both the things I wanted. Emotionally I needed to be at home. In time I became Licentiate of the College of Speech Therapists. I'd had the time I needed at home and so when I qualified I had no problems with the thought of leaving home. I remember saying to myself 'Where will I go?' I stuck a pin in a map. It turned out to be Salford. That was adventurous, wasn't it?

PR   It's certainly an exotic way to choose a job.

AH   It was an exotic place to go. Once I had decided, it made me feel free.

PR   What exactly were you appointed to?

AH   I worked at Hope Hospital Special School and at clinics and schools in the surrounding area. Much of this took place in very impoverished circumstances. But it was very rewarding and taught me an enormous amount. I achieved my very first communication breakthrough at Hope with a young woman with cerebral palsy called Sylvia. This was in the days before computers and all the technology that I now fight for. Sylvia couldn't write at all. But I saw that she was able to make one movement consistently. I went to Manchester, into different typewriter shops and one of them gave me an old Imperial typewriter. I got a drumstick and found, as I suspected she could, that if I tied this to her hand she could press the keys of the typewriter and type. That gave me a big zip but it was nothing like the zip that it gave her. You could see the great pride she took in being able to do this. She wasn't just scrubbing along with a pencil making marks which were almost impossible to understand. She knew her writing was as good as, and sometimes better than, the next person.

PR   And then came electric typewriters and WPs.

AH   Oh yes, and my latest battles have been on just those fronts.

PR   How and why did you become a teacher?

AH   Before becoming a teacher, I got married and came to live in Leicester and my first child was born – Katy. I was working part-time in Leicester as a speech therapist. When the post of Head of Speech Therapy Services for Leicestershire came up I thought 'I'll go for it', and I got it. I moved to teaching after that to extend what I was doing. I was able to because I'd done an external History degree through London University.

PR　　And how did that come about?

AH　　I happened to read a book by Jomo Kenyatta – it was his doctoral thesis from Moscow University and was called *Facing Mount Kenya*. I thought gosh, history would interest me. I did a degree in history and used a correspondence course run by Wolseley Hall to make this possible. The only entitlement I have to be a teacher is as a result of that history degree, nothing else.

PR　　How did you manage to find the time to do the degree with your work and your children as well?

AH　　It was just one of those things. I wanted to focus my mind on something because my second child had died soon after birth.

PR　　Presumably you met many teachers both as a speech therapist and as a manager of speech therapists: what, at the time, did you feel about teachers and schools having had the opportunity to see them from a contiguous profession?

AH　　As I matured, I became increasingly disenchanted with the idea of private education. In my case it meant that I left school with a sense of superiority which was entirely unwarranted. While I was a speech therapist I became very committed to comprehensive education and to the feeling that all young people were of equal value. That appealed to my sense of what democracy should be about and that commitment is part of what I am. I think we needed to share what we both, teacher and therapist, knew. From my perspective, the problem was that there were certain things I knew nothing about which they knew about and vice versa.

PR　　In the literature there are numerous examples of education welfare officers, social workers, careers officers who suggest that too many teachers won't listen to and don't value other professions when they come to schools to work with children. Did you find any of that in your work as a speech therapist?

AH　　I think the professions generally are not good at listening to each other. This is by no means just restricted to teachers. I think, for example, to the careers officer the teacher isn't listening and to the teacher the careers officer isn't listening. When I became a head, I worked very hard to implement an integrated approach to education for all the young people at Ash Field and I hope I've succeeded in this. It's a problem for us all to listen to those with other centres of knowledge and expertise.

PR　　What was your first teaching job? Did you use another pin?

AH　　It was not quite like that. I wondered how on earth I would get into teaching because I had done no professional training and had done no probationary year. So the first thing I did, which again was by chance, was to get a job in an adult training centre in Northampton. What I was to do was innovative in its time. It was to improve communication. They didn't see communication as speech therapy. My task was to offer a teaching input with my speech therapy background to the Centre. It gave me a teacher number. I did not plan this. It was chance again. It let me walk into my first teaching job in Stonehill High School at Birstall although I had never taught or even been in a state school.

PR   Were you asked to do a probationary period?

AH   No, no. But Stan Gaylon taught me a lot. He gave me my freedom in creating a remedial department and all the support in doing this that I wanted. I introduced testing across the whole school – verbal reasoning, non-verbal reasoning, spelling, reading a piece of written work – as a basis when all the young people came in. I identified special learning difficulties and provided individual support for those who needed it. I can remember putting all the way around the walls of the classroom Blake's poem 'Tyger! Tyger! burning bright'. The children loved it. Stan Gaylon taught me that if you are going to encourage staff you must give them opportunities to succeed. He also taught me that you can't change a school that does not want to be changed. It was a good lesson. You have to create the environment for change for change to be successful.

PR   And it may sometimes have to be a slow process.

AH   Ever so slow. Also it is often easy to produce paperwork that suggests you are doing things which you are not actually doing.

PR   Can you describe the school itself?

AH   It was an eleven-to-fourteen High School with a twelve-form entry. There were almost thirty children in each group so the school had more than a thousand pupils. The pupils came mainly from four primary schools. My daughter was there at the time.

PR   Did that work?

AH   My elder daughter Katy was happy, and I left before my second daughter Clare joined. But people feel very differently about this. Katy liked the idea that I was at the school but I suspect most children would not. It would not have suited Clare or my son Andrew.

PR   Did you set up the remedial department or were you appointed to set it up? What was your brief from the head?

AH   There was a remedial department but it was very different. The head wasn't the kind of person who gave briefs. I suspect he believed that the most successful way of giving a brief is to get people to think they have created the idea in the first place. He worked to people's strengths. Looking back now I've no idea why he gave me such a free hand. But I think the test system I set up is still being done! It's been in place over twenty years.

PR   In my research I've met other heads who believed in giving their staff a high level of autonomy in what they did. It enables wonderful work at its best but in at least one school that I spent some years studying it also produced awful work in some departments.

AH   I think you are right. But I don't think I could say anything like that about that particular school. All I know is that I was given my chance. I also know that my experience there encouraged me to want to be a head.

PR   Already?

AH   Oh yes. But remember I had had a good deal of experience as a manager in my years in the speech therapy services. As soon as I realized what I wanted, I did the things that everybody did in those days to become a head. You moved on after two to three years. I stayed at this school for three years and in three schools in all for about three years each and then I became a head.

PR   Can you describe briefly each of these schools?

AH   After Stonehill I went to another Leicestershire high school, Brookvale in Groby and there I met Bill Metcalf, another excellent head. It was a new school so it was very exciting. It had been going for about a year when I joined. The head wanted somebody who could be a head of year and take a lead on remedial work. I was able to combine one with the other. I learned a terrific amount from Bill Metcalf. He set and achieved very high standards of classroom practice.

PR   How?

AH   Well of course he had picked everyone himself. The school is now in its fifteenth year and I was glad to see it has recently had a very good Ofsted report. He had a passion for excellence before it became a fashionable word and in doing so ensured we achieved high standards in the classroom and in every part of the school. I remember we would sweat over taking an assembly and in reporting to parents. He read and re-read every report. This is something I now do myself. He insisted that every document that went out from the school should be as good as we could make it. And then I became deputy head of South Wigston High School.

I started on the same day as Eric Bottomly, the new head, was starting which was an interesting experience. This meant a very steep learning curve for both of us. We started at Easter with both of us eager to make our mark. In the summer term we visited all the local primary schools talking about everything from the ethos of the school to our commitment to the need for a school uniform. Shortly afterwards the Leicestershire County Council ratified a directive, from the European Parliament I think, which claimed that the imposition of a uniform was an infringement on human rights. There we were having just told all these primary pupils to come in uniform on the first day. The way Eric handled this was another very useful learning experience for me. He said none of the teachers were to deal with it at all. We would remain a uniform school but only he and I would talk to pupils and parents about it. We did and we remained a uniform school. What it taught me about managing a school is you should be clear that the main responsibility teachers have is to teach well and that they shouldn't be worried by other things if you can possibly avoid it. They should get their zip out of the classroom.

The other main thing that Eric let me do was manage the buildings. At the time women just didn't manage buildings. I learnt how to make sure any work done in the school was done as well as anything I would have done at home.

PR	You were at South Wigston for three years – what happened then?
AH	I applied for headships. I got the third one.
PR	So it came relatively easily? But why did you want to be a head?
AH	Yes, I suppose it did come quite easily. I have never thought about that. As for why, well I find management the most creative thing I do. Of course, I have to be managing something that my heart is in. I get a great deal of sense of satisfaction from using my management skills to improve the quality of what is happening for pupils within the school. I've only had the one headship. I've been at Ash Field for twelve years. It's been a privilege to work there.
PR	Why Ash Field? Did you apply to mainstream schools as well?
AH	Yes, I applied for what was available. I didn't think it would matter what school I managed, not really. Indeed anything I've managed I have enjoyed. Now, of course, I know I got the opportunity to manage a school like no other. I was so lucky. I'm profoundly grateful for the opportunity.
PR	So you didn't decide that you wanted to manage a special school. In fact you applied for both mainstream and special. What happened with the other two applications?
AH	Other people got the jobs. I was interviewed for the three that I applied for and got the third. In those days local education authority officers got to know deputies who wished to be heads and advised governors. I do wonder how governors now choose and I doubt if some governing bodies have the skills and experience they need in such important decisions.
PR	How did you prepare for headship?
AH	I hardly ever go on courses. As I said earlier, I don't go in for this in a big way. But I did go on a 'Preparing for Headship Course' which was run for deputies in the summer holidays of the year that I applied for headships in. It was run by the LEA. I don't remember much about it and I don't remember who took it. Obviously I'm not somebody who remembers my own teachers well.
PR	You do seem to remember your heads quite well and your descriptions of the three of them are all positive. In contrast many of the

heads I have interviewed claim to have learned more about how not
to do things than what to do from their own headteachers.

AH   They are positive. I have also learnt what not to do from them, but it's
not what I emphasize in my own mind.

PR   Can you think of anything that you learned not to do from any one of
them?

AH   I think that a remark you made earlier can be to the point. Giving
staff freedom can sometimes mean there are areas which were not
performing well and might do much better with a different and
perhaps more intrusive style of management. I am a more intrusive
manager as a result. I also think I'm a more supportive manager
because I felt unsupported on occasions. In one of the schools I
worked in a boy had an accident in the playground and was brought
into school by the member of staff on duty. Every effort had been
made to get in touch with his mother but without success. It wasn't
serious as far as we were concerned. He had a big bump on his head
but had shown no signs of concussion. I ended up as head of year
being asked to go home with the child in the evening. Later there was
a big row about the fact that the school hadn't tried to contact the
father at work. I was blamed because I'd taken him home. I felt I was
standing alone. I promised myself I'd never leave a member of staff
unsupported in that way. Headship is not only about creating a
positive learning environment. It should also be about making staff
feel secure. Indeed if you don't you are most unlikely to achieve a
positive learning environment.

PR   Did you feel prepared for headship when you first took it up? What
was it like suddenly finding yourself in the headteacher's chair?

AH   My first problem was I couldn't get hold of the chair. Ash Field is a
weekly boarding school. I had chosen not to live on the site. The
previous head had lived on the site and had therefore not felt the
need to use the room that was meant to be the head's room next to
the school office. It had been taken over by the head of residential
care who was at that stage called the matron. I had the greatest
difficulty in getting hold of that office but I knew I had to. If you
don't get hold of your office, you're not going to get hold of your
school. In the end I had to ask politely then firmly that 'I expect you
to be out by . . . '. And so there was an immediate tension about my
arrival. That didn't bother me, it had to be done.

PR   Can you describe Ash Field? How has it changed during the time
you've been there?

AH   I arrived just as the 1981 Act was coming to fruition. So the school
had to be turned round to meet the new legislation. There was no
question about that, and there's been a roller-coaster of legislation
ever since I've been the head. I've always implemented what I am
legally obliged to do – but I have done so on a sensible rolling

programme. It's meant a non-stop implementation of new law.

Ash Field is a school for young people between four and nineteen with physical and sensory disabilities. When I took it over it had eighty-four young people and was divided into primary and secondary departments. It had a residential wing with eighteen beds. Pupils did some O Levels. Although pupils stayed until they were nineteen there was no separation of the pre-sixteen and post-sixteen phases. It was an excellent school in terms of what was expected of such schools at that time but even without the legislation I would have wanted change. I had, after all, come from a mainstream school, and, indeed, I think one of the reasons that I had been appointed was the feeling, in the post-Plowden era, special schools needed to become part of a continuum in education.

PR   I remember going to a residential school for boys with behavioural problems, and was frankly astonished, not to say appalled, that there didn't seem to be a curriculum and that the head was quite resentful about the idea that anybody should ask him for one. It seemed that these were children to be managed, to be kept happy, but the idea that they could learn anything useful other than a few simple things was regarded as absurd, even improper. 'These are special children, you can't expect them to ....'

AH   I think there may have been elements of that kind of thinking at Ash Field but it was not the whole truth because I took over a school that was top of the league at that time. After all, they were doing some O Levels although the number of O Levels were limited. For example, the idea that there was an entitlement to science was hard to create. I had to insist that there would be science. But it is one thing to say this and another for it to happen. What took longest to get in place was the idea that homework should be a normal expectation. There was a feeling that really you can't put pressure of homework on these young people.

PR   We are talking of much the same thing. My example was of a much more extreme case than yours but the argument was exactly the same – you mustn't put pressure on ....

AH   Whereas I actually think that people work best if we have high expectations of them. The principle of academic excellence being a right for young people less high on the agenda when I came than creating a loving family atmosphere. Pupils were less likely to break sound barriers academically. Over the last few years we have broken sound barriers academically at Ash Field. I think the first young man ever who achieved a university place would agree with us if he was still alive. His name was Ashok Mistry. I organized it through the Open University, and he did his first year of his Maths degree at Ash Field. He got a distinction. I think that that sort of thing wouldn't have happened at all in the past. Neither would there have been any pupils doing ten GCSEs. We have this now. Currently we have two past pupils at university. One is at Sheffield and the other at Derby.

PR How did you turn things around?

AH I didn't begin with the standard curriculum because others were running that. I would define the curriculum as everything you do in a school. In passing I should say I am not at all happy about the endless linking of teaching and learning. I don't think you have to teach for children to learn. To confuse the two is to miss the way learning actually happens.

PR It seems to be a key Ofsted assumption.

AH I think the emphasis they place on this requires some modification. Coming back to your original question, I started reforming things by working on increasing independence in the residential wing. I converted (my legacy as a manager of buildings coming to the fore) the sick room, an area and a little office into a flat for enabling pupils to learn to be independent. So I began with the vision of empowerment through independence, and then I changed the way the residential wing worked. Instead of a very small number, twelve or thirteen, of children using it all the time, now about fifty-five sleep over in the course of a year and even more use it for extended day facilities. That's where I started to implement change. It was in a vision of the whole environment.

PR That's the problem with implementing changes isn't it? If you are not successful first time you have a huge problem.

AH I had to have credibility and the curriculum was already managed by the head of the secondary department and the head in the primary department. The head of the secondary had made the great step of introducing O Levels. I didn't feel I would be successful if I tried to take away their roles from them. On the other hand I got the opportunity to change the residential wing. It was helpful that I had the opportunity to create change through reshaping the structure of the building.

PR How did you make that transition?

AH Very slowly is the answer. I tried several times, for example, to get something like homework in, and I had to work hard to achieve this. There was also a lukewarm response to the possibility of our young people making anything of science. They did biology, you know, and not chemistry and physics. The things contained in what we now think of as the science national curriculum were not on the syllabus. I think the introduction of computers was where I got a toehold. Some computer work was done in the school but I got the opportunity to open a Micro-Technology Assessment Centre in the school which enabled the development of computer awareness right across the whole school. That was instrumental in beginning to achieve curriculum change in the traditional sense of curriculum change.

PR   How did you achieve this?

AH   In part by appointing new staff. There are times when you need to introduce new people if you want to implement change. Unless the key people are interested and excited by the changes and really want to achieve them they will not happen. If people begin by expecting change to be worthwhile then any particular change is much easier to achieve. That was not the ethos I found when I first came. I certainly was very, very interested in change. Let me talk about a particular case. In the early days at Ash Field I had an idea of teaching the science national curriculum through the computer. I even hired a company to come and develop the software. I created a science room again using the idea of changing the physical environment. We built physically accessible work benches for pupils with all the latest technology. The pupils loved it. My view was that if you can get people to share the vision they'll come with you.

PR   What, more generally, was your vision for Ash Field? Did you go in with a vision? Did you have to develop a vision once you were there? Has it changed?

AH   I don't think my vision would be significantly different whatever the school I was managing, only the way I implemented it. My vision is about empowerment. For me education is about empowerment in social, emotional, intellectual, physical and spiritual terms. It is about creating an ethos. It is about enabling young people to enjoy learning and to achieve to their potential. It means knowing your rights and your responsibilities. I would do that wherever I went and whatever I managed.

PR   You could know your rights and responsibilities but still never do anything?

AH   Not at Ash Field. Empowerment is not just knowing your rights, it's about accessing your rights. It's not just knowing your responsibilities, it's about carrying out your responsibilities. It's not just a cerebral activity, it has to be practical.

PR   One of the most interesting heads I have studied took the view that teachers are very good at justifying what they want to do on the grounds that it is in the interests of children, but that if you look closely there is often a very convenient connection between what's in their own interests and what they want doing.

AH   I think if staff share a vision they will subsume their personal wishes and desires to achieve that vision. I think the real problem with teachers, and with many others who work with children as well, is the isolation of one teacher from another and one profession from another. Those who work with children need to do so from a common set of goals and aims. I think if you are working as a team then individual members won't step out of line because all share a vision. If you are running a school of individuals then you should not be surprised to find that the children aren't being empowered much.

PR   Or even a school made up of sets of semi-autonomous groups of teachers?

AH   That's right. But you keep talking about teachers, I'm for the staff team. I'm committed to a team approach that has at its centre a vision of empowerment for children.

PR   How and how far have you achieved this in your present school? How far has it been made possible – because you have been successful in encouraging some members of the staff you inherited to move on?

AH   There's a natural tide that takes people away when they find that they're swimming against it. I let that tide run. Where it was appropriate I encouraged that to happen. But I don't think that was the key really.

PR   What was the key?

AH   You have to use whatever is at your disposal. For me the first thing that was at my disposal was the annual review for the statement of special educational need. What I tried to do was to break down the barriers between professions, a theme which has kind of drifted through our conversation today. I found that the district health authority staff didn't particularly work together – each profession was on its own and teachers and other school staff were on their own. So I took one aspect of the child. The first one was standing. I got a representative of each profession together and suggested that we would work to create a sheet for the annual review that would be headed 'standing' and do so in such a way that all the professions involved would be able to read the sheet and know what we all meant. I know it seems a simple idea but perhaps not in a school for physical disability. It is all too easy for people to think they are using key terms and ideas in the same way as others when they are not. In the case I have been talking about we were all using words and phrases concerned with standing and in sitting, like corner sitting and long sitting, with most people not really knowing what this meant for others. I used that approach on all aspects of the 'whole person' – including, for example, levels of independence in personal matters. In a sense all the professions were in a similar state because each felt that their power base was their knowledge. You must have a sense that the knowledge you share is respected.

PR   A case of 'The Emperor's New Clothes' in practice?

AH   Once everybody was happy that everybody had a lot of expertise which we could all share and with the idea that there was no need to protect it then we achieved a team approach which was very empowering. You can go into Ash Field now and you can get the information about the management of the child very quickly. This is possible only because people aren't worried any more about sharing their professional expertise.

PR   How important is achieving this for mainstream schools?

AH   It's just as important in a mainstream school in its own way. There's a terrible danger at the moment in children having vast numbers of targets with nobody having a clear overview. It looks great on paper but in practice how is it actually working out? I would passionately stress the need to see young people holistically and not just in terms of how successful they are in achieving particular national curriculum aspirations.

PR   What kind of a leader are you? How are you seen by your staff, pupils and parents? How far is this compatible with your own vision of yourself?

AH   I love my job. I'm a very happy headteacher. Not that I haven't been pushed to the very edge, the brink of feeling I just cannot take this any more. I love it. It's been a marvellous joy to me to have been appointed to this job at Ash Field. There has been, and still is, so much to do that there has never been any need to go on for another headship. I wouldn't have thought that I would be particularly liked, but I think most would know I was fair, and that I was for the young people. I think parents would know that I would always be there for them in all circumstances. Children learn best when their families are happy with the school.

PR   You are respected?

AH   Mmm, yes, yes, I'd hope so.

PR   In an interesting paper Day and Bakioglu seem to suggest that there is some tendency for long-serving heads to become more authoritarian in style and increasingly resistant to change. Do you see this in yourself? Have you changed as a head?

AH   I've become, I would have thought, more, not less, democratic. At least in the sense that I now work through a senior management team, not deputies. I'm not a person who says we'll all vote on this – I'm not into that kind of leadership, so I suppose I'd be on the autocratic side rather than the democratic side.

I need to explain what I mean when I said I now work through the senior management team and not the deputies although I'd had great support from them. This was not a matter of choice. Financial pressures meant I decided to give up having deputies. When this happened I thought I was going to be more lonely, and be under more pressure. In practice I found I actually enjoy running the school through a senior management team. It works better and it also feels more democratic. Now I get input on so many things from a much broader base and that information is not filtered in the way it used to be. I now think it's quite easy for an experienced head to not have a deputy. But I doubt if it would be quite as easy for a new head – not least because of the loneliness thing.

PR   Has headship become harder or easier over time for you?

AH   It's easier as you grow more experienced and the longer you spend in a school the more it becomes something you have shaped and created. This also makes it easier. It's easier too in the sense that now I have much more control over the budget than I used to. I have found that empowering.

PR   Do you still enjoy it? Ted Wragg has suggested that you have to be a nutter to want to be a head nowadays. He, and others, suggest that the contemporary head can't be an educative leader any more, in part because he or she is forced to be a manager, an administrator, a budget manager ...

AH   I disagree. You are forced to be those things but that doesn't prevent you from being an educative leader. I'm very, very committed to being this. I have concerns about contemporary developments in education. I believe education must be much more than completing units of work or achieving narrow targets. Education should be about developing a lifelong love of learning. I like to have a clear curriculum focus each year. This year we have had a big push on key stage 3 and 4 reading. It has been extremely successful. We are very pleased with the outcome. We assess using our own battery of tests and we test on an annual basis. As a result we are in a position to measure how successful we have been. Something like 28 per cent of the young people got in excess of a two years' increase in their reading ages during the year. That's a pretty good result but never once in achieving this did I use the word 'target', because I really think that if at the end of the year the young people are saying to me 'I love reading' then I've given them something for life. If they say to me at the end of the year 'I've achieved my targets' I've given them something that's just here and now. I think we have to be very careful not to become beguiled into saying 'Yes, this child is successful, she has achieved her targets'. If we say this too often then young people would have to be forgiven for believing that all that matters is achieving targets – that it did not matter whether they really care about reading or history or science or whatever.

PR   It could be argued that a good deal of what the government has been trying to achieve over the last ten years is associated with identifying and achieving targets in various ways and translating these into league tables ...

AH   Well, I've gone public on my concern about that.

PR   How would you describe what's happened in education over the last decade? How do you see the government's reform agenda and what do you feel about it?

AH   We needed the national curriculum. I just wish they had thought a bit more about it and didn't hand us two different curriculums in rapid succession to cope with. I am deeply concerned about the educational totalitarian superhighway that's developed. It has become an offence to criticize the new orthodoxy or to contemplate doing anything different. But for our democracy to work all people must be educated to the best of their ability and to be educated means to have ideas and to discuss them and to be able to disagree. At the moment it seems that to say you are concerned or disagree with an aspect of legislation means that somehow you are committing a kind of professional crime. Diversity of opinion and diversity of practice seem to be considered to be a bad thing when, surely, diversity is what democracy should be about. I have to say I am horrified at the demand for uniformity in educational practice with which we have all been faced by a government which claims to believe in choice and diversity.

PR   You mean you see a much greater centralization of control in education? Is this compatible with government claims that they are committed to local autonomy and to the creation of an educational market?

AH   I think their aims are fiercely centralizing. Local autonomy and the market – these are notions without real practical content. I'm not quite sure what people mean when they appeal to the idea of a market. It needs definition. It is a word that is much bandied about to mean so many different and sometimes incompatible things. One of the things I say to the staff is 'Keep your independent vision. Don't think that everything I say you must do to satisfy legal requirements is the way you have to *think*. Keep your own vision of what a child is, of what the developing adult is. Don't lose your personal vision because you're subsumed in a plethora of stuff in which you seem to have to march to the tune I'm singing. Most of the time it's not me that's creating the tune. I'm singing what legislation tells me to sing.' I try to keep the idea alive in the staff that this is happening now but how will it all be viewed in ten years from now? Clear independent vision is what counts and is what will prevail.

PR   You seem to believe in the need for a national curriculum. I don't get the impression on this that you are singing to somebody else's tune. How does it fit in with your beliefs in the need for diversity?

AH   I do believe in the national curriculum. I met Kenneth Baker at the time and thanked him for the national curriculum. Having a national curriculum is certainly important in terms of identifying the need for certain specifics but it shouldn't subsume so much. What I object to is that it has increasingly absorbed our educational thoughts and people are not judged on what they are offering to children as a whole but on how well they are serving up the separate parts. There doesn't seem to be any room left for the exercise of independent professional judgement, not even, for example, in the framework Ofsted inspectors must use to write their reports. The attempt to make a judgement on the basis of the child's whole experience is not emphasized. It's much more about selecting from certain stock phrases that fall within the word-processing packages identified to describe prescribed aspects of provision.

PR   What would you say to those who would argue that your view much better suits those who 'provide' education than for those who 'consume' it?

AH   I don't mean that there shouldn't be any rigour. I would prefer to see 'on the spot', shorter, more frequent checks by inspectors to ensure quality education rather than massive inspections often known about and planned for by schools more than a year in advance and costing tens of thousands of pounds.

PR   Can we consider the arguments currently taking place about levels of achievement in mathematics? What do you feel about this debate?

AH   How can any government be so critical of the teaching profession? We have been struggling against the most extraordinary odds during most of their time in office. If we really have been less successful than other comparable countries in maths, and I don't necessarily accept that we have, then we should look to the government and to society to take a share of the blame and not just to scapegoat teachers.

PR   There is some suggestion that standards of achievement in maths are much higher in a number of countries, such as Taiwan and Korea, where the per capita unit of resource in schools is much lower than the UK. How do you respond to such arguments?

AH   Resources are very important but consistency of experience is what makes education successful and measuring and comparing units of resource with achievement when society is inconsistent is really merely a way of cutting budgets for schools. If you study what happens in Taiwan I think you will find that pupils have a level of consistency of experience our students do not get. In Taiwan children are taught the decimal system and experience the decimal system in the world they live in. The roads are measured in kilometres, the weight is in kilograms, liquids are in litres. Here, for over twenty years, governments have demanded we taught only the decimal system while outside school the world has worked in miles, pounds and ounces and pints. Even eggs continue to be sold by the dozen. Education cannot be blamed for this. So the comparison is not a reasonable one. To an extent this is a cultural matter. Education is deeply located within a culture.

PR   In so far as the kinds of countries we are talking about do enjoy high standards of pupil achievement, to what extent do you accept the argument that this reflects the high regard in which education is held? Has, in your view, respect for education in the UK diminished during your years as a teacher?

AH   I don't know. I do think that the constant running down of teachers can be very damaging. If you keep saying how bad so many teachers are and how awful so many schools are, then the children, quite reasonably, easily use it as an excuse for poor performance.

PR   It is often said that the Irish, the Welsh and the Scottish regard education more highly than the English do. So it might actually be an English disease, essentially?

AH   I think it is.

PR   Have you had your Ofsted inspection yet?

AH   No, I haven't.

PR   Can I put to you what is often taken to be the key Ofsted question? You have talked about the high quality of the things which go on in your school but how do you know this actually happens and what is your evidence for this?

AH   Well, there are different ways of saying you know about such things. I know it by the level of empowerment of the pupils. I have been inspected under the 1989 Children Act and their empowerment shines through the report. So I've got a kind of objective affirmation of what I believe to be the case anyway. In addition, I have evidence for my belief that our young people are empowered because I can see it when I consider the outcomes of their annual reviews. At these, their parents are present but the review is usually conducted through the pupil so they learn early on how to handle people discussing them. They are encouraged to make a real input into the review. This is important. When you have a special educational need, and especially something like a physical or a sensory disability, you live in a world where a lot of the time you are directed. This approach helps young people to control their lives.

PR   Do you try to see it systematically in other ways? Do you collect work in or visit classes?

AH   I do go around the classes all the time frequently with parents. I expect pupils to be able to tell parents what they are doing and why. Also all our pupils have records of achievement which I frequently look at. In addition we have a standard format for preparing schemes of work. I can check these at any time.

PR   Well, that focuses on the young people and their needs. What of staff and appraisal?

AH   We have appraisal. We are now introducing appraisal for support staff. Teachers are all on an appraisal system. We use a theme-based approach. So the first round for teachers was the collection of evidence of pupils' learning. I've found that we have been able to grow as a school from the theme approach. We had some fun because, at first, we did not always succeed in collecting the appropriate evidence. I say 'we' because this was true for us all in one way or another. Understanding this brought the staff together. We learned from it, and moved on. It allows you to treat the whole thing with a sense of proportion and with humour. This makes it possible to really open up on key issues. If you create a system which encourages everybody to go back into themselves and to batten down the hatches, then nobody grows. The day support staff have just had their first tranche of appraisal. The issue they have focused on is the management of pupils' equipment.

PR   Do you link that into a formal system of development planning for the school?

AH   Yes. It is within the framework of the development plan. Although I have to say that the development plan isn't what it used to be. I now have a development plan which identifies the things which I know we are already beginning to tackle successfully. The real development plan is in hopes and dreams of our discussions and it is not written down. For example, the development plan for this year says we will implement the new assessment, recording and reporting policy. We've agreed this because we know we are well on the way with this already. But we all know that we have other things that we are now working on and these will go into next year's development plan. I used to see the development plan as a very creative thing. It used to identify things we might succeed at, that we might attempt to do. Then people started asking 'Where's your evaluation of your development plan?', 'Why haven't you got an action plan for this or that?' Well, the reason was that if you took this too literally you would end up with a forest of action plans with people bored out of their minds and no inspiration left. So we have got round that one.

PR   Who knows of the hidden but real development plan? Do you share it with the governors? In that context who do you see as your manager(s)? Who do you feel accountable to?

AH   Firstly, to my conscience. If I betrayed my educational vision, if I could not channel legislation so that it fits with what I believe, I would be very unhappy. If, for example, I sold out on my commitment to pupil empowerment for a mess of pottage that would grieve me greatly. Secondly, to the young people in my care and their parents. Thirdly, to my governors. But then I've got a superb chair of governors, Councillor Mrs Margaret Berridge, who helps me to make this possible.

PR   I was hoping you would talk about the governing body.

AH   I have a superb governing body. They help create my vision and they each have particular tasks which they take on. For example, one deals with everything for me in connection with the residential wing. Another deals with the Micro-Technology Assessment Centre. They each have a specific aspect of the school and its work for which they take responsibility, sharing with us what we are doing.

PR   What makes your chair of governors superb?

AH   We think alike which is always helpful. In today's world you should never become a head with a chair of governors that you can't walk shoulder to shoulder with in educational terms. As a local councillor she's given a terrific support to all aspects of special education in Leicestershire. She is always there for me. I tell her everything. She never hears about what is happening at Ash Field from somewhere else.

PR   How do you think the governors see you? What do they expect of you?

AH   Probably 'What is she going to do next?'. For example, last year I fought very hard for communication aids for pupils when they leave school. It was a very big fight. I won, needless to say, or I wouldn't be telling you probably. So I think that they expect that kind of . . .

PR   Did they support you on it or did you have to convince them?

AH   They did support me. One of the governor's sons uses a communication aid. It was high-risk strategy. I run two things, the Micro-Technology Assessment Centre, which is a service to the whole authority, and the school. The context of what I was telling you about was that the first pupil with a communication aid issued by the LEA following an assessment at the Centre was leaving school. His statement would therefore cease and the communication aid could be returned to the Centre for use by another pupil. It had been given to him to access the national curriculum. I tried to get Social Services or Health to take responsibility for the provision of the next communication aid which would be for the rest of his life but I couldn't get either of them to do it. Anyway, when there were six weeks left before the young man left school I knew I could not leave things any later. I wrote to Virginia Bottomley who was then the Health Minister and asked her which body should provide the communication aid. I got in touch with local television and local newspapers and they came. I even rang the *Daily Mirror,* and I think a junior minister came down. I didn't see who came but I won and provision is now being made which has ensured that all the young people who have left Ash Field since then and who need the communication aids got them. They didn't tell me I'd won. But the following Saturday as I was coming out of the Grand Hotel in Leicester I saw that the *Leicester Mercury* was on sale. The *Mercury* had supported me. I can never thank them enough. I went over and bought a paper and I cried. The unswerving support of the governing body had given me the confidence to fight.

PR   What do you feel about the LEA? Do you think too much power has been taken away from them? Is the balance about right now or have things gone too far?

AH   I think things have gone too far. In some respects I feel the City of Leicester may not have got the emphasis it required as part of Leicestershire. Now it's getting unitary status and I will work for it with all the energy I've got. LEAs are controlled by local democracy.

The quangos taking their place have no such control. This worries me. Before the moves to diminish the power of local authorities if I had a problem I could phone up Clive Hadfield, who was then assistant director responsible for special educational needs, and get help on almost any aspect of what I did. There is no one I can ring up now with the same broad bank of experience of SEN.

PR   Do you see much of your adviser?

AH   I have got a very good adviser, Judy Dunning. We are allocated so many hours a year of her time and I treasure every one of them. It is so useful to be able to bat educational ideas around, test the water, explore my vision against that of somebody else whom I respect and trust.

PR   Two last questions. First, what do you feel about SEN policy and the way this has changed? Have things improved? Second, what do you see happening in the future, and what will that mean for you and your colleagues?

AH   I think the major improvement has focused on entitlement. In the past the idea that pupils with special educational needs in whatever form – sensory impairment, physical disability, learning disability, behavioural difficulty, whatever – had a curriculum entitlement was not something which was much considered. What does need further attention is policy on statements in terms of who and how many are allocated, how they are determined and what they entail.

PR   Even the process of determining new statements is a very expensive activity.

AH   It is both very expensive and very bureaucratic. I don't think those two things are unconnected. I think it is an over-cooked biscuit but for certain young people it does set out what they need to have in order to achieve their rights. I don't know if it will continue.

PR   And, of course, decisions on levels of statements tend to be resource-led rather than need-led with considerable variations as between different LEAs.

AH   That is why the notion of entitlement is more important than the existence of a statement. In my view it is developments in the thinking and practice of curriculum entitlement which have contributed most to the improvement of quality in special education. To an extent statements have ensured that entitlement actually happened. You had to come up to the annual review able to say what was happening. Whether these reviews really need to take the form they currently do is, however, much less certain. One of my concerns is that integration is becoming increasingly hard to achieve.

PR   What do you mean?

AH   It is becoming harder to get a child into a mainstream school. Ash Field has 120 pupils now. It had 84 when I came. We see a lot of young people with SEN in mainstream schools when we are trying to achieve integration and have an appreciation of the nature and quality of the provision which they are receiving. Some schools of course are excellent but in many the provision is poor. Pupils are over-protected. The quality of the expertise available to support schools is limited. Things have not really improved. It is becoming increasingly difficult to achieve successful integration because in an age of league tables many schools don't want the worry of taking young people with the low scores in school tests.

PR   There are examples in other countries where it does seem to make a difference – in parts of Canada, for example – but there they are talking about large amounts of money on a sliding scale according to the nature of the need.

AH   I am totally committed to integration but I have moderated what I mean by it. I am now totally committed to it only when it can be achieved *effectively*. My cousin and his wife are doctors in Canada and we have talked about these issues. They were not entirely happy about the Canadian experience. There are some things that are very difficult to achieve with high levels of integration. Take, for example, sport. At Ash Field one of the things that gives me great joy is our young people writing for their annual reviews, say, 'My favourite thing about school is football and hockey' when all they can move in their entire bodies is one hand which shifts the joystick of their electric wheelchairs. But when it comes to break or lunch-time they are out in the playground driving about in their wheelchairs playing one of the team games. Now that, for them, is a shared experience with their peers on equal grounds. This is something you can't give in a mainstream school. If you haven't got twenty young people of roughly the same age all wanting to play hockey and all as disabled as they are in Ash Field then you cannot replicate that feeling of team games however determined you are. This is just one example. The opportunity for choosing a boyfriend or a girlfriend is another. So I think whatever we do about integration there will always be a place for a centre like Ash Field. We all like to be, don't we, for at least some of the time with people who share our circumstances and our interests in a very intense way. If we have this then we are happy to be integrated with the rest of the world on other occasions. We don't want to be without one or the other, do we?

PR   How do you keep up to date? How do you manage stress? How do you stay sane? How hard do you have to work?

AH   I have got fantastic staff. But it is hard. I would say I work for about sixty hours a week. My main support are my office staff, my senior management team and my residential management team. The difficulties that come my way usually can be downloaded on one of those groups. They are very good about accepting this. They are very tolerant of my need. So that is one of the ways I manage. Then my three children are very good to me and I've got a wonderful chair of governors and a good governing body. I couldn't ask for more really.

PR   Have you any hobbies?

AH   Family history – but my big hobby, gardening.

PR   You've certainly got a beautiful garden.

AH   Which you didn't expect to see but you did. Reading, history, that sort of thing. As for keeping up to date I don't bother about it. I use a filtration system. Also I meet with groups of other heads. That I value greatly. It is a good way of keeping up to date because everybody knows a little bit of something we all need to know.

PR   Was it a good decision to become a head?

AH   Yes, great. I love it. I'm already thinking about the next thing we need to make progress on at Ash Field. It's maths focusing on different ways of assessing numeracy and on trying to ensure improved progression in numeracy. We are also focusing next year on reading in key stage 1 and 2. I don't think I've slowed down, not even a tiny little bit.

PR   So you are still eager and enthusiastic? What do you say to those who say to you 'I'm thinking of becoming a head'?

AH   I say become a head only in a school in which you are fairly sure that you and the chair of governors see eye to eye. Know your strengths and weaknesses and then decide what skills you are going to need and where you don't have them make sure that they exist in other members of your team. Never think you are going to get to the end of the list of things you have to do. Each day requires a reordering of priorities.

PR   Have you ever met anybody who you've thought would be better off not being a head?

AH   I have. They have often needed people to like them too much. That above all else. They also weren't clear about why they wanted it. They wanted the position but lacked vision. But the major fault would be to want, too much, people to like you.

CHAPTER 9

Re-discovering the joy of learning: managing inclusion and EBD in a primary school

CHRIS MORGAN with Steve Rayner

Chris Morgan is Headteacher at The Goetre Junior School, Merthyr Tydfil, South Wales. He has held his current post since 1984 and previously been deputy head in two other junior schools in South Wales. His interest in an inclusive approach to SEN has grown since his appointment as head at The Goetre School. He has worked in a number of primary schools, both in England and Wales, and has been involved in leading school and LEA projects aimed at teacher development. Chris is a keen musician and is able to boast on-the-road success as lead singer of an over-forties rock band!

SR   Could we begin by you telling us about your personal background – home, school, higher education and people who perhaps had a significant influence on your life?

CM   I didn't have a very academic start to my life – I was born in Aberfan, one of three brothers, and the brother closest to me failed the eleven-plus and went to secondary modern school. Education did nothing at all for him, yet he managed to retire comfortably at the age of forty-two, and now sadly is passed away. My other brother went to a comprehensive school. I was the one who went to the grammar school.

I don't look back on my primary education with any joy. I was caned regularly. I was what you would probably call a 'naughty boy'. I didn't really get a good start for secondary education. In the grammar school I attended, there were three ability streams, A, B, and C, and I was in the C stream until it changed when some pupils were transferred to the technical school. The class arrangements were changed to two ability streams, A and B, and I was in the B stream. Somehow I managed to pass five or six O Levels, and then later I added one or two more to that list. I was supposed to take my

A Levels, but I hadn't prepared for them. I then broke my wrist shortly before the examinations. They took the plaster off my arm to give me the chance to write but I didn't pass, and anyway to be honest, even if I could have written properly, I probably wouldn't have passed.

I applied to teacher training college in Swansea and they must have been short of numbers because they accepted me. However, they lost my application forms, so I didn't go until the following year. I had a funny year, during which I was supposed to be re-taking my A Levels at school, but I was on the bread van more than I was in school. My family owned a bakery and we all helped. I went through teacher training college, after starting a year later. I had a good social life but I didn't do very well academically. I didn't attend many lectures, but I did have ability and I got through using that ability. I got into several scrapes with the authorities, and appeared several times in front of the principal. I had a serious personality clash with the head of science, who was the subject tutor for my 'main method'. I relied upon my ability to achieve 79 per cent in the end of year two exams. The senior lecturer virtually accused me of cheating, which I can honestly say I did not, and she told me that I wouldn't do as well in the final examination. She was right because she failed me! I didn't obtain the teacher's certificate.

I had, however, been accepted for a job in Surrey, at a school near Camberley, Mytchett Primary School. I moved to Surrey as one of a group of eight rugby-playing Welshmen going to make a living in England. Surrey LEA still took me, in spite of my failing my final year at college, but paid me two-thirds of a full salary. Early into my first year in teaching, the LEA adviser came to evaluate my teaching performance, and he was very pleased with what he saw and recommended me for full pay. I've been indebted to him ever since!

This 'success' motivated me to return to college for a day to re-take my final examination to try to obtain my qualification. Luckily, there was a new external examiner, who didn't allow the head of science to partner him in the formal assessment. I was also fortunate enough to identify a species of water spider, in the practical examination, which everybody else missed, that made me look good. Overall, my scientific descriptions were excellent and the examiner looked upon me kindly and I passed.

I continued working in Surrey, met and married a Welsh lady, who was working in a school in Kidderminster at the time. The school I was in was a good school. I was in charge of PE. The school had a good catchment area, although there was one element of 'London slum clearance' children. They were not many in number but they were the characters of the school. The school was then reorganized to form a first school, so I transferred to a middle school in the same area which was brand new and most of my timetable was PE.

After two years at the middle school, I went in to see the head-teacher who offered me a head of year post, and I replied that I couldn't accept it because I was off back to South Wales. I told him I was going to resign because I couldn't afford the mortgage on a house in Surrey now that my wife was pregnant with what was our first child. We returned to South Wales and I found a job teaching in a local school here in Merthyr. I stayed for about seven years at Twynyrodyn School. It had very poor facilities at that time, and poor staff who did very little, and I found that quite hard to accept, I've always been a hard worker, in spite of all of my faults. I found the children delightful. The parents were very supportive and that school should have been the best school in the area, given its catchment.

I decided to apply for a deputy headship and in fact applied for two at the same time. The interviews ran at the same time and another local teacher and I were twice both shortlisted. My colleague was appointed as the deputy headteacher of the larger primary school and I was appointed to the smaller primary school. During that year the headteacher of the larger primary school died, and the colleague who had had gone there was promoted to the headship. I was lucky enough at that time to have a headteacher who didn't obstruct me and was supportive and agreed when I said that I thought I should apply for the deputy headship in the bigger school. I applied and got the job and spent three years there.

SR   Chris, you say that going back to school-time for you isn't necessarily positive, that you weren't a successful pupil. Did you have any positive experiences of school, say for example in sport?

CM   I wasn't any good at sport in school because sport was either football in the primary school or rugby in the secondary school or virtually nothing. My eyesight was pretty poor at that time and I wasn't very big. I was quite a skinny child. I did play in the rugby seconds at grammar school but with no great success. My interest in sport really started at college. That is one good thing I can say about college. But again it wasn't formal college sport, it was really student union activity which triggered my passion for sport and introduced me to things like volleyball, badminton and basketball which we hadn't had any experience of at school.

Well – we moved down to Surrey after college together, there were eight of us and we shared common interests and a friendship. We all played rugby and basketball. We still meet. I think the group prob-ably did play a big part in my life at that time. I don't make many friends, but I'm quite close to the friends I do make. I've got a lot of acquaintances, and I'm quite well known, and if you were to walk round the town with me, you'd see lots of people saying hello to me. But, you know, there's a big difference between a friend and an acquaintance and a friend lasts for a lifetime!

SR   It was interesting that you commented positively about the 'London slum children' as an element in your first school. Do you think there has always been a sense in which you have enjoyed the 'challenge' of teaching children who generally come from problematic backgrounds and are a little more lively than most children?

CM   I think I look back at my education which I didn't enjoy and one of my aims is to give children an enjoyable learning experience, which is not just 'fun' for the sake of it, but to help make the learning effective. There are some educationalists who think if the children are happy and having fun, they're not learning. I think the truth is the opposite. I don't care how much criticism of modern teaching methods goes on, the education the children have now is far better than the education I had to endure in the 1950s.

SR   You were talking, before I interrupted you, of your progression from teaching into management and to deputy headship. During that period of time was there any formal preparation or training for headship?

CM   There was absolutely no formal preparation offered by the LEA I worked for or the schools I worked in, and the headteachers gave me no real help. I decided I had seen a number of people who I didn't respect professionally doing the job and I thought, I could do that job and I think I could do it as well if not better. Then I thought I had better prove to myself that I was serious about the idea and I needed to become more academic. I took a BEd, which I completed in two years and a term. I then decided to take an MEd, straight away without a break, and I was lucky because of the support I received from the lecturer who had supervised me. I completed the MEd in two years. I then left study for a while then returned to it and started a PhD. That was when I actually began the job here as a headteacher and I became interested in teacher appraisal, which was the focus of my research. I had to stop the research, however, because of pressure of work. I'm still convinced I have the ability to do the PhD, but regrettably I don't have the time to do it.

I suppose I progressed to deputy headship despite and perhaps even in spite of the system, rather than with any positive support or guidance. There was no real planning and certainly no preparation. I said earlier on to you that my career has been a little like a pin-ball caught in a rapid ricochet from side to side, quick fire and without any definite direction. I've gone for some jobs that I didn't get, and there were no reasons why I didn't get them. I've gone for other jobs I didn't think I'd get, and I've got them. I think the underlying motivation for applying to headship was that I'm competitive and I wanted to prove that I was better than some of the people for whom I'd worked. I obviously also had a family as well and wanted more money. Teachers don't get paid all that much money at the end of the day.

SR How would you describe the first year of headship in a new school? What were your feelings when you began your first headship?

CM I didn't feel worried or nervous. I'm not like that – I did feel I was facing a challenge. I definitely had a honeymoon period. I think anybody coming in to take up the headship of this school would have experienced the same reception, and I suspect it really wouldn't have mattered how badly I'd done in that first year. I do remember realizing the staff had been here for many many years. Most of them had only taught in this school, or possibly had taught for one or two years somewhere else, for instance Birmingham, and then returned to South Wales. It was very difficult to move them.

I was a lot younger then most of them too. I think there was only one, or maybe two teachers younger than me, and the rest were much older than me. I made it quite clear from the outset that I was going to change things, that if they could give me good reasons why something shouldn't change or why I shouldn't do something, then I would take that into account. However, at the end of the day, I was the 'boss' and things were going to move. I was blunt enough to say to them that if they couldn't handle that they were best advised to look for a different job in another school.

I had one teacher whose discipline was too 'rough' and so I got rid of him. I gave the LEA fourteen pages of complaints, and he went. I got rid of another lady because of her health record which I wasn't convinced was genuine. Some staff decided they wanted to retire. I don't think they did this because of a dislike for me. Many are still friends, and one gentleman still comes back to the school regularly as a school governor. However, the time had come when they were going and there was significant change in the teaching staff. I appointed quite young teachers, in fact, I've appointed a lot of young teachers on probationary years and I've not at all regretted it. There have been one or two who had a difficult first year but they have all come through and done well and contributed a great deal to the school.

The other thing I remember was the reputation of the children, because of the nature of a nearby council estate, which is the school's catchment area. It has a very bad reputation for violent crime and social problems. I was determined to be the 'boss' in my own school. The first pupil I sorted out was the so-called 'hard man' of the school, not that an eleven-year-old can be a 'hard man'. However, perhaps I should add that the young man is now doing eight years for beating a young boy almost to death. He was showing a glimmer of this behaviour in one of my first whole school assemblies. He started to say something or other at the wrong time and I just walked through the children as they sat in front of me on the hall floor. One of the teachers later said it was just like watching the parting of the Red Sea, with children parting to the left and to the right. I just picked the lad up and carried him out of the hall. I have never ever had to do that again, I suspect it is a bit of school legend.

I don't often have to 'lose my temper' either, although there is an occasional situation where I'll pretend to lose it. When I've tried all the nice positive ways, used up all the understanding, extended the support, I will then put on a show of righteous anger, and when I put on a show, I make sure it has the desired effect. If I do have to sort somebody out I make sure I do it effectively, otherwise it is a waste of time and effort. I'm not a 'softie' in that sense, because I do think there are occasions when you have tried everything else, or a sympathetic ear isn't appropriate, when you may not see using a cool, calm manner as the right strategy, when reason is not going to work, and you've spoken to the parents, and the child needs a boundary clearly set. I will do it and I will make sure it is done really well. But, as soon as this is done, mind, I'll work at helping that child get back up again and start putting things together.

SR   Is there any similarity in that approach to how you manage staff – I don't obviously mean in exactly the same way – but is there a parallel?

CM   At my last staff meeting somebody mentioned that my reputation as a headteacher was as somebody who was always praising my staff. I do. I will take them aside and have a chat with them sometimes when they need a gentle reminder or a guiding touch, but most of the time I am praising them and praising them. I am always trying to say to them, look, we have got this record in the school, we're doing this, we're doing that, right, we know there's a language problem, but remember to ask yourself how many other teachers could come and do what you are doing. They do sometimes get down, you see, when they look at the results after the hard work, and it hasn't had the expected results, nothing like it would have done if they had been teaching in a different school with a different school population.

SR   Can we go back to the previous question? I forgot to ask when going through the period of application for headship what your feelings were about the selection process.

CM   Right! Right! In the old days, Merthyr as it was, before it became Mid Glamorgan, was regarded as a place where what political party or other 'fraternity' you might belong to, if it was the right one, would do you a lot of good in any promotion selection. Politics played a real part in career advancement.

Now, when Merthyr became part of the reorganized Mid Glamorgan LEA, we were given a very enlightened District Education Officer and he was great. He was very fair and changed the system.

People who were then working hard won recognition and promotion was a natural part of that process. There was an open discussion about an individual's professional development and career opportunity. The interview procedure was not a hidden agenda or prescribed selection. However – that was the way I had experienced it – because the new education officer was not involved in some of my interviews. I remember being interviewed by the 'old' Chief Education Officer and the Chairman of the Education Committee. I actually had three minutes to answer two questions, and then I learnt I had been successful and was appointed the deputy headteacher of one of the biggest primary schools in Mid Glamorgan. It was farcical.

The district education officer then became the deputy director for the LEA, and then the chief education officer for Mid Glamorgan. The whole situation was changed and very much improved. However, when Mid Glamorgan was broken up at the beginning of this year, the re-organization of the LEA has meant the creation of a new unitary authority based upon Merthyr, and a much smaller LEA. I have to admit I found myself thinking about the 'old ways', the fairness of the system we have grown accustomed to, and what we might be moving towards, now the LEA has returned to the control of our local politicians. I hope we retain much of the system we had developed under the Mid Glamorgan Local Authority.

SR   Looking back over your time as a headteacher, which is around thirteen to fourteen years now, all in this school, what do you think have been the high and low points of success for you?

CM   I'd like to start on the lows which really coincide with the early period of headship. I felt, when I started, that some of the staff and the school were in 'a rut'. They were static and failing to win any recognition for their work. It was a case of well that's the Goetre School, you know, up on the Gurnos Estate, never mind up there as long as there isn't a big problem, you know what the kids are like and as long as the kids do not create a nuisance down the hill, well they are forgotten. People here weren't being shortlisted for promotion. I'm not conceited enough to say that they should all have deputy headship at some point in the future now, but they all have an equal opportunity, and there are one or two who deserve to be on a shortlist and I know they will be looked at and they will be there or thereabouts. It wasn't like that – they weren't getting anywhere in spite of ability and talent.

The nice thing now is that this school is recognized, not just in Mid Glamorgan, but throughout South Wales and even wider a field as a centre of excellence. For example, staff from this school were invited to take part in a project involving the use of good artwork in the local museums recently, and that was well publicized and we did very well. Our SEN Co-ordinator was on television not so long ago being interviewed in a programme giving advice to parents on how to select a school for their child when they have SEN. We are due to be on another programme on art in the near future for the BBC *Zigzag* series on schools television. It is scheduled for some time next term. Staff from this school have been used as examples of good practice and have been involved in work with tutors on different educational courses.

Three members of staff have been promoted in the last four years, which I think is a good reflection on what is going on in our school and marks a high point of success for my headship. We're being used all the time by other schools, who ask us if they can come and visit, and see how we are getting the results we do achieve, in spite of the odds, with the 'school performance track' giving us an 'uneven start', and this being reflected in the actual position in the league table we occupy. In spite of the Standard Assessment Test results, we are regarded as an effective school, a successful school, and that in essence represents the high point of success in my career.

I know I have previously mentioned some specific projects in which awards have been won by the school. I think this is part of the same success. Our extra-curricular activities are rightly recognized as a great strength of the school. We have a lacrosse team, which is unusual for a primary school, or any school this size, and we actually got into the quarter-finals of the Welsh Schools Cup last year. We employed a young lady last year who came from an independent school background and she brought an interest and an expertise in lacrosse. We've got a ceramics club, art clubs, the brass section, the strings section. We have a number of different clubs, a great many, so I decided some time ago to apply for an award from 'Education Extra', which is a London based charity. They gave us a certificate of distinction for our achievement and a gift of five hundred pounds and asked us to take part in an adult literacy programme.

I think they asked us because they could see we were a go-ahead school that showed a lot of initiative. We were the only school in Wales to be asked! They gave us five thousand pounds in year one, which I used to employ three young teachers, and we had something in the region of twenty-five families involved in the scheme. They then gave us two thousand five hundred pounds this year, and I managed to increase it to five thousand pounds again, by winning matched funding with the local TEC.

Now we've got forty-five families involved, so that's grown appreciably, and given us the strength to involve Merthyr College, who have sent us two teachers on Tuesdays, when we have adult learning classes in computing, numeracy and literacy. There have been about fifteen adults coming to the classes, including the grandfather of one of our pupils with SEN. These kinds of add-ons to the school curriculum reflect a depth of learning here, and are a source of satisfaction for me which I suppose are again a high point of success in my career.

Again – in a similar way – high points are created by our success in other competitions we take part in, and they are not only sporting events. I mean, you really expect a primary school this size to field sporting teams, and fairly successful teams, because it has a fair few youngsters from which to select. However, we have had success in art, information technology, and language competitions. We've done well in many of these competitions, on occasion winning regional recognition.

SR If we pause for a moment and think about the high points of success, which, as you describe them, are clearly interwoven into the achievement and reputation of the school, above and beyond this could you tell me how you set about identifying and measuring the success of the school and of the headteacher in school?

CM The league tables don't matter very much to us and less still to our parents. They'll come to this school with their children whatever, because it is here. There are some parents who don't mind if their children can't read or write very well, but if I stop their child going on a school trip because they've been misbehaving or they're told that their child has been stopped from having their crisps, they'll come down to school post-haste to find out why! So we're not worried about having to look over our shoulders at neighbouring schools in case we lose our children to them or from a fear that our parents may decamp. I'm not sure that other schools would actually want some of our children or their parents, in terms of academic ability, SAT results, league tables and 'entry selection', which is all a terrible indictment on something or somebody, isn't it?

We measure success firstly in terms of maintaining a calm, orderly and happy atmosphere in school. Secondly, we measure success by the good discipline in school which leads to effective teaching and learning in the classroom. There are lows, and we are not a problem-free zone. I am not suggesting that everything always runs smoothly. We've got measures in place recording the number of pupils who enter school needing language support, particularly, that number is always very high. It can fluctuate between 55 and 85 per cent of the children as they come into school. When the children leave us after four years, we usually have that figure down to as low as 5 per cent of the same year. In some years we manage to get it even lower, which in anybody's book is academic success.

In terms of the SATs, given the new grade descriptions, we have discovered that we have very few children described as having a 'bright future'. These children have been returned with an asterisk next to their name, and a brighter future forecast, and in our latest returns, we had only 26 per cent of the year identified with an asterisk. There we are, you see, 74 per cent of that year forming one huge educational 'black hole' with no brighter future. That's like tarring this 74 per cent as children with no future! A lot of them will go on and succeed – some of them in academic terms – some of them in terms of making money and getting a job. It is criminal to label them in a negative way and virtually write them off.

SR   Does that mean, really, I would be justified in saying to you that I thought what you have got here, Mr Morgan, is a 'special school'? I mean by 'special' special in the sense of the word which suggests extra-ordinary, added value, on top of the usual, and what you have here is a very very big special school?

CM   We regard ourselves as a 'special school' which has 'mainstream' pupils in it. We don't use that fact as an excuse and claim that we can't do anything or that's the reason why some might regard us as failing in academic terms. We say, this is our population, that's the reality we work with, and we see what we can do with it. We are often surprised that when we do set our sights high we end up being achievers with the children taking everybody else by surprise with what they produce.

SR   What particular vision for the school do you have and how does it play a part in your headship?

CM   We have two statements in our 'official documents' or headed stationery. We came up with these statements together as a staff. One was my own idea which the staff agreed to, the other was an idea the staff created. The first statement is on our letter paper, and declares that we are 'caring for our future'. We wanted this because we saw our role as 'caring for and about our pupils'. We want them to have a future, and a far better situation then many have at present. We want all our children to have a brighter future, and not just the academ-ically gifted.

A lot of children who weren't academically gifted in the past had muscle power, but now all the muscle-power jobs have gone. Mind you, there are not a lot of brain-power jobs left either, with a lot disappearing as information technology changes the working world. It becomes more and more important that if these children aren't going to find full-time employment, it is important to help them develop interests which they might go on to use constructively. It might help to keep them off the streets and out of trouble, as well as give them some self-confidence, self-worth and dignity. So we offer them a great deal in the way of extra-curricular activity. The kind of things I mentioned before, sport, art, lacrosse, computers and so on, giving them something to do.

The discipline policy contains the second 'mission' statement which declares that 'the road to heaven is heaven'. I don't believe in the sort of education I endured, where I was caned, repeatedly, and virtually tied to a desk for two years, and constantly being coached in the completion of speed tests in preparation for the eleven-plus examination. This was justified, at the time, by the argument that this would guarantee a brighter future in the shape of a grammar education. I never saw any of that brighter future in school, it just never happened.

I want the children in this school to have a happy education which they enjoy. In a sense, what I want is for the children to travel to wherever it is they're going, but have every opportunity to enjoy the trip. I think learning is going to be far more effective if they are happy, enjoying themselves, when they are far more likely to be positive and motivated. They are far more likely to make progress and achieve. It really does seem to work and success breeds success. We have a large population, many of whom are coming to school from a wide range of background, but I can say that all of them, with the exception of around nine or ten, are generally positive in school. The nine or ten are not necessarily negative or disruptive, but there is that moment, now and again, when they've got to provide some self-discipline, and they fall down.

SR   Do the staff really share the headteacher's vision in this school?

CM   Yes – they do because everything is taken up in a whole school approach with the staff fully involved. We talk about it all before we do it. There are one or two staff who will agree on it and then drift away from it. My job then is to go and remind them and that's what I do. If I say that we must be positive with our discipline, I'm not telling them they can't have a little shout now and again because that works now and again, and sometimes it is appropriate, now and again, but it is not appropriate all of the time. You see, some of our children come from an aggressive home background, and they can out-aggress anybody or just shut off. They get it all of the time. I mean I had a little boy in here the other day and I spoke as softly and kindly to him as I could, telling him how disappointed I was in him, and he burst into tears, bless him. I could have shouted at him all day without any effect, he would have just stood there staring at me. I didn't want to make him cry. I was quite amazed but that's the way it goes sometimes, you win some by losing some.

SR   Describe the kind of head you are – as a leader – as a manager.

CM   Well, this is the most difficult question in the interview schedule. What did somebody once say, something like, to see yourself clearly is to see yourself as others see you? I asked two of my colleagues yesterday and my secretary today to describe what kind of head-teacher they thought I was, and they found it very difficult. They are straight people and I don't think they'd 'bullshit' me, if we're allowed to use that word. I just think it is really very difficult to pin down an answer.

Hard-working! Hard-working is one thing, and I pride myself on that because I've always been hard-working, although not always in an academic sense. I do think I'm considerate and caring. I think if my colleagues have a problem I will share it and assist if it is at all possible. There have been occasions with divorces and breakdowns in relationships, or bereavements, when I've been quite under-standing. I'm also a positive person and if a teacher comes to me with a new idea I usually say yes and sometimes that will be to our cost because we do all work very very hard and doing something new is usually an extra rather than something that replaces something else.

At the end of a term, we can, as a staff, be on our hands and knees, and we nearly always need the holiday. But then again, the staff is such that work carries on during the holidays – I come in on Saturday and Sunday mornings – and I came in during the half-term break after a three-day school trip to Disney World in France. While I was here I noticed at least seven or eight teachers in at different times during that same week. We do work hard and I sort of lead the way, if you like, by example. I suppose there is a general expectation and attitude to our work which says something about our professional pride. I do think the staff think, well he's doing it so we'll do it as well, you know, I don't tell them they must work hard and not do it myself.

SR   How would you describe your management style?

CM   My first thought is to describe my management style in terms of a sporting analogy, and I have had this idea of management for a long time. I have often thought of myself as a 'tracksuit manager'. The original idea I had was of myself as a manager who mixes it with the players on the training ground, works the team, shapes up method and tactics. I see this style working because there is a clear and sufficient knowledge of the game demonstrated by the manager enabling him to command the respect of the players as he sorts out the game plan. I have to admit, however, to failing to live up to that ideal self. There has been such a great increase in the workload, and so many changes to manage, that I haven't been able to be as involved in the teaching. It is fair to say I think that I am far far more remote from the staff than at any time since I've been a headteacher. I am also the eldest member of staff now, which is perhaps something else!

The change has been forced on me, you know, I've got far more things to do which keep me sitting in front of the keyboard, or sitting at my desk, filling in forms, or on the telephone, and so on, which all adds up to less and less time on the classroom. Issues which need my attention are a priority. It is not easy at all. I don't know whether I'm doing more harm than good by trying to be in the classroom or that I should give it up in the first place. I do do what I call the 'lap of honour', which is my way of describing lesson observation and monitoring. Even this is often difficult to manage because I'll arrange to visit a class in advance, and then the problems start, the drains will block, or a window is broken, or a pupil has an accident and needs to be taken to hospital, or a parent has arrived in a crisis which can't be dealt with by someone else without the danger of the problem escalating. I need really to have a non-teaching deputy headteacher. We did have one for a while, when the finances permitted, and that worked really well. You see, I would like to get into the tracksuit far more often than I do these days.

SR   Do you think with experience things have become less difficult for you as a headteacher?

CM   It is not as difficult now to deal with challenges because I've got my own team. You see, I picked them all and you pick people you want to play in your team when you are a football manager. You do the same thing when you appoint a teacher – so that makes life less difficult. I'm far 'older' now, and perhaps a little wiser, and when I work with the children well, there's thousands of strings to my bow as far as discipline goes, from being the 'nasty' headteacher, which doesn't happen very often, to the cajoling headteacher. It is a fact that you often get better results with these children from difficult backgrounds by 'praising them up' and saying this, that and the other at the right time. I still find it difficult with all of the case reviews I am supposed to attend. I probably go to a conference or review several times a month, and sometimes more frequently. So – I suppose there are always difficulties which you manage that leave you wondering if things are any easier.

SR   The extra demand on you is a direct reflection of the SEN element in your school population?

CM   Yes. Other schools will have some of this, but nothing like on the same scale as we have here. There is a school just over the hill, not even half a mile away down the road, and the headteacher there will have nothing like the same number of case conferences to attend. I do find, you know, that sitting in these meetings, taking decisions, acting like God, is hard. We put a kid into care just three weeks ago, but on that occasion I didn't feel so bad about it because that family already had two other children in care and this was a third and the reasons were very clear. But sometimes you have children, and you know, you think who am I to make this decision. If there was somebody doing the same thing with my own child, then I wouldn't be very happy. I do still find this aspect of the job very difficult.

SR   How do you think the staff would describe you as a headteacher?

CM   I don't know because the two I asked yesterday found it very difficult.

I hope they would say he is hard-working. I don't mind if people don't like me. I'm thick-skinned enough to put up with that, but I do hope they respect me and I think they do, because I'm having a series of discussions with staff at the moment to discuss professional development, and in one discussion this morning I asked that very question. I said to the teacher that I had talked through aspects of her professional practice, and I had pointed out one or two things she needed to change, now she had the opportunity to do the same. I asked her if she could give me a straight answer, and asked her what I was doing as a manager to irritate her. She replied that there was nothing at the moment but as soon as I started she would tell me. I thought that was fair enough, and I also thought it was a worthwhile acknowledgement of my approach to the management of the school.

SR   How do you enable effective teaching and learning which takes place in your school? Do you see any changes in this aspect of your work?

CM   Right! This is where my argument with Mr Woodhead, the Chief Inspector of Schools, comes into our discussion. Smaller classes make good teachers better teachers, and they also make poor teachers better teachers, but importantly, they won't make a poor teacher a good teacher. I also think that larger classes make a good teacher less effective and will make a bad teacher much more less effective. I think class size does matter because it is directly linked to the learning experience, as well as the teaching task. For example, the amount of preparation, the amount of marking, the amount of individual attention you can manage to give to children in the classroom, the activities you can set up for children, are all proportionately determined by the number of children in a classroom. Class size matters a great deal!

I am funded for a workforce in this school against 'average salary', and I have to pay 'actual salary' to the teachers, which means I have a little bit of leeway in our budget planning. We have a young staff which leaves me in this relatively good position on staff salary cost. I have as a deliberate decision gone 'over-staffed' by two to three teachers, and we maintain small class sizes as a deliberate policy. Our largest class has twenty-eight children in it. Our smallest class has seventeen pupils in it. A number of classes have around twenty to twenty-one pupils. Our special needs classes have fifteen children in them, which is really too many for having one adult in the classroom and the kind of SEN presented by the children. The staff-pupil ratio was geared originally for children with moderate learning difficulty. We do have a lot of children presenting emotional and behaviour difficulties as well as additional language problems. Overall, however, you can see that we have used the budget to put our policy into practice.

We also do a huge amount of INSET. We are probably, according to one LEA advisory teacher who spoke to me recently, one of the biggest customers for INSET within the LEA. It's partly because we are a big junior school, and so attract a reasonably good sized INSET grant, but even so I do think it has more to do with our belief in the value of this kind of activity. I think we should always be encouraging teachers to strive towards professional development and continue learning about learning. I think that because we are a large staff, while there's never anybody who is good at everything, we are all good at something, and we organize a good deal of development work to capitalize on our own expertise.

More formal approaches on School INSET days can include specific subjects, for example, we had a morning recently on one teacher demonstrating how we can use the concept keyboard in our teaching. There's a bit of INSET going on in school most of the time and it literally breathes life into our practice and into the process of teaching and learning which takes place in the classroom. We also run 'special weeks', for example, we have a 'language week', when we invite poets in residence, authors, illustrators, and we bring in supply teachers to release our own teaching staff, and they then work with the experts, to see how they can enhance the learning experience for the children. When we finish one of these special events, which can very often grow from the planned one week to run into a fortnight of continuous activity, we usually have a performance or display of work. But I like to stress that the outcome or product of the week is not as important as the experience. While we have the product and there is a celebration of the work achieved as a result of the week, it is my view that it is the process and not the product which is really important. What I don't want happening is a teacher panicking because they want to produce a spotless display, or a perfect performance, whether it is a play or a piece of music. The process is the all-important thing.

SR   Is that your approach to school, generally, that is, you are not as concerned with results and appearance and outcome as you are with experience and process? If I put that another way, would your attitude to inspection be 'you find us as we are', rather than building up to the test and putting on a special performance?

CM   What we're doing for the Ofsted inspection, in terms of preparation, is accept that we are going to be criticized on certain things, for example, certain results in the area of language attainment, but we're going to try to make sure the things that we should be good at and should be in place, are in place. We are trying to have our 'panic' now, before Christmas, so that we can ease up after Christmas in the immediate run-in to the inspection.

My own attitude to the Ofsted inspection process is that it is a 'sham'. Those schools that can put on a good show for a week will 'beat' the inspectors , even though inspectors say they are not fooled. An inspection should really be a 'school audit'. The inspectors should come into school without prior warning or notice, or at least very little notice. If they really want to see the school, that's the only way to do it. They should just arrive with the minimum of notice and carry out their assessment. This present arrangement of a year's notice creates a lot of unnecessary stress for teachers. I've already got two people showing signs of stress because that's the way they are as people. They are not ineffective teachers, they are in fact very effective teachers, but they do tend to worry, and they've been worrying about this inspection now for almost a term. How can that be a good thing?

Colleagues are telling me too that it takes about a year to recover from the inspection experience. So, in effect, you are having two years 'knocked out' by an Ofsted school inspection. I must say that it can often appear to be a 'charade', rather than a positive school development. You know, one school in Merthyr borrowed every policy statement from another school in South Wales, and ended up with a better inspection report.

I see one difficulty in the Ofsted process as the 'snapshot' nature of the assessment. It is only going to give a still-shot picture of the school in action. One of the additional factors which will probably be missed in our school inspection is that next year will be full of changes in staffing which are bound to affect the smooth running of the school. If they had come to inspect us this year, it would have been great, because everything we've touched this year has 'turned to gold', so you know, it is just one of those things! But you can't tell me it is a fair or accurate assessment of the quality of a school.

SR   In summary, then, as the headteacher, do you think you are as personally involved as much as you would like in the teaching and learning process in school?

CM   No. I'm afraid it's less and less because of the changes that have come in, and you know, I think I'm often addressed as the manager of the school nowadays, instead of the headteacher. My teaching skills have become less and less important, perhaps they shouldn't be, but I just don't have the time to demonstrate the point. I certainly do find it difficult to find time to do the things I once most enjoyed – working with the children.

SR   To whom is a head accountable? Who do you answer to and how do you manage this accountability?

CM   I'm supposed to be accountable to the school governors, the LEA, the parents of the school and the pupils, who some call the 'customers'. In the situation we have here, the LEA's authority is more or less totally delegated to the governing body, so yes, I'm accountable to the LEA but strictly speaking, all of that accountability is taken up by the governing body. But in areas like this, and schools such as this, the governing body has never actually realized a full quorum to set up a sub-committee. I have a very interested chairman of the governors, who comes into school on a regular basis, and is very helpful if the drains are blocked, or there is dangerous equipment which needs immediate attention. He will support me and he knows how to pull strings to get things done. One other governor, who is an ex-teacher from this school, comes in quite frequently, but this is really on a social level, and he runs the school pool club.

The governing body really let us get on with the work of teaching, learning and the school curriculum. We are regarded as the professional body. I must admit that's the way I like it. However, I always secure agreement and the permission of the governing body for our policy and planning. But the truth is I'm given a fairly free hand. If we take appointments as an example, I always make the final decision when we appoint a teacher. I do have a lot of freedom, and clearly while I like it that way, it is all going to fall on my head if I get a bad inspection report. The governors will rightly turn around and say that they gave me every chance and look what happened.

I think I am also accountable to the parents and the children. I particularly feel that accountability to the pupils, you know, because I want to give them the best I can all of the time. I am lucky that I have a staff who are prepared to do that too. The parents are rather atypical in that they're not pushing their kids to do well at school. They are not all like that, mind you, because I'm not tarring them all with the same brush, but the majority of them are quite happy if the children are happy and having extra things, such as trips to see Santa Claus, or a camping trip, or Disneyland or whatever. They are less interested in the academic side of school.

If we have parents' events, on social occasions, like carnival, Christmas plays, class assemblies, we'll have high levels of parental support. If we have a parents' evening to explain the NC or a Drugs Evening when we have Drug Aid in to explain the dangers, we get a very low level of parental response. Open evenings are a bit like a curate's egg, some classes will see up to 80 per cent turn-out from parents, and often well above 50 per cent, other classes will have only around the 10 to 15 per cent level of attendance. Sometimes parents will turn up for one class open evening then we will not see them for the rest of the year. It is very very unpredictable.

SR   Is working with parents a big part of your workload and do you think that is different to other schools in the area?

CM   I have a doctor's surgery most mornings and definitely on a Monday morning. I am very often the only one they can talk to when they have a problem. I do think that is different to many of my colleagues in other schools. I have worked in other schools, in Merthyr and elsewhere, and I know the difference. I know you might say, well Chris that might be because you're a 'caring headteacher' who has developed this kind of 'community school'. Well, I'd say yes you are right, but it is more than that, and if the parents can't identify with me and the school, you see, then you're going to stir up a hornet's nest for yourself. When you lose the trust of the parents, that's when you begin to see concerns on the governing body, and we've seen the way in which some schools are torn apart by conflict between the governing body and the headteacher, or where the governing body virtually run the school. There has been one, two, no three schools in Merthyr recently where the governing body has got rid of the headteacher – perhaps justifiably, I don't know.

So – I don't want them to get rid of me yet – because I'm still here, enjoying the job and I want the money. But the main thing is I want the parents on our side so that we can all work together for the children. In the main, we do have that, and yes, I do listen to the parents, and I do think I'm caring and helpful, although I have to admit, sometimes, I have a job not to laugh when they are describing to me some of their problems. I could write a book. For example, we had a mother in last week, and it was quite important, because she explained that her ex-husband has suddenly re-appeared after simply vanishing seven years ago. He had just walked out of the door without a word and now he is back. We are concerned that he may turn up here and try to take the children. We have procedures to keep the children safe.

SR   You must have a similar problem with divorce and family breakdown raising difficult issues of access, parental authority and security?

CM   Yes . . . if the divorce is done in a constructive manner, and the needs of the children are taken into account, it is then OK. It is the stability of the house that is more important, not the number of adults that are in it. Quite often, people judge it the other way around, they say, divorce, single parent, problems, and you see, that's just not the case. We have had families here, where the background has been very stable, and the children have been very happy, even though there has been a number of men passing through the house, because the mother is so strong and powerful and she keeps things together. Up here, you know, quite often the grandmother is the person who keeps things together. It is the stability of the home background which is more important, not the number of adults, who represent the key factor. However, quite often we have young mothers who haven't got a clue and they come along for advice, for example, over free dinners, and this that and the other, even financial and medical problems.

SR   You seem to be describing yourself in the role of a 'counsellor', Chris, which I suspect is a natural part of the job as headteacher for the reasons you've stated. Perhaps we can focus for a moment on you! I know you suggested that the job seems to be getting harder with an increasing workload – how do you manage to maintain your own professional and personal well-being while you manage that change?

CM I . . . I found that I was beginning to get bogged down, where life was becoming only school. I mean ... I used to coach rugby on two evenings a week, down at the rugby club, and obviously, be involved with the team on a Saturday. The other evenings in the week were devoted to gymnastics. Gradually, one by one, all of these interests stopped because school was growing bigger and bigger, that is, the job was growing bigger. I was getting bogged down with school, and I was getting all 'het up' over this, that and the other, and I'm not that kind of person, I'm not an anxious person or somebody who worries. I prefer to get by, using my sense of humour, having a laugh and a bit of a joke.

However, during the time I've been a deputy headteacher and a headteacher, my parents have died, my parents-in-law have died, one of my brothers has died. I have also had some close friends fall seriously ill and because I'm the only cousin still living here now in what was a large family, I've inherited the role of the 'caring figure' who is still at home. The duty of organizing funerals, for example, has fallen to me. So – I can laugh this sort of thing off, have a bit of a joke, and so on but I do hear a lot of my colleagues talking about stress, and lots of them are beginning to take an extra drop or more, you know, and I find myself dropping into the pub straight after work. I go to get a complete break from education. I don't go to drink with teachers very often and I just get away from it. I laughingly 'front' a rock group too, with some other teachers as it happens, but we only talk our interest in music, never education or schools. It is a sort of get-out, which the sporting interests used to be, but it's only been going for six months or so, and yes, it is going well, maybe too well.

SR You're still hitting the right notes then, Chris?

CM Yes. It is becoming very silly really, you see, we did one gig last week in a local pub, and it's led to five new bookings. People were there and saw it and liked it and now we're booked for performances in Bristol and in Swansea, so I suppose you could say we're on tour. That's got to be carefully managed, so that it doesn't run out of control. It has to remain an interest, a relaxation. Once it starts to create its own pressures, then it will have to stop. We have a younger member of the band, on the drums, who works in a shop, and he's dead keen, perhaps not surprisingly, and wants the band on the road. But – as I say – it has got to be handled carefully.

SR What about your professional well-being? I suspect most headteachers are bad at maintaining their own development, choosing instead to focus upon the INSET provision for their staff. How do you manage this aspect of your work?

CM   Now then funnily enough we were discussing this issue the other day. We were revamping our schemes of work, and there is a formula now that has come out which is a fairly standard format across the different areas of the curriculum. I realized I didn't really know what this formula was, and then, even the way the schemes of work are actually structured at the planning stage, because I've not been on a schemes of work course, as have most of my staff. I've never really had to teach a scheme of work to a class over the school term, or year, you know, it is very easy to lose touch if you're not careful. In fact, that's one of the reasons why I'm trying to get back into the classroom.

I have been criticized for being absent from school too much. I have been away because I am one of the 'stronger' characters amongst the local headteacher fraternity, and as a consequence, I am serving on a number of working bodies. I serve, for example, on the SEN Steering Group, which makes decisions about the children in the area, the placement provision and very often addresses the SEN of children with exceptional needs who are placed in 'out-of-county' provision. This is important because it is very very expensive. I only missed one of these meetings in the last year or so, and it immediately affected the SEN provision here. This helped the staff realize how important it is to represent the school and for me to be involved in activity outside the school. It has eased the kind of criticism I was beginning to receive for being away from school.

I am on the steering group for the Education Forum, which our new Director of Education has set up, where headteachers have a constructive part to play in the decision-making at an authority level. I am also the schools cluster co-ordinator for this area. I am asked sometimes to give presentations, lectures or talks, like the lecture I gave in Poole, Dorset, last year on the subject of education, schools and the new unitary authority. I have also been down to London once or twice to give similar talks. I am very keen that schools such as ours are represented, or otherwise it tends to be the more middle-class view that is always given, and decisions are made or taken, and I am keen to promote our side to the decision-making group. This activity helps to celebrate and publicize the sort of work we do here in school and to raise the profile of the staff, thereby increasing self-worth, self-confidence and the ethos of the school. I think it is also good for the school and the local community to see us involved in the 'bigger picture'.

I do try to control the number of times I'm away from school. I obviously don't want it to be so often that it interrupts the running of the school. I think that cuts down on the opportunity I have to attend more conventional INSET courses. The courses I have opted to attend have lately been on management, for example, the SIMS courses on information technology. I try to keep in touch with curriculum development. Every teacher that goes on an INSET course has to come back and give a presentation to the staff and have to give me a written report. I get that sort of second-hand information, which does help keep me in touch, even if it is by proxy, and it is one way of keeping abreast of new development as well as monitoring the relevance of our INSET programme.

SR   Ted Wragg says 'You don't have to be a "nutter" to join the "barmy army" but ... '. Do you think headship has become much more difficult and do you enjoy it?

CM   Those who are not 'nutters' probably do become 'barmy'. Those who can't laugh, have a joke, and relax a bit are fast becoming 'barmy' in more ways than one and end up cracking up! They become stressed, break down, and are going out of the profession on early retirement. Merthyr has got about twenty-four primary headteachers, no, about thirty headteachers if you include all the nursery schools, and eleven of those headteachers retired this summer, over a third of the heads in this local authority! Two of those eleven, sadly, have died since they retired, a matter of a few months, and while one of those two heads was a lady who had cancer, and it was an expected death, the other person just dropped down dead. Everybody thought she was fit and well and were shocked! It stops you in your tracks and makes you think, doesn't it?

A lot of my colleagues, as I said, are turning to drink to help them relax, and I suspect if they are not careful, we might have the making of a new problem amongst those in headship. They are beginning to talk about having a few drinks each night when they get home. Some are even talking about regularly knocking back a bottle of wine or two in one evening. The warning signs are there, but I do see myself as the kind of person who has a good sense of humour, likes a laugh, and like some of my friends, I suppose I am a bit 'daft'. I don't think being a headteacher has turned me that way, but perhaps it has been a useful qualification for the job. I think it is important to keep a balance. I never ever take work home. Never! Even if I do have to stay at school until six o'clock, half past six, I'll stay in school, I never ever take work home. I'll come in on a Saturday morning or a Sunday morning, quite regularly. My wife is a teacher but I don't talk about school with her.

I think the job has and is going to get more difficult. It's more than just an increasing workload, it is about managing change but also about being faced with new and additional responsibilities, new tasks that have to be carried out. I'm doing a lot more things which are central to the job for which I was never trained. Overnight, I went from handling seven thousand pounds to buy pots, paints, paper and books, to handling two hundred and seventy thousand pounds for the school budget, and managing staff employment, health and safety, buildings and grounds, and so on.

The job does seem to sometimes resemble a juggling act, with lots of balls thrown up in the air, or maybe spinning plates on the end of sticks, but the trouble is there does seem to be an ever increasing number of plates being given to me. There are conferences to attend, all the administrative tasks I need to complete, free school meals, the computer side of the finance, the school returns, and so on and so on. For example, I now know we were funded too much last year because we claimed for fourteen kids who didn't materialize. Well, the LEA has clawed back the money we received for these kids and we're facing a loss of twelve thousand pounds. That's a deficit before we start.

The cleaning contract has just gone up in price to three thousand pounds. Now that's a fifteen thousand pounds deficit before we make a start. That's a big concern because that equates to half a teacher. Now – these sorts of problems are on my mind all of the time, and I've got teachers who really should be promoted and given extra responsibility points, and I've already had two of them come to see me and ask for a promotion. I've had to say to them that I am sorry but I can't give it to them even though they deserve it because I just don't have the money. I also told them that I might have to make someone redundant in the Summer Term. I might be lucky on that, though, because as I have said we have one lady who might be leaving us because of a change in her personal circumstances.

SR   So – are headteachers increasingly finding themselves between a 'hard place' and 'the rock' of educational needs in their schools?

CM   Yes, I think they are! In Merthyr, the predictions are that we will be facing, next spring, a 3 to 5 per cent cut in the total budget. Now, on top of inflation, and a deficit inherited from last year, that's going to mean that this school is facing a big problem. We're a school with a big budget, so I can't imagine how some of the smaller schools are going to fare.

SR   Out of interest Chris, do you think there is still a need for schools to have a headteacher?

CM   I think you can go two ways on this question. You can have the headteacher who is going to be the 'manager' looking after finance, shaping general policy, dealing with the outside agencies, such as advisers, education officers, the various organizations, and other members of the local community as well as the governing body. Then you can have a non-teaching deputy headteacher who will lead and manage the day-to-day implementation of the school curriculum. I think it is important that the school manager has a background in education. I think this is important because of, one, 'street credibility', and two, the need to be able to understand the pressures which are part and parcel of the classroom teacher's job.

If I draw a parallel with the management in the National Health, hospital managers are accountants, and have no medical training at all, and they therefore fail to understand or take into account medical factors when they take decisions. Decision-making in hospitals, in my view, does not seem to consider the implications of policy-making on the professional practice of doctors, nurses and medical care. I wouldn't want a headteacher who would create that kind of situation in a school. I really do think the manager in a school should have a background in education, who has had training and experience in education.

There will always be a need for somebody in the position of leader or manager in a school. I don't think you could run a school as a 'head-free zone'. I am, especially with the young staff we have here, the lead, the 'beacon' which is out in front lighting the way, charting the course and pointing out the right direction. They are the crew, I suppose, pulling on the oars, driving the ship forward on its voyage.

SR   Do you think that the function you serve is not only to provide the 'vision thing', if you like, but also to provide a very practical steadying hand on the tiller, which reflects an experienced hand?

CM   Yes. I've had years of experience teaching in different schools, in different areas of the country, and lots of my teachers here have only taught in this school. I do think there is a time when teachers should move on and I've often said to my colleagues that now is the time for them to move. Hence, the fact that we have had one young lady go to Canada on an exchange two years ago, and we now have another lady going to Australia next term. I think this is good for the staff and the school. We've had three teachers in the recent past move on to deputy headships, and as I say, I think it is a good thing because it prevents the 'pool' from becoming stagnant. We have a throughput of people with different talents, and we all learn a little from each other. We have, by and large, youngsters on the staff, although we have on occasion appointed experienced teachers, and we do try to keep a balanced staff team.

At the moment we do have a problem, in that we have an imbalance in terms of gender, with only two male teachers on a staff of seventeen. I don't think that's at all healthy. We will be looking to change that and we tried to change it during the last set of interviews. We were looking for a male teacher but the fact of the matter was that a young lady who was amongst the candidates was the best applicant. She got the job. At the end of the day, I want the best person for the job, whether or not they are male or female. I think it is good if up here, with many of the children who come from a home where there is no man as part of the family, that we have male teachers who can act as a male role model. I try to do this rather deliberately when I walk around school. I don't just walk down the corridor and not speak, I'm talking to the children all of the time, even though, mind you, I can't remember their names half the time.

So – I think it is good to have a throughput of staff in school, and I've been impressed with the young ladies that we have had here. I say young ladies, but we have had a young man as well, and to be quite frank, I find it flabbergasting to hear the government at present talking about changing the teacher training arrangements because we've had newly qualified teachers from Exeter University, Cardiff, Camarthen, and they have come into the school well prepared for the job.

SR   I'd like to focus if we may, for the next ten minutes or so, on the SEN dimension in the school. I have already said I have gained the impression of this school as a 'special' school. Indeed it reminds me of one or two special schools in which I have worked, although quite obviously it is what it is, a mainstream junior school. In the first instance, what fundamental changes do you think have taken place in special education and what does this mean for headship and special education in this school?

CM   Let me give you some facts first, which will tell you more about the nature of SEN in the Goetre Junior School. We have seventeen classes, fourteen of which are mainstream, three of which are designated an SEN unit for children with moderate learning difficulties. They are not separate to the school, but are fully integrated, and that's why I prefer to call them classes rather than a special unit.

We have had this SEN provision as part of the school for thirteen years, in fact, since I have been the headteacher. We started with one class, then added a second, and then a third which now officially comprises the 'SEN Unit'. It was expanded by the LEA because it was cheaper than transporting pupils elsewhere, and far cheaper than building a new special school. Theoretically we have forty-five pupils on roll in the special classes, and previously all of these pupils would have been statemented. However, the number of pupils statemented for SEN in Mid Glamorgan was dramatically reduced last year as a result of the Welsh Office telling the LEA that it had too high a percentage of the school population statemented. The result was a de-statementing exercise which magically removed a number of statements from many of the children in the special classes.

We now have three youngsters with a statement, one of which has got medical problems as well as complex learning difficulties, the other two with severe EBD as well as associated learning difficulties. We've noticed that the majority of children being placed in the special classes are not pupils with MLD, but generally pupils with EBD and who present complex learning difficulties. There are no children here with physical disabilities, because of the nature of the building, with its steps making it entirely impractical to bring in wheelchairs and move children with mobility problems.

In the mainstream classes, we have an intake of between 50 and 80 per cent of children presenting learning difficulties. At the moment, we've got two hundred and fifty pupils out of the whole school population identified as having SEN, of which one hundred and fifty are registered at stage 3 of the SEN Code of Practice. There are thirty-two pupils registered at stage 2 of the Code, and forty-six pupils on stage 1 of the Code. The latter are pupils who have 'come off' the language support programme, but who we still deem to be 'at risk'. I have to all intent and purpose, if we re-consider your earlier comment, probably described a 'special school' to you.

The changes and the reform we have experienced in the last few years has obviously put SEN into the 'limelight'. The 1993 Education Act, especially, has created new responsibilities for us. The appointment of a SENCO, duties of the governing body, observance of the SEN Code of Practice, and the development of individual education plans (IEP) as part of an annual review system, to name but just a few. We are supposed to have an IEP for every individual on the SEN Register. It is totally impossible in a school this size. If you only have a small school or a unit, well then it makes sense, because I do think it is educationally sound and a good idea. We have had to develop a 'Group Educational Plan' (GEP), in which we action-plan programmes for pupils with SEN. When the GEP is insufficient, because there is an obvious need for greater individual detail, we then implement an IEP.

We have a SENCO with a full-time teaching commitment and as a consequence, she cannot meet all of her responsibilities as a SENCO. We seek to 'free' her for a morning a week, but this has been under 'attack', for various reasons. This year she has taken a mainstream class rather than a special class, just to help her preserve a balance in her perspective and experience. It is very easy to lose a sense of 'normality' when you work in special education, and expectations and a sense of levels of attainment can become skewed. So – she has come over to teach a mainstream class for the year and a young teacher who was expressing an interest in special education had replaced her as a teacher of a special class. I was worried that this young lady might make the move to special education and then find she was trapped in work that didn't suit her. The exchange gives her 'work experience' in SEN without that kind of commitment. She will be in a better position to make up her mind and I think the experience will add to her professional development. This two-way exchange is a recent innovation in school but one about which I feel very positive.

SR   Does it perhaps illustrate one of the advantages of integrated SEN provision, in so far as an interchange of staff can lead to professional and curriculum development?

CM   I think so and it is taken as read that there is collaboration and a continuous interchange of pupils and staff between the classes in school. There are various activities and programmes going on which simply assume this level of integration. I don't think the children see the special classes as separate to the school. We make a point of involving the special classes in any school event. In fact, the special classes often lead in running a school event. We recently had a special class run the school harvest festival celebration. They are involved in sports clubs, teams, and other extra-curricular activity. We have children in the school choir.

The captain of our lacrosse team last year was a pupil with SEN who was in one of the special classes. I'll admit that choice was partly tactical, in so far as he wasn't chosen purely on ability, but he was one of the most loyal members of the team, always made practice, and could not be faulted for motivation or effort. He literally grew six feet during his captaincy, you know, because he was there, and he shook hands with everybody when the team received its awards, and a deserved accolade. He was in the team on merit, and he proved to be a good captain. He also benefited from being part of the whole school.

We have the three special class teachers working together as a team. I think this is important too, because it prevents the typical problem which can easily occur in a primary school, when one special class finds itself isolated and remote from the rest of the school. Now, that is most definitely not the case here. The SEN teachers share their expertise with the other staff and this is necessary because the staff all have children with SEN in their class. In fact, the exchange of ideas, expertise and perspective is a two-way process which strengthens the school in a number of ways, not least, in terms of professional and curriculum development. Everybody is in the same staff room, they do duties together, they have a laugh together, they attend the same school staff meetings, they have their differences of opinion, they go for a drink together, and they have the same headteacher.

SR   Does the nature of Merthyr as a distinct kind of community add to the 'specialness' of this school?

CM   Well – Merthyr is a distinct community and the school's catchment area is unique even within the Merthyr community. The topography of South Wales has made us rather narrow in many ways, because we can't see anywhere else as we are down in the valley. We tend to be slightly hypocritical sometimes, and a little prejudiced about the world outside. In truth, I think we probably have more in common with the mining communities of the East Midlands, Yorkshire and the North East then we do with the sheep farmers of North Wales.

I do think we have a fractured society here in Merthyr, and we have a disaffected sub-group within the community, the delinquent element, the nuisances, who are not the 'hard men' of the area, but are nevertheless dangerous and violent. It is this group who beat up old ladies, mug people, rob, and are very much into the drug culture. The local boys, you see, the real 'hard men', will deal with things in their own way, and keep themselves to themselves, and they are part of the black economy which thrives on the estate. I mean many of the families up here have got things I'm still saving up to buy, but the kids will go without a pair of shoes. Now the disaffected sub-group I'm talking about are not part of the traditional community, they are dislocated from it. When you mix this with alcohol and diazepam, which leads to aggression, that's when the trouble erupts. Yes – I think the community and the geography of Merthyr has a part to play in making us that little bit special.

SR   Does the drug problem surface in school?

CM   We have had one young girl on 'speed' and a young boy on diazepam. In both cases, they were taking drugs as a consequence of pressure from older children. The girl violently assaulted another girl in school. The boy just flaked out. We get parents coming in on drugs, mostly 'downers', prescribed drugs for depression. If I think they're totally 'out of it', I'll phone social services.

I think the worst experience I've had with drugs happened one Saturday morning. It was before we had the fence erected as a security measure. I was sitting here working when I heard this banging on one of the school doors. I went down to see what all the commotion was about, to find a little girl aged about seven, another girl aged about four and another child in a pushchair. The mother was sitting on the grass in front of the door taking drugs in front of the children. I phoned the police because you are a bit wary these days, handling women, and the police took so long to arrive that they had left. I mean what upset me the most was that the little girl was looking after them all, even the mother. I didn't know whether to keep them with me or what to do but in the end they disappeared down the subway. The police spent an hour looking for them but without success.

SR   How do you wish to see your own school develop? What will this mean for the head?

CM   Right! The first thing is because of changes in the personal circumstances of some of my staff, I know we are going to see a considerable turn-over of staff. I also know that we have a budget problem looming next April, which is going to raise the question of staffing levels and funding. I have already decided what I propose to do, and staff don't know yet, but when one teacher leaves at Christmas, and a second teacher goes to Australia, I'm going to disband one class and increase the size of year four classes. Now year four classes are still comparatively small when taking into account average class size in the school, and even after collapsing the two classes will still only average twenty-seven or twenty-eight pupils per class. I hope these changes will help me with balancing the budget in April and leave me in a stronger financial and organizational position, or at least, in a more stable position for next year.

SR   Is there any scope in your opinion for additional funding for the SEN element in school?

CM   I keep making noises about that all the time, but to be blunt, it is a waste of time. There is no money. The pot for the education funding isn't any bigger and it is all committed. As I have already said, the authority is facing an across-the-board cut next year. Merthyr haven't administered education or social services since 1973, and they are facing the two big spenders who don't earn a penny. Last April there was a massive row between the councillors and the headteachers because of proposed educational cuts. We were successful in fighting a rearguard action because we threatened them with parental opinion. We won't get away with that again next April. Social services bore the brunt of the cuts this year. They had to find savings of up to one million pounds. Quite honestly, I don't think the local councillors saw it coming, and I can quote one of them telling me that he thought the borough would be awash with money. So it has all been quite a shock.

As far as school goes, I just want to maintain the 'status quo' over the next year, and avoid being 'knocked back' by the financial stringency we are going to experience. If we level out over the next two years or so, I would like to see two or three teachers promoted, and generate some fresh staff turn-over in school. If I'm honest, I think it is time I moved on too because I've been here for thirteen years, which is too long. I wouldn't like the school to be content with staying the same, because it has been my experience that when a school tries to stay the same, it usually slides backward and there is a drop in professional standards. I'm happy that this school is innovative and I want it to maintain this vitality. When we have talented teachers leave we have successfully filled the space with new people.

I think the special classes will remain unchanged. I am arguing with the LEA that we shouldn't be providing for children with severe EBD. I think the LEA needs to provide for them in a better way. Our special classes are not meeting their SEN. Some of them have come from observation units where there are six or seven pupils with two adults in the classroom, and then suddenly they find themselves in a class of fifteen pupils with one adult. Some of the children in the special classes are obviously not presenting MLD, but are pupils with EBD, and they prevent teaching and learning taking place. We have also noticed that they set a role model for many of the other children, and the behaviour of the group deteriorates in a kind of levelling-down process. It can become a tough uphill battle for the teacher.

SR   Do you really think your school is 'special'?

CM   There are two ways in which I do think our school can be considered 'special'. I do think we are special simply because we do special things. I'm delighted that we are beginning to receive some recognition as a result of this 'specialness'. I also see us as a special school in another respect, and that is because we have pupils with SEN. They are not only pupils with learning difficulties, but there are many pupils here with SEN that related to personal and social development.

Many of the pupils in this school are directly affected by what happens on the estate. Last night there was a violent scene when a fire engine answered an emergency call after a house was attacked. We have had serious beatings and even murders on the estate. It might not affect that family of our pupils, but when it is happening around them, just up the road, or perhaps to somebody they know, it has an effect. The last murder we had left this school really buzzing for over a fortnight. The estate is on the television, in the news, and the result is excitement, notoriety and the wrong kind of energy in the classroom.

SR   To sum up Chris, given you are serving a particular kind of community, is an integrated provision the best way to meet the SEN of children in school?

CM   I think inclusive education is the way to do it, but it still must depend upon the nature of the SEN of the children. For example, we couldn't meet the needs of children with physical disability because of the nature of our building. I also should repeat my previous point, and say that integrated education must be appropriately resourced or it will not work. We can resource MLD classes without too much trouble but we are not resourced to work with children who present more severe learning difficulties or EBD. If we had more resources, then perhaps we could do this, and in my opinion that would be preferable to segregated provision which might mean taking children out of the community and labelling them as different.

I think another problem with integration, however, is what happens to pupils when they transfer to secondary school at the age of eleven. Pupils with SEN often fall through the safety net in secondary school because of lack of support. I think it is a difficult question. If

I say I have only once permanently excluded one child, who did have special needs, but was excluded after a second serious assault on a member of staff, I have excluded four other children for a fixed period of time and they came back and settled down and that was very pleasing. We have also only had to have one child with SEN moved to a special school because we couldn't handle him. He came from such a disturbed background it is difficult to even begin to try to describe it. Now I think that that record illustrates that we are quite successful in meeting the needs of our children.

However – when our children enter secondary school the support is often not there, and the changes occur, resulting in absenteeism, bullying and victimization from the peer group. Now, that is when I am left thinking there is a need for a special educational response, and a place for the special school. I also think there is a need for a special school to deal with those children who have extreme or severe SEN with which we cannot cope and there is equally a need for a special school for the children who cannot cope with mainstream school.

SR   At the end of the day, then, you seem to visualize the ideal provision for SEN as a diversity of schooling, centred around the community, which is coherent but enables a flexibility of placement. It should also be integrated in the sense that it removes negative labelling and segregation and supports children within the mainstream school and the wider community. Is that right?

CM   Yes, but crucially, mainstream schools which raise their 'threshold' to accommodate SEN must have the resources required to do it. Considerations like numbers of pupils, staffing ratios, staff expertise, INSET, curriculum, must be taken into account. My staff, after all, are expected to have trained to work with MLD. We can gear up to deal with EBD. But the key factor is the resources with which to do it. If you are going to establish an inclusive educational system which will integrate pupils with SEN into the mainstream community, you must be prepared to find the resources to support it and to make it work.

CHAPTER 10

Owning headship: an exercise in common sense and leadership

EDNA ROSS with Steve Rayner

Edna Ross is recently retired after forty-one years of service in education. She has taught in primary, secondary and special schools. She served as a deputy head (for six years) and headteacher (for fourteen years) at Slades Farm School, a residential and day special school in Bournemouth for pupils with Emotional and Behavioural Difficulties. Her career spans a wide breadth of teaching experience, including five years as a colonial service education officer in Nigeria. A theme running throughout her work has been involvement with pupils experiencing learning difficulty. Edna is busy now in 'retirement' managing diversified farming, including fruit growing, equine accommodation and holiday cottages.

SR   Could we begin by your telling me a little bit about your personal background and of anyone or anything you think may have had a significant influence on your career?

ER   I started school early in life because my mother died when I was two years old. My father was also unwell and I think he wanted to get me into school as early as possible. We lived in a small village where people were very accommodating. I remember being very enthusiastic about the idea – starting school. I remember too the excitement – being told I was to start on the next Monday – but the enthusiasm evaporated by the time Monday arrived. Nevertheless I was bowled along and made an early start to school.

From what I remember, I did reasonably well all through infant and junior school, although I should mention that I did attend several different schools. We moved, initially because the house in which we lived was marked for demolition. It was to be knocked down to make way for a new road. We moved right away from the area for a while, then we moved back again, to Rochdale, and then subsequently moved away to Blackpool. My father was ill for most of the time during my early childhood but all in all, I must have moved school about five times, which really is not very much if you think of some service children who are here, there and everywhere.

I then faced the scholarship examination and passed and went to the grammar school. It was an all-girls school, in fact all the schools I attended were single-sex, in those days even the junior schools were all girls. I went to The Collegiate School for Girls in Blackpool. It was a very well known school at that time, with a very good reputation. I know it was a girls' school, but there was a boys' grammar school which served as a brother school to our own school, and one of our most famous 'old boys' was Alistair Cooke. I would always point him out to people as an 'ex-pupil'. More recently, for what it's worth, one of our famous 'old girls' is the lady who is in charge of the Child Support Agency. She was obviously much younger, and at the school much later. She gave an interview on television and went back to her schooldays at the Collegiate, a good solid base from which she developed her ability to enter management.

SR   Is that true for you too?

ER   In retrospect, yes, possibly; however, I could have definitely got far more out of my time there. Looking back on it, yes, it was a very good education. I did well, academically, until the third year. Really, you've got to put the work in after that, haven't you? Before that you can get by on 'natural nous' as you pass through junior school and into the early years of secondary school. From then, you really do have to start to work and I simply didn't make the effort. I wanted to leave school. I'd had enough of it. I wanted to finish with it. I wanted to get a job. It didn't interest me, not in the least. Indeed I did leave school after I gained the school certificate. I left school and went to Technical College to follow a secretarial course, which lasted for about a week. I didn't like that at all and went back to school and spent two years in the sixth form going on to do my A Levels.

SR   During your school years, was there anyone you recall having an influence on you?

ER   Yes. I think Miss Lever, a talented teacher in my junior school. She used to write plays for children. She was presented to the Queen, who is now the Queen Mother, and the plays she wrote were superb. They were the sort of the plays that you would re-live again and again, as you become totally engrossed. All the children enjoyed them. They used to vie and fight and clamour to be part of them. It was very exciting and a tremendous boost to the imagination. I often wonder what became of Gladys Lever. I'm sure she didn't become an Enid Blyton or anything, and she'll be dead now, but I do wonder.

For good or bad, I do remember vividly the headmistress of the school. She was a mountain of a woman, absolutely huge woman. When she spoke, she put the fear of God into everybody, pupils and staff alike. There were three 'mortal sins' at Miss Dobson's junior school. They were telling lies, playing truant, and stealing. I don't think that anybody who attended Miss Dobson's school would ever lightly say an untruth, or pick up anything that didn't belong to them, without fearing the thunderbolt which they know would strike them down. Possibly, although I am sure many people my age will say this, if there was more of that fear and awe in school today, you would not have the number of disruptive pupils who can't be managed. I'm sure Miss Dobson would manage many of them!

SR   Is that true too for the levels of violence which are reportedly increasing in the classroom?

ER   It's not just school is it? It is a change in society as well isn't it? Society was a lot different in those days because there was this element of awe, an element of fear that if you did something wrong, then retribution would surely follow. In books, in plays, films, crime was always solved, murderers always caught, you know, there was never any suggestion that crime paid. Now in this day and age, it does pay, doesn't it? It's not just true, either, for the criminal element. It runs right the way through society, the object is to take the risk, and get away with it. Does conscience play a lesser part in forming our behaviour these days?

SR   Did Miss Dobson have an impact upon your own teaching style?

ER   No, I don't think so, although I've used Miss Dobson many times since I've been a teacher. I've spoken of Miss Dobson in assemblies and narrated some of the things she did and some of the things she used to say. I've had children sitting open-mouthed, incredulous, accusing me of making up this story of an ogre of the past. But I wasn't or have never been a 'Miss Dobson' as a teacher. I simply couldn't successfully copy someone else's 'style'.

In the same way, I couldn't be a Peter Lawrence as a headteacher. Peter Lawrence was the headteacher at Slades Farm before I took up the position. I remember people asking me 'are your ways different to his?', and as I said at the time, if Peter Lawrence had a naughty boy, he would advance on him until his rather portly 'corporation' would bear down on him, leaving no space between himself, the boy and a wall. Then Peter would talk to the boy who had no choice but to listen. Well – I couldn't quite manage that particular strategy even if I wanted to use it.

We were talking about influential people and I must mention another teacher, a woman called Joan Wilkinson. She was a teacher in my third, fourth and fifth year at grammar school. I know it was at the time that I became disinterested in school and I didn't work, generally, but I did work for her. She was a very good teacher. She taught English and I did enjoy the subject. I went on to take the subject at A Level and I think Dr Wilkinson had a lot to do with it.

I went from school to teacher training college, not because I had any burning ambition to be a teacher, but on returning to the sixth form, and after some time had passed, we were faced with the expectation of making a decision about our career development. We were asked to make choices and I didn't have a clue. The head-teacher advised me to come up with something, and she was talking to me about teaching as one example. She told me that if I was in an office, like girls who had left school before the sixth form, I could expect to earn between two pounds ten shillings and three pounds a week, but if I qualified as a teacher, I could expect to start on three hundred pounds a year. It was a very big incentive and there was no escaping the fact that it seemed a well paid job.

It all just fell into place, almost by accident, because the money was attractive although I didn't really have any desire to enter teaching. I think there was an undercurrent of chance, which continued to run for me throughout my career. It really was that same current which carried me forward towards headship. As I've said to you before when we've chatted about these things, so often now you're asked to plan your career, aren't you? Where do you expect to be in five years' time? I have to confess that's something I've never given a moment's thought to, ever. I have just gone along with the opportunities as they have presented themselves. It does seem sometimes as if those opportunities have gathered pace like a big snowball and I have got caught up in it.

SR   When you were at college, was there anyone who stands out in your mind as influential?

ER   Staff no, friends yes. Some are still my friends today. We sometimes meet and we stay in contact. We expected to earn a good salary as a teacher! We were trained to do the job and there were lots of teaching jobs at the time. There was no question of difficulty in finding work. You were wooed from the first day of gaining a teaching qualification. LEAs wanted you. I suppose looking back I can't really say I learned very much at college. The teaching experience in schools helped but the course was not a relevant preparation for the world of teaching.

SR   As you describe your early education and life, I can't help thinking about the fact that your parents died when you were young. Do you think this played a part in encouraging you to make a career out of teaching?

ER   It's hard to say. It's a little bit like 'what would have been', isn't it? No – not really – I was one of many orphan children at the time. I was growing up in the war years. It was not strange or unusual to be an orphan. My brother and I coped, went on, and did. I think we were both extremely fortunate to have had my mother's sister, who brought us up, and I must say even now as I look back, I think she must have been an absolute saint.

My aunt had no children of her own yet within a couple of years she acquired a ready-made family of two stepsons, a nephew and a niece – all in all, a very disparate group! Although they were very poor, and accommodation was the two up, two down house so common in those days, there was never a hint of 'can't afford' or 'no room to take them', and no such things as support from social services or benefits from the DSS. We had an abundance of 'love', which I must confess was never really appreciated until very much later. I remember my aunt telling me that she hadn't had any sort of education herself. She used to tell me that her only memories of school were fear. She was always frightened when she was at school. I found this very difficult to understand because I hadn't really experienced it myself.

After college I applied to several LEAs. You were expected to apply to a minimum of three LEAS, and I applied to Lancashire, Preston, and Manchester. All three replied and said yes, but I chose Lancashire. I went, initially, to a school called Penwitham County Secondary School just outside Preston. I used to queue up for the bus, look out of the window at the passing scenery as the bus trundled along country lanes for the best part of an hour. I would then get off the bus in the bus station and stand in another queue for the local bus. People just don't do that any more, do they? I would get off the bus and finally walk the rest of the way. That was my first job!

I was part of the teaching pool for Lancashire LEA. This meant that you were placed in a school where the need existed and not necessarily on a permanent basis. My first school was only for a year and then I subsequently moved to a junior and infant school. However, I do remember that first year. When I first arrived at Penwortham School, I arrived to find that there was a gentleman there who had just been appointed to take charge of the children who had difficulty with learning, what we call Special Educational Needs today but were then called 'backward children'. I remember, he had a book, Schonell's *Backwardness and the Basic Subjects*, which he always carried around with him. He took the older children who were all grouped together in a withdrawal class. I took the younger children who also had SEN.

This was my introduction to teaching. I was given the 'naughty' difficult children, the 'slow learners' or disaffected in my first year of teaching. Well, in the middle of the first term, this teacher went sick, so I had the most difficult children together all in one class. I did a year there, then I moved to the junior and infant school, again at Penwitham. It suited me fine because right from the start I had been harbouring an ambition to go abroad. I was determined to find a teaching post overseas and I reasoned if I gained as much experience of teaching across the age range as I could, this would strengthen my application. So I taught junior and infant classes during the entire second year of teaching at Penwitham Junior and Infant School.

I started to look for overseas jobs and saw a position advertised in *The Times Educational Supplement* for a teaching post in West Africa. The advertisement stated that candidates had to be of a minimum age of twenty-five years old, have at least five years' teaching experience, and hold an Honours Degree from a British or Commonwealth university. Well – you know how when you're young, you're very brash! I was twenty-two years old, I'd been teaching for two years, and I didn't have an Honours Degree, but I applied for this job, and I got it! I can only think that nobody else applied. The job was in Nigeria. My friend used to say to me, well, there you are, people don't apply for jobs in West Africa, they're transported there! But I looked forward to it. I remembered the films of equatorial Africa, such as 'Sanders of the River', and had pictures in my mind of the pith helmet, the flowing river, the exotic animals and the jungle. I was entranced by vivid images of romantic Africa.

I really did have a great time there. It was before the days of independence. I should really have been twenty-five years old and I should really have had more experience to have made it all really worthwhile and to have made the most of the time. I stayed there for five years and taught in The Government Girls' School in Kano. Girls' education at that time in Nigeria was very much in its infancy. What they used to do was to send out Education Officers to the villages to try and persuade the village headmen to send their girls to be educated because their value would then be enhanced. The girls would be sent to school in Kano. The school was an old American Air Force billeting next to the airport which had been converted into a boarding school. It was called The Government Girls' School and Women's Training Centre.

It was in many respects very similar to a traditional English education. Most of the staff were white English people, who had suddenly found themselves teaching children who could be and often were extremely difficult. The village headman tended to send the most difficult or problematic girls in the village to school, to knock the rough edges off them and to have them out of the way for a while. I had moved from Lancashire, where I had been teaching slow learners, to Nigeria, where I again found myself teaching difficult children.

Can you imagine, I was young, alone, inexperienced, and arrived in Kano after the most wonderful, adventurous voyage out to Africa. I mean you wouldn't have the same experience nowadays, they would just arrange for you to get on a plane and fly there. I was on the ship for four weeks with government officials and missionaries for company. We sailed out to West Africa, and when we arrived we disembarked then transferred to a train at Lagos and travelled north up-country to Kano. Then suddenly, the next day, there I was, facing my class, a sea of black faces looking at me, all alike, and I was given a list of names which I couldn't pronounce. That was all the preparation I had – a list of names.

Well – half of the children couldn't speak English and I couldn't speak any of the local language. Looking back, I do wonder what we were really pretending to do, what we were really achieving. I did learn an awful lot about 'Usuman dan Fodio and the Fulani Rebellion' and the 'The Rise and Fall of Timbuktu' because it was no use teaching the history of Henry VIII and the Tudor Dynasty. I learned to make groundnut stew as opposed to teaching the kind of standard lesson we had had as schoolgirls in England, which was making Brown Windsor Soup.

Relationships were clearly very important, perhaps as important if not more important than the content of what you taught. I mean, you taught everything to the children, you had to be responsible for the whole curriculum. You also had to run clinics. It was a boarding establishment, you lived on the premises, you had to present yourself at the clinic to administer health-care. I had no experience of this sort of thing, particularly tropical disease. The girls often experienced attacks of 'guinea worms' which would break out all over the skin. We used to wrap them around a match stick and turn them a little bit each day. I remember there were two big bottles of medicine from which we would dispense medication. The first was 'Mist-Alb'. The second was 'Mist-Expect'. If the problem was below the waist you would dispense from the 'Mist-Alb' bottle, if it was above the waist, you would dispense from the 'Mist-Expect' bottle. I really had to grow up very quickly!

During those five years in Nigeria, I got married. I became pregnant with my first child and came back to England. But by that time, things were beginning to change in Nigeria. The country was following Ghana down the road towards independence. The whole atmosphere was changing. There was an increasing number of people shouting for freedom. It was a little bit like South Africa after Nelson Mandela took over, with a lot of people experiencing great disappointment because they expected a utopian brave new world. They were destined to be bitterly disappointed, of course, because it couldn't be changed all at once.

Well, it was the same in Nigeria, there were a lot of young people who wanted their place in life, and rightly so, I'm sure we would have felt and behaved in the same way. They wanted the foreign nationals out of their country and wanted to manage things for themselves. But then you had the older people who took a different point of view. I recall one old man saying to me that he remembered how it used to be before the British rule. Well, of course, what happened was there erupted a dreadful, terrible civil war, some three or four years after independence. A truly dreadful war.

SR   So it was a good place to have worked but the right time to leave it and return to England?

ER   I think it was an ideal place to be if you were single without any responsibility. However I didn't particularly want to have my baby there because I had seen too many babies die. It was so easy for you to fall ill and then you were dead. There was very little in between. We came back to Lancashire. My husband has always had a series of 'projects', or so it seems, which he has started at various points throughout our lives, and we started one in Preston where he went into business for a while.

I felt the need to do something else, away from the business, so I looked to teaching. I rang up the nearby LEAs to ask if there were any teaching vacancies. Within two or three days I found myself in a special school for children described then as an Extra Sub-Normal (ESN). The school had had to get rid of a teacher very quickly because she had developed an inappropriate relationship with some of the girls in her class. She had gone on Friday night and I was there in the classroom on Monday morning. The children were quite difficult as you might imagine but I stayed there for a term. While I was working in the special school I successfully applied for another post in a mainstream school called Stanley School. I subsequently moved there and spent a very happy period which had to come to an end because my husband had to move in his work. We moved to Dorset where we have since lived.

On arrival in Dorset I immediately began looking for another job. We moved at the beginning of the summer holidays so I was planning to look for work in the September. It was just at the beginning of September when Miss Goodman, the deputy headteacher of Boscombe Secondary Modern School, came knocking on the front door. She asked if I would come into school the following day. I did and I was given the difficult children there. Initially, I only taught for four days a week, but when I didn't go in on the Thursdays, nobody else wanted my class and the children were very difficult. Eventually they asked me if I would teach full-time. They wanted me to come in on Thursday too, so I agreed.

SR   But Edna, Bournemouth is a nice area, I can't imagine there being naughty children here!

ER   Well – one or two – one or two! They were lively kids and I think we had a good relationship. It was in the era when the Beatles became famous. I remember having some good fun. We could have a good laugh together. It was during the time I was there that the government brought in legislation preventing pupils from leaving at

Christmas. I had this group of difficult children, all looking forward to leaving at Christmas and suddenly they were told they had to stay on at school until Easter. I remember telling them 'Don't you take it out on me, it's not my fault, I'd have you all out at Christmas if it were up to me!'

But we got on all right together and there was no great harm done. They would do things for me which really at the end of the day is what it is all about, isn't it? Good relationships! It's no use relying upon the principle of 'you will do this because I say so'. You'd end up saying that all day long until you were blue in the face. It was about building a good relationship and an important part of this was to have some fun. It was always better when there was some fun.

Boscombe County Secondary School eventually closed. It was amalgamated with Beaufort School which has also since closed. I didn't want to travel across Bournemouth to Southborne which was where Beaufort School was situated. I made it clear I didn't want to stay in the new school. At the same time, Alma Road Special School approached me. The head asked me to go down and see him. I vividly remember going to see him. I had my daughter in one arm and a basket in the other arm. I had made up my mind that I was going to have a break. I fully intended to say this, but when I met Malcom Head, the headteacher, who was a lovely man, he greeted me with a huge expression of relief. He told me how pleased he was that I was going to join his staff at the start of next term, and I didn't feel able to refuse.

SR   When did you first make a move towards senior management?

ER   Well – I carried on at Alma Road after the first year because a vacancy occurred and I went for the job. Malcom Head retired and Roy Roland replaced him. I then had the opportunity to go to Southampton to do a Diploma in Special Education. I thought this was absolutely fantastic, wonderful. I mean somebody actually paying you to go away and study. I hadn't intended to leave Alma Road, and it was Bill Lewis, a colleague with whom I was friendly, who really was responsible for bringing this period to an end and steering me along the road to deputy headship. He mentioned to me that the LEA were building a new special school called Slades Farm School not far from where I lived. Peter Lawrence was going to move from Westbourne Special School as the headteacher and was advertising for a deputy headteacher. He suggested that we should both have a go and see what happened. He popped down to Portman House, the LEA office, and picked up a couple of application forms. He gave me a set, we both applied, and I got the job. I was very surprised. I didn't expect it. I was later told that it was the references which carried the day. I'm sure I didn't interview brilliantly. It was Peter Lawrence who later told me that it was the reference, but you know, you get a job, don't you, because you're the best of a bunch on that day at that time. There's more than a slice of luck involved.

SR   Did you have any inclination to climb the rungs on the career ladder before Bill Lewis mentioned the deputy headship at Slades Farm School?

ER   No – definitely not – not at all. I had been promoted while I was at Alma Road Special School. I was given a post of special responsibility. I was given the role of teacher in charge of senior girls. I suppose that was my only experience of 'management' but you have to remember that you didn't have the same structures of management in school then as you do today. You received the post, took on the extra responsibility, but this was in addition to the normal and full teaching programme. There were some very difficult problems, but overall you just carried on with the teaching day. There was no sense of management, middle or otherwise. The management, that is management in the sense of being responsible for the work of other staff, was left to the head and deputy.

SR   Were there any particular people or events which influenced your decision to progress from deputy headship to headship?

ER   Well … There was the fact that the headteacher decided to retire, thereby creating a vacancy! In that sense the vacancy presented itself, courtesy of Peter Lawrence. I did take on a lot of things during my deputy headship which I simply continued to do in my headship. In that respect, the deputy headship was a good grounding for headship. I became a deputy headteacher to a head who was six years from retirement and was very much looking forward to it. He used to say how many governors' meetings he still had to attend, and when someone is counting down in that manner, well you know that's when they have other things on their mind. He was a wonderful person, a tremendous character, who contributed an awful lot simply by his presence in the school. However, I seemed to do most of the organizing in school. When the school first opened we weren't even going to have a timetable, and each class teacher was going to be responsible for the daily programme of their own group.

It was the kind of approach I associate with an archetypal EBD headteacher, their philosophy would be reflected in an approach which would be about 'flying by the seats of their pants' or 'making decisions on the hoof', or facing the staff each morning and asking the question, 'what are we going to do today?' I couldn't accept this approach. I felt very strongly that we needed to have a structure for the curriculum, a firm foundation upon which to build an approach to teaching and learning. It was important that everybody knew where they were supposed to be and what they were supposed to be doing, so that if they veered away from it, and the timetable wasn't written in tablets of stone, it was possible to easily return to it. I also thought there was a need to use to the full, the skills of specialist subject teachers appointed to Slades Farm School. We should, I strongly felt, deliberately stay in line with the curriculum in mainstream secondary schools.

I was aware of the fact that this was the secondary education of these children and it had to be as good an education at Slades Farm School as it would have been elsewhere. I am talking about a period before the national curriculum, and the structure provided centrally by legislation and curriculum prescription, and it was not as easy then as it is now to accept the need for planning, structure and accountability. But we did have the timetable right from the beginning. I devised the timetable which provided the structure for the school. I looked at the staff we had, considered their strengths, and organized a timetable which would make sure that the children who attempted reintegration into mainstream education, when appropriate, would not be completely disadvantaged in a secondary curriculum. In many respects, I suppose I ran the school on a day-to-day basis. We had the structure, we had the timetable, we knew what the pupils were supposed to be doing, and we drew up programmes of work while we also developed the aims of the school.

SR   Were you also the disciplinarian of the school?

ER   I think as far as the children were concerned, Peter Lawrence had this very strong appearance and personality and he filled that role very positively. However, as far as the staff were concerned, that very clearly became my role. I was, I suppose, the curriculum leader and a kind of personnel manager. If Peter Lawrence wanted a member of staff talking to or given some 'guidance', then I was asked to do it. I remember on more than one occasion some very difficult problematic situations in which, to put it delicately, I had to intervene and was instrumental in sorting out the problem. I can't really go into detail but it most certainly involved me in 'senior management' right from the start.

But as I say, Peter Lawrence was a super man, I felt involved and I felt that he appreciated my work. I must repeat that point. I really did feel appreciated and I remember John Littson, an Education Officer, speaking to me at a Leeson House weekend. The Leeson House weekends were INSET weekends for special education before the days of INSET, Baker Days and the rest of the government's reform. We organized them through the membership of the National Council for Special Education (NCSE) and they were very well supported.

Well I remember John Littson chatting with me at the end of one of these weekends and telling me that he was very pleased and heartened by the way Peter Lawrence had spoken about me to him. I thought that was very good. There is nothing like being appreciated, is there? I did feel, for a long time, appreciated by the headteacher and the LEA. I do think that in those days, when you were more obviously a part of the LEA, a 'family', and if you felt you were appreciated, you responded accordingly.

SR   During this period did the encouragement you describe play a part in moving you towards headship? What other factors played a part in forming your ideas on headship?

ER   Well – the important thing is acknowledgement and appreciation. It has to be because the school leader is only as strong as the team which they lead, who after all are the people dealing with children. It's not easy being with these children from day to day, and on a minute-to-minute basis, without a significant break. I think one of the duties of a headteacher in any school, but particularly an EBD school, is to reduce as much as possible the stress of trivia so that people are not going to be worn down by the job. I didn't want any of the staff to feel, and I'm not talking about incompetence here, that they could not face the day-to-day wear and tear of teaching children with emotional and behavioural difficulties.

I'm talking about the day-to-day stress of dealing with pupils experiencing severe emotional and behavioural difficulties, and the fact that I have known of some schools where teachers would die before admitting they have problems managing a particular pupil or class. They simply wouldn't admit it because they would feel it was something they thought only they were experiencing and that it would be an admission of failure. I was quite prepared to admit to, and even make a joke about facing the task of managing difficult behaviour. The kind of thing I mean would involve making light of a bad experience with a difficult class, or a difficult pupil, or declaring just how difficult I had found the morning, or the lesson.

I remember a senior teacher approaching me shortly after she had started at Slades Farm School, and saying that she had thought she was the only person to have these feelings and experience the difficulties I had openly expressed. My response immediately was to say it happened, and it happened to everybody, and the thing was to ride over it, and sort it out in the end. It takes far more skill and commitment and courage to do that than to walk into a classroom and teach a group of docile, amiable, compliant children who are ready to respond to your every word, doesn't it? In an EBD school, by definition, you simply don't have this opportunity to teach on 'automatic pilot', and you learn to live with it.

I can remember one day visiting the local comprehensive school, where I had to meet a teacher, and she was actually teaching in a classroom to where I was directed. I went along the corridor, looked through the glass section of the door and saw rows of uniformed girls sitting facing the front, completely attentive, whilst the teacher was explaining something to the class as a whole. No interruptions, no one out of their seat, no interference with other pupils and no evident lack of concentration. I was mesmerized and wondered about the effect of just one disruptive or disturbed pupil being planted in such a bed of tranquil industry. We were, at the time, thinking about a pupil being reintegrated to that particular school but it seems to me that it also illustrates the difference that exists between the 'world' of learning in some mainstream classes, and the 'world' of pupil management in a special school for children with EBD. They are very different!

I could see absolutely no point at all in a headteacher, in addition to this stress experienced at one time or another by all teachers, putting further unnecessary pressures upon the teaching staff. Now, given the recent reform introduced by the government, the way education has developed has seen a growing number of pressures bearing down upon teachers which previously a headteacher was able to control but I'm afraid that is probably no longer possible. The headteacher is obviously going to have to manage this rapid change but is not able to control it.

SR   So if I was a conscientious teacher in your school Edna, and I successfully managed a specific project, how would you respond to me?

ER   I would have obviously very much appreciated your effort and I hope I would have said so. I would have then given you an opportunity, for example in a staff meeting, to talk about the project, explaining what you had done, and how you had done it. I would want to disseminate 'good practice' to the rest of the staff. I would also want to see the children involved. I would want them to have their turn, for example, to present their account as a school assembly. I would want this to be a celebration of positive experience linking the project to the whole school. The idea would be to celebrate the whole event. Something good, whenever it happened, would not just be taken for granted, but passed on, made the most of, celebrated. After all, in an EBD school you really cannot afford to overlook the good, any success at all, but hope that it will be continued or lead to further success. The positive experience really does need to become a positive habit and it won't happen without working at it.

SR   How would you describe the first year of headship in school?

ER   I wasn't looking to be a headteacher. It was not an ambition. I was not saying it was something I would be in so many years' time. I became a headteacher because I happened to be there as a deputy head-teacher, when the headteacher retired. I was there and it seemed the sensible thing to do, to apply for the headship. I didn't know that I would get it. I certainly wasn't full of confidence. It had filtered through to me that they were looking for a man. They wouldn't be allowed to say that now, would they? They were looking for a man because it was principally a boys' school. They also preferred some-one new coming into the school. But having said that, I had nothing to lose. I can only presume that the 'right young man' from outside didn't turn up. It was around about the same time, a new head had been appointed to Westbourne Special School, and another had been appointed to a special school that wasn't an EBD school, and there seemed to be a pattern of appointment, as they were all bearded chaps in their mid thirties with a dark beard. I remember saying to the Chief Education Officer a little while later that if I had gone to the interview and there had been a bearded gentleman in his mid thirties amongst the candidates, I wouldn't have bothered staying for my turn.

SR   Was it an easy transition, from deputy headteacher to headteacher?

ER   I was in the school I knew, with staff I knew, and pupils I knew – I don't know whether that made it any easier or harder. A lot of people asked me, initially, what I was going to change. There was a great expectation that there was going to be lots of change. I made it very clear that I wasn't going to change anything for change's sake. I emphasized that we would change things when the need arose and not for the sake of appearance. I didn't experience any of the difficulties some people describe when they move from the deputy head's role to that of the head in the same school. It might well be me, not recognizing any of that, but I do think that the staff were not displeased that I was appointed and that might have helped. I also think my years as a deputy head served me well, and as I've already said, I didn't find myself doing anything that was greatly different.

SR   What advice would you give to a member of staff who was seriously considering application for headship?

ER   Well – my advice would be different now to what it might have been, say some ten years ago, because we now find ourselves in a very different climate. I would say be absolutely sure it's the job you want to do and you are not simply being attracted to an idea of status. I would urge the person to familiarize themselves with the real job and see what it does entail. Now, so far as I was concerned, the deputy headship did that for me. I'm equally sure it doesn't for everybody.

I do know of one example which occurred a few years ago, where a deputy headteacher was in post for a number of years in a special school within the LEA, and worked with a headteacher who in his own words gave him 'nine years of hell'. The deputy did become the headteacher, and when we would meet as heads, he would look back and say the best thing the headteacher did for him and the school while he was the deputy, was to have a heart attack. Now that comment was a bit harsh, but to actually say something like that reflected a tremendous depth of emotion. The deputy, as I have said, went on to become the headteacher in the same school, but what he clearly didn't experience was the positive opportunity and experience I gained serving as a deputy headteacher, and it was his few months as acting headteacher which gave him the only preparation he actually experienced for headship. He would repeatedly talk about his deputy headship as nine years of hell and I couldn't even begin to describe any part of my own deputy headship in that way.

I always felt that Slades Farm School was my school. You did feel, very much, that it was a place you enjoyed going to, felt at home in, because it was a comfortable place to belong. That sense of ownership, that personal feeling is very important. I know it's said that as a headteacher you shouldn't say 'my school' but should say 'our school'. I wouldn't deny the importance of staff belonging to the school. I think that all the staff felt in their own way that Slades Farm was 'their school' or, just like me, 'my school'. It has always been a place I've enjoyed being at, going to, and I didn't begrudge the extra time I gave to it during the holidays or after hours. I enjoyed working with my colleagues. There were problems, of course, you do get the 'sane' and the 'dotty', you experience the 'good' and the 'bad', but it was always a feeling of satisfaction that lasted.

SR   What, in particular, are the high and low points of success which feature in your experience as a head?

ER   Well – I worked fourteen years as headteacher, and altogether twenty years of senior management at Slades Farm School. High points? Let's see what I've written down in my notes. 'Individual and school success'. Moments of shared success and its celebration. Whether it's one particular thing we all shared, like a pupil returning to mainstream and doing well, or theatrical productions which have been staged at school, or concerts, events which have proven to be absolutely wonderful on the night, even though the trauma we had to live through during the rehearsals and the disruption and upheaval in school, and on some occasions in the staff room, had left me pulling my hair out! I would often seem to be left asking myself why we were doing all of this to be given the answer on the night.

I also think that a high point or positive part of the job were the relationships I developed over the years with colleagues, not only in school, but with fellow school heads, LEA officers and other people. We all felt we were part of something definite, a community, which is something now lost. The changes in the last three or four years have created a very different climate, with different values and attitudes to our work.

One of the low points in the job came quite recently, and involved the media's response to our Ofsted inspection. It wasn't the actual Ofsted inspection which made me feel low, nor the Ofsted report, but the media response to that report. I can only put it down to my inexperience in dealing with the media. I was totally unprepared for their belligerent attitude. Praise in the report was completely overlooked, yet the slightest criticism was blown up out of all proportion. If I was to face the same situation again, I would have my report prepared and ready for any media enquiry. I would be able to say to a newspaper reporter, here you are, the report is more or less written for you. I couldn't imagine the scene where we became, in the words of the Inspection Team Leader, 'lambs to the slaughter'. I couldn't envisage that a report on Slades Farm School would be considered newsworthy, especially six months after the event. I was taken by surprise and it is true to say this is one way in which the educational climate has changed, dramatically, during the last three or four years.

The experience of the media reporting on the Ofsted inspection was a definite low and since then I have very literally regarded anything reported in the newspapers with a great deal of scepticism. I don't mean that I took it extremely seriously, I didn't have sleepless nights or worry about it, but I was cross on behalf of my staff. I particularly remember my deputy headteacher feeling sickened by the whole experience. I certainly think it was the start to his questioning his own position and job and led to him leaving the profession. He came out of the inspection 'smelling of roses'. He was given an extremely good report and thought of extremely highly by the inspection team, but the way in which the school was treated and the attitude which seemed to underpin the inspection process made him ask himself what it was he was actually doing teaching exceptionally difficult children. The job was hard enough without exposing himself to the further pressures of an Ofsted report and the public press. He couldn't see the sense or fairness in it and his response was to say to me, if this was the way it worked, thank you very much but no thanks.

Another low point was the case of a particular young boy we had a few years ago who we had successfully reintegrated into mainstream school while still retaining the support and placement as a boarder at Slades Farm Hostel. I had such high hopes for him. He was doing well in mainstream and it all seemed to have worked. When he was at his best, he was a super kid and now he's serving a life sentence for murder. I was sickened by that because I felt that if I had been given the right support at the time, and if we had not created this modern climate of 'thought' which is that children must have everything they want, and no child tells a lie, which I was getting from social services, things would have been different. The boy was bright enough to take all of this on board and use it. There were times when this youngster just needed somebody to sit him down and say to him he would not do this, or not do that, and that he would do as he was told, end of story, without feeling there was another agency he could run to which would countermand everything in order to 'meet his needs' and in effect to 'suit his every whim'.

SR   How did you actually measure your own success as a headteacher?

ER   I don't know. You did the job to the best of your ability. I never wanted anybody to leave school, at the end of the day, feeling low, which if you like, was my policy. Whatever happened during the day did not warrant taking it home like a weight on the shoulders because I didn't and I didn't want anyone else to do it. I used to ensure that we all got together as a staff at the end of the day and sorted out anything we needed to in a light-hearted way. It's hard to say how you really know whether you are truly doing a good job. On some days I felt I was doing well, on other days I felt that I was doing a poor job. I know that on a couple of occasions I overheard people saying I was doing a good job – but I would move away from the conversation because it wasn't really meant for me to hear. I do remember thinking, however, oh well that's good isn't it! I suppose you draw a picture of your own performance from the way other people see you at work.

SR   What vision for the school did you have? How did it play a part in your headship?

ER   I think it has to come back to doing the best you possibly can for the children, hasn't it? As I said earlier, this is where the children are getting their secondary education. We were not a therapeutic community. I wanted every child who came to Slades Farm School to benefit from a good education. We were not there to provide a cure for a medical problem. How can you cure children from being themselves? Is there really such a thing as a cure for children with emotional and behaviour difficulties? I would have liked to have said that we were successful in making their behaviour more socially acceptable, but you can't say 'cure'! You can perhaps stop certain patterns of behaviour and hope to 'lessen' the severity of other behaviours, but generally the education counted as a priority. I mean I don't really know any therapy other than hard work. I felt that crucially there was a need to work towards success – nothing succeeds like success.

SR   Didn't you also use 'humour therapy', Edna?

ER   Well – I had to didn't I! But if the children were successful and they became used to getting their 'kicks' out of 'measures of success', there was every chance they would look to that rather than getting their 'kicks' from swearing, acting up, being the class clown. The aim was to find something, work out what would provide the measure of success that could lead a child to further success.

This really takes us back to the importance of relationship building, and a need to avoid an 'us and them' situation. I was often struck by the same explanation which occurred when I would talk to a new pupil about how their difficulties first started. It would invariably involve a person, either in pre-school days, or very often, boil down to an unpleasant relationship with 'that teacher'. Of course, there was the occasional difficult personality, an individual who found trouble wherever they went, but nearly always, I find myself listening to a story about 'the teacher who had picked on me'. It was nearly always an account of a teacher-pupil relationship breaking down, which in turn led to a more general breakdown of personal relationships. After all, I had the same as a pupil, I bet you did. I could say that while I was at school there were teachers with whom I had a good relationship, and then I could say, there was this certain teacher and other people in school with whom I would not co-operate. At the end of the day you had to have pupils doing things because they were happy to do them for you, not because you had laid down some dictum, or pointed, or shouted, or yelled or threatened them.

I remember we had this understanding with the class of senior girls I taught, before I became the headteacher. There were some 'beauties' in that class, who kicked, and screamed and shouted and would have their own way. We developed an 'attitude' and an arrangement that if they wanted something they had to make a good case for it. That's a good training for life – isn't it? If you want something – can you put a good case for it. It became such a habit that they would say automatically, 'Let's sit down and discuss the matter'. I remember one girl who came to us in an awful mess. She had been responsible for the death of a baby. The pupils in her old school found out and ganged up on her. She turned out all right in spite of this tragic influence in her background. She had a very good sense of humour and we developed a good relationship. Well – she would be the first in the class to say we should sit down, pull up the chairs and discuss the problem. Let's talk it through and make up our minds about it. Now – that's civilized behaviour – don't you think? It wasn't just for the classroom, it gave the girls a way of behaving in the school and outside school.

SR   Did this approach also feature later in your approach to school management?

ER   Yes. I think it did. I think very often you've got to say, sit down, get it off your chest, let's sit down and discuss it. Let's see if we can sort it out.

SR   What kind of headteacher were you?

ER   I wasn't autocratic. I didn't go around feeling that people had to touch their forelock or doff their hats by virtue of my position.

SR   Didn't you enjoy the status and the power of the position?

ER   Oh yes! Yes of course I did. I very soon realized after I had retired that I was moving from a position which carried a certain amount of status to one of an unpaid labourer which was a long jump, from there to here. I suppose it probably encouraged me to carry on teaching for longer than I might otherwise have done. I suppose that thinking about it, I placed a great deal of importance on the atmosphere in school. I was always very pleased when people wanted to come back to Slades Farm. It is a little like the fruit-picking business we run here during the summer, where I've found that people want to come back again because they find the atmosphere friendly and relaxing. I think it was important to create the right kind of setting. School needed to be a place where people could feel comfortable, whether you were a pupil or a member of staff. Can you imagine if you had a school where teachers didn't want to come to work?

SR   Do you think the atmosphere created reflected your own management persona?

ER   Well – you'd like to think that you had contributed. I wanted the children to enjoy coming to school and for some of them that was asking a great deal. I wanted the staff to enjoy coming to work. I mean, there is enough of the 'other' in the first place, as you know, in an EBD special school. I have worked in a school which was unhappy, and although I wasn't there for very long, it was awful. The head-teacher was resented, several of the staff felt under-valued, they felt that they worked very hard but didn't get anywhere. There was an undercurrent of unease which affected the atmosphere in the school. I felt, what a shame! What a pity! Consider how much of your life is spent at your place of work. It's too much to go there feeling bitter and resentful. It just won't do!

SR   How did you enable effective teaching and learning which took place in your school? Do you see any changes occurring in this aspect of a headteacher's work?

ER   Now, people can write what they like in records, can't they? You saw what was going on, you had the visible signs of what the children produced, what they would bring and show you with pride, although you would occasionally have the others too, those pupils brought to you to see the extent of their work. There would on occasion be the pupil brought to you with a book, and you would look at it, look at the teacher, look at the pupil, and think, help, why have they brought this pupil to me. Did you ever have a situation like that, when you weren't one hundred per cent sure why the teacher had brought the child to see you, and whether to praise the work for good effort, or criticize it for lack of quality?

There were a number of indications of achievement, end results, work completed by individuals, improvement in pupil behaviour, which were reflected in reintegration programmes to return pupils to mainstream school. These clearly provided evidence of behaviour change, resulting in individuals behaving in a more appropriate way.

There were academic results too, but in an EBD special school, the most important evidence was 'value-added' evidence, which reflects good teaching and learning within the context rather than in a league table.

I would say that in the earlier days of headship I was much closer to the classroom and the children. However as time went by, the distance between the classroom and my office did seem to become much greater. A big change came with Local Management of Special Schools (LMSS) and with it a responsibility for school finance. It opened up a whole new dimension to school management. Indeed, looking back over the entire period of headship, I think it is true to say that there were a tremendous number of 'extras' introduced to the job of managing a school and nothing taken out.

At the beginning, I had the luxury of being able to spend time in the classroom and around the school. I would often take a group out on an educational visit. As time went by, these opportunities lessened tremendously. It was a shame really, but it happened. The 'fun' things lessened and you spent more and more time in frustrating meetings, and I'm not a 'meetings person'. We would waste a great deal of time talking about wretched abstracts like the policy described in that press cutting I showed you a few minutes ago, describing a new SEN policy for the LEA. Well, it's not new, because I remember spending hours talking about the very self-same thing. We would often spend far too much time juggling with words, only to end up with what we had first proposed. We really didn't need to see all of the effort and energy consumed in meetings but that was the way things were organized. Perhaps the process was necessary, but as time went by it did seem that most 'new' things were simply 'old' ideas being re-invented.

In order to produce something really revolutionary, we would have to see a dramatic U-turn in society as a whole. I did think there was an awful lot of wasted resources in education. I've always thought education had been adequately funded – but all too often badly organized and managed. I have held to that opinion all through my headship.

I didn't go to the Special School Headteachers' Association in Dorset (SHADD) meetings banging my fist on the table, complaining I wasn't being given enough money. In my way of thinking, I believed I was given a sum of money, and my job was to manage with it. I wonder if that's perhaps a 'female' response rather than a 'male' response? Maybe I should have banged on the table, but my approach I suppose has been one of 'put up or shut up'. I really didn't participate in the table-thumping or the loud protests in which some of my colleagues, especially more recently, engaged.

SR   To whom is a head accountable? Who do you answer to and how do you manage this?

ER   I think that within the school context, and within yourself, you are ultimately accountable to the schoolchildren. On the other hand, if you're looking at accountability in a different sense, I think you can probably trace the developing notion of accountability we are faced with today back to the speech by James Callaghan which opened the 'great debate' on education in this country. I think too that this also marked the beginning of the movement toward 'parent power', 'parental choice' and the idea of a service to parents who are also exercising their right to select a school for their children. And of course, we are all accountable to our employers, to the LEA, although this form of accountability has most certainly changed. At one time, the LEA was totally in control of the educational system and the schools within that system. This has changed dramatically in the recent past in a way which would once have been considered inconceivable. However, if you talk about accountability generally, and look at the media, or read the newspapers, what you realize is the greatly increased powers of the governing body in the management of a school.

I was always very lucky with my governing body. They didn't cause me any trouble at all, being very supportive, and clearly interested in the well-being of the school. They were very clear in the way in which they perceived their role and their relationship with me as the headteacher of the school. When I say I couldn't fault them at all, I feel and felt then very much aware that they were being asked to do too much sometimes, given that these were people you had plucked from 'normal' life, already working hard with their own jobs to do, and were expected to do so much for no payment. They really did a very good job, taking up extra responsibility for no obvious reward. If it was possible to make it a pleasant process, I was determined to do it.

I can remember having to organize our own clerk for the meetings of the governing body, a role which previously had always been filled by an officer of the LEA. We found a lady who had actually clerked for school meetings as a person hired by the LEA. I recall her leaving us at the end of her first meeting as our clerk, and as she was about to go, telling me that she only wished all the meetings she clerked were as pleasant, productive and enjoyable as the one she had clerked at Slades Farm School. Certainly the governing body and the staff who attended these meetings were united and working to one end. I shake my head in bewilderment at some of the recent reporting on school issues where we see the governing body in conflict with the headteacher. It really is no way to manage a school or an educational system, is it?

SR   Am I right in thinking that you now see the headteacher placed at the centre of a network of different strands of accountability?

ER   Yes, very much so and I think more so towards the end of my career. I started to notice signs of stress appearing in staff which I'd never seen before at Slades Farm, which probably reflects some of these changes in accountability. Relationships which had previously been very good seemed to deteriorate. While this may have been the sign of added pressures, I shouldn't place too much emphasis on it. After all, I had seen similar things in my experience before I became a headteacher.

I suppose these kinds of things have always happened. I remember one such occasion, when I had to deal with a staffing problem as the deputy headteacher. We had a teacher who had fallen head over heels in love with another member of staff who unfortunately was a homosexual. I had been away on a trip to return to find that the first member of staff, a lady, had walked into the second teacher's classroom and slapped him across the face in front of the children. She didn't stay with us after that, I obviously had a chat with her and pointed out that I did not see how her career could continue under the same roof as her colleague. So I suppose personalities, clashes, they do occur, but significantly, I felt the pressures on teachers were beginning to increase.

SR   How did you manage your own well-being, both professional and personal well-being?

ER   I think I've said to you before that the NCSE was a great force for good in its heyday. We got good attendance at meetings, we used to arrange good speakers, held good debates, where we sat down and thrashed out our problems and shared in a professional perspective. We also clearly had an educational system to which we belonged in those days, which we certainly don't have today. When we held our Leeson House weekends, we all contributed to the programme, to the planning and its organization. I also used to feel that it was all worthwhile.

Latterly, this was replaced with membership of various working parties, or INSET sessions, which quite honestly I felt involved playing games. It was the game of 'let's pretend' and there was no real purpose or connection with teaching and learning. For example, and rather sadly, I remember one such occasion a few months ago, shortly before I retired. It was a session led by an Educationist who I had known for a number of years. I liked him as a person, and had a great deal of time for him. I felt quite simply embarrassed. He was standing there spouting utter rubbish and I knew he was losing the respect of all of the people who were there, listening to him. I had to contain the tremendous urge to interrupt him and say stop before it is too late. He had an unenviable task, as he talked of pupil rights, and how we could find ourselves on the wrong side of the law, and perhaps I should recall this event more charitably, but it was sad. It is sad, when professionals tie themselves up in knots as a result of enforced change, but it will continue, and go on changing time after time, because, you know, issues are earmarked as a 'priority number one' but they don't stay that way. The number of times I've heard that phrase. Then months later, the issue is as dead as a dodo!

SR   Ted Wragg says 'You don't have to be a "nutter" to join the "barmy army" but ... '. Do you think headship has become much more difficult and do you enjoy it?

ER   It really depends on your definition of 'nutter'. What does he really mean – a masochist? I do think the job has got harder because of the amount of extras which it has attracted. I've mentioned a big one just a moment ago, LMSS. I didn't spend hours and hours on it, I didn't think that sort of thing was necessary or appropriate, but nevertheless it was there and had to be done. It was necessary to look at staff salaries, and it became a big issue, particularly when you started to consider 'who you could afford' when really you should have been saying that you wanted 'the best teacher for the job'. I mean that's something that had never ever happened to me before. Issues like staff salaries or how many toilet rolls you could afford to buy or to be without, it wasn't something that as headteacher was part of the original brief.

I also think that attitudes and values in society at large have changed which have made things harder in school. I think we reached the stage some time ago now where you take a professional risk of allegation and complaint if you give a pupil a dirty look. It seemed to me we also reached the point where there is no longer such a thing as an accident and somebody always must be blamed. I mean the kind of thing which involves an irate parent ringing me up to complain that their child has a bruise on their knee. Well, you know, so do I, as it happens, more than one, and it is all part of living.

If I give you an example: it has recently been reported in the news that a twenty-year-old claiming to have suffered post-traumatic stress syndrome as a result of bullying at school was awarded thirty thousand pounds in an out of court settlement. Needless to say, I have no time for bullying; consider it abhorrent, and always requiring serious attention. But can you imagine the floodgates opening after this and the subsequent effects upon headteachers, governing bodies and school. I should say, too, that in the final couple of years of my headship, the response 'I'm being bullied' became the very fashionable excuse for every misdemeanour in school. I overheard one child, on one occasion, ask another child to hit him so that he would have an excuse to abscond, as there was somewhere he wanted to go.

I find it extraordinary, generally speaking, to see the defences or excuses people will make now to explain away difficulties or alternatively how quick people are to seek to blame somebody else for a problem. Yes – I do think some of the additional pressures in school are very much reflected in the changes we see in society. I do think we have lurched away from 'Miss Dobson's day', when lying was a 'mortal sin' for which if you were found out you were publicly caned. We have moved to a way of life that involves making excuses, telling lies and getting away with it.

SR   What about your own personal well-being?

ER   Well I do think it is important to leave school at school. I have the farm animals here and I have always looked after them. I get up reasonably early to feed them. I would do this on a school day and during the holidays. I have also always had my family. What I really didn't have was enough hours in the day. I didn't believe in worrying. I still don't believe in worrying. It doesn't resolve anything.

SR   What fundamental changes do you think have taken place in special education? What does this mean for headship and special education?

ER   I'm not really sure about this question in a specific sense, as it applies to Slades Farm School, especially now that I have retired. However, in a general sense, I should think that the greatest change and probably the biggest challenge for special education is parental expectation and the shift of power and increased demand of parents for that expectation to be realized.

SR   Did you experience any of that change in your final period as a headteacher?

ER   I don't know that I did but in a sense, I probably contributed to a high level of expectation because I required the best of the pupils. It may have been unrealistic at times, but luckily I didn't experience the 'complaints upsurge' which is reported in the press. I didn't have parents asking why their child hasn't received individual tuition eight hours a week because it is detailed in the statement of SEN and they should be getting it. The Educational Psychologist, Mr X has explained it to them. I always knew whether a child was statemented for individual tuition, but teacher resources didn't always allow us to provide the prescribed tuition. I could only do my best. In a sense this proves what I said previously, you can write almost anything, but in truth the practice can be entirely different.

SR   Do you think the recent reform has improved provision for children with emotional and behaviour difficulties?

ER   Not necessarily. Let's take the police for example, I have had them coming into school in circumstances they would never have done before but they had to because they had no choice. They had to follow up what a child had alleged. Everybody is forced to presume, now, that there will be a case of sexual or physical abuse behind every allegation. I had another example of an allegation of sexual abuse to deal with which was followed up by a social worker attached to a young girl. She had alleged that a male member of staff had sat at the lunch table and felt her leg. He had in fact sat at the table, but only for a short time, during which his hands were busily engaged with a knife and fork eating his meal. He certainly wouldn't have stayed there for longer than he needed. Now whether his knee brushed this young lady's leg or not, I really don't know, but a sexual assault? The allegation meant a formal investigation was completed. It is silly really, because we're creating a set of rules which are not helpful in working with children, especially young children or children who are experiencing emotional and behavioural difficulties.

SR   Do you think that 'common sense' has been thrown out with the baby and the bath water?

ER   Common sense! Common sense! Common sense was my first school rule, and consideration was my second. This is a thing I repeatedly stated to the inspectors who came into my school, we exercise common sense. A lot of the strict prescribing of policy rules and guidelines would simply not be necessary if people exercised common sense. I'm sure that they are necessary to a far greater extent than I ever really thought, but in many respects, I do feel that common sense has gone out of the window.

I went into a school a few months ago, and there was this large notice on the wall in the entrance hall, stating there was no bullying in the school. It wasn't a fact but it did seem as if that was being claimed as well as a declaration of policy. Well, to my mind, dealing with the problem as and when it arose was far more important than having a big notice stating that as far as the headteacher was concerned there was no bullying in her school.

SR   What changes do you see as important for Slades Farm School and special education?

ER   I'm going to have to go back a little bit in order to answer that question because I've been retired now for two terms. I think this makes the answer hypothetical, but priority number one at Slades Farm School was managing the change to senior staff, both at the level of senior teacher, deputy headteacher and headteacher. Clearly that meant a huge change for the school. However, if I was still there, I think the most important priority would have been to see an admissions policy for the LEA established. In my last two years there, a lot of time went into discussing an admissions policy, and at the end of the day, in spite of countless meetings, nothing was achieved. The thing that I know is now creating great problems is the impact of Local Authority reorganization in the Bournemouth area. There are two EBD special schools, but the other school is now GMSS and exercises far greater say in the referral process which leads to placement of pupils. The other school is, as a result, taking first choice in admitting pupils and Slades Farm is consequently receiving children who are more generally difficult and who are presenting exceptionally severe emotional and behaviour problems. This is obviously unfair but it is also a problem which needs resolving. I do think there will always be a need for Slades Farm School.

CHAPTER 11

Making the mark: leading the way for special education

ROB SAMMONS with Steve Rayner

Rob Sammons is currently headteacher of Montacute School, Poole, a grant maintained special school for pupils with severe learning difficulties. He was appointed in 1982 and has more recently overseen the school's transition as a pilot school in the local management of special schools scheme to grant maintained status. Rob has worked in mainstream and special education, although most of his career has been in special schools. He has held posts of responsibility in special schools in Birmingham and Dorset, as well as serving as an acting LEA Senior Inspector and Advisory Headteacher for two separate periods of secondment. He has been very involved in continuing professional development, including work as a part-time lecturer as part of a fellowship at Rolle College, Exmouth. Rob is a qualified Ofsted Inspector and an LEA Appraiser Trainer.

SR   Could we begin with your personal background – home, school, higher education and people who perhaps had a significant influence on your life?

RS   Born just a stone's throw away from the County Ground in Edgbaston and lived almost in the backyard of the cricket ground. I was born towards the end of the war. My father was in the RAF at the time and we lived in a flat for the first two or three years of my life. My father was based at several RAF stations across the UK. We then moved to a council house in King's Norton. I had a lovely childhood, and have very fond memories of that time, for both my sister and myself.

    I really did have a lovely childhood. King's Norton was like a small village even though it was part of Birmingham. It was a 'village community', and where we lived backed on to green fields, the canal and a park. My sister and I were very happy throughout our childhood. We both loved school – we went to King's Norton Primary School. Mum and Dad would let us wander – in a way you'd never be able to today. The council estate was built post-war, was full of young kids, and it was a good place, a good time in which to be children and to grow up.

I passed the eleven-plus and went to a new technical school. The technical schools were an educational innovation of the time and very popular in Birmingham. I went to Bourneville Technical Grammar School. There were about five or six similar schools in Birmingham, all of them fairly new. I wasn't particularly good at school, academically, but I was passionate about sport. All sports! I represented the school in as many sports as I could manage – every school team except cricket. I was captain of most of them and represented the county in rugby.

Dad has always been a big influence on my life. My father was an insurance agent. He worked very hard. We didn't see very much of him as kids. He was nevertheless a huge influence in the house. I don't mean by that in a disciplinarian fashion. He shaped our view on life and created a set of standards, moral standards and attitudes, values which we all shared. We were really brought up by Mum – she went out to work and we would let ourselves in like many kids, but then she would be there. Dad was always out at work collecting and selling insurance. But in spite of this we were a very close family and looking back I can only repeat that we had a great childhood.

Dad was a 'Christian', not in the religious sense of the word, but in the sense that he was a good man. He'd do anything to help someone in a bit of trouble. He had a nice personality, he was good with people and he was basically a giving person who was prepared to help and support those who were less able or fortunate. I mean 'Christian' in that sense. He was a very strong family man. Because he was a 'people person', and had all his life dealt with people, he was able to use his innate qualities of humour and sympathy. Like many successful businessmen he combined a nice personality, humour and under-standing, with an eye for business and was something of a manipulator, in the nicest sense of the word, in order to make money. He was very much the person who'd get involved in helping people. The street in which we lived, even the council estate as a whole, was a community. We would have, what seemed at that time, huge bonfire parties for the whole street, and other things like that, with everyone taking part.

SR   How does this kind of value system fit into your great interest in sporting achievement?

RS   I don't know! But Dad was a sportsman. A cyclist. A racing cyclist for Bromsgrove. He was also very involved in sport during his time in the RAF. He did a lot of running and played a number of team games. He won a lot of medals. He has always been an achiever, but I don't think to the same extent as I have been in sport, probably because he didn't have the opportunity. He came from a very poor family. He lived near Ryland Street, which is no longer there, in Birmingham city centre. He has recently written a very interesting book about his childhood in Birmingham. He describes passing the scholarship and going to King Edward's School, Fiveways, and writes about how he had to put cardboard in the bottom of his boots to go to school. He was mixing, every day, with millionaires' sons, yet came from a very different world. He had a challenging childhood – it was, all in all, an unhappy childhood.

Dad would be very much motivated by success in business. He will still, even now, mildly disapprove of me not having a proper job. He would hope that perhaps one day I would do something important and earn some money. Teaching has never been that kind of proper job, and becoming a headteacher has never made any difference to this belief. He'd still put five pounds in my pocket because he thinks I need the money. But that's his idea of success, you see, and I may have inherited some of that – I'm extremely competitive – and while dad wouldn't be as competitive in a sporting sense, he would be as competitive in the business sense, so maybe I've channelled it in a different direction.

SR   What about your own educational career? Academic achievement?

RS   Average! I just did like other kids really. I passed the GCEs with as little effort as was required. I never ever really picked up a book during my whole time at the grammar school. I certainly never read one from start to finish. I worked my way through O Level, A Level, just doing what I had to do.

After I left school I did a year as a student teacher, you could then. Really, if I have any skills at all, it lies in art. I wasn't sure whether I wanted to go to art college or teacher training college. I remember taking the advice of a young teacher who'd just joined the school while I was in the sixth form. He had joined as a new PE teacher. He knew I was keen on sport, and suggested I go to his classes and help him in the final months of the sixth form. I ended up working with his classes and I liked it. I then decided to do student teacher work which lasted for a year, then left Birmingham to go to teacher training college at Cheltenham.

SR   You clearly enjoyed the year!

RS   Yes. It was good. I worked with the top class in a junior school with kids who were getting ready to move up to the secondary school. It was a great time. I fancied teaching and made enquiries about the student teacher scheme. You did it off your own bat – just applied to the LEA. They placed me at The Meadows Primary School at North-field. Harry Walker, the ex-BBC swimming commentator, was the headteacher. That was by the by, I didn't go there because there was a sporting connection.

I went from there on to teacher training college for three years, for PE, and I didn't like it. I liked the teaching experience, Cheltenham was lovely, but I didn't like the course, the ethos of the place. Perhaps it was because I was a year older. I'd bought my own car. I completed a year in school as a student teacher. I was used to looking after myself and I found some of the attitudes and parts of the course childish. In those days, a lot of the guys who were teaching in colleges were ex-services or with a similar background. The college was run on military establishment lines. I was caught there totally ill at ease with the ethos. I suppose it was a chore, something I had to do, to work through the course and complete the teacher training. I think it was a mistake, doing the PE. I should have taken art. I loved sport but I got terribly bored teaching PE. I only taught PE for two and a bit years, then packed it up.

SR So – the two and half years you mention were at your first school?

RS A comprehensive school, in Harborne, in Birmingham. It was in the days when you applied to an LEA rather than a school. I was accepted by the LEA and they gave me a choice of schools. Their approach was they needed a PE teacher in a number of different schools, you were invited to visit them, then expected to tell the LEA which one you would like to work in. I can't remember what my thoughts were, exactly, at the time, but I knew one of the schools I visited because I had completed a long teaching practice there. It was a great school. I had thoroughly enjoyed my placement there. It was what would be described as an inner-city school today. It was The George Dixon School. It was a great school but I remember thinking, well, I've been there, I've done that, and it was a lovely teaching practice but I need to go to a new place. I went to the comprehensive school at Harborne. It was a new school and offered a new challenge which appealed to me.

SR Did it provide you with a good experience?

RS No! I didn't enjoy it at all. It was a good staff, lovely kids, but the set-up of the school was poorly designed. The result was fourteen hundred kids packed into a single building. I felt the concept of the school was ill-founded. It was a Roman Catholic comprehensive school. In fact, it was the Roman Catholic comprehensive school for Birmingham. It took kids from all over the city. I watched clever kids become ordinary kids and children who were not very able being ploughed under by the system. The only way to succeed in that school was to be exceptional, you had to be very very clever, or very very bad. I didn't feel working there suited me.

SR You left teaching then as a consequence?

RS Yes. I went to play golf for about a year. I got a job with an insurance company just collecting around, which gave me enough money to pay for the mortgage and essential bills. If I had to collect money from any additional insurance I sold I earned commission. It was enough to pay the basic bills. We didn't have any kids at that time. I played amateur golf and earned money by gambling. I didn't get paid for playing golf – it was strictly amateur – but I played in lots of tournaments and there were several ways of earning money while you played. There were prizes, games awards, and, on the course, bookies were willing to give people the opportunity to gamble. In fact, I did quite well out of the gambling, betting against my own performance, playing people for a stake, say fifty to a hundred pounds. It was good money at that time.

I stayed at this for about a year, maybe slightly longer, but during the second winter made a new contact in education. I was helping a mate renovate a cottage. While I was doing that, a friend of a friend told me that the head of the school at which my wife had worked as a physiotherapist had lost his deputy headteacher to the Inspectorate. Greg Davies. He was subsequently to become Senior Inspector for Hereford and Worcestershire. He'd been seconded to the Inspectorate in Birmingham. They needed a man to teach some PE. I was asked if I was interested. I went along not realizing the school was for the physically handicapped (PH). I said I'd do it, certainly up until the Easter, a period of six weeks. I stayed a lot longer. Thoroughly enjoyed it. Wonderful time. The school was Wilson Stuart, a campus on Perry Common. It was a campus provision for SEN made up of several schools. It was at that time a provision for the partially sighted, for the deaf, and partially deaf, and a school for PH.

SR   Did you only work with PH?

RS   Yes – except that PH as a category covered a wide range of disability. In the time when I went there, around 1972, the nature of the disability presented by the children called PH included 'delicate' children, 'school phobics', there were a few lingering cases of post-polio children, and some thalidomide children. A lot of the children went for ordinary lessons at Perry Common Comprehensive, and would subsequently progress through school to go on to college and university.

I was also there while we experienced a transition between the mid seventies and the latter seventies, when there was a marked increase in the number of spina bifida children, hydrocephalus children, each group presenting special educational needs associated with learning difficulty. This was closely followed by an increase in children suffering from cerebral palsy and more massive brain injuries which meant working with more severe learning difficulty as well as the physical handicap. All in all we had a terrific range of SEN.

It was a fantastic school. A fantastic headteacher. In terms of my own career, educational perspective, there is no question in my mind that the person who had the greatest shaping influence on me was this headteacher. I think he was such a 'brave' headteacher, who took risks – which invariably worked out. I mean, who would take a bloke off the golf course and ask him to come and work for six weeks, and tell you that you aren't going to have a class, and that he wanted you to go out, get around the school, play with the children, just float, get to know them. He did that with me, and he did it with other staff too, when it was appropriate.

He gave people a lot of space within which to grow, and then used it. He would fit you into an appropriate niche. I realized later that he was a very good manipulator. He would manipulate people beautifully. He saw niches which would fit individual people. He gave me a chance to try several different things and one of those was the early floating role, working with some of the more profoundly handicapped children, working across the school, obviously, much of it to do with PE, and later working with the leavers' group. It was a progression of different, quality bound experiences. I have never been a good classroom teacher because I've never had to do it. I've had a lovely range of mixed experiences in schools but couldn't hold a candle to the classroom teachers in this school.

SR   I suspect that might be more than a modicum of false humility?

RS   Not at all – I think teachers here are very good at their job and quite honestly I'm not as good as them at that job. But I've had the chance, through working with various people, to try lots of different things. Even here, during my time in Dorset, I've had the opportunity to do extras, and that's quite an honour, really. Maybe that's why I do my job. I'm probably better at my job than they would be because of the range of experience.

SR   So that has helped you in the task of educational leadership and school management?

RS   I think it gives you a chance to appreciate all the different jobs held by staff just that little bit better. It just isn't a question of delegating things and saying well, now you just need to get on with it. I have done all of those jobs, often not as well as most of my staff, but nevertheless I've done them. I know what's involved in the job and maybe it gives me a better idea of what's required when I'm shaping up my direction for school development.

SR   How would you sum up the effect upon you of the headteacher at Wilson Stuart School?

RS   As I try to answer that question, memories of him flash across my mind. What I see is this little bloke who was held in such enormous esteem by everybody who came into contact with him. You have to remember that Wilson Stuart School in those days was a very highly respected special school in a period when Birmingham was a very highly respected LEA. Frequent guests to the school were people like Gulliford, Tansley, Wedell and others who were famous names, educationalists. They came to Mitch, worked with us, and so obviously held him in high esteem. It didn't matter who you were in the system, everybody was a little in awe of Mitch, who held very firm views on education. I would never dream of arguing with him over his views. I greatly respected his views but more than that, I respected the way he would temper all of that business, the professional respect, with the highest personal regard from us all, as a friend and a colleague.

SR   Would you like to think some of that rubbed off on you, Rob? Would you see yourself as a similar kind of headteacher?

RS   Well ... I'd like to think so but I know better. I just think he was a great, great example and a very good model for any teacher.

SR   When did you decide on senior management Rob? Was there a particular turning point in your career?

RS   Well ... I've said it before, but quite honestly, I had no ambition at all. People pushed me in the right direction, and I've really relied on that to happen. Mitch was one of those – he pushed me onwards in the right direction. He encouraged me to go to Birmingham University – I took an advanced diploma with Gulliford. It was a great time – I thoroughly enjoyed it. I couldn't claim to have come out of it with a whole body of new knowledge but the thing it did for me was that it fundamentally altered the way I looked at issues, making me much more analytical. In other words, it didn't give me any specific answers, but it taught me the kind of questions to ask.

After I'd finished at university, Mitch told me about a deputy headship going at another special school where he was a governor. It was an SLD school. He said that I ought to be interested because I should go on to become a headteacher. Tansley had said the same thing to me – he was particularly good at encouraging people. Well – I took all of that with a pinch of salt but when I did stop and think about it, I realized I had a lot of experience by then in working with severe learning difficulty because of the range of SEN we were experiencing at Wilson Stuart School. There were the kinds of SEN I've described to you already, and which we would both associate with children experiencing severe learning difficulty. I went to look and was interested. It was a very small school – Selly Oak Special School. We catered for about fifty-five pupils. I applied for the job and got it.

The day after I was appointed, the headteacher, who was a lady of the old school, a lovely lady in every sense of the word, said to me that she was going to retire. She explained to me that she had been planning this for a while and that I ought to know, because the way that Birmingham worked, it was certain that I would be asked to act as the headteacher for a period of time. She also pointed out that this would be good for me. The upshot of this situation was that she suggested that I start in this role immediately, and that's the way it worked. Although I should add that she didn't let go immediately – she wasn't that sort of headteacher or person. I wasn't interested in anything controversial, like the petty cash box, or the 'stock cupboard key', at least, not for some time. She kept a very tight control in that respect!

I remember how all of the staff were required to apply to the head on a Friday afternoon for their resources. She would personally distribute these resources. I can see her now giving out the powder paint, spoonful at a time, colour by colour. She distributed other resources in the same way. But, in every respect, I started to pick up the running of the school. When she retired, by which time she had actually relinquished the stock room key, I did become acting headteacher, which went on for about nine months. It was great!

I didn't go for the headship at Selly Oak. Birmingham in those days had a clear policy on internal promotion – it did not happen. They made it very clear to me that I would not be offered the job because Birmingham did not promote deputy heads to headship in the same school. I can accept that – but in a sense it didn't matter to me – we had a great time during the period of my acting headship, perhaps even longer, as I took on the running of the school. It was a period which was marked by taking the school forward and making things happen and sometimes standing back and watching them happen.

The school had been operating in a world which was determined by the Mental Deficiency Act, and in which pupils were described as emotionally young, untrainable imbeciles. Taking the school from that era, where there were fifty-plus children with only one qualified member of staff and an ancillary in one village hall, into becoming a school where we gave a lot of thought to the curriculum and teaching method was a great experience. It was really great. It was like having the chance to experiment without any obvious accountability, an Ofsted, or something, hanging over your head. We were able to say that we are not just going to hold the fort for the period, but we're going to shape up a direction and take things forward.

SR   Was that a good training ground for headship for you?

RS   Yes. Yes it was. I mean, it was a little artificial in the sense that I wasn't really the head. The staff were great. They treated me with a great deal of respect and even more support. They literally joined the challenge. I offered them the challenge of taking the school forward. What we could have done was just mind the shop for the interim period, but I argued that we could, alternatively, say let's try something out, let's do something different and look for school improvement. We could ask ourselves how we wanted the school to develop, how we wanted to set it up. If we set it up for the new headteacher coming, what we had got right would stick, and what we got wrong, the new headteacher would change.

SR   What happened next, in terms of your career advancement?

RS   I came here, almost immediately, to Montacute School in Poole.

SR   So – that must have meant your applying for headships?

RS   Well – yes – but I've been very lucky and I didn't apply for terribly many jobs. When the new headteacher arrived at Selly Oak, I realized how much I'd enjoyed the job, particularly the shaping of the school. I just fancied doing the real thing. I started looking straight away, I had a couple of interviews before finally arriving here at Montacute School.

SR   This was really your first headship. It's been a long headship. I wonder if I can take you back to the first year of headship. Can you recall the first year, and its challenges, and more especially, whether the previous nine months had prepared you for the 'real thing'?

RS   Well, it certainly helped prepare me. I suppose in retrospect I have to say that the first year was pretty much smooth sailing. There's a lot of luck in headship isn't there? It was in an era, around 1982, where there weren't really many pressures being brought to bear upon you from outside of school. I know it's something of a blunt statement, a generalization if you like, but it is nevertheless true. I just think people thought we were a bunch of do-gooders. I think that people still think this, generally, about special schools. I mean, you do a good job when you work in a special school, in spite of all of the pressures from outside, but it amounts to more than just banging the drum. I keep all of my diaries from my first year in headship. I've still got my diary from 1982. The thing that I always find hard to believe is that there's hardly anything in it. There is truly very little in it.

I remember thinking the similarity between Selly Oak and Montacute was close. Montacute School was built in the 'Health Services' days, in 1968. It wasn't really too long after that that I arrived, about fourteen years, and the school was still staffed principally by unqualified staff. There were only a couple of qualified teachers even in 1982 when I arrived here. There was no formal curriculum. There was very little co-ordinated method throughout the school. One member of staff didn't work with the next member of staff. There was no staff discussion about the nature, or the aims of the school, or an approach to the children. The staff simply came to work, cared for the children, and whilst I wouldn't want ever to think that we care or love the children any less, it's not enough!

It was a great opportunity, Steve, it was like having a blank sheet. It was like someone saying, here Rob, here's a headship, and there's no pressure from Ofsted, or the LEA, or any other pressure of that sort, no pressure other than that which you create for yourself, have a go. I have to say, perhaps a little complacently, that I didn't find the first year difficult at all. It was very smooth sailing.

SR   If we were to move the focus from the first year and look at the fourteen years of headship here at Montacute, can you see highs and lows across that period?

RS   Yes. I've had two breaks from headship. I had a fellowship at Exmouth, at Rolle College, which lasted for a term. It was useful and enjoyable. I also spent a fairly long period in secondment working for the LEA Inspectorate – it was really quite a long break from headship, a year or more – then another period standing in for a sick colleague.

In terms of lows, well there are a lot of lows, but I've been fortunate that some of the awful things that can happen in schools have not happened to me. There are some truly dreadful things can happen in schools and their staff, and their heads, and while we do have sadness when children die, and that happens more regularly than I would wish, while we have lows of that kind, and the odd staffing difficulty, which certainly do get to you, I haven't had anything truly dreadful happen.

In a general sense, of course, I do have lows from time to time. I have lows because the workload increases an enormous amount. The greatest, most frequent low I experience, I think, is when I realize that I don't spend enough time talking to staff, and sometimes you feel you are trapped on a merry-go-round of finances, meetings, and other administration. Actually, you catch yourself saying 'This surely isn't my business, my business is children, and I don't want to be a businessman'. The administration can dominate and this results in a fairly consistent, recurring low. But I am lucky, I haven't had too bad a time even during the lows, and in spite of some massive arguments and battles with the LEA.

SR   In some respects, perhaps, Rob, I think headship can take on the appearance of a series of battles which you aim to win, and even begin to feel like a war. In all of this, would you say any particular success stands out for you during this period of headship?

RS   I think if we accept that analogy, and it isn't all like that, but if I've led the school through a war, and if it's a war I've helped to win, it's been a war with the LEA. I was for many years the chairman of the Special School Headteachers' Association in Dorset (SHADD), partly, I think, because of my experience with the LEA Inspectorate which gave me a knowledge of the internal workings of the LEA. What that gave me as well was a clear insight into the unfairness, inefficiencies, lack of professionalism, and lack of commitment to special education.

There was in a sense, when I returned to my own school, the taking up of a banner on behalf of special education. For several years, I fought a running battle with the LEA over the low esteem in which special schools were held, and the low status education officers and elected members would often give to special education. I'd like to think that we won some of the skirmishes along the way. If you translate success into money, over the last ten years we certainly won a lot more money from the LEA. I know this is a crude measure of success, but I think we also won more respect and an improved status, although I have to say it is still relatively poor. I remain very critical about the overall organization of special education in Dorset.

SR   Have you always had one eye on special education in Dorset, Rob, as well as one eye on your own school?

RS   Well – I don't think they are the same thing, so the answer to that question is yes and no. By nature, I'm ever such a selfish person. There is no dilemma at all for me, whether I'm dealing with an obdurate member of staff, or obdurate councillor, or anything else, it really doesn't matter, it can be a parent, you name it. The important thing to remember is children always come first. There is no dilemma, no doubt. It's easier to operate when you have a clear focus of this sort – isn't it?

I am by nature a selfish person, and so more generally, that will be for Montacute School, and the children here. If I'm facing the Chief Education Officer, or the Chairman of the Education Committee, or other people at County Hall, or in the new Council, and the issue is special children, I'm quite happy to fight for them all because in that sense, they are one and the same, they all need a champion, and they haven't had one in Dorset. Involvement on this front used to take me out of school quite a lot, but very much less now, because I am no longer the chairman of SHADD, and we have recently become a grant maintained special school (GMSS).

SR   What kind of headteacher are you?

RS   Well – I think my staff would describe me as fairly average. I think they would say I try and that I'm committed. I think they probably see me as a 'benign dictator'. I do genuinely try to encourage a democracy but none of us here are stupid, and the general rule is the fundamental rule I remember stating the very first time I met the staff, fourteen years ago.

They were all sat around the staff room in a big circle by the retiring head and introduced to the new headteacher on his first visit to their school. I remember saying that I was very sorry that they'd got me because they hadn't got a clue about me, they didn't know a thing about me. I could be the greatest thing ever but it might just as likely be that I had been dumped by my LEA who were glad to get rid of me. We all know that sometimes that's the way references work. I said that they didn't know me from Adam and that we were working from a clean sheet. Whatever I'd done which was good or bad was in the past, and I stressed that same thing applied to them.

I then went on to say that I hoped they would call me Rob because I hoped we would be able to talk and work together as a staff. If I asked their opinion, I wanted them to give it, but there was another side to the coin, which was if they didn't express an opinion, I would assume they didn't have a view, and make up my own mind. I also said that if I didn't want their opinion I wouldn't ask for it, because I would have made up my mind and this would happen if there was an issue in which I very strongly believed. In fact, that has very rarely happened. It happened in the first week over what seemed on the face of it a trivial issue. I think it would seem trivial to most people, but it was not for me. It was about the way in which we ate at lunch-time.

The school had a system which involved everyone sitting at long trestle tables, and food was served out of huge pots with big utensils at the head of the table. I was horrified. I just had to change the way we ate straight away. I didn't discuss it, and there was no trouble over it, none at all. I think the staff respected the fact that I'd only said the week before, if I wanted an opinion I would ask for it, and please give it to me, but if I didn't want an opinion it was because I was going to do it my way.

SR   I know that the idea of a senior management team is important to you. I wonder what that means in terms of your management style and your own management approach?

RS   It's interesting really because I'd like to think I talk to people, listen to people and when I ask for their opinion, I value it and respect it. I'll use other people's views to shape up decisions which need to be made and that's generally true. But I wasn't really prepared for how difficult that would prove to be as we worked it up into a structure for a senior management team. The SMT is made up of three heads of department, the deputy headteacher and myself. Only five of us in the team but there have been quite a few skirmishes, and what I wasn't prepared for were people coming to a meeting and then all of a sudden fighting for their own corner. It was quite challenging, I had thought it would be cosy and friendly, and laid back, but it hasn't been quite like that at all.

We meet after school every Wednesday. It is really beginning to work well now, with everyone having the chance to float ideas and an open exchange of viewpoint. We all float ideas, some of them outrageous, and they get knocked down. It is really about plotting and planning together but I know I wasn't ready for people suddenly taking up their business, their own agenda, and fighting in a focused way, which reflected an aspect of the school, their own particular corner.

SR   When was the SMT started – fairly recently?

RS   Yes, relatively so – it has been running for about three years. We previously ran with the head and the deputy head, during a time when we did a lot of planning and curriculum development. We shaped and pushed and prodded the curriculum through in a direction which we decided. We unashamedly manipulated the staff to work towards that end, even though it did mean at times that they found themselves travelling down a road which they discovered was a dead end. They did that on several occasions. Through all of that period it was only the two of us behind the driving wheel.

No – when I think of it, it has been surprisingly hard work setting up the SMT, but very very fruitful. I'm very pleased with how it's working. For example, in all of our appraisals, and obviously I'm privy to all of the appraisal information, and actually appraise all the senior staff, people have said without exception how they are pleased with the development of the SMT. I know I did in my own appraisal. We are working at it and trying to improve the process, and it has meant a lot to all of us, and all in all, it has been a very effective change in our approach to management.

SR   What particular vision for the school do you have and how did it play a part in your headship?

RS   One thing you can't do is just hope to shape and keep shaping the vision which sustains the school from an internal stimulus. To keep shaping, adapting and keeping up to date as a school from an internal focus or stimulus is not possible. It just doesn't work that way and one of the problems with our staff is that we are settled, we are very good, but we are all getting old together. You need to think about issues like the balance of the staff team, bringing in new colleagues, getting yourself out to other schools and further educational establishments. You need to think about training opportunities, reading books, about talking to people, and about going to conferences. You've got to take all of these things seriously because they do keep you informed.

We found ourselves early on in our own curriculum development work desperate for this kind of input. We have always tended to plough our own furrow here, in Dorset, and we don't have that much in common with our neighbouring special schools, not in terms of curriculum development. It is really important to maintain external input for this work, for the life of the school. Almost all of our support staff are on university courses at the University of Plymouth. We are very happy to get national speakers in just to speak to us. We've done just that several times.

SR   At the heart of all of this, is there something which exists which can be called your vision – the vision of the educational leader?

RS   Well, I do think – over time there is such a thing. It has become more shaped by the staff than it was previously, but inevitably there isn't anyone who can perhaps take the overview in the same way as me. I'm sorry to say this but I've actually taught for longer than anyone here in school, and there's no one who has my experience. There are some people here who have great ideas, we have some very good innovators, but I think they still need a lead from the top, some one who is providing the vision as you describe it.

I hope that most of the time I can provide that vision, but I am aware that I cannot always do it. It needs an outsider's perspective, or another professional perspective, and that's why we need external people to come in and help us to shape up, as it were, our corporate view. I like to think, I don't know if it's pompous of me to do so, that I still have an overall vision of the school that the others take from me. It would be interesting to ask them, it's not something I have asked. It would be very interesting to find out.

SR   Is it possible to think in concrete terms about the 'vision', or 'corporate identity' as you call it, for Montacute School? Can you sum it up in a few words?

RS   I don't think it is possible in a few words, but the question does bring to mind one expression which we do often use here. I do keep repeating it and have done over the years. One of these days I'm jolly well going to have to order some stickers which will say 'Our business is children'. It's important that we never forget it – that's what our business is about and we should be clear about it. We still care for them, we should still cherish them and be ambitious for them and all of the rest that goes with it.

The aims of the school reflect a lot of careful thinking and staff discussion. We have spent a lot of time working on them and although they are few in number, covering say no more than a side of A4, they are a clear expression of our values and our vision. If you really force me to think up a phrase, it would be something to do with allowing children every opportunity to develop a high self-esteem. I think that is very important. It is one of the things, interestingly, that parents always say to me and just recently the chairman of the governors said it, last week in fact, while we were working on a document. He explained to me that what he thought about his own son was that his son knew his own strengths and weaknesses, and he realized, too, that he was quite clearly different to other children, and so on, but while he knew what his place in the scheme of things might be, he had a very positive high self-esteem. I think that this is good and I think that is what we should see as a fundamental aim of the school.

SR   A different question: you've described how in the last three or four years, extra administration has taken you away from working directly with children, from the teaching and learning which lies at the heart of school life. How do you enable the effective teaching and learning which takes place in your school? Do you see any changes in this aspect of your work?

RS We have been much more prescriptive in some ways as a staff in our approach to teaching and learning. This reflects a general standard we have imposed upon ourselves as a staff because for years we've worked very deliberately at building up a first-rate curriculum and I think quite rightly, we felt that we were well on the way to achieving an excellent product. What's happened in a fairly dramatic fashion recently, say in the last three years, is that we have agreed we have a well developed curriculum, but we needed to pay much more attention to what we actually do with that curriculum in the classroom.

We decided we needed to look at how we implemented the curriculum. As a result, there has been a self-imposed prescription set up by the teaching staff. They have gone about examining their own method and developing a whole school approach to planning, record-keeping and teaching method. We have, as a staff, looked at how we go about working towards our stated curriculum aims, and which method should match what learning activity. Consequently, over recent years, issues to do with preparation, planning and organization are in place.

Even prior to this more recent work, we had a system for recording teaching plans and programmes of learning, in which all staff were involved, not just the teaching staff. This has meant that planning files come into senior staff for monitoring purposes as a matter of course, it is expected. Staff are used to people coming into the classroom to observe them, it's part of the appraisal process, but it also takes place in a number of additional ways. Department heads will observe lessons as part of their remit, which is aimed at reviewing and developing our method and general approach to teaching and learning and to the special education of our children.

SR Are you pleased with these emerging structures, Rob? It seems to me, in some respects, to formalize many of the things I suspect you did anyway, but in an informal manner. Is the change for the better?

RS I think it is a good thing. I think it does formalize the process, as you describe it, because one of the things I can remember saying as a group, agreeing as a staff, was that none of us doubted that if anybody asked me how I monitored the performance of teacher X, I would be able to give a fairly accurate summary of the teacher's performance and a satisfactory explanation as to how I arrived at that judgement. It would have been on an informal basis, and it would have involved impressions gathered over a period of time, as you visited classrooms, often regularly, and working alongside colleagues, as you do, and the information which is gathered occurs almost automatically and you build up a fairly accurate picture of what is actually going on in the classroom.

It is right to say that many of the recent changes formalize the process, but I think we have become more comfortable with sharing our professional world, of being held accountable, and of collaborating in a positive way. I think we have also got to become more comfortable with it anyway, because the system in general now demands it. We have to accept this recent upsurge in forms of accountability – it is part of the real world. When Ofsted descend upon the school next May, we jolly well ought to be able to say that this is what we do, come and watch us, this is what it's about, come and see it happen, come and see if what we think is happening is really happening.

SR   To whom is a head accountable? Who do you answer to and how do you manage this accountability?

RS   The children! No doubt in my mind. I know the answer is a little abstract – I mean, how can you prove you're accountable to an ideal? In real terms, as a headteacher or a school, how can you prove you're accountable to any child? I believe that in the whole way I deal with a child, or act on behalf of a child, I should never ever forget it is the child I am actually responsible for, and whose interests I am serving. If I am speaking to an education officer, or an educational psychologist, or governor, or another teaching colleague, or a member of the support staff, I never forget that it is the child and their interests which are paramount. If any of us begin to feel that we may fail them, parent, governor, teacher, then surely we should be able to face the child, a child, and say, 'We're actually going to do the right job by you sunshine'.

SR   Do you think that you would give a similar answer if you were working in mainstream education or another part of special education, say with emotional and behavioural difficulties?

RS   Well – I've got no experience of EBD. I would hope I would feel the same way. What I do think is how it is a great pity that the current system invests so much in ensuring that we are accountable to other people. For example, we're accountable as a GM special school to the Funding Agency for Schools (FAS) for the money we receive and spend. I'm directly accountable to the governors as the headteacher of the school for several functions of my job. I'm accountable to the parents and have to report to them formally as laid down in statute, but in truth, whilst that's a straightforward response and perhaps the 'right' answer to your question, the real answer is I am more accountable to the child than any of these other people or bodies I have mentioned. At the end of the day, if I was doing anything that was consequently preventing me from meeting the needs of the children, of a child, I ought to be professional enough to say 'no' to the FAS, or say 'you are wrong' to governors, or take issue with a teacher and tell them 'you are not doing your job'.

SR   How do you manage to maintain your own professional well-being and development?

RS   I think I probably handle stress less well than I used to and maybe that's got something to do with the fact that there is more pressure involved in the job today. Some of that pressure at Montacute is of our own making, and that kind of stress I can handle. For example, I don't find it as stressful as others might that we work long hours, as we do here, because the nature of that pressure is self-imposed. We have elected to put that stress on ourselves. I think there is an ever increasing weight of responsibility on headteachers now – you only have to listen to the news or pick up a newspaper or listen to any parent or governor to quickly realize how many new pressures are building and being placed on the shoulders of the headteacher.

Every time Gillian Shephard opens her mouth, there's another task lined up for the headteacher. Similarly, every time you pick up the newspaper, there is another piece of news targeting the teaching profession, blaming it for the poor performance in one or other part of the economy, and criticizing teachers for being trendy, bad spelling, increased crime, getting it wrong. There's a sense in which these intangible pressures can start to weigh more heavily, and it is so easy to take some of it on your own shoulders and think 'hold on, is it worth it?' or 'what has this all got to do with me?'

SR   What do you do to manage this stress?

RS   Well – I do my best. One of the best cures for me at this school is to wait for nine o'clock. As you know, my office is at the front of the school, next to the main entrance, and at nine o'clock, every morning, whether I've had a bad night, or am having a bad day, whether I've got the whole world on my shoulders, whatever happens, the kids start charging through the day and want to see me. I think that's what it is all about and that's what keeps me going during a low. If I've got a suit on, they'll come in and say, 'Well Sammons, are you coming to work today?' They just bring you down to earth, bring you around in the best possible way.

I think it is fair to say I've never really thought about my own well-being but I will admit, of late, I have had occasion to think, and I've said to myself, 'You're under pressure sunshine.' I still play sport, a game of squash, I exercise, and enjoy it. I guess your own personal private life becomes more important too as the pressure builds, as a way of maintaining a balance. I am more self-conscious, now, about stress than I ever was, Steve – that's a fact.

SR   What about professional development? I presume that given everything you've said, it's as important for you as it is for your staff?

RS   Yes. Undoubtedly! I've been ever so lucky, Steve, I've had lots of challenges, and you know yourself that one of the privileges of headship is that you can present yourself with new challenges, which is not always easy for teaching colleagues and that's why I think we take it very seriously here. The teachers are not in a position some-times to effect change for themselves and I think it behoves senior management to make sure that they do get the opportunity to experience challenge and work to effect change. Senior manage-ment should actively look after teachers' professional interests as well as those of the institution.

Headteachers are luckier, they can effect change for themselves in their working situation. If I'm having a particularly bad day, in truth, I can always go up the road for a cup of coffee. You simply can't do that if you're teaching. I can always say, for example, do I really want to go to that meeting in London? Or I can think again, and recon-sider the day out, a break from routine, you know, that sort of thing.

In that general sense, opportunities do occur. The chance to become qualified as an Ofsted Inspector is one such example. I did it because I thought it would be in the interests of the school, but it is just that sort of development which opens up new avenues for me and brings to bear a new perspective on our work. A good example of the same thing is the number of contacts I have with the University of Plymouth which I have used over the last ten years or more.

The Ofsted Inspector role has also been useful and interesting. I have been involved in two inspections. I found the Ofsted training interesting too as well as hard work. We paid for the training out of our in-service training budget because we thought it would add to Montacute School. We felt it would help us to sort out what would be expected of us in an Ofsted inspection and also give us an insight into the Ofsted perspective.

Whilst that was the background to my involvement, I have to say there were other folk in the group on the course who were in jobs which relied upon their successfully qualifying as an Ofsted inspec-tor. There were for example some Hampshire inspectors present who literally had to pass. It was not pleasant watching that process unfold. In fact it was very unpleasant. I guess looking back I was very complacent about the whole experience.

The inspections have been worthwhile, however, interesting and useful. Perhaps because of my background, I went into the inspec-tions with a little more humility than some of the other inspectors in the team. I don't know, but I do say this, and I've said it to our staff repeatedly, the two inspections reassured me and gave me a healthier view of the ability of inspection teams to complete an inspection of a school in a fair and efficient way. I'm not sure I'm a fan of the Ofsted process, but the two teams I worked with worked very hard to pick up what was good in the school. They were not there to focus singly upon what was bad. They would obviously pick that up as part of the process but it was not an overriding feature of their work. They were also very good at their job.

The team was staffed by some very conscientious and able people. The two inspections were of community colleges, and it was very hard work, very hard work. There was an enormous amount of preparation, hours and hours, lots of reading and I didn't really enjoy watching teaching colleagues under pressure. If I was able to give them feedback, I did, in some small part, and when it was positive, it was very enjoyable. At other times, feedback wasn't so good, but at the end of the day, that's what it is all about.

SR   In some respects we have touched upon this question already but I'd like to return to it now. Ted Wragg says 'You don't have to be a "nutter" to join the "barmy army" but ... '. Do you think headship has become much more difficult and do you enjoy it?

RS   I remember a conversation with you about what kind of advice you'd give to a teacher who is considering application for headship. I think I would say even more definitely now that ... just be absolutely sure it's what you want to do because with the territory come some very unpleasant and difficult tasks.

What you see happen much of the time, unfortunately, are people who are good teachers moving on because they are good, through middle management to deputy headship and then to headship, who never ever should have left the classroom. They are excellent teachers, enjoy being with the children, and draw a great satisfaction from that side of the job. That's all I would really want to say to them, just be absolutely sure. If you are sure, and you want to go ahead, perhaps Ted Wragg's right, maybe you've got to be mad in order to convince yourself you really want to do it!

SR   As a footnote to that statement, is it still possible to enjoy the job in spite of all the pressure?

RS   Well – yes – I think it is – of course it is possible. When children here at Montacute come to you, there is a constant delight in that relationship. I love going into schools, anybody's school, because the kids are just so funny. Colleagues too! Certainly when I'm away with colleagues, or with other teachers, there's a lot to laugh about, a lot of fun to be shared. At the end of the day, if you set yourself a target and achieve it, of course, there is still just as much satisfaction in it. I just think, however, that everything is a bit harder earned nowadays. I do feel that more than perhaps I did – that I now earn every single penny of my salary.

SR   All of that seems to suggest that there have been some big changes in special education, say over the last five years or so, or maybe longer. What do you think have been the biggest changes, and which have had the biggest impact on your job?

RS   Before you start to consider this, you have to put this into the context of the LEA in which I have worked as headteacher. I suspect were I in another LEA, certainly in some LEAs, the answer would be different. The root of my biggest problem in headship here has been money! I say that unashamedly and with emphasis. The problem has been about money and the lack of status given to special education. If I say that the biggest challenges in my recent career were implementation of LMSS, the advent of the national curriculum, and now GMSS, they are clearly the big issues which have affected everybody.

However, in other LEAs, the introduction of LMSS would not have been as big an issue, because the school budget and education finance figures have been there for all to see. I can look at an equivalent school to my own in a neighbouring LEA, and I see the level of funding as a stark contrast to Dorset. In fact, I am thinking of one particular example right now, as it happens I have the figures recently to hand, and the level of funding is exactly double what this school would get if it were maintained by Dorset LEA.

Now, managing a special school is not that difficult if you have a decent budget. It is a real challenge, speaking euphemistically, if you are trying to run a budget which has 93 per cent of its total committed to staff salaries. Maybe GMS would not have been an issue for Montacute School had we not been in Dorset. There are, as a matter of fact, more than a third of Dorset's special schools in the grant maintained sector.

Nevertheless – if I can push these issues to one side, because they may not be as important in other LEAs, although they are clearly very important to special education in Dorset and important in my own career – the NC is by far the biggest issue we have faced in the last few years. We are passionate about the curriculum here. We have spent a lot of additional time working on the curriculum. We have worked after school, three evenings a week, because of our commitment to total teaching time during the day. We're very interested in curriculum development and initially we were vociferously critical of the NC. We made a big contribution to the Department for Education on the NC. They came to visit us to see what we were doing and as a consequence we did feel that we contributed to the recent curriculum review. In fact, I was asked if I would become a member of a SCAA team with Dearing. In point of fact, I didn't go in the end, but we felt part of the process and as a consequence felt that the curriculum was more relevant.

We hope in some small part we managed to contribute to the change. We were an afterthought initially, the NC originally was ill conceived, it was totally inappropriate for us. It would never have happened if Mrs Rumbold had not put her foot in it and effectively said that these sort of children were uneducable. I think, more recently, we've seen great progress on this front, and it has meant a great deal to children in special schools like Montacute. They now have a clearer and more meaningful entitlement. It is just not sufficient, or good enough to care for them. As good as that it is as an aim and a practice, it is not enough. The children have a curriculum entitlement and teachers have got to teach them.

SR How does the movement from the LEA to GMS affect you and your school?

RS The NC is by far the biggest issue. GMS is a means to an end. It's a necessary evil. I feel that the governors and staff of this school can do a better job with the limited resources available than the LEA has managed over the past few years. The LEA has never shown any respect for special schools and GMS is a means to an end. The important thing is the point of delivery and this means asking the question what does it mean for the children? What it means for the children of Montacute School is they now have more teachers, more staff working with them than they did last April when Montacute was an LEA school. They have tens of thousands of pounds of new equipment to use, computer hardware, software, special apparatus. There is literally tens of thousands of pounds' worth of equipment money, in general, going into the school.

SR What about the 'nuts and bolts' of this change in status? Are you spending more time on administration?

RS Yes – undoubtedly – but it's merely a means to an end. It's got to be done. You don't receive the 12.7 per cent of the money the LEA spent for nothing. Someone's got to do the LEA's job. That's me, the administrative staff, and the governing body. We have two school secretaries, just as we had in the first year of the LMSS pilot scheme. There is simply more work for all of us. But what it means is the kids get a better deal.

SR To sum up, does this mean as a school you have a far greater control over your own destiny?

RS There is no question about it! We own the school and we are the employers. It's not bad is it? We don't have enough money but we have more than we had before. In cash terms, excluding the 'sweeteners', if you like, we have had £70,000 more this financial year to spend on pupils. Well, that's a very persuasive incentive for change, isn't it?

SR How do you hope to see your own school develop in the next five years or so?

RS I see that as a twofold question. The first part refers to the continued processes of following the work already in place. A continued emphasis on the point of delivery and what is happening in the classroom. We want to get better at doing that and we're working hard at it. We also want to look around the school and improve the appearance and school ethos.

To some extent, you tend to concentrate on one thing, for

example the classroom teaching and the curriculum, and you forget that you're sitting there and you have three holes in the wall behind your head. It is then, naturally, that you start to think, hold on, what does that say about us and the esteem in which we hold children? We don't want them to have to work in an environment which is unpleasant. You sometimes forget to look around. It's partly about that, but it's a bit more than that, because importantly, you've got to keep looking at your performance and keep saying 'Are we really doing the best we can? We've got the material now to teach and do a good job.' I do believe we have got something good here, high quality special education, and we are delivering it in the best way possible.

SR   I find that emphasis very interesting because I think I see signs of a growing interest out there in schools in curriculum process.

RS   I do hope you are right! I find that prospect exciting, it's great, because the process is dynamic. There are ideas to generate, to develop and to follow through. I think, however, that there is another part to the question. The second part of the question is about the wider challenge that is always facing a school. It's rather an abstract concept because it is bound up with looking to the future. It is in effect saying we don't actually know what the educational landscape is going to be like in two years' time.

For example, five years ago, I would not have dreamed we would have twenty children in the autistic spectrum of SEN. It is a new challenge for us and the school has got to develop in a way which means it is flexible enough to meet the needs of a wide range of disability. If we can be adaptable, and meet the changing nature of the SEN continuum, we will be moving forward, not standing still. If our curriculum is as good as we think it is, then any children with SLD should be able to come to this school, fit into the curriculum, and have their SEN met and as individual learners be challenged by us.

CHAPTER 12

Leadership in special education: towards a reframed zeitgeist

Three questions on theory and practice

The question of leadership, *per se*, naturally leads one to ask further questions about the theory and practice of leadership in special education. Any such consideration seems to naturally fall into two parts: the first, an examination of general management context, that is, special education; the second, an examination of the individual differences which impact upon the exercise of management and leadership performance. Such an approach, hopefully, leads us to a third set of considerations which relate directly to some of the issues and principles that lie at the heart of managing SEN provision.

The 'special' nature of SEN does, arguably, distinguish it from what is sometimes described as normal, or mainstream provision. This, we would argue, is so in spite of a prevailing belief that SEN should be 'normalized', a view which has gathered strength over the past twenty years, and is epitomized in the UNESCO document issued after the conference in 1994 at Salamanca. A second characteristic of special education is its diversity. A very great variety of different disabilities, categories and perspectives exist under the umbrella of SEN provision. There is even a contemporary debate within the professional world of SEN Co-ordinators (teachers with middle management responsibility for SEN provision in the mainstream school) as to whether the most able or gifted pupil should be regarded as forming part of the SEN continuum. As against this, the domain, traditionally, has been deficit-based, and concerned only with those who are less able or disadvantaged in some way.

The consequence of such diversity, for those who would lead, is that special schools, or other SEN provision, can differ quite sharply. The expectation that SEN provision is or should be a coherent and single entity is, it seems to us, often seriously over-emphasized. Indeed, the single universal feature of special education is probably this very characteristic – its diversity – often expressed in the form of a pervading concern for the individual person. The variety of need, and its concomitant expertise, should never be underestimated. This is despite the current zeitgeist for normalcy or mainstreaming.

Considering context

As we have previously stated, leadership and management in special education are greatly neglected as subjects of research or as topics in the literature of educational management and leadership. Given the continuing scope of SEN provision, and, perhaps more importantly, the continuing expansion, albeit of a changing nature, of that provision, there is a strong case for knowing more about how this provision is managed and led. What is self-evident is the existence of a number of separate issues for management and leadership which, while perhaps not unique to special education, take on a particular shape or nature contrasting with that to be found in a mainstream school. This is reflected in a number of different ways: the ethos of a special school, as compared with a normal school, for example, is very often distinctively different and immediately recognizable. The nature of the school day, with various elements reflecting a particular learning need, or educational perspective, can readily characterize the distinctive institutional identity of a special school. It is even possible to generalize, perhaps not without some risk, and suggest that specific kinds of special school appear to attract particular kinds of headteacher. Certainly, it is our view, on the basis of the studies which are reported in this book and in others, that a relationship exists between the philosophy and style of the headteacher and the nature of the school.

Special schools are by nature small, and may perhaps be perceived as close relatives to the primary school. Even a large special school will generally have on roll no more than a hundred pupils. However, SEN provision is often now more complex than just simply a special school. Boundaries have become blurred, principally because of policy stimulated by the Warnock Report (DES, 1978). The idea of a continuum which is relative as well as dynamic reflects the Warnock 'concept of SEN', underpinning policy implementation over the last fifteen years. This has resulted, not surprisingly, in the emergence of policy and provision that attempts to provide a parallel continuum of resource. Initiatives involving the establishment of outreach to support pupils with SEN in mainstream schools, the creation of support services, and the clustering of schools around a special school, represent only some of the many developments which have added complexity and diversity to SEN provision.

The leader in special education

Whether there is actually a case for stating qualitative differences in the professional context, or indeed the nature of headship, in mainstream and special education remains open to debate. The discussion in the following section will address several perceptions of becoming a leader in special education, and more generally, the nature of this special educational context, which might be tentatively described as an SEN paradigm. What we would argue for is the existence of several features associated with leaders in the SEN context which to varying degrees has been affirmed in our and other research. These features reside principally in perceptions of (1) the SEN context and/or (2) the professional leader. They include:

- a high value placed on relationships and personal growth;
- a need for professional expertise and a knowledge of specific areas of SEN;
- a high regard for curriculum process rather than subject content;
- an indication of good levels of teaching competence in their professional career;
- prior experience of mainstream education as a virtual prerequisite for effective management in special education;
- a positive regard for education and its value for children otherwise identified as refusing school or less able to access academic learning.

We have little doubt that successful leadership in the SEN context reflects the personal and professional values and beliefs held by the headteacher. This is, in large measure, evident in the conversations reported in this book although to substantiate such a claim fully it would be necessary to engage in the kind of second and third level studies of leadership and management proposed in our opening chapter.

However that may be, the key importance, for example, of *vision* reflects this centrality of leadership persona in school development, and as a process involves the head in envisioning the staff, as well as continuing to reinforce their own vision. In this respect, there is a commonality to the leadership vision for special education, which reflects the nature of the SEN paradigm. In some of his work, Rayner has suggested that this includes the following elements:

- *the individual pupil* – a prime concern for the individual pupil;
- *the SEN continuum* – an expression of a dynamic continuum of special educational need;
- *the SEN dimension* – an understanding of a scale of inversion, in successful SEN provision, in terms of economy, intensity and locality;
- *parental partnership* – a sensitivity to and appreciation of parental activity in the provision made for pupils with SEN;
- *inclusion and reintegration* – an awareness of the issues relating to provision aimed at supporting SEN in the mainstream setting.

The question of a qualitative contrast between managing provision within special education and ordinary education is enigmatic. Few, surely, would seek to deny the existence of commonalities as well as substantive differences, in terms of task and context, between the various phases of education. Heads do, on occasion, successfully switch from one phase to the other, and some SEN provision is continuing to evolve in such a way, with traditional boundaries being eroded, that may conceivably make this exchange easier.

Yet several heads, in our conversations, insist that the differences are more important than any similarity. Ashdown, for example, cannot imagine attempting to lead a secondary school, nor even a different kind of special school. In his view, professional experience must be relevant experience, as a prerequisite for successful leadership in special education. Clarke, on the other hand, with extensive experience in both mainstream and special schools, explains how ideas and strategies developed during headship in a large comprehensive are, in his view, equally applicable to the running of an EBD special school. He does make the point, however, that the movement between phases of education is one-way, and once a special head, always a special head! O'Hanlon's research (1988) into marginalization takes on a haunting lilt as the implications for career progression and school leadership are considered. Evans and Morgan, however, seem to see little difference in running the integrated SEN provision within, respectively, their mainstream secondary and primary schools, to an approach to 'normal' mainstream management. However, both display an understanding of SEN provision which demonstrates an expertise which is readily associated with leadership in special education.

Aspects of this SEN expertise and experience are reflected in all the conversations which are reported in our research study. As such, a number of interesting issues recur which further describe the SEN paradigm and perhaps lend support to the notion of a qualitative difference between 'ordinary' and 'special' education. These issues are:

- *Integration* – Clarke's vision of his school winning the 'best kept village' competition for an educational community reflects a commitment to integration and the clustering of provision for pupils with SEN in an inclusive arrangement. His argument for such an inclusive approach echoes the views of several of the other headteachers who would prefer to see the same kind of approach (Evans, Morgan, Craig). However, the issue of integration also raises doubts, and a belief that a special response will always be needed within a school setting to meet the needs of some pupils (Ross, Craig, Haigh).
- *Child-centredness* – several heads stress and re-stress a need to keep the image of the individual child and their SEN in the foreground of any vision of special education. Abrol and Hinchliffe make similar passionate statements to this effect, linking their

arguments to their professional values and their vision for the special school.

- *The 'experienced curriculum'* – a new academic emphasis for the pupils and an awareness of a 24-hour curriculum marked the beginning of Hinchliffe's incumbency at Ash Field School. Task definition was grounded in her vision for special education and the need for staff to 'share' this philosophy. In some respects, it almost seems as if the leader is busy laying the foundation for reshaping the institutional self-concept, if such a construct can be said to exist. An emphasis upon the whole curriculum relating to the whole child, but more particularly the category of SEN presented by the child, recurs repeatedly in the various explanations we were offered about the 'true' nature of special education.

- *Administration and assessment* – identification and assessment lie at the heart of special education. This fact probably explains the close relationship which exists between special education and educational psychology. It is also clearly illustrated in the title and content of the recently introduced Code of Practice for the management of SEN in mainstream schools (DfE, 1994). The 'system' for SEN is an obvious concern for the leader in special education. Heads of special schools can use this 'establishment' creatively, to match resource to need, or can be frustrated by the very same system which prevents resource meeting need. All the heads in our study talked about this aspect of leadership. Ross interestingly identifies this aspect of SEN activity as dominating her final years as head. She explains: 'if I was still there, I think the most important priority would have been to see an admissions policy for the LEA established. In my last two years there, a lot of time went into discussing an admissions policy, and at the end of the day, in spite of countless meetings, nothing was achieved.' Evans refers in detail to this as a key task in managing inclusive SEN. Morgan repeats similar points when discussing the SEN element in his school. Craig, of course, is dealing with the issue as a first priority, as part of his service's raison d'être.

- *Policy, provision and practice* – the funding of provision and its organization to resource systems designed to support pupils with SEN is a recurring theme in our research. Every head referred to the mismatch between need and resource, as well as the task of managing resources to sustain current provision. But their concern for resource was by no means limited to the practical task of administration. The way forward, the future both for their own schools and for special education, and their vision of what special education can and ought to be, included a consideration of resource, its deployment, and how meeting the needs of individual pupils should be best developed.

A final note

In summary, perhaps the most interesting feature of the collective vision of the heads who are the subject of our study is a shared tendency to see the 'big picture', and place their own work in their own school or unit within the larger context of special education. This may reflect an insight into leaders' perceptions and possible realities, even a substantially reframed zeitgeist, for moving towards an inclusive special education in the twenty-first century.

References

Ainley, J. (1995) 'Effective schools: where to?', in *Leading and Managing*, 1(1), 28–44.

Ainscow, M. (1991) *Effective Schools for All*, London: David Fulton.

Ainscow, M., Hopkins, D., Southworth, G. and West, M. (1994) *Creating the Conditions for School Improvement*, London: David Fulton.

Best, R., Ribbins, P., Jarvis, C. and Oddy, D. (1983) *Education and Care*, London: Heinemann.

Brundrett, M. (1998) 'What lies behind collegiality, legitimation or control?: a critique of the purported benefits of collegial management in education', in *Educational Management and Administration*, 26(3).

Chapman, N. (1994) 'Caught in the crossfire: the future of special schools', in *The British Journal of Special Education*, 21(2), 60–3.

Court, M. (1994) 'How far have we come in women's employment in education?', in Manson, H. (ed.) *New Zealand Annual Review of Education*, 4, 9–24.

Court, M. (1997) 'Reconstructing "the principal": professional/parent partnership and devolution dilemmas', paper presented at the Professionalism: Rethinking the Work of Teachers and School Leaders in an Age of Change Conference held in Oslo, 20–22 May.

Davies, L. (1990) *Equity and Efficiency?: School Management in an International Context*, Lewes: Falmer.

Davies, L. (1994) *Beyond Authoritarian School Management: The Challenge for Transparency*, London: Education Now Books.

Davies, L. (1995) 'Who needs headteachers?', keynote paper given at the BEMAS Annual Conference 1995, 23–25 September, Oxford (unpublished).

Davies, L. (1996) 'The case for leaderless schools', in Watson, K., Modgil, S. and Modgil, C. (eds) *Educational Dilemmas: Debate and Diversity*, London: Cassell.

Day, C. and Bakioglu, A. (1996) 'Development and disenchantment in the professional lives of headteachers', in Goodson, I. and Hargreaves, A.

(eds) *Teachers' Professional Lives*, London: Falmer.

DES (1978) *Special Educational Needs. Report of the Committee of Enquiry into the Education of Handicapped Children and Young People*, London: HMSO (The Warnock Report).

DES (1988) *Education Reform Act*, London: HMSO.

DfE (1994) *Code of Practice: On the Identification and Assessment of Special Educational Needs*, London: HMSO.

Fish, J. and Evans, J. (1995) *Managing Special Education: Codes, Charters and Competition*, Buckingham: Open University Press.

Gardner, H. (1995) *Leading Minds: An Anatomy of Leadership*, New York: Basic Books.

Gronn, P. (1993) 'Psychobiography on the couch: character, biography and the comparative study of leaders', in *Journal of Applied Behavioural Science*, 29(3), 343–58.

Gronn, P. (1994) 'Educational administration's Weber', in *Educational Management and Administration*, 22(4), 224–31.

Gronn, P. (1997) 'Leadership from a distance: institutionalising values and forming character at Timbertop, 1951–1961', paper for the Conference on Values and Ethics at the Centre for the Study of Leadership and Ethics, University of Virginia, 2–4 October.

Gronn, P. and Ribbins, P. (1996) 'Leaders in context: postpositivist approaches to understanding educational leadership', in *Educational Administration Quarterly*, 32(3), 452–73.

Hallinger, P. and Heck, R. (1996) 'The principal's role in school effectiveness: an assessment of substantive findings, 1980–1995', paper presented at the 8th Annual Conference of the Commonwealth Council for Educational Administration, Kuala Lumpur, August.

HMI (1988) *Secondary Schools: An Appraisal by HMI*, London: HMSO.

Jermier, J. and Kerr, S. (1997) ' "Substitutes for leadership: their meaning and measurement" – contextual recollections and current observations', in *Leadership Quarterly*, 8, 95–105.

Kerr, S. and Jermier, J. (1978) 'Substitutes for leadership: their meaning and measurement', in *Organizational Behaviour and Human Performance*, 22, 374–403.

Kets de Vries, M. (1989) *Prisoners of Leadership*, New York: Wiley.

Kets de Vries, M. (1995) 'The leadership mystique', in *Leading and Managing*, 1(3), 193–211.

Kets de Vries, M. and Miller, D. (1987) *Unstable at the Top: Inside the Neurotic Organisation*, New York: New American Library.

Mortimer, P. and Mortimer, J. (1991) *The Primary School Head: Roles, Responsibilities and Reflections*, London: Paul Chapman.

Nias, J. (1972) ' "Pseudo-participation" and the success of innovation in the introduction of the B.Ed.', in *Sociological Review*, 20(2), 169–83.

Noble, T. and Pym, B. (1970) 'Collegial authority and the receding locus of power', in *British Journal of Sociology*, 21(4), 431–45.

Ofsted (1993) *Improving Schools,* London: HMSO.

O'Hanlon, C. (1988) 'Alienation within the profession: special needs or watered-down teachers? Insights into the tension between the ideal and the real through action research', in *Cambridge Journal of Education,* 18(3), 297–312.

Pascal, C. and Ribbins, P. (1998) *Understanding Primary Headteachers,* London: Cassell.

Podsakoff, P. and MacKenzie, S. (1997) 'Kerr and Jermier's substitutes for leadership model: background, empirical assessment, and suggestions for future research', in *Leadership Quarterly,* 8, 117–25.

Rayner, S. (1995) 'Restructuring reform: choice and change in special education', in *British Journal of Special Education,* 21(4), 166–9.

Ribbins, P. (1985) 'Qualitative perspectives in research in secondary education: the management of pastoral care', in Simkins, T. (ed.) *Research in the Management of Secondary Education,* Sheffield City Polytechnic: Sheffield Papers in Education Management, 3–53.

Ribbins, P. (1997a) 'Heads on deputy headship', in *Educational Management and Administration,* 25(3), 295–309.

Ribbins, P. (1997b) *Leaders and Leadership in the School, College and University,* London: Cassell.

Ribbins, P. and Marland, M. (1994) *Headship Matters,* London: Longman.

Ribbins, P. and Sherratt, B. (1997) *Radical Educational Policies and Conservative Secretaries of State,* London: Cassell.

Riddell, S. and Brown S. (eds) (1994) *Special Educational Needs Policy in the 1990s: Warnock in the Market Place,* London: Routledge.

Scheerens, J. (1992) *Effective Schooling: Research, Theory and Practice,* London: Cassell.

Schon, D. (1983) *The Reflective Practitioner,* New York: Basic Books.

Sinclair, A. (1995) 'The seduction of the self-managed team and the reinvention of the team-as-group', in *Leading and Managing,* 1(1), 44–63.

Thody, A. (1995) Review of Davies (1994) *Beyond Authoritarian School Management,* in *Educational Management and Administration,* 23(3), 215–16.

Thorp, J. (1986) 'Accountability versus participation', in Hughes, M., Ribbins, P. and Thomas, H. (eds) *Managing Education: The System and the Institution,* London: Cassell.

UNESCO (1994) *The Salamanca Statement and Framework for Action on Special Needs Education,* Paris: UNESCO.

Walters, B. (1994) *Management for Special Needs,* London: Cassell.

Wragg, T. (1995) 'You don't have to be mad to try this … ', in *The Times Educational Supplement,* 20 October, 60.

Young, S. (1997) 'Heads dash to quit early', in *The Times Educational Supplement,* 18 April, 1.

Index

The ten headteacher subjects of the book are indicated in bold type.